Decolonial Mourning and the Caring Commons

Decolonial Mourning and the Caring Commons

Migration-Coloniality Necropolitics and Conviviality Infrastructure

Encarnación Gutiérrez Rodríguez

ANTHEM PRESS

Anthem Press
An imprint of Wimbledon Publishing Company
www.anthempress.com

This edition first published in UK and USA 2024
by ANTHEM PRESS
75–76 Blackfriars Road, London SE1 8HA, UK
or PO Box 9779, London SW19 7ZG, UK
and
244 Madison Ave #116, New York, NY 10016, USA

First published in the UK and USA by Anthem Press in 2023

© 2024 Encarnación Gutiérrez Rodríguez

British Library Cataloguing-in-Publication Data
A catalogue record for this book is available from the British Library.

Library of Congress Control Number: 2024933744
A catalog record for this book has been requested.

ISBN-13: 978-1-83999-248-3 (Pbk)
ISBN-10: 1-83999-248-4 (Pbk)

Cover Credit: Encarnación Gutiérrez Rodríguez

This title is also available as an e-book.

For Juan José and Pepa,

the theatre director,
Telat Yurtsever.

To the spirits, souls and minds.
¡Están Presente!

CONTENTS

ACKNOWLEDGMENTS

This book is the outcome of numerous encounters and political struggles and the sharing of pain and desire for a world where many worlds are at home. The feeling of mourning has been with me throughout my life—every time I lost a loved one, but also when grief inhabited my space due to racist, misogynist, transphobic, queerphobic and colonial violence targeting communities and producing genocides, feminicides, terracides and ecocides. Walking together or bearing witness in mourning with these communities and following their political struggles, particularly their political communal labor of mourning, has helped me arrive to the observations, reflections and *sentipensar* present in this book. My parents' wisdom, their sentient being in the world, their sense of justice and their sharpened analysis of injustice, as well as their relentless work, embracing an Andalusian spirit of communal living, have also given me the strength and capacity to continue in their path. It is at this juncture that this book has appeared, taken shape and after years of work become what it is now. In this journey, numerous colleagues, students, friends and family members have accompanied me and given me strength to work with and through grief.

First, I would like to thank all the organizations and collectives whose words I have listened to. They have enabled me to reflect with them and pay tribute to their communal political labor of mourning. They are many, and I am grateful especially to Caminando Fronteras, #NiUnaMenos, Women in Exile, #SayHerName and AAPF, the Arslan family, Genç family, the Tribunal NSU-Komplex Auflösen, Initiative 19. Februar Hanau and the Bildungsinitiative Ferhat Unvar. I am also indebted to Cana Bilir-Meier for her generous sharing of her work with me. During this process, the analysis of scholars such as Kimberlé Crenshaw has been decisive in forming my perspective, while my friends Gladys Tzul Tzul, Yuderkys Espinosa Miñoso and Rhoda Reddock have enriched my theoretical approach and shaped my path through this journey. I am also indebted for the research to the institutional support I have received: I am grateful to the University of Alberta and to Michael O'Driscoll, Carrie Smith and Sara Dorow for facilitating a visiting adjunct faculty position there, which enabled me to begin the research for this book. Further, my discussion with my colleagues at the Chair for Critical Studies in Higher Education Transformation at the Nelson Mandela University, André Keet, Dina Belluigi, Jenny du Preez and Luan Staphorst, has inspired my argument. Additionally, I would like to thank my colleagues at the Institute of Sociology, Justus Liebig University Giessen (JLU), particularly Andreas Langenohl, Nicole Zillien and Thomas Brüsemeister, for helping keep me afloat in this process, as well as my team at JLU: Andrea Silva-Tapia, Çiçek Tanlı, Daniel Heinz, Johann Erdmann, Moschda Sabhezada, Johannes Reusch and Sarya Ataç. Furthermore, the constant and embracing support of Andreea Racleş and Sebastian Garbe has enabled me to continue the writing of this book. With Sebastian and Andrea Sempértegui I had also the chance to discuss one early draft of a chapter for this book, I am grateful for their insightful comments. I would also like to thank my colleagues at the Graduate Centre for the Study of Culture (GCSC), especially Ansgar Nünning. I am also thankful for the institutional support I received from the Maria Sibylla Merian Centre Conviviality-Inequality in Latin America (Mecila) and the intellectual contributions of Sérgio Costa, Barbara Göbel, Susanne Klengel, Marcos Nobre and Barbara Potthast. I am grateful to my colleagues there, in particular Juliana Streva and Susana Durão, for their brilliant inspiration. Finally, my move to Goethe University Frankfurt has given me a new intellectual environment and a wonderful team; here I would like to thank especially Onur Suzan Nobrega, Oscar Herzog Astaburuaga, Juan Esteban Lince Salazar and Valérie Bignon. I had the opportunity to present chapters of this book at the conference "Racism, Border Struggles and Disobedient Knowledge in Times of Multiple Crises" at the Swedish School of Social Science, University of Helsinki, where I benefited from the insightful comments of my colleagues Suvi Keskinen and Ann Phoenix as well as other participants. Incredibly valuable, as well, was the feedback I received about the chapter I presented in the Visualizing Care Series panel "Epistemologies of Care," organized by the Revaluing Care in the Global Economy research network at Duke University. The observations of Riikka Prattes, as well as Jocelyn Olcott and Tania Rispoli, have enriched my thinking about mourning in regard to care work and ethics. I would like also to thank Matxalen Legarreta Iza for inviting me to collaborate with her and her colleagues in the Transforming Care Network. This book would not have been complete without the attentive eye and commitment of Michele Faguet. I am also grateful to Shirley for her numerous readings and comments as well as her support throughout the process. Finally, I would like to thank my friends Selçuk, Aron, Christoph, Susanne, Luzenir, Ainhoa, Adrià and especially my sister, Angela, for her immense support.

Chapter 1

INTRODUCTION: ENTANGLED MOURNINGS

heimkehr, traueratem

einen augenblick einsamer
atmet oleander
vor dem gittertor jasmin
einen augenblick einsamer
atmet
der zikadensang
einen augenblick einsamer
kindstage aus:
ganz abgeschiedener sommer
ganz nachtgeborene notkunft
ganz luftgewobene trauer

das grab zum dichten nah
(Oliver 1997, 26)

On 21 June 2015, I walked down the sunny streets of Frankfurt. It was a pleasant day, but I knew that nothing would ever be the same again because my father, **Juan José Gutiérrez Cabello**,[1] had died at midnight. Scarcely two years later, I lost my mother, **Josefa Rodríguez Santana**, as well. My father had wanted to die in his village, Bollullos de la Mitación, in the Spanish province of Seville, but my parents' lives ended in Germany, where they had arrived as *Gastarbeiter*[2] (guest workers) in the 1960s. Since their passing, I have been inhabited by mourning—embedded in my everyday, mundane activities. In this journey, my eyes have been opened to different articulations of political work, embracing the communal labor of mourning.

This book is the product of an endless, individual and collective, process of mourning. It engages with decolonial mourning by bearing witness to the political grief work of contemporary struggles against migration-coloniality necropolitics. It departs from the mourning for my parents, their histories and struggles in Germany as Gastarbeiter, while it also engages with the struggles against necroborders in Europe; the intersectional feminist movements against feminicide in Central and South America or *Abya Yala*;[3] the struggles against state and police misogynoir violence of #SayHerName[4] in the United States; and the resistance of refugees and migrantized[5] people against the coloniality of migration in Germany. Here, in particular, I attend to the intense political grief work of families, relatives and friends who have lost their loved ones in racist attacks from the 1980s until today. I have read blogs, homepages and newsletters; listened to podcasts, webinars and Sound Cloud episodes; and attended—and sometimes organized—gatherings, rallies, political events and lectures. I have paid close attention to how families, relatives and friends articulate, analyze and grapple with their respective experiences of loss. My mourning has been traversed by their grieving practices; their thoughts have nourished my seeing. It is in this entanglement of affect and thought—thinking through feeling, or *sentipensar*[6]—that I have borne witness to their accounts. Sentipensar has theoretically and methodologically textured my path through the political labor of mourning as the presenting of those lost. I engage with what Ashley Noel Mack and Tiara R. Na'puti (2019), drawing on María Lugones (2010), call "intersubjective witnessing," a heuristic decolonial approach that decenters my authorial position by privileging the voices of the communities of resistance as theory. Their analysis of the contemporary forms of racist and cisheteropatriarchal violence guide me in the understanding of the political communal labor of mourning. Bearing witness to the stories and accounts of political organizations, families, relatives and friends, but also engaging with the historical, cultural and social analysis of mourning and *Trauerarbeit*, or grief work, this book explores decolonial mourning as political action, affective labor and a site of necropolitical social reproduction. It traces the historical material fabric and the affective texture of a grieving caring commons, while it follows the building of a conviviality infrastructure against migration-coloniality necropolitics and for reparative justice.

Coloniality-Migration Entanglements

On 3 October 2013, a fishing boat carrying 500 people seeking refuge in Europe sank near the coast of the Italian island of Lampedusa. Three hundred and sixty-eight passengers lost their lives. The co-founder and vice president of the Archivio delle Memorie Migranti/The Archive of Migrant Memories,[7] Ethiopian-born Italian filmmaker Dagmawi Yimer, published his video *Asmat*[8] in 2015, commemorating the victims of Lampedusa by naming "each and every one, to make us aware of how many lives ended on one single day, in the Mediterranean sea."[9] As Yimer writes in the post "Nomi senza corpi":[10]

Nomi senza corpi (Names without bodies)
On 3 October 2013, many young people with names such as Selam (peace) or Tesfaye (my hope), left us all at the same time.

Naming our children is a way of telling the world about our hopes, our dreams, our beliefs, or about the people and things we respect. We choose meaningful names for our children, just as our parents did for us.

For years these names, and their load of flesh and blood, have left their birthplaces, going far from home, composing something like a written message, a message that has reached the threshold of the Western world. These names have defied manmade boundaries and laws, have disturbed and challenged African and European governments.

If we can understand why and how these names fell so far away from their meaning, we might be able to transmit an endless message to our children, grandchildren, and great-grandchildren.

Although the bodies they belonged to are gone, those names linger on because they have been spoken and continue to live even though they are removed from their human constraint. Deafened by a chaos of poisoned words, we can't hear them. But those syllables are alive because they have been inscribed in the cosmos.

The film's images give space to these names without bodies. They are meaningful names although it might be difficult for us to grasp their meaning.

It is necessary for us to count them all, name each and every one, to make us aware of how many names lost their bodies on one single day, in the Mediterranean sea.

(Dagmawi Yimer)

Yimer's words linger in my mourning for those[11] who lost their lives while attempting to reach the coasts of the European Union. His insistence on naming the victims reverberates throughout this book. The deaths of refugees en route to Europe underline the historical responsibility and accountability of this continent, where I live and am a citizen. My mourning for my parents, on the other hand, brings Germany's Gastarbeiter history to the fore (Klee 1972; Kourabas 2021). Both the loss of my parents and Yimer's commemoration of those who drowned in the Mediterranean highlight the questions of how we mourn for these losses and how these two moments relate to one another.

The relationship between my mourning for my parents and for those deaths in the Mediterranean reveals entangled histories of migration and coloniality. It is in this coloniality-migration entanglement that the question of decolonial mourning surfaces at the juncture of biopolitics and necropolitics. The lives of my parents were marked by a specific historically and locally situated articulation of racism, related to the Gastarbeiter history in Germany and Spain's peripheral and liminal positionality in the 1950s to 1980s Europe. In comparison to other articulations of racism in Europe such as anti-Black, anti-Muslim, anti-Roma, anti-refugee racisms, my parents' experiences were denoted by their Southern working class and peasant positionality in a Fordist Europe. At this time, Spain, particularly the region my parents were from, Andalusia, was characterized by a lack of industrial development, expansive agricultural extractivism and a poor educational system with high levels of illiteracy. Furthermore, the Francoist dictatorship killed, imprisoned and pushed democratic and progressive political forces into exile.

Both of my parents began working at an early age as children—my father at age 10 and my mother at age 12. My father was employed as a day laborer on the land around his village owned by *latifundistas*, or large-estate owners; later, he also labored in construction. My mother was precariously employed as a seamstress in a small business in Seville. As rural and urban working-class Andalusians, both my parents worked for over two decades before arriving in West Germany in 1962 as part of the migrant labor recruitment scheme known as the Gastarbeiterprogramm (guest worker program) (Chin 2009). My mother had heard from friends that Germany was looking for workers and went to one of the recruitment offices[12] in Seville (Bhagwati, Schatz and Wong 1984; Sánchez 2001; Sánchez Alonso 2001; Petuya Ituarte et al. 2014). Similarly, my father also learned through friends about the possibility of working in Germany. Both my parents fulfilled the recruitment criteria: they were unmarried, in their early 30s and passed the mandatory health check. My father was sent to labor in the coal mines of Bavaria's Upper Franconia, while my mother, along with approximately 30 other women from Seville, as well as women from Greece and Turkey, was recruited to the same region by the porcelain factory Oscar Schaller & Co. Nachfolger.

The Gastarbeiterprogramm was a temporary employment scheme in Western Germany based on binational agreements with Italy (1955), Spain and Greece (1960), Turkey (1961), Morocco and South Korea (1963), Portugal (1964), Tunisia (1965) and the former Yugoslavia (1968). Workers were recruited for one to two years for the mining, manufacturing, hospitality, gastronomy, cleaning and nursing sectors on a rotating system (Mehrländer 1984; Park and Fehling 2003; Chin 2009; Lee 2014; Ahn 2020). However, companies often extended their employment contracts; thus, the envisaged short-term working period for most migrant workers became a long-term project. Most workers established families and homes in Germany, as did my parents, who met and married in Germany, where I was born. Like most migrant workers of that time, my parents eventually left Germany and returned to Spain in the late 1960s with the promise of secure employment. However, the Spain they encountered on their return had changed very little. Still under Franco's dictatorship, the country was afflicted by profound economic inequality and regional disparities between rural and urban industrial regions. The southern region of Andalusia, long marked by the extractivist logic of the compartmentalization of land into *latifundios* (Arenas 2015; Vigil-Villodres 2021)—large estates usually owned by wealthy families from Madrid or northern Spain who belonged to the military, political or business elite classes of Francoist Spain—was characterized by precarious work conditions, unemployment and restricted access to education. In contrast to Madrid, Catalonia and the Basque Country, Andalusia's industrial development was limited. Migration from Andalusia to these regions and abroad provided the best option for most of the poor rural and urban populations. After living precariously in Madrid for a few years, my parents returned to Germany shortly before the introduction of the *Anwerbestopp* (the end of recruitment) in 1973.

During the Spanish Civil War, Andalusia experienced the destruction of its democratic parliamentary system and the persecution, incarceration and exile of republicans, among them Marxists and libertarian anarchists (Lidia 1997; Richards 1998; Martinez López 2014). With the socialist government's introduction of the Ley de la Memoria Histórica de España (Law of Democratic Memory of Spain) in 2007,[13] this history came to the fore, but in small villages mass graves of republicans and antifascists remain undetected to this day (Ruido 2002; Ferrándiz 2009; Villaplana Ruiz 2010; Renshaw 2016; Chaves Palacios 2019).[14] Contemporary research on Andalusia addressing internal colonization (García-Fernández 2021) disregards not only the history of emigration but also the role of Spanish colonialism in settler migration to the Americas. The erasure of this history in official Spanish historiography represents a symptomatic amnesia in the public imagination of the modern Spanish state. My parents' migration and that of the Gastarbeiter generation in general have also been largely excluded from official accounts of Spanish history. When migration studies emerged in the 1990s, the research reflected the contemporary immigration to Spain from former colonial-settler migration territories in Latin America, the Caribbean, Northern Africa and other territories in Africa, Asia and Eastern Europe (Suárez-Navaz 2004). The emigration and exile movements (Márquez Macías 1995) between the late 1930s and the 1980s from the Spanish Peninsula to other parts (see, c.f., Sánchez-Alonso 2000, 2012) of Europe, Latin America and

Australia remain underresearched until today. But also the connections of these migratory movements to Spain's colonial history remain unseen.

After a new wave of Spanish migration in 2007 and 2008—which continues today due to the global financial crisis and its concomitant economic and political crises—the topic of emigration and immigration was revisited in media, political and scientific debates in Spain. However, my parents' emigration remains rather marginal in these historical accounts. Mourning for my parents brings this memory into focus by recalling the pain, suffering and struggles of the Gastarbeiter generation while also embedding this experience within an analysis of European colonialism. It is in this regard that the Gastarbeiter becomes a cipher of a specific conjuncture of racism and articulates a particular dimension of the coloniality of migration.

The Gastarbeiter and the Coloniality of Migration

Throughout their lives in Germany, my parents encountered everyday and institutional racism against Gastarbeiter. They were often spoken down to, shouted at and ignored and learned to navigate a system that neither acknowledged nor respected them. They would often see walls painted with the slogan "Ausländer raus" (foreigners go home).

Their experience of violence against Gastarbeiter marked my parents' time in Germany. Subjected to processes of differential inferiorization, reverberating within the dynamics of colonial difference, my parents were subordinated in German society as the other of the nation. Their individual skills, qualities and professional experiences were disregarded and their labor formed part of the unskilled migrant proletarian "reserve army" serving Germany's post-1945 economic and industrial development. In other words, the Gastarbeiter was the pillar of Germany's 1950s and 1960s *Wirtschaftswunder*.

Veronika Kourabas (2021) discusses the logic of Gastarbeiter recruitment as a utilitarian device. Though my parents were not (post)colonial subjects and were members of a nation with a colonial past and present, their status as Gastarbeiter in Germany positioned them within a framework of European internal coloniality. As migrant workers, they were subjected to migration control policies circumventing the limits and potential of their mobility and residency. Their access to the labor market was determined by their usefulness or disposability as labor. As Gastarbeiter from the Southern and Eastern European peripheries and South Korea, Tunisia and Morocco, these workers were confronted with racial and cultural stereotypes, constructing them as the subordinated other of the nation.[15]

As Gastarbeiter, they were perceived and dehumanized through the prism of utility, culturally objectified as "inferior" beings and politically excluded from citizenship rights. Their workforce, considered unskilled, was used for the low-paid sectors such as the manufacturing, gastronomy, hospitality, health, cleaning and care industries (Karakayalı 2008; Bojadžijev 2012). My parents already experienced subalternity as members of the working class and peasantry in Andalusia,[16] but being guest workers in Germany brought a new dimension of differentiation through their objectification as Ausländer (Gutiérrez Rodríguez 1999). Between the 1950s and 1990s, the Ausländer in Germany marked the nation's racialized and migrantized other, relegated to a position of inferiority in terms of educational skills, professional capacities and personal autonomy. While most of the migrant workers who arrived in Germany between the 1950s and 1970s were from countries with a low literacy rate, the majority of them had previous work experience and training in the agriculture, construction, textile and service sectors (Erel 2009 and Tsianos 2002). They were trained, experienced workers whose skills were not recognized within the German labor market, which classified them as unskilled workers.

The children of Gastarbeiter experienced similar attitudes in the 1970s and 1980s: We would stand at our parents' sides as translators to make sure their voices were heard. We would often experience sanctions and disciplinary measures in response to our fierceness and resistance. I remember how the neighbors would call the police because they said we were too loud, or how our food was accused of being too smelly. Children at school would shout, "Ew, you stink of garlic." In the 1980s and 1990s, German scholars described what my parents' generation experienced as xenophobia (Bade 1987; Jäger and Link 1993; Thränhardt 1995; Wimmer 1997), analysis of racism and colonialism by the Black and African diaspora in Germany was absent from scientific and public debates at this time (Oguntoye et al. 1987; Hügel et al. 1993; Ayim 1996; Michael 2015). Yet, literature, poetry and short stories written by authors with migration biographies openly addressed racism against Gastarbeiter at this point (Biondi 1979; Biondi et al 1980, 1981, 1982, 1983; Teraoka 1987; Özdamar 1990; Chiellino 1995). One prominent example is "Mein Name ist Ausländer/Benim Adım Yabancı" (My Name is Foreigner) by the Turkish poet **Ertan Semra** (2020, DE/176), who set herself on fire in Hamburg in 1982 to protest systemic racism:[17]

Mein Name ist Ausländer,
Ich arbeite hier,
Ich weiß, wie ich arbeite,
Ob die Deutschen es auch wissen?
Meine Arbeit ist schwer,
Meine Arbeit ist schmutzig.

Das gefällt mir nicht, sage ich.
Wenn dir die Arbeit nicht gefällt,
"Geh in deine Heimat," sagen sie.

I work here /
I know how hard I work /
Do the Germans know this? /
My work is hard /
My work is dirty /
If I don't like this, I say it /
If you don't like it /
Go back to your country, they say.

José F. A. Oliver, the son of Andalusian migrants, also addressed this process of differential inferiorization by dissecting the German word "Fremd:wort" (foreign:word) (Oliver 2000, 9):

Das so leicht nicht sag- /
bar ist und wird /
aus den Angeln /
gehobene Nähe

That is not so easy /
to say and becomes /
unhinged intimacy

These writers voiced the sentiments of a generation fighting racism against Gastarbeiter in Germany. In the early 1980s, numerous migrant groups organized against the rise of anti-migrant racism. Amid debates around the new Ausländergesetz (foreigner law) across party affiliations, anti-migrant sentiments appeared widely in the media; a group of scholars in Heidelberg even issued a "warning" about the increasing *Überfremdung* (foreign infiltration) of the German population (Mecklenburg 1996). In 1982, the German government deliberated about the introduction of a "Rückkehrprämie" (return bonus) for migrants willing to return to their countries of origin (Schneider und Kreienbrink 2010). Headed by Chancellor Helmut Kohl, the conservative government passed this law in 1983, prioritizing *Ausländerpolitik* (foreigner politics) as a main point on the state agenda (Dreß 2018).[18] Racist attacks on refugees and migrants increased given this anti-migration climate. The 1980s also witnessed the inception of feminist movements headed by migrant women in Germany, termed more recently as "Migrantischer Feminismus" (migrant feminism) (FeMigra 1994; Gutiérrez Rodríguez and

Tuzcu 2021). Feminist migrant groups organized against racist patriarchal migration policies, while also critiquing the representation of migrant women in German scholarship and media as objects of research that were portrayed in an ahistorical manner, lacking any political agency, social subjectivity and cultural autonomy (see also Gutiérrez Rodríguez 1999). In sum, as the case of the Gastarbeiter demonstrates, it articulates a specific temporal-spatial coloniality-migration entanglement (Gutiérrez Rodríguez 2021) that I have elsewhere termed the "coloniality of migration" (Gutiérrez Rodríguez 2018a).

Temporal-spatial entanglement: The coloniality of migration

The analysis of temporal-spatial entanglement focusing on spatial relationalities and the interrelations between time and space has received attention in the last few decades in science and technology studies, archaeology, material culture, human geography, world history and postcolonial and decolonial studies. For example, Karen Barad's (2003; 2007) work, drawing on feminist scholarship and the philosophy of technology, focuses in particular on the relationship between space and agency. Sharpening our view on the interface between ontology and epistemology by discussing "intra-active" dynamics in human and nonhuman interactions, she complicates the relationship between matter and discourse by analyzing "agential intra-action" (Barad 2003, 814) as "the sedimenting materiality of an ongoing process of becoming" (Barad 2007, 439). As Barad (ibid, ix) argues, "[to] be entangled is not simply to be intertwined with another, as in the joining of separate entities, but to lack an independent, self-contained existence. Existence is not an individual affair. Individuals do not pre-exist their interactions; rather, individuals emerge through and as part of their entangled intra-relating." For the understanding of the temporal-spatial entanglement configuring the relationship between coloniality and migration, this perspective is relevant as it addresses "the mutual constitution of entangled agencies" (Barad 2007, 33) This notion of material bodies performatively produced through entangled intra-actions leads us to consider the relevance of space. Yet, in our analysis of coloniality-migration entanglement, the temporal dimension is equally relevant.

Following Achille Mbembe's (2001, 229) analysis of "colonial entanglement" that defines "socio-political dynamics [...] constantly shaped and mediated by multiple, overlapping modes of self-fashioning in which the past and the present function relationally," coloniality-migration entanglement relates to the overlapping of temporally interconnected spaces. The entanglement of coloniality and migration is shaped by political conjunctures, embedded in historical connection, producing specific social contingencies. The European history of colonialism and its continuation through the development of migration policies and emigration movements to settler-colonial states is fundamental to understanding the coloniality-migration entanglement (Gutiérrez Rodríguez 2021). In this sense, Mbembe's analysis of the postcolony as longue durée,[19] composed of the different temporal moments of age and duré, requires that we complicate our perception of time as static, lineal and monodirectional. Thus, for example, age does not denote a "simple category of time, but a number of relationships and a configuration of events—often visible and perceptible, sometimes diffuse, 'hydra-headed'" (ibid.). This hydra-headed phenomenon is composed of historical processes that have lasting effects on the configuration of the present. Therefore, for Mbembe (ibid., 14), our present social reality "encloses multiple durées made up of discontinuities, reversals, inertias, and swings that overlay one another, interpenetrate one another, and envelope one another" producing "an entanglement."

Introducing a differential analysis of global capitalism that departs from the methodological presumption of the "historical structural heterogeneity" of Latin American societies, the Peruvian sociologist Anibal Quijano (2000a,b; 2008) determines the coloniality of power as a longue durée. Analyzing the impact of European colonization and imperialism on the establishment of a hegemonic global power system organized along the matrix of race, Quijano develops an approach to the global expansion of capitalism based on racism. This approach reminds us of Cedric Robinson's (1983) work on racial capitalism. In his engagement with radical Black thinkers such as W. E. B. du Bois, C. L. R. James and Richard Wright, Robinson explores the logic of capital accumulation and production by considering the entanglement between colonialism, slavery and capitalism. While Robinson and Quijano seem to coincide in their analysis of the constitutive character of racism for European modernity and the development of Eurocentric white supremacist settler-colonial states, they differ in their focuses. Robinson centers his analysis on the United States, while Quijano concentrates on Latin America. Within this context, Quijano (2000a, 55) differentiates four dimensions of the coloniality of power: (a) "the control of labor and its resources and products; (b) sex and its resources and products; (c) authority and its specific violence; (d) intersubjectivity and knowledge." Maria Lugones (2007) critiques Quijano's dimension of "sex and its resources and products" by addressing the coloniality of gender. As she notes, Quijano's focus on "sex" prioritizes a biological differentiation, naturalizing the colonial binary gender system, imposed by the European colonial forces in Abya Yala. In dialogue with Black scholars, such as the Nigerian sociologist Oyeronke Oyewumi (1997), and Indigenous scholars, such as the Lebanese-American Laguna-Sioux poet and activist Paula Gunn Allen (1992), Lugones argues that the binary gender matrix is imposed as a disciplinary tool of governance and social regulation by European colonial forces in settler-colonial societies. The coloniality of gender as an intersectional framework of analysis is constitutive for the coloniality of power (Lugones 2008a,b, 2020) and draws attention to the entanglement of cisheteropatriarchy and racial capitalism. Following a similar analysis, but differing in their theoretical and methodological scope, feminist activists and intellectuals from Abya Yala—such as Julieta Paredes (2010, 2013), María Galindo (2021), Mujeres Creando (2015), Silvia Rivera Cusicanqui (2010), Breny Mendoza (2014), Yuderkys Espinosa Miñoso (2014, 2022a), Gladys Tzul Tzul (2019a,b) and Carmen Cariño Trujillo (2019, 2022)—propose a critical anticolonial or decolonial analysis of gender.

The coloniality of migration engages with Quijano's analysis of the coloniality of power, Lugones's critique of the coloniality of gender and Robinson's examination of racial capitalism. Yet, as we will see throughout this book, contemporary struggles against migration-coloniality necropolitics, including anticolonial, decolonial, abolitionist and intersectional feminist and antiracist struggles against incarceration, necroborders, feminicide and racist killings, shapes my understanding of the current articulation of the coloniality of migration. The coloniality of migration matrix is characterized by the implementation and development of a global system of differentiation and racialization on which social hierarchies are established in distinctly local ways along the cipher of "the refugee" and "the migrant". For an analysis of contemporary intersectional forms of racism, the perspective of the coloniality of migration is central. It attends to new forms of colonial differentiation and categorization of individuals and populations produced by asylum and migration discourses and policies that contribute to the subordination and dehumanization of people by subjecting them to an objectifying logic of racial or cultural differentiation within a cisheteropatriarchal ableist capitalist system of exploitation. In short, the coloniality of migration describes the reactivation of colonial residues of the logic of cisheteropatriarchal ableist racial capitalism, manifested in the governance of migration, migration policies and laws as well as in the cultural production of Europe's racialized-migrantized other. In this sense, the Gastarbeiter denotes a moment of political conjuncture and historical contingency of the coloniality of migration as expressed within German Fordist and Postfordist society. In comparison to France and the United Kingdom's (post-)colonial labor migration recruitment in their respective colonies between the 1940s and 1960s, Germany recruited its workforce from regions with authoritarian fascist regimes and extreme economic disparities. These regions, as we have noted through the example of Andalusia, were often shaped by the dynamics of European internal coloniality, creating specific local forms of racialization and differential subalternity. In the context of Gastarbeiter recruitment in

Germany, as we have previously seen, the logic of colonial othering was activated through the coupling between Ausländer, as an exclusionary category defining exteriority to and cultural difference from the nation, and Gastarbeiter, as a utilitarian workforce recruitment model. Setting decolonial mourning within the framework of the coloniality of migration as an articulation of the coloniality-migration entanglement leads us to consider the intra-relational character of mourning and its multiple sites of resistance.

Mourning Sites

Rememory—Eingedenken: Memory and Doing

The politics and labor of mourning actualize the lives lived. Decolonial mourning engages with Toni Morrison's *rememory*: the actualization of memory through the work of remembering and telling a story. In Morrison's 2019 essay "I wanted to carve out a world both culture specific and race-free," she describes how rememory engages with the historical and societal circumstances that shape existence. Likewise, her novels address the effects of a "racialized society" and the affective harm this produces. Thus, writing as rememory is for Morrison (ibid.) "not simply recollecting or reminiscing or even epiphany. It is doing [...]." Rememory, then, connects with practice; it is about reassembling or postulating other ways of living, speaking and seeing that go unnoticed or are silenced in official national historiographies. As Ashraf Rushdy (1990, 303) notes, rememory connects to a "primal scene [...], an opportunity and affective agency for self-discovery through memory." For Rushdy, rememory surfaces at the juncture of psychology and narratology. It represents working through the experiences of the self and the search for words. In Morrison's case, the process of writing is the act of rememory, endowing the narrative with a "mimetic quality," which Rushdy (ibid.) defines as "a remimesis." This means Morrison's rememory is a political act that acknowledges the experiences of suffering caused by racism but also resists racism through writing. Rememory is a communal act that mirrors commonly shared experiences and articulates a sense of self inextricably tied to its community. Rememory offers healing, creates legibility of experiences and enables their public recognition and understanding.

Morrison's concept of rememory resonates with Walter Benjamin's *Eingedenken*. Translated into English as "remembrance," Eingedenken is a neologism that Benjamin introduces in *Über den Begriff der Geschichte* (2010) (*Theses on the Philosophy of History*), written between 1939 and 1940. With this term, Benjamin focuses on the moment of hope as resistance, while facing the Shoa and the rise of fascism in Germany. Following his seminal *Passagen-Werk*

(1982) (*Arcade Project*) and his reflections on Charles Baudelaire (2017) and the construction of history (1965), Benjamin's Eingedenken implies what Heinrich Bleicher-Nagelsmann (2020),[20] echoing the German philologist Hans Mayer[21] (1992a/b), describes as "die Hoffnung im Vergangenen" (the hope in the past). Mayer and Bleicher-Nagelsmann interpret Benjamin's Eingedenken as an elaboration of the initial remarks of Ernst Bloch (1918) in *Geist der Utopie* (orig. 1918; 2018) (*The Spirit of Utopia*) and *Thomas Münzer* (1989) on the dynamics of the past in the shaping of the present. In fact, Bloch introduces this term, contrasting remembering as a static moment with Eingedenken as a future-oriented act. Thus, as Bleicher-Nagelsmann (2020) concludes, the focus lies not on what the past dictates but on the potential for a different future. It is the "Jetztzeit"—the now-time—that shapes the attempt to reconstruct history (Benjamin 2010).

For Benjamin, the term Eingendenke is a *Gedankenspiel*: an intellectual exploration that is not conceptually determined.[22] It relates to other German words that are etymologically and semantically similar, such as *Gedenken* (remembrance) or *Andenken* (commemoration). In contrast to Hegel's understanding of *Erinnerung* (memory), Eingedenken refers to how memory influences our thinking and actualizes our present. As Benjamin noted in the *Arcades Project*, Eingedenken challenges the positivist assumption of historicity by conceiving history as shaped by yearnings for happiness in the past, overshadowed by the present experience of suffering but indicating a possible future. Eingedenken works within a dialectical movement where the past is materialized in the present. This is not just a temporal relationship but also a spatial one. As George Ulrich[23] notes, "the conceptualization of Eingedenken is to Benjamin intimately related to a rethinking of the structure of experience." Thus, "the conceptualization of Eingedenken involves negotiating a complex dialectic of loss and liberation." Eingedenken is a "composite concept" (ibid., 30) that relates memory to a practice that might produce a different historiography based on thinking (*denken*) through remembering (*erinnern*). Ulrich (ibid., 29) considers Benjamin's idea of the relationship between memory and practice, as articulated in Eingedenken, as a form of "dialectics at a standstill"—"where the contrasting moments are not continually mediated and resolved (ibid) but rather 'flash together' in points of heightened tension" (ibid., 31). He traces the concept of Eingedenken through three stages: (a) "a moment of remembrance," (b) practice, marking a "paradoxical strategy" and (c) political stand. Decolonial mourning relates to these three stages as (a) an act of remembrance, (b) a communal practice and (c) a political demand for reparations (ibid.). As such, it evolves within the dynamics of "dialectics at a standstill" by expressing a present moment of grief, while articulating memories of the past and their actualization through contemporary practices of resistance. In this sense, my mourning for my parents traverses the mourning for those human beings that seeking refuge in Europe have lost their lives in the Balkan routes and the Mediterranean. It is this memory of my parents' Gastarbeiter experience in Germany that informs my witnessing of the deaths of people facing border necropolitics and the coloniality of migration in Europe. In this regard, mourning as labor and political action is driven by rememory and Eingedenken as acts of remembering and resisting modern colonial intersectional violence as we will also see when we attend to the analysis of feminicide and misogynoir state and police violence of #NiUnaMenos, #SayTheirName and Women in Exile.

While decolonial mourning historically and politically delineates a politics of memory, it ontologically relates to epistemologies of resistance (Medina 2012), particularly from Indigenous, Black and Women of Color cosmologies and relationality (cf., Tzul Tzul 2018a,b; 2019a,b; Espinosa Miñoso, Gómez Correal and Ochoa Muñoz 2014; Altamirano-Jiménez 2013; Kermoal and Altamirano-Jiménez 2016; Todd 2017; Leyva Solano and Icaza 2019; Mendoza 2014, 2015; Mendoza and Paredes Grijalva 2022).

Additionally, decolonial mourning also connects to Arturo Escobar's (2020; 2018) relational ontology of *sentipensar con la tierra* (thinking-feeling with the earth). Drawing on the Colombian sociologist Orlando Fals Borda (2015), Escobar develops a pluriversal approach to human-nonhuman relationships, resonating with the Zapatista Movement's credo of "otro mundo es possible" (another world is possible), where many worlds exist (donde quepan muchos mundos).[24] Connecting to the local struggles of *campesinos* (rural workers), Fals Borda (2015) develops sentipensar to conceptualize feelings and emotions as a dimension of an intelligible understanding of society. In fact, as Gabriel Restrepo (2016) argues, this concept establishes a different approach to the role of emotions in occidental philosophy, which largely prioritizes the Cartesian *cogito ergo sum* and neglects the role of feelings (Jaggar 1989). By emphasizing the synthesis between feeling and knowing, sentipensar focuses on the intertwining of affect and practice. With this term, Escobar addresses new worlds and forms of knowing based on Indigenous feminist (Cariño Trujillo and Montelongo González 2022) analyses of multispecies relationships, and as Marisol de la Cadena (2015) defines it, "co-labor" (co-work). Arising from the immediacy of living and doing, sentipensar emerges from and with the earth. Land, plants, animals, rivers and winds are not just external to human life; they are inextricably connected to it. In her 2021 doctoral dissertation "Grieving Geographies, Mourning Waters," Meztli Yoalli Rodríguez Aguilera connects this thinking to grief and mourning and raises the question of ecocide and grief as method. Exploring the environmental devastation of the Chacahua-Pastoría Lagoons on the Pacific Coast of Oaxaca, Mexico, she questions its economic, social and emotional impact on Black and Indigenous women. While my own monograph does not directly engage with questions of ecocide, terracide or extractivism, I do seek to engage with the analysis and theoretical framing of relational ontologies, planetary connections and cosmologies in other ways. In writing this book, I am indebted to sentipen-sar/thinking-feeling and committed to acknowledging the entanglement of memory, thoughts, affect and political practice. My grieving for my parents has wandered along these pluriversal routes by bearing witness, listening to stories of sorrow and being present in struggles against necropolitics and necroborders.

Necropolitics–Necroborders: Structural Violence and Resistance

Some scholars have addressed the question of mourning by analyzing the dynamics of necropolitics (Mbembe 2003)[25] in the context of EU migration and border regulations (cf. di Maio 2013; Albahari 2016; Stierl 2016; Ticktin 2016; Rygiel 2016; Danewid 2017; De Genova 2018; Smythe 2018; Horsti and Neumann 2019). Over the last two decades, racist images of people drown-ing in the Mediterranean while attempting to reach European shores have appeared daily on television and social media. As I have argued elsewhere (Gutiérrez Rodríguez 2018b), these images do not engage the empathy of spec-tators or move them to act. Rather, they succeed only in converting dehuman-ization and cruelty into a routinized image of the racialized other as a signifier of thanatopolitics or necropolitics (cf. Sontag, 1977; Brown, 1987; Mortensen and Trenz, 2016; Friese 2018; Smythe 2018; Barry 2021). Racialized bodies floating in the water; young children dying on the shore: such images are set within a racist iconography (Tate 2015) and scopic relationship (Gelbin 2010) portraying the racialized other as nonhuman (Wynter 2003; Weheliye 2014)—as bodies related to death and allowed to die in public view.

This routinized media representation does not draw attention to human lives; rather, as Édouard Glissant (1997) discusses in the *Poetics of Relation*, the other appears within representation, signifying exteriority to the hegemonic self. Its presence is defined in relation to the hegemonic self through mech-anisms of annihilation-negation of the existence of the other. Coloniality and racism compound this othering, where the other is racialized, inferior-ized and reduced to "thingness" (Césaire 1950; Fanon 1952; Dussel 1995; Mbembe 2013). While simulating compassion, the use of these images subjects the lives of those who have died to the necrophilic desire of the hegemonic gaze. In her reflections on the afterlife of slavery and the use of images and accounts in public discourses and representations, which reiterate the violence and cruelty inflicted on enslaved bodies, Saidiya Hartman observes (Hartman 1997, 3–4),

> the casualness with which they are circulated, and the consequences of this routine display the slave's ravaged body. Rather than inciting indignation, too often they immure us to pain by virtue of their familiarity—the often repeated or restored character of these accounts and our distance from them are signaled by the theatrical language usually resorted to in describing these instances and especially because they reinforce the spectacular character of black suffering.

These images and accounts are placed in the "zone of non-being" (Fanon 1952), where Blackness is confronted with anti-Black racism (Gordon 2005, Maldonado Torres 2007). However, as Glissant (1997) notes, the zone of the nonhuman and nonbeing is one of a right to opacity (Davis 2019; Bachir Diagne 2020), where life takes place, subjectivity is formed and resistance is organized and continued. In this regard, Hartman (1997, 4) invites us to witness "the face of the world-destroying capacities of pain, the distortions of torture, the sheer unrepresentability of terror" not by becoming voyeurs but by reading the dominant account against its grain and attending to the truth of the subjects who have suffered this violence. In other words, *by witnessing* their agency and resistance.

Within this context of necroborders, Alessandra di Maio (2013) has introduced the term "Black Mediterranean," drawing on Paul Gilroy's (1993) "Black Atlantic." This term posits the Mediterranean as a site where the European continent is confronted with its history of transatlantic slavery and colonialism, while also emphasizing African diasporic agency. It denotes the ambivalence between oppression and resistance condensed in the crossing of the Mediterranean by Black people subjected to migration and asylum control laws that produce what di Maio calls "Black death." Following di Maio's argument and embedding the death of Black people in the Mediterranean within an analysis of racial capitalism, S. A. Smythe (2018) critiques the accumulation logic behind the enumeration of those who have died or survived the Mediterranean crossing. As Smythe (ibid., 5) notes referring to Katherine McKittrick's (2014) "mathematics of unliving," the construction of Europe's "necropolitical machinations of callous and dehumanizing statecraft" continuously reiterates "patriarchal White supremacy." All of Europe is complicit in this statecraft, "be it for their withdrawal of funding, their past colonial exploitation and gross historical underdevelopment or their current militaristic and neoliberal practices in Africa, which have exacerbated migration across the increasingly treacherous route" (Smythe 2018, 6). At the same time, Smythe (ibid., 7) emphasizes that rather "than existing solely as a metaphor, a fixed geography or a paradigmatic site of loss often referred to as a 'wet cemetery,' the Black Mediterranean is a variegated site of Black knowledge production, Black resistance and possibilities of new consciousness."

Besides the media spectacle of racialized and migrantized lives, the representation of these deaths in the Mediterranean appeals to humanitarian discourses (Fassin 2012; Ticktin 2016) for the white audience. They are visually and discursively portrayed as the inevitable outcome of a natural catastrophe or the actions of criminal smuggler rings. The orchestration of fabricated compassion unfolds within these discourses while the EU negotiates further controls of maritime borders, with some European member states patently refusing to allow refugee ships entry to their ports. As Miriam Ticktin (2016) notes, while the discourse on humanitarianism creates an object of compassion assumed to be innocent, its very presence disrupts the normative order. Detached from any moral sense of receptivity (Butler 2015) or ethical response to act in responsibility,[26] the relationship of the hegemonic white European racialized self (Danewid 2017) to the suffering and death of the racialized other is one of affective disconnection. As will become clear in this book, decolonial mourning disrupts this disconnection by addressing the ethical principle of a caring commons based on the realization of mutual dependency. In other words, decolonial mourning stresses ontological relationality and material interdependency through grief-resistance.

Grief-Resistance

Mourning as an ethical condition (Butler 2004; 2009; 2015), as antiracist politics (McIvor 2016; McIvor et al. 2021), as feminist struggles against war (Athanasiou 2017) and against necroborders in Europe and the United States (cf., Stierl 2016; Lewicki 2017; Squire 2015; 2020) is about resistance. Maurice Stierl (2016) links mourning to political activism through what he calls "grief-activism." Drawing on Butler's work on mourning and Jacques Rancière's notion of the political as a site of precarious connections, contradictions and ambivalences in neoliberal post-democratic times, Stierl explores his own political work as an activist in WatchTheMed Alarm Phone[27] as grief work. Likewise, in her engagement with political work on the US-Mexico and Italian borders, Vicky Squire (2015; 2020) has noted how advocacy and political work involve practices of mourning. Some of these practices are directly related to bereavement and funerals, such as painting crosses or grave dressing. Other practices are more indirectly triggered by feelings of grief, such as the creation of humanitarian corridors supporting the rescue, medical and legal infrastructure that enable the crossing of borders, as I will discuss in the next chapter in relation to the NGO Caminando Fronteras.

Christina Sharpe (2016), on another level, introduces wake work following Hartman's focus on agency in the afterlives of slavery by attending to "the wake." The wake is a "flow" that "cuts through all of our lives and deaths inside and outside the nation" (ibid., 3); Sharpe introduces the wake as a point of inflection between "care," thinking, and "Black non/being in the world." On "defending the dead," Sharpe (ibid., 10) asks:

> What does it mean to defend the dead? To tend to the Black dead and dying: to tend to the Black person, to Black people, always living in the push toward our death? It means work. It is work: hard emotional, physical, and intellectual work that demands vigilant attendance to the needs of the dying, to ease their way, and also to the needs of the living.

The "vigilant attendance to the needs of the dying" exemplifies (ibid., 11) wake work, that is, "grief, celebration, memory, and those among the living who, through ritual, mourn the body of the dead person from death to burial and the drinking, feasting and other observances incidental to it." In this sense, "new ways to live in the wake of slavery, in slavery's afterlives, to survive (and more) the afterlife of property" (ibid., 18) are imagined. While wake work is "attentive to mourning and the mourning work that takes place on local and trans*local and global levels" (ibid., 19), it also "troubles" conventional forms of mourning as commemoration by insisting on "modes of attending to Black life and Black suffering" (ibid., 22).

Decolonial mourning resonates with Sharpe's wake work while considering mourning as a democratic principle (McIvor 2019; 2021), mourning as a site of feminist struggles (Athanasiou 2017) and mourning as political activism (Stierl 2019). As my own work does, these authors depart from Butler's inspiring and critical analysis of mourning as an ethical condition. Grief, particularly what Butler defines as transversal grief, mirrors a common realization of "the apprehension of the precarity of others" (Butler 2009, xvi). As Butler writes, the "apprehension of the precarity of others—their exposure to violence, their socially induced transience and dispensability—is, by implication, an apprehension of the precarity of any and all living beings" (ibid.). Thus, "even if my life is not destroyed in war, something of my life is destroyed in war, when other lives and living processes are destroyed in war" (Butler 2015, 43). Butler echoes here Esteban Muñoz's (1999, 73) assertion on communal mourning that "we do not mourn just one lost object or another, but we also mourn as a 'whole' by feeling that we are losing a part of ourselves." This existential realization constitutes the moment of "receptivity" as an "ethical obligation" to mourn for the lives of others. Butler's reflections on mourning draw on Emmanuel Lévinas's concept of altruism, departing from the dual logic of self and other. While altruism derives from empathy for the other, it operates within the self/other divide. This dichotomy is rooted in liberal occidental thought. As Fanon (1952), Wynter (2003) and Glissant (1997) observe, liberal occidental thought is organized around the dualism of self and other. The constitution of the sovereign self is established through the negation of its alter ego, the other. Historically, this logic is reflected in violent processes of dehumanization, annihilation and genocide, designating the other as inferior through the attribution of colonial, gender and racial difference. Decolonial mourning moves away from this logic of self-duality by approaching grief work as relational and pluriversal.

Decolonial mourning embraces a planetary cosmological thinking that acknowledges that each individual life is interdependent and connected to the well-being of other human beings and planetary inhabitants, such as animals, plants, rivers and mountains. Decolonial mourning is sustained by multispecies and planetary relationships. As we will see in Chapter 4, it draws on genealogies of knowledge based on Indigenous epistemologies, relational ontologies and cosmologies from Turtle Island (North America) and Abya Yala. Following the Maya K'iche' political theorist and activist Gladys Tzul Tzul's (2018b) understanding of the interdependency between life and death, this work is inspired by her thoughts on the cycle of life. This book then charts a perspective on mourning that goes beyond lamentation and lays open the labor of mourning attached to the rhythms and rites of life connected to death. I argue that pluriversal grief work is work that is necessary to repair past, present and future lives (Chapter 4) within a circular understanding of temporality (Rivera Cusicanqui 2012, Sempertégui 2021a; Espinosa Miñoso 2022b).

While decolonial mourning is connected to vulnerability, suffering and loss, it also emerges from centuries of intersectional struggles. It is a form of "rexistência" that Andreea Sempertégui develops in dialogue with women from the Achuar, Shuar, Sapara, Kichwa, Shiwiar, Andoa and Waromi communities of the Ecuadorian Amazon. Through this perspective, Sempertégui engages with rexistência (Sempertégui 2021a), a struggle for life as resistance. Sempertégui looks everyday practices, connections and networks through which autonomous, self-determined and sovereign communal living takes place. The term rexistência has inspired me to think about decolonial mourning as a form of resistance intertwined with our daily life practices. It is an attempt to resist while living under necropolitical conditions such as those articulated by necroborders, feminicide and the coloniality of migration. As resistance practice, decolonial mourning highlights Europe's responsibility and accountability while demanding reparative justice, as I conclude in Chapter 7. Decolonial mourning calls for an analysis of the systemic character of structural intersectional violence rooted in European colonialism and raises the question of reparations. It does this by engaging with mourning as political work, following the multiple struggles of decolonial trans, queer and feminist movements against necropolitics (Snorton and Haritaworn 2013; Haritaworn, Kuntsman and Posocco 2014; Valencia 2010, 2018; Valencia and Arnaiz Zhuravleva 2019; Segato 2017; Sagot 2017; Cariño Trujillo 2020).

Political work

Drawing on Bonnie Honig's discussion of the abuses of "sentimental rhetoric" in politics—particularly by populist and authoritarian forces— David McIvor, Juliet Hooker, Ashley Atkins, Athena Athanasiou and George Shulman (McIvor et al. 2021) attempt to think through the potential and limits of the politics of mourning. In complicating the politics of grief and grievance, particularly in the United States, they are interested in mourning practices as a field of political negotiations. For example, through a focus on "psychic tax," Hooker (McIvor et al. 2021) discusses the need for democratic states to make reparations to those communities subjected to racism. Though this book does not engage with psychic tax per se, it reflects on demands for reparations for communities experiencing intersectional violence. The impact of this violence on subaltern, racialized, migrantized and impoverished communities was aggravated during the Covid-19 crisis (Zinzi and Moon 2020; Neely and Lopez 2022). Throughout the pandemic, state commemoration mourned the victims of Covid. However, the understandings, practices and social relations of, or on, mourning vary between cultural, political and national contexts. As I have argued elsewhere (Gutiérrez Rodríguez 2018b), these state commemorations perform national communion by including some populations and excluding others. Behind these public rituals of state commemoration lies not only the performance of national unity (see critique in Honig 2009; McIvor and Hirsch 2019) but also what Butler (2004; 2009) calls the "metrics of grievability." Or, what Esteban Muñoz (1999, 74) has addressed as the "various battles we must wage in their names," when it comes to mourning "the lives of people of color, lesbians, and gay men."

While some bodies are publicly mourned, other bodies are omitted in these official acts of remembrance. The absence of national mourning for those who died in the Mediterranean reflects this divide. The lack of a wider publicly stated official mourning for these losses, though remembered by their families and friends, as we will see in Chapter 2, speaks of national amnesia and affective disconnections (see also critique from Utlu 2013). Similarly, we will attend in Chapters 4, 5, and 6 to the political labor of communal mourning that disrupts the matrix of denial and abandonment of those who lost their lives to feminicide, misogynoir, state and police violence and the necropolitics of the coloniality of migration. Trying to understand this dynamic, through her analysis of Serpil Temiz Unvar's words "not this time," Çiğdem Inan (2022) suggests that we reflect on "the relationship between dispossessed mourning, negative affectivity, and fleeting resistance" (Chapter 6). In the context of racist violence, Inan notes that mourning is caught in "the work, paradoxes, and difficulties of a politics of grief" when the mourner is confronted with constant "public withdrawal and annulment." Yet, as Inan states, this realization transforms pain and "the knowledge that for this grief there will be no public reciprocation, condolence, or testimony" into a "resource for social change." Dispossessed mourning becomes a site of radical politics for antiracist racialized and migrantized communities. While attentive to dispossession, decolonial mourning understands mourning as affective labor and political action, as care work that is constantly done on the level of the individual, family, neighborhood and community, and contributes as such to social reproduction. As we will discuss in this book, the communal political labor of mourning forges a caring commons, creating, maintaining and supporting the conviviality infrastructure of rexistance.

On another level, as George Shulman (McIvor et al. 2021) notes, right-wing populisms are utilizing the politics of mourning in reactionary ways. As Gilroy (2000) observes in his analysis of postcolonial Britain, conservative and right-wing discourses engage with politics of commemoration to evoke a glorious imperial past. Grounded in national myths of cultural authenticity and monoethnic origins, these discourses mobilize what Gilroy defines as "imperial melancholia," which imagines the nation as white, Christian and monocultural. The history of colonial imperialism and Britain's involvement in the transatlantic slave trade, resulting in its contemporary diasporic connections, is erased from the performance of national mourning. The politics of mourning works here as an affective vehicle for constructing the imaginary of Britain as an insular white nation, detached from its colonial imperial past and present (Hine, Keaton and Small 2009). In settler-colonial societies, the commemoration of the past is related to the establishment of white European settler communities as the origin of modernity (Tuck and Yang 2012). Imagining European white settlers as agents of history, industrial development, economic progress and scientific advancement, as Eve Tuck and K. Wayne Young (2012) note, promotes the oblivion of the genocidal history of settler colonialism. Countering official amnesia, decolonial and

Indigenous feminist movements, such as Idle No More[28] in Canada, as well as scholars and activists in Abya Yala, such as Xochitl Leyva Solano, Rosalba Icaza, Lorena Cabnal, Betty Ruth Lozano Lerma, Aura Cumes and Irma Alicia Velásquez Nimatuy, place resistance to colonial modern necropolitics at the forefront of their mourning politics. Following Laura Rita Segato's (2016) analysis of feminicide as a new form of conducting war, these authors emphasize the centrality of sexual domination in the display and exercise of colonial violence (Leyva Solano 2019, 14). As Leyva Lozano states, war is defined in plural ways (ibid., 79, my translation):[29]

> [...] To a certain extent, by pluralizing the notion of "war" we are attempting to decolonize and depatriarchalize it by expanding its experience, perception, understanding and interpretation and emphasizing how "wars" today are also present in the micro, the everyday, the interstitial, enacting multiple forms of violence and death in the plural form.

This book attends to the analysis of this plurality of violence when it looks at the political labor of communal mourning—the intersectional struggles against different forms of entanglements of everyday structural violence. Addressing these systemic forms of violence through decolonial mourning entails looking at quotidian acts of grieving, their political implications and disruptive force. The political labor of communal mourning puts demands for reparations at the center of the political agenda, as I will discuss throughout this book and particularly in Chapter 7. As we will see, political movements like #BlackLivesMatter, #NiUnaMenos, #SayHerName, Refugee Strike and Women in Exile; movements against racist violence in Germany, including Unraveling the NSU Complex and Initiative 19. Februar Hanau; and numerous initiatives campaigning for the investigation and prosecution of unsolved racist murders work along these lines of communal affective labor.

Communal affective labor

The political communal labor of mourning challenges the hegemonic politics of mourning on two levels. First, by breaking public silence and countering state historiographies' erasure of the systematic killing of Indigenous, racialized, migrantized, trans, queer, feminized, crip, homeless and impoverished bodies. Second, by organizing political protest in the form of living-resistance by honoring the presence of the lives lived in contemporary struggles against cisheteropatriarchal racial capitalist necropolitics. The political communal labor of mourning draws attention to the fact that *where* we mourn and *who* we mourn for is historically embedded and related to hierarchies of power and modes of exploitation, contested by communities through grief and struggle.

Decolonial mourning is not just a reminder of our common vulnerability and the experience of dispossession of communities subjected to necropolitics and structural intersectional violence, or the recognition of "loss as an occasion for radical imagination and futurity" (McIvor et al. 2021, 169). Rather, it is about the materiality of our lives in a triple sense: as (a) affective labor, (b) relational ontology and (c) social reproduction. As affective labor, decolonial mourning speaks about connections and the immediate work that is required to live with loss. As relational ontology, it addresses our multispecies interdependency and interconnectivity, in particular the relationship between life and death, the human and nonhuman. As a site of social reproduction, it is foundational for the establishment and recreation of our social relations. As affective labor turned into political action, decolonial mourning represents an immediate act of transformative reparative justice, embedded in a long-term struggle for dignity, respect and reciprocity. It draws attention to the spatial and temporal entanglements in which our lives unfold, connect and disconnect.

Mourning as a form of subversive politics is not a straightforward one: it goes beyond what Athanasiou (McIvor et al. 2021) terms "dissident mourning." As McIvor et al. (2021, 168) argued, "mourning has its ambivalences" and deals with the messiness of an internal and external world. As practices of mourning are embedded in a historical societal context, they can become part of reactionary, racist and fascist politics, conjuring up false unity and mobilizing racial, gendered divides. They can also be confused with a therapeutic approach that seeks absolution for wrongs or "a connection to a possessive form of love" (ibid.) where mourning is understood as sacrifice. Nevertheless, I subscribe to the aim of McIvor et al. (2021, 169) to examine "the value of a critical concept of mourning or the promise of mourning as a means of organizing or engaging in praxis." In other words, I am interested in mourning as a progressive political communal practice.

In this vein, decolonial mourning as political communal affective labor is not the equivalent of Honig's (2009) "mortalist humanism" or "lamentation politics." Rather, following Athanasiou's (2017) "antagonistic mourning,"[30] decolonial mourning surfaces as a moment of personal unease turned to politics, when mourning results in working with and against agony. In this sense, decolonial mourning also resonates with Sharpe's (2016) wake work as accentuating the ambivalence between suffering and struggling embodied in the practices of mourning. Thus, decolonial mourning underlines the moment of living and striving against all odds under conditions of necropolitics. Attending to these social antagonisms and inspired by the double bind of Sharpe's (2016, 22) wake work, which she describes as "the modalities of Black life lived in, as, under, despite Black death," decolonial mourning focuses on the anticolonial, antiracist, trans-queer-feminist communal affective labor of mourning.

Book Outline

This book develops the concept of decolonial mourning by first looking at death, grief and mourning. Departing from Sigmund Freud's Trauerarbeit, Chapter 2 traces mourning as affect and interrogates the social meaning of the practices of mourning connected to attitudes toward death. It discusses communal grieving practices in order to understand Trauerarbeit as a set of material and relational acts required to work through the constant presence of death in life. Trauerarbeit is grief work, accounting for the pain of loss, while paying tribute to the lives lived. As reparative work, decolonial mourning engages with previous generations and delineates a common justice project, engaging with the lives of present generations and those still to come. As such it articulates the cycle of life, connected to death (Tzul Tzul 2018b).

Chapter 3 discusses the labor of mourning as political action and draws on Hannah Arendt's *vita activa* in a decolonial reading that employs intersectional feminist and antiracist critiques. I examine the potential of Arendt's notion of political action while critically dissecting her dichotomy between labor and work. I then consider mourning as emotional and physical work connected to reproductive labor. In other words, mourning as political action is related to the work of a caring commons. Chapter 4 focuses on mourning as affective labor and a site of necropolitical social reproduction. By thinking through social reproduction, I attempt to understand mourning as affective labor that addresses lives impacted by necropolitics. The political labor of communal mourning is reproductive in biopolitical ways, while resulting from the societal conditions of necropolitics. In this sense, mourning as affective labor speaks about social reproduction at the interstices of life and death. This argument is further developed by engaging with the political grief work of intersectional and decolonial feminist movements against feminicide that focus on the connection of land, body and territory (Cabnal 2017; 2017; Colectivo Miradas Críticas del Territorio desde el Feminismo 2017). Attending to the politics of mourning articulated by Latin American feminist movements against feminicide around the #NiUnaMenos campaign—particularly in Argentina and Mexico—this chapter raises the question of decolonial mourning as relational ontology. In chapter 5 we bear witness to the political labor of communal mourning by paying close attention to Kimberlé

Crenshaw and the mothers, sisters and friends of the African American Policy Forum #SayHerName campaign. In doing so, this chapter introduces *bearing witness* as methodology and *accountable listening* as method, thus engaging with mourning as intersubjective practice. Following Lugones's (2008) intersubjective witnessing and Mack and Na'puti's (2019) witnessing as a methodology of imagining and building Women of Color Coalitions, I situate my mourning for my parents alongside my bearing witness to the mourning for the women remembered by #SayHerName. I further develop this work of intersubjective mourning in Chapters 6 and 7, when I bear witness to the political mourning of families, relatives and friends of those who lost their lives to racist murderers. As an act of transformative justice, bearing witness is connected to collective and individual seeing, listening, speaking, remembering, documenting, denouncing and demanding an end to racist, trans and misogynist state and police violence. As already mentioned, chapter 6 bears witness to racist attacks and killings in Germany from the 1980s to the present. Mourning with the families, relatives and friends who lost loved ones in racist right-wing attacks but also to police custody and state *Lager* (imposed confinements for those seeking asylum in Germany), I bear witness to the accounts of the Arslan family in Mölln and the Genç family in Solingen, the mourning activities of the political self-organized and advocacy group Women in Exile e.V., and the demands of antiracist political groups in Germany for an end to state and police racist violence. Drawing attention to questions of accountability and reparations, Chapter 7 concludes by defining decolonial mourning in communal political terms by thinking through reparative justice and projects of common justice. On these grounds, decolonial mourning addresses multiple struggles against structural intersectional violence, seeking justice for the lives lost of family members, relatives, friends and members of community. In this vein, decolonial mourning calls for an end to colonial racist feminicide, necroborders and the coloniality of migration. It is in dialogue with decolonial, anticolonial and abolitionist transfeminist claims as well as planetary multispecies reparative goals. Let us begin this journey by exploring Freud's Trauerarbeit, or grief work.

Notes

1 Throughout this book, by writing the names in bold, I am paying tribute to my parents and the daughters, mothers, fathers, brothers and other relatives that have lost their lives to racist intersectional violence.
2 This term was introduced in December 1955, when German labor minister Anton Storch and Italian minister of foreign affairs Gaetano Martini signed a binational agreement for labor recruitment in Rome (cf., Knortz 2008). Financially supported by the US Marshall Plan, the guest worker program recruited laborers on a rotational

basis for a limited period of time to help rebuild the German economy (cf., Chin 2009; Croce et al. 2017; Zölls 2019).

3 In the Kuna language, *Abya Yala* means "land in its full maturity" and refers to the Americas. See Emilio del Valle Escalante, "Self-determination: A Perspective from Abya Yala," 2014, https://www.e-ir.info/2014/05/20/self-determination-a-perspective-from-abya-yala/.

4 See #SayHerName, the African American Policy Forum (AAPF), https://www.aapf.org/sayhername.

5 "Migrantized" refers to a person who is perceived and labeled as a "migrant" by the nation-state, which is often related not to an actual migration but to one's family. The adjective "migrantized" emphasizes the societal process of being interpellated by the state but also reinscribed by political, cultural, scientific and media discourse as a migrant. It thus highlights the process of being made a migrant. Within the context of low-paid labor migration, this designation connotes processes of othering, constructing the nation's other as inferior.

6 Here I am particularly indebted to Yuderkys Espinosa Muñoz's methodological and epistemological engagement with sentipensar. See Espinosa Muñoz (2014, 2022a); but also Xochitl Leyva Solano and Rosalba Icaza Garza eds. (2019) *En Tiempos de Muerte: Cuerpos, Rebeldias, Resistencias.* I am also inspired by Orlando Fals Borda's (2015) participatory action research as a "sentipensante" sociological methodology and Arturo Escobar's (2018, 2020) approach to committed research along these lines.

7 See https://www.archiviomemoriemigranti.net/?lang=en; see also the discussion by Thompson and El Tayeb 2019.

8 See https://www.archiviomemoriemigranti.net/films/co-productions/asmat-names/?lang=en.

9 Ibid.

10 Ibid.

11 In 2016, the IOM listed 5,143 dead or missing; in 2017 the figure was 3,116 and in 2018 it was 2,299. Between 2018 and 2022, the figures were 1,449 in 2020; around 1,885 in 2019 and 2021; and 1,283 on August 2022 (see http://migration.iom.int/europe/). As Butler discusses in *Frames of War*, the use of numbers in media representation suggests the idea of an inevitable truth. Yet, as she notes, numbers are used strategically, and some numbers are omitted in media representation. In this regard, the question arises of when a life counts. Further, as Katherine McKittrick (2014, 17) argues, the numerical representation of Black bodies reinstates the objectification of human beings by objectifying them through practices of enumeration of dead and dying bodies. She writes (ibid.): "The slave's status as object-commodity, or purely economic cargo […] acts as an origin story," where "historic blackness comes from: the list, the breathless numbers, the absolutely economic, the mathematics of the unliving." S. A. Smythe (2018) expands upon McKittrick's argument by analyzing the numerical media representation of dead Black bodies in the Mediterranean. As Smythe (ibid., 5) notes, this media representation is a "recurrent practice of enumeration, of counting people without being accountable to them. Such enumeration conforms to the logics of accumulation that structure racial capitalism. In the case of contemporary Mediterranean crossings, the counting of people who die or survive by the International Organization for Migration or various social and mass media entities reveals the quantified abstraction of Black and/or migrant lives."

12 The documentary film on the Spanish emigration in the 1960s to Germany *El tren de la memoria* (2006) by the film directors Marta Arribas and Ana Pérez provides good insight into the German state infrastructure of advertisement and recruitment of migrant workers in Spain; see the interviews with Heinz Saidel and Hans-Peter Sieber.

13 See law, https://www.boe.es/eli/es/l/2007/12/26/52/con.

14 On the 19th of October 2022, the Ley Democrática de la Memoria (20/2022) was instituted, see: https://www.boe.es/buscar/act.php?id=BOE-A-2022-17099.

15 Stuart Hall, Chas Critcher, Tony Jefferson, John Clarke and Brian Roberts introduce this analysis in their reflections on the use of racist rhetoric by the media and politicians during the early stages of Thatcherism in Britain. See *Policing the Crisis* (London: MacMillan, 1978).

16 Under Franco, Andalusians were portrayed in the Spanish media in stereotypically folkloric and patronizing terms as illiterate, ignorant and fun-loving people; in television series and films they usually appeared either as maids and peasants or individuals dedicated to idleness. In fact, during this period media representations of Andalusians were often conflated with anti-Roma racist representations. Anti-Roma racism in Spain goes all the way back to its nation building in the fifteenth century and has been manifested in several anti-Roma pogroms since then (Rios Ruiz 2003; Gallardo Saborido 2010; Garcés 2016; García Sanz 2018). The construction of Spanishness (*Hispanidad*) is based on the annihilation of the Iberian Peninsula's Roma, Muslim, Jewish and Black past and present (Lowney 2005; Martin-Márquez 2008). Moreover, Andalusia represents the liminal border between Spain and the African continent (González-Ferrin 2006, 2017; Calderwood 2018; Hirschkind 2021).

17 See the collection of Semra Ertan's poetry compiled by the author's niece Cana Bilir-Meier and her sister Zühal Bilir-Meier (2020): *Mein Name ist Ausländer | Benim Adım Yabancı. Gedichte | Şiirler* (edition assemblage. See also interview with Semra Ertan: https://www.berlinartlink.com/2021/04/06/cana-bilir-meier-interview-semra-ertan-poet-activist/ as well as the interview with Ayse Gülec (2018), and the radio-book by Canar Bilir-Meier (2017) *Semra Ertan. Her Own Voice / Kendi Sesi / Ihre eigene Stimme* as well as the short film by Cana Bilir-Meier: https://vimeo.com/90241760.

18 See *Zusammen haben wir eine Chance* (2018), a documentary film by Nadiye Ünsal, Tijana Vukmirović and Zerrin Güneş (Berlin: Verlag Yılmaz-Günay).

19 Mbembe draws on the French Annales School historian Fernand Braudel (1949): the longue durée marks a historical process interlaced in the configuration of the present. Braudel differentiates time on three levels as a short episode, a medium-term conjuncture or a longue durée. This approach to time (Lee 2018) is defined by a "differentiation of a relational plurality of social times – the short-term events or episodic history (for instance, political history), the medium-term conjunctures (such as, among others, economic cycles), and the *longue durée* of structures (the organizational regularities of social life)" (Braudel, quoted in Lee 2018, 71).

20 See Heinrich Bleicher-Nagelsmann, "Zeitgenosse Walter Benjamin – Erinnern und Eingedenken," Conference: *Erinnerns und Eigendenken*. 23 October 2020. Cologne: Hans-Mayer-Gesellschaft. See https://www.hans-mayer-gesellschaft.de/dokumentation/ and https://nrw.rosalux.de/dokumentation/id/43262/walter-benjamin-erinnerung-und-eingedenken.

21 See inaugural lecture, Hans Mayer: *Vorlesung zum 100. Geburtstag Walter Benjamin.* University Leipzig. https://www.grimmchronik.com/hans-mayer-zum-100-geburt-stag-von-walter-benjamin/.

22 See Charlotte Odilia Bohn. 2019. Historiography and Remembrance: On Walter Benjamin's Concept of Eingedenken. *Religions* 10, no. 1: 40. https://www.mdpi.com/2077-1444/10/1/40 (accessed April 2023)

23 See George Ulrich (2001): "Unforgiving Remembrance: The concept and practice of *Eingedenken* in Walter Bejanmin's Late Work," doctoral dissertation submitted to the Department of Philosophy, University of Toronto, p. 28.

24 See Comité Clandestino Revolucionario Indigena, Enlace Zapatista, https://enlacezapatista.ezln.org.mx/2018/01/01/palabras-del-comite-clandestino-rev-olucionario-indigena-comandancia-general-del-ejercito-zapatista-de-liberacion-nacional-el-1-de-enero-del-2018-24-aniversario-del-inicio-de-la-guerra-contra-el-olvi/; and Ana Esther Ceceña (2004), "Los desafíos del mundo donde en que caben todos los mundos y la subversión del saber histórico de la lucha," *Revista Chiapas* 16, https://chiapas.iiec.unam.mx/No16/ch16cecena.html.

25 Mbembe (2003, 14) defines necropolitics as a systemic project based on "the generalized instrumentalization of human existence and the material destruction of human bodies and populations."

26 For further discussion, see Jacques Derrida on responsibility for the other, *The Gift of Death* (1995) and Gayatri Chakravorty Spivak, "Responsibility" (1994).

27 For further information see *Watch the Mediterranean Sea Alarm Phone*, an online mapping platform to monitor the deaths and violations of migrants' rights at EU maritime borders: http://watchthemed.net/.

28 See Idle No More: https://idlenomore.ca.

29 [...] pluralizar la noción de 'la guerra', de alguna manera, estamos intentando des-colonizarla y despatriarcalizarla a partir de expandir su experiencia, percepción, comprensión e interpretación para enfatizar como 'las guerras', en los tiempos actu-ales, también se dan en lo pequeño, cotidiano, intersticial e involucran diferentes formas de violencias y muertes, todo en plural (Leyva Solano 2019, 14). (Translation in English mine.)

30 Through the case of the political struggle of the feminist movement for peace, Women in Black, Athanasiou engages with mourning as shaped by social asymmetries and power relations, prescribing but also limiting the potential of progressive politics.

Chapter 2

TRAUERARBEIT: DECOLONIAL MOURNING

Introduction

On 9 November 2017, the German newspaper *Der Tagesspiegel* published "Die Liste" (The List): the names of 33,293 persons who lost their lives in the Mediterranean between 2013 and 2015. The List was compiled by Istanbul-based artist Banu Cennetoğlu in collaboration with the Amsterdam project United for Intercultural Action, a network of NGOs working against nationalism, racism, fascism and supporting migrants and refugees. In 1993, this network of volunteers began to uncover the names and personal details of those unable to "legally" access the European Union as well as the circumstances leading to their deaths.[1] In a 2018 interview with Charlotte Higgins featured in *The Guardian*, Cennetoğlu comments on the hurdles she encountered while seeking funding and institutional support for this project. Since its appearance in *Tagesspiegel*, The List has been published in Greece, Bulgaria, the United States, Germany, Switzerland, Turkey and the United Kingdom. In the interview, Higgins (ibid.) classifies the work of Cennetoğlu on two levels: as (a) an act of mourning, "a lament" and (b) "practical work" manifested in the compilation of the material.

As I will argue throughout this chapter, Higgins's differentiation between mourning and work is common to modern occidental thought. Yet this divide has been complicated through peoples' beliefs, understandings and practices throughout history. Mourning is work or *Trauerarbeit* (grief work): a series of activities that deal with pain, memory, care and social reproduction and stand at the center of our lives. Despite the taboo around death in twentieth-century Northern American and Central European urban industrial settings (Gorer 1965; Ariès 1975), the twenty-first century is marked by the return of death (Gatti and Martinez 2020) and an increasing preoccupation with communal mourning (Butler 1997, 2020; Muñoz 1999).

This chapter follows these observations by raising the question of mourning as labor—as everyday activity shaping our common lives. I explore Sigmund

Freud's Trauerarbeit as decolonial practice, emanating and surfacing at the entanglement of coloniality-migration. Deriving from practices of resilience and resistance, grief works through the pain of loss while pragmatically dealing with the impact of necropolitical realities. The labor of mourning is characterized by its immediacy to life, its maintenance and its reproduction. It counters thanatopolitics and contours new future paths. Decolonial mourning manifests the death-life continuum (Rodríguez Aguilera 2021) while engaging with the reproduction of the cycles of life (Tzul Tzul 2018a) through communal political practices of resistance (Leyva Solano 2019; Ortega 2019). As such, decolonial mourning relates to multiple forms of rexistencia (Sempértegui 2021) and Christina Sharpe's (2016) wake work.

Witnessing the grief work of the Spanish sea rescue NGO Caminando Fronteras (Walking Borders), this chapter approaches this understanding by engaging with the sea rescue's political labor of mourning. Transforming "dolor en justicia" (pain into justice), Caminando Fronteras makes mourning a political act. Departing from this observation, I identify cultural formations of mourning by engaging with (a) the affective texture of grief, (b) the historical expressions of death and (c) the social practices of mourning. In other words, decolonial mourning expresses 500 years of anticolonial resistance (Mamani 2019), as the struggle of this particular organization against necroborders illustrates.

Necroborders: Dolor en Justicia

Caminando Fronteras was established in 2002 with the aim of creating networks of supporters and advocates for human rights on the Western European-African border. In their 2020 annual report #DerechoAlaVida2020 "La vida en la necrofrontera"[2] (#RightToLife 2020: Life on the necrofrontiers), the organization introduced the term "necrofrontiers"[3] to describe how restrictive migration and asylum policies in Europe and binational European-African border control agreements result in the systemic killing of migrants. Considering that the coast between Western Europe and North Africa is a complex one traversed by military, economic and political interests, Caminando Fronteras notes that the number of people disappearing in this area has increased due to policies prioritizing controlling borders rather than rescuing people.[4]

The sea rescue focuses on four crossing routes in the region between the northern coasts of Africa and the southern coasts of Spain: (a) Alborán: the coasts of Almeria, Malaga and northeastern Morocco; (b) Argelía: the coasts of Almeria, Murcia, Cartagena, the Balearic Islands, Tunisia and northwest Algeria; (c) Canarias: the coasts of Ghana, Senegal, Mauritania and southern Morocco; and (d) Estrecho: the route connecting Ceuta and other parts of Morocco with the coast around Cádiz. Two of these crossing routes— Argelía, via the Mediterranean, and Canarias, via the Atlantic—have been prominent in recent years and are both extremely dangerous. In 2022,[5] 2,390 people were registered to have died on their route to Spain. As the report "La vida en la necrofrontera"[6] notes, the dismantling of protective measures and the precarious conditions of the rescue operations at sea led to systemic failure in responses to calls for rescue. In some cases, the length of time in delivering help resulted in the unnecessary loss of lives of people that might have been saved by technical control and infrastructural preparedness. Furthermore, the report notes that the Covid-19 pandemic has exacerbated the precarious living conditions of populations in societies already experiencing extreme economic inequalities, propelling the search for employment and economic opportunities abroad. Additionally, political struggles in the Maghreb, Mali and Senegal have brought about the persecution of political dissidents, pushing them to seek political asylum in Europe. Other regional factors, such as the 2014 fishing agreement between Senegal and the EU,[7] allowing EU vessels from Spain and France to fish in Senegalese waters, have contributed to a deterioration of the living conditions of families relying on fishing in Senegal. These diverse social, economic and political elements have necessitated the emigration of families and young people from Africa to Europe (Jabardo Velasco 2006; Bledsoe and Sow 2013; Baizánnand González-Ferrer 2016; Vickstrom 2019).

It is within this context of necroborders that necropolitics has become the principle of governance on the European-African border. Specifically targeting persons from the Maghreb and the African subcontinent, the mechanisms of surveillance of this border, as already mentioned, do not prioritize the saving of lives.[8] Rather, as Caminando Fronteras argues, these mechanisms operate within the logic of structural racism and contribute to the disappearance of those individuals whose bodies are marked by the politics of racial devaluation and dehumanization, exercised within the dynamics of the coloniality of migration (Gutiérrez Rodríguez 2018a). The NGO pointedly summarizes the situation:[9]

> This institutional racism [...] goes out of its way to save white occidental citizens, but [...] ignores all calls for help from migrants of the Global South; [it] is not merely an ideological product, it is a business.

Studies revealing the connection between the arms and security industries, the militarization of borders and organized crime networks demonstrate how an increase in border and migration control restrictions is actually a lucrative business (cf., Burroughs and Williams 2018; Campesi 2018; Cuttita 2018). This business, according to Caminando Fronteras, involves "detention, deportation, torture, sexual aggression, murder and kidnapping." All of these are elements of structural intersectional violence operating in congruence with political conjunctures. The militarization of the border, a lack of respect for human rights and the racist, misogynist, ableist, transphobic and queerphobic culture extensively represented at the necroborder reflect the persistence of colonial hierarchies within modern societies. Furthermore, these articulations of structural intersectional violence are coupled with modes of (re)production, extraction and circulation of racial capitalism. In its racialized heteronormative and homonationalist form, necroborders target cisgendered as well as LGBTIQ+ people and members of dissident activist groups and communities (cf., Snorton and Haritaworn 2013; Ricard 2014; Haritaworn, Kuntsman and Posocco 2014; Mole 2021; Danisi et al 2021; Ataç, Rygiel and Stierl 2021).

Within this context, Caminando Fronteras confronts state violence and entrepreneurial profit maximization coupled with criminal ventures by engaging with the grieving process of individuals and communities, among other activities. Walking together (*caminando*) with the relatives and friends who have lost a loved one, the organization works with social media and provides 24-hour helplines for inquiries about missing persons or information on a person's whereabouts by tracking their movements between the northern coasts of Africa and the southern coasts of Spain. The political work of mourning deployed by the sea rescue also offers support and protection, as well as possibilities of "restauración y reparación de los Derechos Humanos" (restoration and reparation of human rights). Insisting on the defense of these rights, Caminando Fronteras claims the right to mourning, which entails psychosocial sustenance, the investigation of the causes of death and access to the legal system. Additionally, they organize the repatriation of the dead bodies, the denunciation of killings and the identification of missing and murdered persons, enabling families, friends and communities to process human rights violations claims at the border. In this context, support for the victims' families and friends is pertinent, especially because in the search for information on the disappearance and retrieval of loved ones' remains, the actions of families, relatives, friends and the NGO itself are often criminalized by state authorities.[10]

In other words, Caminando Frontera's response to necroborders is the political organization of communities in grief by demanding a right to life (*derecho a la vida*), the visibility of the victims and the mechanisms of victimization (*victimas y victimarios*)[11] and reparative justice in the sense of "grief justice" (*dolor en justicia*). As stated on their website,[12]

The deaths and disappearances of people at the borders open deep wounds in their families and communities. The disappearance of a companion is a form of torture with no closure, due to not knowing under what circumstances they lost their lives and where their bodies can be found. The death of a loved one, confirmed only when the body is found, results in an incomplete sense of mourning for families who are thousands of kilometers away and unable to give them a proper burial. Additionally, the legal, economic and social problems that arise for the families of the victims at the border are a burden they must endure for the remainder of their lives.

As Caminando Frontera notes, the communities and families of mourners organize an annual public gathering to grieve for their loved ones, render justice to their loss and bear witness to their perilous journeys. *Dolor en justicia* transforms the profound pain caused by the border-control-industrial complex into "truth, reparation and justice." Supporting families, friends and advocacy groups in their attempts to prosecute the authorities and individuals responsible, the NGO offers legal advice and support when claims are litigated and informs the media about the losses and disappearances on the routes from Africa to Europe.[13]

Drawing attention to the role of mourning as a force of transformation and collective political practice, Caminando Fronteras introduces us to an analysis of state violence from the vantage point of networks of resistance. As I will develop further in the book's concluding chapter, their work contributes to the building of communal political mourning networks—one site of a conviviality infrastructure—through which "people as infrastructure" (Simone 2004, 2021) forge and maintain a form of creolized conviviality (Gutiérrez Rodríguez and Tate 2015; Gutiérrez Rodríguez 2020). The activities of bearing witness, speaking justice, demanding investigation of the crimes committed, asking for the official accountability of the perpetrators and commemorating the names of the persons lost and missing are embedded in a communitarian understanding of mourning. Transforming grief into political action, through the act of mourning, enables the uttering of the right to justice. Set within this context of struggle against necropolitics and necroborders, decolonial mourning works against violence and returns dignity to the lives lived and to the families and friends of the deceased. It speaks about practices of communal caring and the potential of a caring commons, unfolding through gestures of love, compassion, condolence reciprocity, recuperation and reparation, embracing the conviction that when the life of another person is attacked or lost, one's own life is also threatened.

Let us join Caminando Fronteras in paying tribute to the lives of **Kanaté Soulayaman**, **Mbene Diop** and **Larisa**.[14] Karatoum Karamogo lost her 12-year-old son, Kanaté Soulayman,[15] on the Canary Islands route on 19 December 2019. The family was separated during a moment of confusion while boarding different *pateras* (dinghies). Karatoum and her daughter reached the Canary Island Las Palmas, but her son's boat never arrived. On 14 August 2020, the sea rescue recovered his body; by then Karatoum Soulayman was living in one of the inhumane refugee camps on the island. During her time there, she had repeatedly and unsuccessfully appealed to the authorities to search for her son. As a refugee woman, she felt stripped of her right as a mother to properly mourn for him. Caminando Fronteras supported Karatoum in her search for justice as well as the family of Mbene Diop.[16] A 21-year-old hairdresser from Senegal working in Morocco, Diop was identified on 5 May 2019 by her brother, who lives in Malaga. She had decided to join him in Spain via the Estrecho route. In Algeciras, a city in the province of Cádiz, her brother had thanked the NGO for accompanying him and his family. As he has said, "a part of the family died with Mbene. At least I am not the same. Our pain, and that of so many Senegalese families, is immense." Mbene's brother considers that they were lucky to have recovered her body, while other Senegalese families are still looking for their loved ones. Larisa,[17] a young woman from the Ivory Coast, lost her life while trying to reach the coast of Cádiz with 11 other people on 12 January 2017. Her sister Estelle, who lives in Switzerland, traveled to Algeciras to identify Larisa's body. Caminando Fronteras accompanied her throughout the journey, which they recollect on their website:[18]

> Despite everything, Estelle affirms that in Algeciras she felt accompanied and protected. Her sister was bid farewell by a large group of people from the city, who take to the street after each tragedy to publicly mourn for the dead and demand accountability. Larisa was buried on a rainy Saturday in February. A mass was held after her body was laid to rest near the sea where she died, in keeping with her mother's wishes.

Turning mourning into reparative justice, Larisa's family, together with other mourners, returned dignity to her life while also demanding political consequences and the right to public mourning. As Estelle tells Caminando Fronteras, "it is complicated to speak about all this, but it does good to speak about Larisa. I am happy, because each time we talk about her we are paying homage to her life."[19] Keeping our thoughts with the families and relatives and remembering the names of the lost loved ones, we bear witness to their mourning.

Estelle's comment introduces us to the affective dimension of mourning within the coloniality-migration entanglement. To explore this dimension we will next draw attention to Silvan S. Tomkins and Eve Sedgwick's understanding of affect and Philippe Ariés's and Geoffrey Gorer's cultural critique of Western attitudes toward death.

Cultural Predications

Affective Texture: GRIEF

In an article co-authored with Robert McCarter, Silvan Tomkins (1964; 2008) has identified eight primary affects:[20] (1) interest-excitement, (2) enjoyment-joy, (3) surprise-startle, (4) distress-anguish, (5) fear-terror, (6) shame-humiliation, (7) contempt-disgust and (8) anger-rage. He attributes the bodily responses to and sensation of grief to the feeling spectrum of distress-anguish. Like other affects, grief is classified in Tomkins's barometer as a density of stimulation (Tomkins 2008, Vol. II: 3ff.), which describes the relationship between emotion, body and mind. Grief is often expressed by corporeal reactions to pain such as tears, articulating an emotional state of mind related to sadness. Tomkins is particularly interested in how the body reacts to different stimuli. The body, Tomkins argues, seeks to satisfy its needs triggered by feelings that stimulate its response. For example, the body's reaction to hunger will be to calm this corporeal reaction by eating. In the case of grief, the body's reaction to pain, articulated through tears and lamentations, could be soothed by means of embraces and emotional support. In fact, for Tomkins, affects are visceral: they are bodily stimulations linked to corporeal reactions. The body acts but also reacts to the sensation and intensity of feelings in visceral ways; for example, feelings are reflected in facial gestures. Considering laughter in the case of joy, stillness in the case of sorrow or crying in the case of sadness, facial expressions mirror the inner life of our feelings. In the previous mentioned article with McCarter, Tomkins (1964, 120) has noted that the "inner bodily responses are the chief site of the emotions."

For Tomkins, affects are relational: they refer to a range of feelings and emotions that are interlaced and result from the dynamics produced by a set of spatial and temporal assemblies. Within this entanglement of emotions, feelings, space and time, affects surface in reaction to other affects. Feelings and emotions as sites of affect revolve in circuits of stimulation, sensation, intensity and satisfaction. Affects are impacted by corporeal stimuli, and at the same time these reactions are permeated by affective sensations and intensities. When it comes to grief, as related to distress-anguish, the temporal intensity of the sensation of pain varies according to the temporal-spatial entanglement and its corporeal impact in relation to other affects. For example, crying as a corporeal reaction can vary in duration and intensity depending on the interaction between pain and distress. The distress of sudden grief might result in deep pain, leading to an intensity of sorrow, while the distress of sudden pain might result in an immediate corporeal reaction unrelated to sorrow. As Tomkins (2008, 6) notes, the distress of sudden pain, "may be a concurrent realization of the transitory nature of the pain and distress, whereas in sudden grief the same distress response may be accompanied by an awareness of the greater distress that is soon to follow and of the permanence and irreversibility of the loss as well as its future consequences." The relationship between expectation, future consequences and the irreversibility of pain might influence the feeling, expression and perception of grief. Thus, grief is not just mediated by drive stimulations but also by social meanings, conventions and expectations. If we consider grief as an affect arising from stimulation and resulting in the expression of a visceral corporeal reaction to a feeling of pain, distress or sorrow, mourning as the response to grief can be a soothing and transformative act. Both grief and mourning articulate the connection between body and mind. The two stages of sorrow—grief as the immediate reaction to the pain of loss and mourning as the corporeal, practical and intellectual response to grief—both evolve within an affective texture.

Cultural theorists working on affect in the late 1990s emphasized the biological dimension of affect. Eve Sedgwick and Adam Frank (1995a) adopted Tomkins's analysis of primary affects by focusing on the corporeal material texture of feelings and their impact on bodies. Going beyond an analysis of representation concentrated purely on the discursive text, they suggested that attention needed to be paid to affect. As Sedgwick and Frank (1995b) argue in their essay "Shame in the Cybernetic Fold: Reading Silvan Tomkins," Tomkins invites us to leave the psychoanalytic script and engage with the visceral expression of feelings. The realization that corporeal reactions are not immediately connected to cognitive abilities enables us to understand the relational ways in which mind, emotion and body interact and are mutually interdependent.

Following Tomkins's framework, in *Touching Feelings: Affect, Pedagogy, Performativity*, Sedgwick (2003, xiii) develops an approach to corporeal materiality by exploring "promising tools and techniques for nondualistic thought and pedagogy." To highlight the difference between a representational approach and one guided by the analysis of affect, Sedgwick introduces the differentiation proposed by Renu Bora (1997) in their analysis of literary texts. Addressing what lies beyond the discursive perception of the text, Bora draws attention to the texture, the fabric and matter of what constitutes the text. Marking the material foundation of the text by adding an "x" to tex(x)ture, Sedgwick borrows Bora's understanding (cited in Sedgwick 2003,19) of tex(x)ture, denoting "the stuffness of material structure" to address, "the kind of texture that is dense with offered information about how, substantially, historically, materially, it came into being." For Sedgwick (ibid.) the uncovering of affect in the text reveals the "scars and uneven sheen of its making" like in "a brick or metalwork pot." It moves the textual analysis away from the fixation on epistemology by turning our gaze to its ontological becoming. Uncovering the affective loops, Sedgwick suggests that we should consider touching feelings by introducing "cutaneous contact" as a basis for analysis. Proposing an analysis of the societal dimension of affect, Sedgwick (ibid., 19) is attentive to how affect is "attached to things, people, ideas, sensations, relations, activities, ambitions, institutions, and any number of other things, including other affects." Sedgwick connects with Tomkins's concept of affective assemblies to acknowledge the relational character of affects: the relationships of independence, dependence, interdependence, control and transformation between affects.

For the understanding of grief, Tomkins and Sedgwick's analysis draws our attention to the corporeal (re)action to the intensity and sensation of loss, pain, suffering and sorrow, while also considering the cultural predication and social emergence of the transmission and circulation of affect. In *The Transmission of Affect*, Teresa Brennan (2004) follows this thought by uncovering the mutual interdependency between affects, things, bodies, spaces and relations. When it comes to grief, this perspective makes us aware of the role of affective assemblies, connecting sensations and intensities to practice. Mourning as a practice resurfacing from the corporeal response to grief emerges from the combination of affects, thoughts, memories and actions. Therefore, for Tomkins (2008, 266), "the loss of a loved object through death may instigate aggressions as well as distress and fear, but aggression will not return the lost loved object nor will it free me from the painful grief work of successively reducing the joy and distress, in the hopeless yearning of mourning." Combined with other affects, the practices of mourning evolve within affective dynamics, energies and (re)actions in multiple ways. Telling us about a corporeal reaction that the mind addresses by seeking solutions to its pain, the deep sorrow related to grief might unleash impotence or even aggression. In response to it, the practice of mourning might soothe the painful actuality connected to loss while interacting with a range of dispersed and agonistic feelings related to the social infliction of death.

Historical formations: DEATH

While grief is articulated by the corporeal affective stimuli triggered by the pain of loss, mourning expresses how it is dealt with pragmatically and cognitively. As a historically contingent and geopolitically situated practice, mourning varies through time and space. Drawing on the Annales School and in particular Fernand Braudel's notion of longue durée, the social historian Philippe Ariès (1975) argues in *Western Attitudes toward Death* that the way we mourn is linked to our specific historical and social context. Focusing mainly on urban regions in France and England, Ariès notices how attitudes toward death and practices of mourning vary through regions and historical periods. In the twelfth century, for example, death was considered destiny, a transcendental force determined by nature that exceeded human will, and mourning was linked to the public display of communal lamentation and redemption. During medieval times and the Renaissance, the focus shifted from the moment of loss to the relationship between the mourner and the deceased. From the eighteenth century on, notions of selfhood connected to memories of the deceased took center stage in bereavement rituals; this was further accentuated in the nineteenth century. Funerals became public sites of the display of social distinction through the performance of specific rituals and the exhibition of garments and adornments. As Ariès (ibid., 68) writes, "the death which is feared is no longer so much the death of the self as the death of another, *la mort de toi*, thy death." Thereafter, mourners and their relationships to one another through the event of death became the focal point. This is what Foucault (1984) characterized as the main feature of the modern subject "le souci de soi" (caring for one's self in relation to the other). For Ariès, mourning is a site of individual performance (ibid., 67)—"the most spontaneous and insurmountable expression of a very grave wound"—but also of social distinction.

The solemn official commemorations of the deceased are connected to melancholic or heroic remembrance of the death of others. Cemeteries became key public sites for the display of social differences through their architectural composition and compartmentalization and the arrangement and decoration of tombs. These sites and objects exhibit the financial resources and social standing of the mourners. Ariès situates these public manifestations and paraphernalia around death, bereavement and mourning, shaped by the projections, aspirations and yearnings of the mourners, within what he calls the era of "hysterical mourning." In this manner, mourning as a public site of official commemoration and private sentiments constitutes a significant object in the study of the social psyche. This was acknowledged by not only literature and painting but also psychoanalysis, which emerged in the late nineteenth century. Freud's work on mourning and melancholia is decisive here as it establishes the relationship between the individual and loss at the center of his study of the modern psyche.

During the twentieth century, the denial of death that became dominant in the public sphere led scholars such as Geoffrey Gorer (1965) to conclude that death had become taboo in advanced capitalism. In *Death, Grief and Mourning*, he discusses attitudes toward death in the United States and England in the 1950s and identifies a social tendency to keep death and mourning out of the broader public view. While until the nineteenth century, death, mourning practices and rituals were conspicuous in the public sphere, in twentieth-century Fordist societies, the social sphere of death was progressively perceived as a private matter, especially in white middle-class urban settings. In the second half of the twentieth century, practices and technologies of public mourning largely disappeared in highly individualistic urban societies. Considering Gorer's observations, Ariès (1975, 90) writes, "outward manifestations of mourning are repugned and are disappearing. Dark clothes are no longer worn; one no longer dresses differently than on any other day." Likewise, demonstrating grief in public through communal stages of lament or sorrow is avoided. As Ariès (ibid., 92) notes, a "single person is missing for you and the whole world is empty [...] one no longer has the right to say so aloud." Furthermore, in cases where these sentiments are stated publicly, they might be considered inappropriate and seen as signs of mental fragility. Death is kept away from the public sphere as it might disrupt the promise of happiness of capitalist consumer culture, since "[by] showing the least sign of sadness, one sins against happiness, threatens it, and society risks losing its *raison d'être*" (ibid., 94).

Concluding Ariès (ibid., 91) remarks that twentieth-century industrial societies are characterized by a "flight from death." The public perception of mourning in Western urban institutional settings is guided by the maxim that "society should notice to the least possible degree that death has occurred" (ibid., 90). While family members, relatives and friends may mourn in the private sphere, life must go on without disruption. Additionally, mourning should not endure beyond the official acts of commemoration and bereavement. One of my childhood memories from Seville in the 1970s is a group of hundreds of people dressed in black, walking in silence behind a hearse, blocking traffic and interrupting the daily routine; such images have largely disappeared from our everyday lives. Bereavement and mourning are today private rituals, attended only by those in a familial or intimate relationship to the deceased. This attitude toward death as detached from the public sphere has led to an increased invisibility of grief, while death has become an object of state governance, as Dominique Memmi and Emmanuel Taïeb (2009) also conclude in their analysis of attitudes toward death in the early twenty-first century.

Focusing on the role of biopolitics in institutions and referring to Agamben's sovereign power of "letting die" and Foucault's (1979) biopower centering on the administration of life, Memmi and Taïeb suggest that we look at the state's dynamics of impeding death (*ne plus faire mourir* and *ne pas laisser mourir*).

State measures preventing deaths are reflected, for example, in the increasing suppression of the death penalty. At the same time, the state has also come to mediate self-assisted suicide or attempted to reduce deaths through public health measures and the governance of the self-body-productivity nexus (cf., Brunnett 2009; Bröckling et al. 2010; Sänger 2015; Fassin 2020). Simultaneously, questions regarding "social death" (Patterson 1981) have redrawn the border between life and death (Das and Han 2015). In television and social media series, figures of the "living dead" in the form of zombies, ghosts and spirits denoting the death-life continuum have gained in popularity (Desprét 2011; Gatti and Blanes 2020). Considering the media industry in particular, there is a paradox when it comes to the public representation of death. As Donald Joralemon (2016) discusses regarding the United States at the beginning of the millennium, the expansion of social media, together with technical and medical innovations, has brought death and the dead back into public view.

The focus on the governance of death, "thanatopouvoir" (thanatopower), as Taïeb (2006a) terms it, increasingly organizes contemporary societies. As Memi and Taïeb (2009, 10) note, thanatopower attempts to understand how biopower is connected to the state's interventions and investments in organizing the social field of death (see also Gatti and Blanes 2020). Memmi and Taïeb address the paradoxical instance of regulation, connected to what Memmi (2004, 136) calls "la biopolitique déléguée" or delegated biopolitics. They (2009, 10) consider that the state administration of death reveals the "apories de la bio-politique" (aporia of biopolitics), reflected in its twofold character of promoting birth and regulating death. Following a similar analysis of death and life as intertwined, Gabriel Gatti and María Martínez (2020) discuss lives at the liminal stage of social death. Departing from research on "social disappearance," they question the porosity of the divide between life and death when "bad deaths" or "bad lives" are at stake. A special issue of the journal *Death Studies* edited by Gatti and Martínez addresses areas where death seems to govern life, such as immigration detention in the United States (Inda 2020), border lives in the Spanish colonial enclave of Melilla (Kobelinsky 2020) or the deportation machine and mass incarceration of refugees/asylum seekers in the United States (Fregoso 2020). The journal articles raise the question of how the governing of death and "death spaces" stand at the center of "modern Western humanity." "Political death," "social death" (Patterson 1981) and "muertas en vida" (the living dead), as Rosa-Linda Fregoso (ibid.) phrases it, circumvent the lives of people attempting through flight and migration to achieve freedom from exploitation, terror and persecution.

Looking at how necropolitics systematically targets non-normative bodies (cf., Haritaworn, Kuntsman and Posocco 2014), Marietta Radomska,

Tara Mehrabi and Nina Lykke (2020) make similar observations. Exploring Queer Death Studies (QDS), they link necropolitics to extinction and "ecologies of death" (Mehrabi 2020; Radomska 2020) and raise issues of "responsibility, accountability and care for/in the (dying) more-than-human world" (MacCormack 2020). QDS problematizes human-nonhuman relationships such as "nonhuman animal death" and radically rethinks abolitionist practices along these lines. Death and mourning form the core of queer theory's genealogy. Referring to Mel Y. Chen, these authors connect queer preoccupation with life and death back to radical queer AIDS activism and ACT UP. Nonetheless, as Jin Haritaworn, Adi Kuntsman and Silvia Posocco (2014) demonstrate in their anthology *Queer Necropolitics*, the question of death is connected to what C. Riley Snorton and Haritaworn (2013) also refer to in borrowing Henry Giroux's "biopolitics of disposability." From this angle, these authors draw attention to racial homonormative politics targeting the lives of queer and trans people of color.

Death as an organizing principle of the present has also become apparent in the wake of the Covid-19 pandemic crisis (cf., Chakraborty 2021; Comas d'Argemir and Bofill-Poch 2021; Garcia-Sainz and Legarreta 2021). Taïeb's (2006b) thanatopower has come to the fore in the governing of life and death through extensive state investments in vaccination and the introduction of rules regarding hygiene, self-care and the care of others. Mourning has received more attention in the public sphere through the forging of communities of mourners and the creation of numerous commemorative events (Cipolletta, Entilli and Filisetti 2022; Scheinfeld et al. 2021). Moreover, as this book demonstrates, mourning practices as communal political work are an organizing principle of people's lives in communities suffering from colonial, racist, misogynist, ableist, transphobic and queerphobic violence and the inhumane conditions of the coloniality of migration and racial capitalism.

Social practices: MOURNING

The Covid-19 pandemic crisis has sparked personal initiatives and company offers to organize mourning events for family members, relatives and friends who could not personally bid farewell to those lost, due to lockdown measures (cf., DeBerry-Spence and Trujillo-Torres 2022). Thus, the pandemic has placed acts of public commemoration on the nation-state agenda once again (Millar et al. 2020). These acts were more visible in the first year of the pandemic, while in the second year the silence around the dead due to Covid has been more noticeable. The British sociologist Toni Walter (2020) notes that while the research field dealing with death, dying and bereavement has received increasing attention, mourning as a public matter remains rather marginal. In general, contemporary Western societies seem to be shaped by a paradoxical attitude toward death, grief and mourning.

While mourning remains largely relegated to the sphere of the private, death, particularly the death of the other, has become a popular media currency. Populating television and computer screens (Sontag 1977; Brown 1987; Mortensen and Trenz 2016), these media images, as I have argued in the introduction, contribute to a normalization of gendered racialized deaths and the immunization of spectators against the affective potential to feel visceral pain. Such media representation of death does not contribute to a common sense of mourning that might be connected to combating racial, cispatriarchal, ableist, capitalist necropolitics by paying tribute, bearing witness and demanding justice for the lives lived. Instead, the production of media images of "ungrievable" bodies evolves within the dynamics of what Édouard Glissant (1997) defines as the "logic of the One" or the "duality of self-perception": the reiteration of the hegemonic self's fantasies and projections. While simulating compassion, the inflammatory use of images of racialized bodies struggling for survival or the objectification of singular lives as part of an unidentified dead mass serves the necrophilic desire of the hegemonic white gaze. At the same time, these images are instrumentalized for self-serving humanitarian goals, distracting and silencing the accountability and responsibility of state institutions and actors for these deaths. A humanitarian discourse (Fassin 2012; Ticktin 2016; Cuttita 2018) is thus created through the object of compassion, alluding to what Gloria Wekker (2016) defines as "white innocence": the creation of European nations performing the oblivion of their colonial-imperial past and contemporary necropolitics. Contesting this form of self-serving white European compassion and capitalist expansion of a death industry, communal forms of mourning such as those I will examine in this section shed a different light on the potential of mourning as a transformative collective force.

Mourning is a (re)action to the pain of loss, a transformative force that turns grief into action. The German word *Trauer* does not differentiate between grief and mourning, whereas the English language's distinction between grief and mourning enables us to distinguish the corporeal reaction from the cognitive response to the pain of loss. Though Trauer engages with the pain of grief, mourning as a practice in the German term "betrauern" departs from the divide between the subject of mourning and the object being mourned for. "Betrauern" refers to an intersubjective relation, the subject-object dyad, in which one mourns the loss of a significant other or object, indicated by the prefix "be".

Practices of mourning mirror our emotions, the inner world of our self and the expectations and norms around death and bereavement in society. Mourning articulates the subjective sensation and social enactment of working through grief. As we have seen, for Tomkins (2008) the affect of grief is expressed in bodily reactions such as trembling legs or uncoordinated responses like stuttering or blankness of mind. The act of mourning channels these corporeal reactions according to a relational script, drawing on personal feelings and social expectations. In mourning, the subject in grief actualizes and revises its relationship to the deceased. In the acknowledgment of love for the lost person, the subjects of mourning mirror themselves in relation to the lost. As Petra Strasser (2003) notes, the act of mourning articulates an intersubjective moment between an inner and external dialogue with those lost, opening new potential for the interpretation of one's own subjectivity and relationships. Thus, as Strasser (ibid., 49) argues,[21]

> Loss is also reflected in the mourner themself: as themself and a social body. In sorrow, the mourner finds an expression for themself and an expression that addresses the significant other. In the act of mourning, there is always a social gesture. Thus mourning contains creative potentials, but it can also symbolically trigger psychological conflicts or an attempt to solve these conflicts. Mourning that is experienced, lived and shown creates a new community.

The process of mourning evolves in connection with different social moments and creative activities related to grieving and represents a process of labor that is never completed. Though the pain might lessen, the act of mourning endures. Mourning is an integral part of our lives, an activity that never ends. According to Tomkins (2008, 290), mourning as a feeling varies "not only by virtue of varying combinations with different memories, thoughts, perceptions, and actions, but also because of varying combinations of primary affects, as well as because of varying transformations of the affective responses themselves." This understanding of mourning as a relational, creative and transformative force leads us to consider communal mourning.

Communal mourning

The reflections of Ariès (1975) and Gorer (1965) on Western attitudes toward death draw on examples from contexts with high levels of individualization in white urban middle-class settings in Britain and the United States. Their studies consider neither gendered forms of mourning nor mourning practices in multifaith, Indigenous, Black, Latine and other racialized communities in

Britain or the United States. Nor do their studies consider practices of mourning in Mediterranean regions. C. Nadia Seremetakis's (1991) study on women's mourning practices of lamentation in Inner Mani, a southern region of Peloponnese Greece, complicates Ariès and Gorer's observations by introducing feminized communal practices of mourning in the rural Mediterranean.

Proposing a diachronic analysis of mourning, Seremetakis focuses on a series of laments in the form of lyrics that express Inner Mani women's love, respect and appreciation for their lost loved ones. As these laments reflect the Inner Mani's community death and mourning rites and thus the social life of belief systems, Seremetakis opts for a cultural analysis that begins with the "optic of death" (ibid., 15). Asking whether theory can, "shift from the familiarization of death to the defamiliarization of the social order by death" (ibid., 14), she interrogates Ariès's observation on death as "the deep structures of premodern social life" (ibid.). She challenges a linear temporality in the process of mourning and adopts Ariés's methodological framework of the longue durée, developing a diachronic analysis that reveals the parallel existence of so-called premodern and modern elements. At the juncture of these temporalities, Inner Mani women's mourning practices consist of vernacular rituals and belief systems that evade the logic of an established social order.[22] Complicating the chronological divide between the modern and the traditional, Seremetakis interprets laments as communitarian forms of mourning realized through the labor of mourning. As such, the performative practices of mourning embodied by the laments of Inner Mani women are a form of resistance to the centralized practices of mourning propagated by state and religious institutions. Their laments are not Durkheimian (2001) "eccentric" events that mark the exception to an established social structure; rather, following Ariès, the laments express and enact the social order established by the community of Inner Mani and performed by women. As Seremetakis (1991, 14) states, "the defamiliarization of social order through the optic of death is precisely the central task and cognitive orientation assumed by Maniat women in their performance of death rites."

Seremetakis's study introduces us to mourning as gendered communal work that defamiliarizes the dominant social order through local practices, their social meanings, popular rhythms and vernacular aesthetics. Connecting to a tradition in anthropology that focuses on death studies as a field of knowledge production and transgression (cf., Panagiotopoulos and Santo 2019), Seremetakis traces the other of modernity in the mores of Maniat women's laments. She (1991, 12) also interrogates "the interplay between the theorization of death and the social context of the theorist" because the "representation of death is inflected with the stigma of a culturally defined otherness that is often erased before it can be brought into ethnographic discourse."

Critiquing individualist self-reflexive operations detached from collective ways of knowing and doing in anthropology, Seremetakis draws attention to the relationship between mourning, mourners and researchers. Within these connections, she constructs mourning as a collective practice, discerning the different genealogies of grieving and its local and global meanings. Thus, as Seremetakis (ibid., 13) argues, death cannot be conceived of in a Durkheimian manner in "a specific culture as a determined component of an overarching social organization." This approach reduces the emotional, affective and relational character of mourning to an effect of a social order. As Seremetakis argues, anthropological analysis needs to engage with the practices and vocabulary that do not form part of the hegemonic text of representation. The focus of her research (ibid., 14) is the "attempt to familiarize the death of the Other by depicting how domesticated death is in the society of the Other." Uncovering the "heterogeneous and antagonistic cultural codes and social interests" that "meet and tangle" in the death rituals and mourning practices of Maniat women, Seremetakis (ibid., 15) uses her examination of the "performance of death rites" to "look at Maniat society through female eyes." By adopting this perspective, Seremetakis approaches Mani women's labor of mourning by insisting on the value of death rites as social practices creating a gendered communitarian meaning of the connection between life and death.

Similarly, Kristin Norget's (2006) study *Days of Death, Days of Life: Ritual in the Popular Culture of Oaxaca* explicitly invites us to consider mourning practices as inserted in communal forms of knowledge and doing. Based on a study carried out in a marginal neighborhood (*colonia*) of Oaxaca, Mexico, Norget's ethnography explores popular Catholic, Zapotec and Mixtec rituals around death. Arguing that such practices strengthen social bonds by creating spaces of trust and reciprocity, Norget's research resonates with Seremetakis's observation on "death rites" as communal practices based on relationality and circular notions of temporality. Norget introduces the notion of a circular temporal rhythm in her study of how communities in Oaxaca connect to death through memories and by keeping relationships alive. Within this temporal framework, death is not perceived as an end but as, "a change, a site of transformation, a moment when relationships among the living, and between the living and the dead" (ibid., 238) are reaffirmed. In the colonia, death is a constant presence in daily public life. This is not only due to the pervasiveness of violence in Mexican society and the omnipresence of death in public life that articulates modern colonial necropolitics or what Sayak Valencia (2010, 2018) calls "gore capitalism"—a specific confluence of politics, police, military and organized crime shaping necropolitical forms of authoritarian neoliberal governance—but also to the cosmological understanding of the connection between life and death in Oaxaca's Zapotec and Mixtec communities (cf., Gargallo Celentani 2014; Leyva Solano and Icazar 2019). As Norget (2006, 239) observes, death is not an exception to life but imbricated in it as a public matter:

> [The] community gathers around so that no one is alone in this moment; no one goes into the beyond unattended; no one loses a family member and then must carry on, as though nothing happened. Grieving is never a solitary act. Nor is it a singularly sorrowful act. The dead remain with the living for as long as they, too, are alive.

Listening to the research participants in her ethnography while also mourning the loss of her own father, Norget (ibid.) recounts how "death" became "an ongoing exchange and a shared memory of belonging" in her fieldwork. This resulted in a "shift of consciousness," a "life-giving ground of connection" and a "process of reciprocity, a sharing, even a merging, of spaces."

Both Seremetakis and Norget explore communal mourning and shed light on the relationship between death and life in communities. As Norget (ibid., 240) highlights, within "such a setting the social idiom of community expresses a social vision that allows the maintenance of an image of wholeness, integrity, and permanence." The connection to death in both communities—Inner Mani and the colonia in Oaxaca—refers to a broader vision on mourning as a communal practice reflecting a specific social order, embedded in a cosmological and ontological understandings of the connection between death and life. Norget (ibid., 240) writes, "death rituals I encountered in Oaxaca showed me the wisdom of regular acts of remembrance and devotion; such acts help the living stay alive by keeping the dead alive inside them." Communal mourning is related to Oaxacan cosmology and Inner Mani women's spiritual knowledge and interrogates the divide between "us" and "them" constructed by media representations of the suffering other. Instead, it shows that the labor of mourning is a form of reciprocal communal political practice.

Political Grief: Decolonizing Mourning

In her doctoral dissertation "Grieving Geographies, Mourning Waters: Race, Gender and Environmental Struggles on the Coast of Oaxaca, Mexico," Meztli Yoalli Rodríguez Aguilera (2021) engages with grief as a method to understand the struggles of Black, Indigenous and Mestizo populations that live around the Chacahua-Pastoría Lagoons on Mexico's Costa Chica. Exploring the relationships between human and nonhuman inhabitants,

Rodríguez Aguilera examines grief and mourning as analytical tools and a conceptual framework for anticapitalist practice. The author's (ibid.) assertion that grieving is embedded in a temporality "that centers slowness and not productivity" resonates with bell hooks's[23] assumption that "to cling to grief, to desire its expression, is to be out of sync with modern life, where the hip do not get bogged down in mourning." Employing her own grief as a methodological tool, she notes (ibid.):

> While grieving, and I am speaking also through my own experience with grief, people need space for processing their emotions, to feel their emotions through the body. Grief occupies a lot of emotional and physical energy, so slowness becomes the way to live and exist. This slowness of existence through grief permits us to also concentrate in the immediate reality: what to eat, what to work on [...]

It is this temporality of grief (cf. Stewart 2020) that structures Black and Indigenous women's resistance in Costa Chica as they witness the death of animals and plants, in short, the annihilation of their living environment. Rodríguez Aguilera (2021, 2) defines this ecocide violence as "necro-mestizaje": "the sovereign prerogative to decide who/what will be allowed to live or left to die." In this region of Mexico, ecocide is connected to environmental racism, questions of territoriality and narcotrafficking violence. Rodríguez Aguilera looks at the grief work performed by these communities in connection to their grieving environment. She notes (ibid., 2) that grief work is suffused with "inner resilience and capacity to hope, dream and resist" and defines grief itself as a "collective emotional expression and agency" that refuses and counters the necro-mestizaje attempt of "erasure and slow annihilation" (ibid., 3). Thus, for Black and Indigenous people on the Costa Chica, grief is "a radical act" (ibid.) in a nation-state that has denied their very existence. In Rodríguez Aguilera's words (ibid.):

> The process of grieving draws Zapotalito women together, sharpens their critique of necro-mestizaje and its toll, deepens their resilience, fortifies their "radical hope," and imbues their righteous political anger with profound emotional force. [...] Through feelings of loss, rage, nostalgia, and sorrow, grief becomes a potentiality for political mobilization against the Mestizo project of disappearance and erasure. Black and Indigenous women repair and re-write their landscape and existence through the creation of counter-hegemonic cartographies, mutual aid projects, and practices of solidarity and care with themselves, their community, and the lagoons.

Rodríguez Aguilera's (ibid.) conceptualization of grieving practices as "a potentiality for political mobilization" speaks to my own understanding of decolonial mourning as political communal labor. It also connects to Hema'ny Molina Vargas, Camila Marambio and Nina Lykke's (2020) proposal to decolonize mourning by considering a pluriversal approach that connects with planetary cosmologies and departs from what Rodríguez Aguilera (ibid., 23) calls the "life-death continuum." As I will argue in Chapter 4 following Gladys Tzul Tzul's (2018b) observation on the cycles of life, decolonial mourning addresses the affective labor that goes into the social reproduction of the entanglement of life and death, while it is also a site of political action. Before we develop this argument further in the next chapter, let us first consider Freud's Trauerarbeit and its colonial/imperial entanglements.

Trauerarbeit: Labor and Violence

As numerous scholars have shown, Freud's analysis of mourning is embedded in a specific historical, political and geographical constellation (cf., Jones 1975; Gay 1988; Nitzschke 1996; Whitebook 2017). Between 1915 and 1917 (Freud 1949), Freud developed his thoughts on mourning in three essays: *Zeitgemässes über Krieg und Tod*, 1915 (*Thoughts for the Times on War and Death*, 1918 and 1925), *Vergänglichkeit*,[24] 1916 (*On Transience*, 1942) and *Mourning and Melancholia*, 1917. These essays address the atrocities of World War I; in the first two, Freud voices his disenchantment with intellectuals who supported the war and regrets the loss of civic values. He bases the possibility for cosmopolitanism, peace and democratic unity on the cultural achievements of European poetry and literature. In this sense, he considers himself a patriot, though he despises the cruelties of war and the chauvinism of the Austro-Hungarian Empire and is anguished over the loss of life in the war. Freud's preoccupation with loss is both personal and sociopolitical: three of his sons were drafted, his family became impoverished and he himself was a target of antisemitism.

Sadly, the experience of antisemitism was nothing new to Freud. When he began his studies in Vienna in the late nineteenth century, he joined the student association Leseverein der deutschen Studenten Wiens (Reading Society of German Students in Vienna) (Nietzschke 1996), a group of students influenced by Arthur Schopenhauer, Friedrich Nietzsche and Richard Wagner. There, he was subjected to antisemitic remarks and harassment, prompting him to abandon this association and to join the Jewish lodge B'nai B'rith instead (Gay 1988), where he met likeminded companions who supported his psychoanalytical work and had also endured antisemitism as German or Austrian Jews. In a 1926 interview, Freud stated (Gay 1988, 448): "My language is German. My culture, my attainments are German. I considered myself a German intellectually, until I noticed the growth of antisemitic prejudice in Germany and in German Austria. Since that time, I consider myself no longer a German. I prefer to call myself a Jew."

As Bernd Nitzschke (1996) and Petra Strasser (2003) argue, Freud's analysis of mourning was formed by his own experiences of antisemitism and nationalism. Following Austria's *Anschluß* (voluntary annexation) by Nazi Germany in 1938, Freud, then 83 and suffering from cancer, was forced to leave the country. He went into exile in London, where he spent the last 15 months of his life. In the three aforementioned essays, Freud addresses the question of mourning in terms of the loss of loved ones and the loss of political principles and ethical values. Set within this context, Freud's Trauerarbeit relates grief to memory work. Nitzschke (2011) draws attention to this dimension of grief work when he discusses Holocaust commemorations in Germany. Confronting the cruelty and traumatic consequences of the Shoa, Trauerarbeit deals with the experience of antisemitic violence. Trauerarbeit can also be a force of transformation—a turning point—where grief becomes practice. This may result in acts of reparation, involving the reflection of the mourner's accountability as a historical subject. Trauerarbeit, in this sense, is committed to working through the wounds, pain and trauma while also addressing the specific historical and social conditions that produced this violence. Freud's Trauerarbeit emerges from a specific historical conjuncture and sociopolitical contingency marked by World War I and its colonial/imperial entanglements.

Colonial/imperial entanglements

Freud's analysis of mourning is rooted in a critical inquiry into Europe's imperial ambitions. Yet, like other intellectuals of his time such as Max Weber, Georg Simmel, Émile Durkheim and Ferdinand Tönnies, Freud does not mention the human atrocities, territorial expansion and extractivist ventures of European colonialism and the transatlantic slave trade.[25] The initiation of the transatlantic slave trade in 1441 and the colonialization of the Caribbean and the Americas in 1492 laid the foundations for a system of global trade, resource extraction and labor exploitation that imposed European languages, cultures, religions, beliefs and knowledge on the colonized territories. As Quijano (2000) argues, this new social order was characterized by a classification system organized around the category of race, differentiating the population in racial terms. Colonial racial exploitation introduced by Portuguese and Spanish colonialism, and further elaborated by the Dutch, British, Belgian and French empires in the eighteenth and nineteenth centuries, laid the groundwork for the development and global expansion of racial capitalism (Robinson 1983).

The 1884 Berlin Conference, also known as the Congo Conference (Hansen and Jonsson 2015), grotesquely illustrates the sociopolitical landscape of the nineteenth century. Convening in the German capital, the imperial world powers—the United States, the Ottoman Empire, the Austro-Hungarian Empire, Belgium, Denmark, France, the United Kingdom, Italy, the Netherlands, Portugal, Spain, Sweden-Norway and Germany—agreed upon the partition of Africa, initiating the so-called "scramble for Africa" that brought the continent under European imperial control (Sauer 2012). The conference was triggered by the dispute between France and Belgium over ownership entitlements to the Congo-Togo region, but also by the Ottoman Empire's declining influence in North Africa and the Middle East (Blumi 2010). Otto von Bismarck, chancellor of a newly unified Germany (1871), organized this conference as both a diplomatic negotiator and interested party (Friedrichsmeyer, Lennox and Zantop 1998; Perraudin and Zimmerer 2010). Germany's central role was clearly guided by its own colonial ambitions (Onguntoye et al. 1987; El Tayeb 2001; Onguntoye 2020), realized by its official annexation of Togo, Cameroon, German West Africa (today Namibia), German East Africa (today Tanzania, Burundi and Rwanda) and German New Guinea in 1885 (Zimmerer 2021). While the Austro-Hungarian Empire was politically neutral in the Berlin Conference and did not directly participate in the territorial annexation of Africa, it did actively partake in the "imperialism of trade" (Sauer 2012, 16) through its diplomatic and military missions.

Set against this backdrop, Freud's reflections on mourning and melancholia go beyond the loss of European soldiers during World War I. Among the millions of deceased soldiers from the French, British and German armies were those conscripted from the French and British empires (Koller 2006; 2011)—a reminder of Europe's colonialism. As Peo Hansen and Stefan Jonsson (2015) argue, Europe's colonial/imperial ambitions in Africa shaped the postwar history of European integration in the twentieth century. As they further note (ibid., 17), "World War I is usually interpreted as a European conflict that expanded into global war. But it was also an event that brought the conflicts of global imperialism back to Europe." The disentanglement of Europe's imperial wars from its colonial venture has consistently been a serious shortcoming of European intellectual thought. Though imperialism would be publicly debated around World War I, leading, for example, to the fissure of the German Socialist Party,[26] the colonization of Africa, Asia, the Americas, Oceania and other territories continued. The handful of intellectuals who protested—among them Rosa Luxemburg (1913)—were silenced in political debates in Europe.

For the intellectuals of the African continent and its diaspora, an analysis of the transatlantic slave trade and colonialism is fundamental to an understanding of modern colonial societies (Gilroy 1993). W. E. B. Du Bois (2007b) and Ida Gibbs Hunt (1923), for example, established a public intellectual exchange on this question for the Black diaspora and African intelligentsia in the 1919 Pan-African Conference they organized in Paris. It was followed by a series of Pan-African Congresses in London (1921; 1923), New York (1927) and Manchester, United Kingdom (1945), which posited that the entanglements of colonialism, racism and capitalism form the core of global societies. The outspoken Jamaican feminist activist Amy Ashwood Garvey added the rights of Black and African women to the agenda of the Manchester Pan-African Congress (Reddock 2022) she co-organized with George Padmore, Ras T. Makonnen, Kwame Nkrumah and Peter Abrahams. As Rhoda Reddock (2014, 504) notes, this conference was "significant to the decolonisation process" and "was attended by many of the future leaders of independent Africa." Reddock (2022, 154) also observes that Ashwood Garvey's speeches as one of the two women who spoke at the conference addressed the call "for freedom and self-rule for the British colonies" as well as the "liquidation of racial discrimination." These debates reflected the anticolonial revolutionary spirit[27] in Africa and the Caribbean that evolved into the anticolonial struggles against European colonial rule in these regions between the 1950s and 1970s. We will now take a closer look at mourning and melancholia by situating Freud's Trauerarbeit within this colonial modern entanglement.

Mourning and Melancholia

In distinguishing between mourning and melancholia, Freud (1917, 242) describes mourning as a "reaction to the loss of a loved person, or to the loss of some abstraction which has taken the place of one, such as one's country, liberty, an ideal." Mourning is a conscious act, an "expression of an exclusive devotion" to the loss of a loved one (ibid., 243). When the work of mourning does not occur in a way that a direct engagement with the pain of loss takes place, the grieving subject rejects or diverts the pain of loss to another object or cause, resulting in what Freud defines as melancholia—a neurotic relationship to grief.

In *The Ego and the Id* (1923) along with his writings about the Great War, Freud reassesses his mourning theory by focusing on the transfer of loss to a new libido object. The ego cannot overcome melancholia because of the constant existence of loss, the endlessness of grieving. The realization of loss as a constitutive part of the modern subject turns mourning into melancholia. The fear of loss becomes aggression toward what is considered the cause of the loss—an object or another subject upon which angst, violence and destruction are projected. The "elegiac ego" (Clewell 2004, 1) bases its autonomy on the rejection and negation of what is considered the root of its fear of loss.

Further developing this in his 1914 essay "On Narcissism," Freud delineates a "topography of the psyche" (Clewell 2004, 46) consistent with his theorization of the subject as "self-centered." Yet, as Tammy Clewell (ibid., 47) notes, the focus on melancholia and mourning "involves less a lament for the passing of a unique other, and more a process geared toward restoring a certain economy of the subject." Freud develops a nuanced theory of ego formation in his later work, while in *Mourning and Melancholia* the focus is on the ego's desire and not on the objects of desire. Freud's later reflections on subject formation consider the ambiguous and contradictory desires of the ego; grief could be converted to other feelings based on a rejection or an idealization of the lost person, animal or object. In the grieving stage, melancholia expresses an idealized world "through the medium of a hallucinatory wishful psychosis" (ibid.), where the griever's lost object of desire and their relationship to it have gone beyond the affective attachment. Thus, in melancholia (Freud 1917, 245), the

> [...] object has not perhaps actually died, but has been lost as an object of love (. . .). In yet other cases one feels justified in maintaining the belief that a loss of this kind has occurred, but one cannot see clearly what it is that has been lost, and it is all the more reasonable to suppose that the patient cannot consciously perceive what he has lost either. This, indeed, might be so even if the patient is aware of the loss which has given rise to his melancholia, but only in the sense that he knows whom he has lost but not what he has lost in him. This would suggest that melancholia is in some way related to an object-loss which is withdrawn from consciousness, in contradistinction to mourning, in which there is nothing about the loss that is unconscious.

Cultural theorists have argued that Freud's approach to mourning and melancholia pertains to his earlier works on subjectivity based on an analysis of the process of individuation, where his dialectical approach to the relationship between society and the individual is at an incipient stage (cf. Clewell 2004). This perspective has guided the critical inquiry of mourning in cultural theory. For example, Judith Butler (2009, xvi) has contrasted the notion of mourning as melancholia with Lévinas's relationality by addressing "the apprehension of the precarity of others" and the realization that "their exposure to violence, their socially induced transience and dispensability [...] is, by implication, an apprehension of the precarity of any and all living beings." Considering mourning an ethical engagement with loss in *The Psychic Life of Power*, Butler

(1997) posits the "reflexive" potential of the subject to engage with "passionate attachment." She acknowledges that Althusser's interpellation theory and Foucault's subjectivation cannot explain why the subject feels the loss and the attachment to the other and thus Butler reverts to Freud's analysis of subject formation. Departing from fundamental relationality as the basis on which the relationship between the subject and the other is forged, Butler's later work (2004; 2005; 2009; 2015) focuses on the relational character of agonistic politics and mourning as ethical relationality. She draws upon Lévinas to discuss responsibility and receptivity as two premises that rely on the experience "of a common vulnerability" (Butler 2020). In assuming that one's life is intrinsically connected to the lives of others, Butler defines precarious life as a moment of interdependency. Thus, the apprehension of the precarity of the lives of others leads to the recognition of one's own precarity.

Butler's analysis shifts our focus on Freud's mourning as melancholia to mourning as the site of the political.[28] Bringing mourning back to the public sphere, she addresses the cultural politics of mourning and argues (1997, 139), "where there is no public recognition or discourse through which such (losses) might be named and mourned, then melancholia takes on cultural dimensions." As David McIvor (2012, 420) notes, Butler's (2005) engagement with mourning as an ethical gesture addressing the subject's responsibility and the common vulnerability of everyone is an incessant "reminder of our constitutive sociality, and undergirds a more generous and humble approach to shared lives together." Positing mourning as political work, cultural theory on the tension between agony and racism sheds further light onto the fraught relationship between mourning and melancholia.

Agony and Racism

Melancholia is triggered by the difficulty of facing the pain of loss, and this avoidance may transform into neurotic behavioral patterns, according to Freud. Contemporary authors such as Paul Gilroy (2000) have addressed racism by analyzing melancholia as entrenched in forms of racial formation and subjugation. Focusing on racism in postcolonial Britain, Gilroy notes the inability of white Britain to come to terms with its violent history of colonization and imperialism. Describing postcolonial melancholia in British society as a societal matrix shaping state politics and popular racism, Gilroy discusses the failure of European nations to take responsibility for colonial genocides, destruction, extraction and ongoing settler colonialism. Other cultural theorists, such as Anne Anlin Cheng (2000), José Esteban Muñoz (2006), Christina Sharpe (2016), Mariana Ortega (2019) and David L. Eng and Shinhee Han (2019), have drawn attention to racial identification as a melancholic act and racism as a structure of violence that produces systemic deaths. Sharpe transcends Freud's analysis of Trauerarbeit and melancholia with her notion of wake work.

Drawing on the 2015 *New York Times* op-ed "The Condition of Black Life is One of Mourning," by the poet Claudia Rankine, Sharpe reflects on mourning by proposing wake work. Rankine's piece pays tribute to the six Black women—**Cynthia Graham Hurd**,[29] Reverend **Depayne Middleton-Doctor**,[30] Reverend **Sharonda Coleman-Singleton**,[31] **Susie Jackson**,[32] **Myra Thompson**,[33] **Ethel Lance**[34]—and three Black men—South Carolina State senator and senior pastor **Clementa Pinckney**,[35] **Tywanza Kibwe Diop Sanders**[36] and Reverend **Daniel L. Simmons, Jr.**,[37] murdered at the Emanuel African Methodist Episcopal Church in Charleston, South Carolina, on 17 June 2015. Arguing that mourning shapes Black families and communities, Rankine draws on the photograph of the funeral of **Emmett Louis Till**. Murdered in 1955 at the age of 14 by a racist mob that accused him of offending a white woman in Mississippi, his funeral became a moment of outcry and protest. Despite abundant evidence, his murderers were acquitted. His mother, Mamie Till-Mobley, requested that her son's coffin be kept open during his funeral, telling journalists "[let] the people see what I see" (ibid.). As a result, numerous photographs capturing Till's "mutilated" and lynched body were widely disseminated in newspapers and magazines. These photographs became a catalyst in the struggle against the systemic killing of Black people in the United States. Till- Mobley's act of publicly displaying her son's dead body announces, for Rankine (2015), a "new kind of logic" reframed by "a method of acknowledgement that helped energize the Civil Rights Movement in the 1950s and 1960s."

The photograph of Emmett Till continues to serve as a reminder for the struggle for Black Lives. For Rankine (ibid.), Black Lives Matter is "an attempt to keep mourning" an ontological moment that underlines the precariousness of Black lives but also "the instability regarding a future." Aligning with "the dead," the politicization of mourning as "recognition" of our "feeling for another" by establishing a day of national mourning for Black Lives Matter speaks to the grief work that, as Rankine (ibid.) notes, "might align some of us, for the first time, with the living." It is this interminable, intense wake work that Sharpe (2016) discusses as the ontological condition of Black lives.

Wake work

Sharpe's *In the Wake* (ibid.) discusses anti-Black racism as a systemic structure constitutive of US democracy. She (ibid, 7) reiterates the question posed by Joy

James and João Costa Vargas[38] about the limits of normative frameworks of justice: "What will happen then if instead of demanding justice we recognize (or at least consider) that the very notion of justice […] produces and requires Black exclusion and death as normative?" Sharpe develops wake work as an analytical perspective to understand the connection between ontology, epistemology, materiality and historicity and the twofold character of mourning as suffering and resistance. Drawing on Saidiya Hartman's (1997) analysis of the afterlife of slavery, she proposes wake work as interlaced with care, memory and political work. Sharpe focuses on anti-Black racism in the United States and proposes that we "think 'the wake' as a problem of and for thought. I want to think 'care' as a problem for thought. I want to think care in the wake as a problem for thinking and of and for Black non/being in the world" (2016, 5). Wake work as radical care work starts from everyday gestures and practices of sharing grief and life. This entails, for example, "a watch or vigil held beside the body of someone who has died, sometimes accompanied by ritual observances including eating and drinking" (ibid., 10) but also "defend[ing] the dead," which means "hard emotional, physical, and intellectual work that demands vigilant attendance to the needs of the dying, to ease their way, and also to the needs of the living."

Understanding wake work as connected to what Rodríguez Aguilera (2021) defines as the "life-death continuum" has implications for our methodological and epistemological work. Wake work uncovers the epistemic violence underlying academic texts, reproducing the representation of Black bodies within the logic of "ontological negation" (Sharpe 2016, 14). Instead, wake work addresses "the ongoing locations of Black being" (ibid., 16) by engaging with the multiple and complex ways of living, touched by moments of suffering and vulnerability but also by instances of resistance, lines of flight and "awakening" (ibid., 18). For Sharpe (ibid.), wake work means

> to continue to imagine new ways to live in the wake of slavery, in slavery's afterlives, to survive (and more) the afterlife of property. In short, I mean wake work to be a mode of inhabiting and rupturing this episteme with our known lived and un/imaginable lives. With that analytic we might imagine otherwise from what we know now in the wake of slavery.

Wake work speaks about communal practices of care in grief, support and struggle, emerging from a specific being in the world, shaped by the experience of systemic annihilation and epistemic violence. While addressing "antiblack violence," Sharpe also warns us about the reiteration of "blackness" as a "symbol, par excellence, for the less-than-human being condemned to death" (ibid., 21). Thus (ibid., 22),

[At] stake is not recognizing antiblackness as total climate. At stake, too, is not recognizing an insistent Black visualsonic resistance to that imposition of non/being. How might we stay in the wake with and as those whom the state positions to die ungrievable deaths and live lives meant to be unlivable? These are questions of temporality, the longue durée, the residence and hold time of the wake. At stake, then is to stay in this wake time toward in-habiting a blackened consciousness that would rupture the structural silences produced and facilitated by, and that produce and facilitate, Black social and physical death.

Consequently, Sharpe's wake work is linked to a consciousness emerging from the experience of the noncitizen and delineating "particular ways of re/seeing, re/inhabiting, and re/imagining the world" (ibid.).

In Sharpe's words (ibid., 16), to "be in the wake is also to recognize the ways that we are constituted through and by continued vulnerability." Thus, wake work represents a form of working through grief. In reference to Freud, Sharpe (ibid., 17) distinguishes "Black being in the wake and wake work from the work of melancholia and mourning." Although wake work engages with "the mourning work that takes place on local and trans*local and global levels" (ibid., 19), mourning in the wake is related to specific historical contingencies marked by the history of colonialism, chattel slavery and anti-Black racism. These moments haunt and shape contemporary moments of mourning in Black communities. By situating mourning within this historical context, shaping the materiality of wake work, Sharpe challenges the Freudian analysis of mourning as a universal phenomenon that exists outside of concrete history. Wake work derives from the relationship between melancholia and mourning but moves beyond it to foreground a Being of the wake and Being in relation to the wake based on the experience of colonial and racial violence. Wake work is more than mourning; it is what Rankine describes as an ontological condition of Black being but also what Sharpe[39] describes, following Keguro Macharia (2015), as "we formations" and Glissant ([1995] 2006, 9) as "knowing ourselves as part and as crowd." The understanding of wake work as communal labor brings us back to consider mourning as José Esteban Muñoz (1999) has articulated it: "riddled with queer possibilities."

Following Muñoz's (1999) thoughts on mourning as a path to the future, Mariana Ortega (2019) examines the potential of mourning as a communal practice for forging a "becoming-with" in her essay "Bodies of Color, Bodies of Sorrow: On Resistant Sorrow, Aesthetic Unsettlement and Becoming-With." Recalling Muñoz's (1999, 74) observation that "we do not mourn just one lost object or other, but we also mourn as a 'whole'—or put another way, as a contingent and temporary collection of fragments that is experiencing a loss of its parts," Ortega proposes citing Muñoz (ibid.) mourning as an "integral part of everyday lives," a "mechanism that helps us" to "take our dead with us to the various battles we must wage in their names—and in our names." Under these conditions, mourning speaks about the material site of pain and sorrow that bodies of color experience through the violence enacted by "histories of injustice and practices of racism and xenophobia" (Ortega 2019, 125). As Ortega emphasizes, working through sorrow, communal forms of mourning can be driven by "resistant sorrow": practices of resistance sustained by a coalitional politics of transformation, striving toward racial and social justice based on what Ortega defines as "becoming-with" (ibid.).

Conclusion: Trauerarbeit as Communal Labor

In this chapter, we have discussed Trauerarbeit as work that results from the affect of grief and from the practice of mourning. We have looked at the relationship between violence and mourning by differentiating between melancholia and working through the pain of loss. I have argued that Trauerabeit is work: it is the transformative force that acknowledges the pain while unfolding different practices of coping, understanding and moving forward with that pain. Rather than residing in melancholia by diverting or transferring the pain to another object, Trauerarbeit directly faces the loss. Though it connects to the analysis of mourning as agony, it is, as Athanasiou (2017) notes, also agon—confrontation with the loss as an articulation of social conflict. As such, it resonates with Sharpe's (2016) wake work. However, wake work, as we have discussed, derives from a specific collective experiencing of the pain of loss. As Sharpe (ibid., 5) notes, thinking the wake means thinking "care as a problem for thought, (. . .) a problem for thinking and of and for Black non/being in the world." Thus, the wake work is (ibid., 10) "hard emotional, physical, and intellectual work that demands vigilant attendance to the needs of the dying, to ease their way, and also to the needs of the living." It this vein, decolonial mourning addresses a relational moment. It recalls Muñoz's (1999) mourning as a "whole" and Ortega's (2019) "becoming-with." Furthermore, as we have seen here, Trauerarbeit derives and occurs within a historical and societal context. While Freud's Trauerarbeit is set within the experience of antisemitism and World War I, Sharpe, Rankine and Muñoz' mourning and melancholia are set within the context of racial capitalism and cisheteropatriarchal entanglements. Their analyses engage with the ontological and material conditions embedded in and resulting from mechanisms of structural violence and systemic suffering. They approach mourning as communal practices of resistance, reminding us of Morrison's (2019) rememory by bearing witness and demanding justice for the lives lived.

Mourning as an ontological condition (Rankine), as wake work (Sharpe) or as "becoming-with" (Ortega) does not just speak of personal grief. These authors approach grief, mourning and melancholia through the prism of structural racial intersectional violence and resistance. It is this perspective on both, structural intersectional violence and communal mourning as resistance, that shapes my focus on decolonial mourning as Trauerarbeit—as political communal labor.

As we have seen, Caminando Frontera's political communal labor of mourning is shaped by the coloniality-migration entanglement and marked by necropolitical violence but also resistance to it. Decolonial mourning as Trauerarbeit addresses this structural violence and suffering by drawing attention to the historical and material conditions that determine interdependent lives and deaths. To mourn for lives and living processes that do not immediately seem to be emotionally or corporeally or geographically related is to recognize that our social being is historically and socially entangled. Decolonial mourning acknowledges Ortega's (2019) becoming-with, while it emphasizes the labor of mourning—Trauerarbeit, or grief work—as a productive force, a necessary societal labor that carries the potential for communal planetary living. In the next chapter, I will discuss how, resonating with Caminando Frontera's work of turning pain into justice, decolonial mourning transforms grief work into political action.

Notes

1 UNHCR, Operational Data Portal, Refugee Situation, https://data2.unhcr.org/en/situations/mediterranean.
2 Monitoreo del Derecho a la Vida 2020, Caminando Fronteras. https://caminando-fronteras.org/monitoreo/monitereo-del-derecho-a-la-vida-ano-2020/ (accessed April 2023)
3 https://caminandofronteras.org/en/life-on-the-necrofrontier/.
4 Caminando Fronteras, https://caminandofronteras.org/derecho-a-la-vida/.
5 Monitoreo del Derecho a la Vida 2022, Caminando Fronteras. https://caminando-fronteras.org/wp-content/uploads/2023/01/Monitoreo-Derecho-a-la-Vida-2022-ES-v2.pdf. (accessed April 2023)
6 Ibid.
7 See https://ec.europa.eu/oceans-and-fisheries/fisheries/international-agreements/sustainable-fisheries-partnership-agreements-sfpas/senegal_en.
8 See also discussion in the refugee networks based in Germany *The Voice* and the *Karawanne für die Rechte von Migrant_innen und Flüchtlinge – The Caravan for the Rights of Migrants and Refugees* http://thecaravan.org/node/2017.
9 "Restoration and Reparation of Human Rights," Caminando Fronteras, https://caminandofronteras.org/quienes-somos/. All translations of Spanish or German citations are mine.

10 Helena Maleno Garzón, a journalist and human rights advocate as well as one of the founders of Caminando Fronteras, has been accused by the Spanish and Moroccan authorities of working with smuggling and human-trafficking networks in Morocco and Spain. This is a distortion of Maleno's humanitarian work in Morocco, where she has regularly contacted the Spanish and Moroccan coastguards to alert them of boats in distress between southern Spain and the Moroccan coast, saving many lives in the process. In 2019, a Tangier court acquitted Maleno after a 15-month trial for human trafficking. In April 2017, a case against Maleno accusing her of having ties to a "criminal organization" in Spain was dismissed. Front Line Defenders: https://www.frontlinedefenders.org/en/profile/caminando-fronteras.

11 https://caminandofronteras.org/victimas-y-victimarios/.

12 https://caminandofronteras.org/dolor-en-justicia/.

13 https://caminandofronteras.org/derecho-a-la-vida/tragedias/.

14 https://caminandofronteras.org/dolor-en-justicia/.

15 https://caminandofronteras.org/el-dolor-de-perder-a-un-hijo/.

16 https://caminandofronteras.org/el-cuerpo-de-mbene/.

17 https://caminandofronteras.org/desaparicion-de-larisa/.

18 Ibid.

19 Ibid.

20 In some writings, Tomkins speaks of a ninth affect that he describes as "neutrality." See, for example, Tomkins and McCarter 1964.

21 In German original: "Das Verlorene ist auch der Trauernde Selbst: als Selbst und als sozialer Körper. Im Kummer findet er hierfür Ausdruck für sich selbst und Ausdruck, der sich jeweils an die, den bedeutenden Anderen wendet. Im Trauern findet sich immer auch eine soziale Geste. So hat Trauern durchaus kreative Potentiale, es kann als Symbolisierung eines psychischen Konflikts bzw. als Versuch der Lösung dieses Konflikts gesehen werden. Trauer, die erlebt, gelebt und gezeigt wird, schafft neue Gemeinschaft," (Strasser 2003, 49).

22 See also David E. Sutton (2004), "Ritual, Continuity and Change: Greek Reflections," *History and Anthropology* 15, no. 2: 91–105.

23 Cited in Rodríguez Aguilera (2022) as hooks 2001, 200.

24 Written in November 1915 and first published in *Das Land Goethes 1914–1916*, 37–38, Stuttgart: Deutsche Verlagsanstalt,1916. Here, *Gesammelte Werke*, vol. 10, 358–61.

25 Portugal initiated the European slave trade with Africa in 1441, when Prince Henry sent a trading expedition there. The triangular trade began in 1444 with Portugal utilizing enslaved workers on sugar plantations in Madeira and building Elmina Castle in 1460, the first fort, where enslaved people were incarcerated.

26 The German Social Democrats opposed Kaiser Wilhelm's imperial policies and debated the meaning of imperialism for capitalism. Ten year later, this debate resulted in the splintering of the SPD into revolutionary and reformist Marxist orientations. While the revolutionary strand would formulate a critique of imperialism as a necessary motor for capital accumulation (Luxemburg 1913, 2015), the reformist strand focused instead on the political dimension of imperialism, concentrating on debates over diplomatic and military strategies (Kautsky).

27 See, for example, the works by Léopold Sédar Senghor, Frantz Fanon, Aimé Césaire, Kwame Nkrumah, C.L.R. James, Eric Williams and Claudia Jones.

28 See also the critical discussion in Eng and Kazanjian 2003.

29 See Cynthia Graham Hurd Foundation for Reading and Civic Engagement, https://www.cghfoundation.org/what-we-do.

30 https://www.postandcourier.com/depayne-middleton-doctor/article_e69ef21a-cd49-11e6-989a-4fde0437dada.html.

31 https://scafricanamerican.com/honorees/rev-sharonda-coleman-singleton/.

32 https://scafricanamerican.com/honorees/susie-jackson/.

33 https://www.postandcourier.com/myra-thompson/article_4b6ced36-c878-11e6-a4ee-cf86ef5610f9.html.

34 https://www.postandcourier.com/church_shooting/charleston-church-shooting-victim-ethel-lances-family-suffers-yet-another-loss/article_71dde510-3513-11e9-b229-631125087d43.html.

35 https://ballotpedia.org/Clementa_Pinckney.

36 https://www.tywanzasanderslegacyfoundation.com/tysstory.

37 https://www.charlotteobserver.com/news/local/article24903601.html.

38 Cited in Sharpe 2016, 7: James and Costa Vargas 2012, 193.

39 Both authors cited by Sharpe 2016, 19.

Chapter 3

POLITICAL MOURNING

Introduction

This chapter introduces mourning as political work. It draws on Hannah Arendt's (1958) approach to action while critically exploring grief work as a site of the political. I revise Arendt's distinction of action, labor and work by engaging with Kathryn Sophia Belle's (formerly Kathryn T. Gines, 2014) feminist and anti-Black racism critique. Offering an understanding of mourning as communal political work, I engage with Gillian Rose's (1992) mourning as intense work and conclude with Athena Athanasiou's (2017) reflections on agonistic mourning.

Labor, Work and Action

In *The Human Condition*, published in the United States in 1958 and translated by the author into German two years later as *Vita Activa oder vom tätigen Leben*, Arendt introduces her analysis of the modern subject as conditioned by work, labor and action. Tracing the historical transformation of the divide between the *polis* as the sphere of the public and the *oikos* as that of the private, Arendt proposes looking at action as a site of intellectual deliberation and political transformation. Revising the occidental philosophical account of the distinction between labor and work from Ancient Greece to modern European bourgeois society, Arendt draws our attention to the distinction in Greek philosophy between theory as *vita contemplativa* and praxis as *vita activa*. Focusing on "doing" as the driver for action, Arendt approaches the sphere of the vita activa that will be translated into German as *tätiges Leben* as the site of the immediacy of the political. The political is intertwined with praxis—with the immediacy of action.

Arendt's definition of political action inspires my approach to mourning as political communal labor. Yet, while Arendt's analysis differentiates between action—as the sphere attached to universal transcendental practices—and work and labor, as pertaining to mundane activities of immediate reproduction—I propose, aligning with Steven Colatrella (2013) and Mika Ojakangas (2020), that we complicate this divide. Mourning as communal political action, I suggest, results in the entanglement of action, work and labor. The activities constituting mourning as the sphere of the political, I will argue, are configured by collective forms of exchange and deliberation but also by the immediate work constituting our daily interdependent lives. Mourning as political communal action emanates from the routinized work and reproductive labor constituting our social relations.

From animal laborans to the commons

Arendt distances herself from John Locke's premise of a society of owners, Thomas Hobbes's understanding of society as "relentlessly engaged in a process of acquisition" (Arendt 1958, 31) and Karl Marx's formulation of a "society of laborers" focused on the logic of *animal laborans*. Instead, Arendt moves beyond the sphere of the social by prioritizing action as the site of political deliberation (Kateb 2000; Villa 2000; Voice 2014). Arendt places the sphere of the political outside the organization of the reproduction of life, which is organized around basic needs and economic and material interests. Thus, while she partially agrees with Marx's diagnosis of modern society as configured by relationships of production, she differs from his view that the potential of transformation and freedom is found in the liberation from the means of production. For Arendt, the field of labor is innate to human nature so to propose that it needs to be overcome to create a society of free subjects is tautological: a conception of society based on labor relations reduces the potential to think about the political beyond the immanence of life. Arendt argues that the political must proceed not from work or labor but from action. Differentiating between labor as attending to biological reproduction and work as the sphere of the creation of tools, Arendt argues that the political is exempt from mundane needs and dependencies. The political resides in the polis as the locus exterior to the oikos, the site of generative reproduction and individual interests. Thus, political action is exterior to the reproduction of human existence; it transcends the immediacy of life and surpasses the logic of the social as a field of struggle and coercion. Instead, political action emerges through critical liberation and the force of speech, uttering the will of the commons in the public sphere.

In Arendt's view, the commons is forged and enacted in the sphere of public deliberation. Using the example of people sitting at a table separating them from the things surrounding them, Arendt relates the political to people's ability to turn objects into tools of communication and instruments for communal action. As she (1958, 52) notes, "to live together in the world means

essentially that a world of things is between those who have it in common
[...]," as the "public realm, as the common world, gathers us together and
yet prevents our falling over each other, so to speak." It is this "community
of things which gathers men together and relates them to each other" (ibid.,
55) that is transformed into a community, elevating the private and ephem-
eral existence of human beings to "worldliness"—a historical transcendence.
Communal action is thus remembered, recounted and materialized through
objects such as paintings, writing and other cultural artifacts. Human beings
are born into this common world, as Arendt (ibid.) writes:

> [...] the common world is what we enter when we are born and what
> we leave behind when we die. It transcends our life-span into past and
> future alike; it was there before we came and will outlast our brief
> sojourn in it. It is what we have in common not only with those who live
> with us but also with those who were before and with those who will
> come after us. But such a common world can survive the coming and
> going of generations only to the extent that it appears in public.

Referring to Ancient Greek philosophy, particularly Aristotle and Plato,
Arendt conceptualizes the political, constituted by public deliberation (speech)
and doing (action). These two elements, as Arendt notes citing Aristotle, represent "a kind of praxis" (cited in ibid., 57), enacted in the *agora*, the site of
assembly and debate of the polis citizens: "men" whose citizenship is established by their possession of land and the ownership of enslaved people and
women. Seyla Benhabib (1993; 2003) and Bonnie Honnig (1995; 2009) have
emphasized this appearance in public space as a performative act that does
not rely on identity politics. In contrast, Kathryn Sophia Belle (2014) and
Ayça Çubukçu (2021) have drawn attention to the historical exclusion of
women and enslaved peoples from polis citizenry and public deliberation.

Arendt's perception of the sphere of political action is oriented toward
an account of Western classical philosophy that some authors have termed
"Arendt's masculine Grecophilia" (Honkasalo 2016). Additionally, Honig
(1995) and Benhabib (1992; 1993; 1995; 2003; 2020) have critiqued her public-
private dichotomy as lacking a social historical analysis of the gendered
division of work. Benhabib draws attention to Arendt's use of the public by
noting that she neglects that the French Revolution's "emancipation of workers
made property relations into a public-political issue" (1992, 95). Furthermore,
women's struggles for political participation in the late nineteenth century
brought the sphere of the private as a public issue to the fore. However, in
Arendt's view, these social struggles have compromised the public sphere by
adding corporeal needs to the public agenda. As Arendt (1958, 73) notes:

The fact that the modern age emancipated the working classes and the women at nearly the same historical moment must certainly be counted among the characteristics of an age which no longer believes that bodily functions and material concerns should be hidden. It is all the more symptomatic of the nature of these phenomena that the few remnants of strict privacy even in our civilization relate to "necessities" in the original sense of being necessitated by having a body.

Working-class and women's struggles for emancipation brought the preoccupation with basic needs—"necessities"—to the public sphere. Arendt perceived this transformation of the public as giving way to the social realm, which is dominated by "the life process" and the logic of animal laborans. Her focus on political action, however, seeks to reestablish the public sphere as concerned with worldly matters and not with the "growing social realm" (ibid., 47). Focusing on the transformation of industrial work through the expansion of automatization, she perceives an increased integration of the sphere of labor into the public sphere. Noting that this expansion has blurred the borders between the public and the private, she nostalgically reclaims the autonomy of the private. Some theorists have described Arendt's critical examination of modernity as "anti-modernism" (Benhabib 1993; 2003). Yet according to Benhabib (1993, 112), Arendt is not invested in a "nostalgic *Verfallsgeschichte*" (narrative of decline); rather her reluctant view of modernism expresses skepticism toward the utilitarian logic of industrialization (Benhabib 2003). Denoting the expansion of the instrumental reason of homo faber, this logic articulates "the coming into being of a man-made world of things" (Arendt 1958, 121). The animal laborans contrasts this view by emphasizing human beings' need for the immediate fulfillment of their basic needs and corporeal "necessities." As Benhabib (2020) notes, labor in Arendt does not address the "highest good; not the good life of the *bios politikos* or the life of contemplation [...], but instead mere life and its sustenance." This perception of the political as exterior to the world of interests (homo faber) and of vital needs (animal laborans) detaches the sphere of the polis from its point of emergence and sustenance, the oikos.

Complicating Oikos: Redefining the Political

If we consider Marx's critique of political economy, Arendt's conceptual differentiation of labor, work and action is misleading. For Marx, social relations lie behind the modes of production and are mediated by political interests and reproductive needs coupled with the logic of capital accumulation. To proceed from a social analysis that disentangles the political from the social is a nostalgic move, as Benhabib (1993; 2003) argues. However, she (2020) reiterates that Arendt's critique of Marx does not oppose his analysis of alienation but rather radicalizes it as "labor." As Benhabib (ibid) notes, "automated or not," labor "is an anonymous process that fails to embody the individuality of the producer, thus alienating her from the very activity itself, it is only the product and activity of work which embody and bear the individuality of the maker." This observation turns Benhabib's focus away from the producer, while honing in on the process of singular creation. As she (ibid.) further states, "Arendt is not dismissing Marx's theory of alienation but what she is showing is that this theory is only intelligible if another model is presupposed." Benhabib (ibid.) suggests that we can understand this model as a "quasi-aesthetic" that works with the senses and "bears the individual mark of the maker." For Arendt, labor produces "anonymous objects, consumed in the process of the reproduction of life" (ibid.). Interrogating these presuppositions, Benhabib (ibid.) raises the question of whether the "hierarchical ontology" that Arendt establishes between labor, work and action represents a "denigration of the private sphere, of the household and of women's work."

Arendt's historical reconstruction of labor, work and action from Ancient Greece to Western European modernity operates within an analytical matrix that reduces labor to the satisfaction of biological needs, work to the fabrication of objects and action to the worldly practice of the commons. In other words, labor and work are not points of reference for Arendt when it comes to political action. As previously argued, Arendt's distinction between the spheres of the private—governed by mundane needs and individual interests—and that of the public—organized by communal political reasoning—does not capture the dynamics and interdependencies between these spheres. Arendt's insistence on the political as a site free of mundane needs and group interests and shaped by deliberative practices of reasoning is based on an idealistic model of society beyond power relations and social divides. The societal model underlining Arendt's argument is based on Athens, the polis of Ancient Greece. As a city marked by the social divide between landowning and dispossessed populations, as well as between citizens (landowning free men) and noncitizens ("barbarians," enslaved people and women), the historical point of reference for Arendt's argument requires further consideration. As Ojakangas (2020) states, this divide between the polis and the oikos disregards the fact that in democratic Athens, the oikos represented an entity of the polis—a space politically controlled and governed through laws and ordinances. Thus, the differentiation between the art of household (*oikonomia*) and the art of politics (*politikê technê*) as two separate domains does not hold if we consider, as Colatrella (2013) suggests, that Arendt's analysis conflated the three distinct historical experiences of ancient democracy, modern democracy and direct democracy. These dimensions attend to different forms of political agency that derive from the struggles against enslavement, patriarchy and labor exploitation. Colatrella thus draws attention to the political work of the enslaved and feminized subject in the oikos, transforming the oikos into a site of democratic action. On a different level, Benhabib (2003) critiques Adrienne Rich's (1979) problematization of Arendt's perception of women's work in *The Human Condition* by favoring a hermeneutic interpretation of this work over what Benhabib considers a simplistic reading that ignores the heuristic context of production of this text; however, the question of how to complicate Arendt's understanding of the gendered division of work remains pertinent. Benhabib (ibid., 4) assumes this task by "searching in the footnotes, in the marginalia, in the less recognized works of thinker for those 'traces.'" She engages with Arendt's (2021) work on the Jewish thinker Rahel Varnhagen to suggest looking at women's presence rather than their absence. Our discussion here will reconnect to Benhabib's (ibid.) question on the representation of women's work in *Human Condition* by complicating the hermeneutic horizon on which Arendt's analysis takes place.

Women's work, enslaved labor: The Other of the polis

Ancient Athenian society was organized by a political elite composed of citizens of the polis. To become a citizen in Athens, land ownership was required, a privilege granted only to men who were neither enslaved nor designated "barbarians." Citizenry enabled the participation in public politics, exercised in the agora, which was predicated on the free labor of enslaved persons and women who took care of these men's basic needs and guaranteed their social reproduction. The political action of the commons in the service of "the freedom of the world" (Arendt 1958, 31) was organized by this culture of unremunerated labor, oppression and enslavement. Addressing such historical facts in our analysis of political action in Arendt's work does not represent a "self-righteous dogmatism of the latecomers" (Benhabib 2003, 3), that is, judging the past from the perspective of the present. Rather, in doing so, we engage with moments of the past relegated to the margins of hegemonic accounts and analyses of European history and society. Tracing these moments and placing them alongside the societal constellation represented in *Human Condition* completes Benhabib's proposed hermeneutical framework of interpretation by foregrounding information that has been suppressed and widening our perspective on political action. To focus on the care and domestic work performed by women and enslaved persons in the polis necessitates that we rethink the idea of political action as purely deliberative. We must consider the sphere of care and manual work—the daily routines serving our social reproduction—as central to the rearticulation of political action that engages with politics in other ways. This addresses political action embedded in the immediacy of life and performed by those excluded from the hegemonic sphere of the political (Rancière 2007).

Thus, Ancient Greece was shaped by foundational antagonisms between the citizens of the polis and those excluded from it. Women and enslaved persons cleaned the home, cooked and organized the lives of affluent male citizens, who could then dedicate their time to free deliberation in the agora. In this way, the social order of the polis was determined by mechanisms of subjugation and exploitation based on the systemic structural violence of a patriarchal system of slavery. Within this context, zones of political autonomy and sovereignty marked by masculinity and private ownership were established for the citizens of the polis, with zones of abjection and servitude designated to the noncitizens, feminized and enslaved subjects, who provided the (re)productive labor that sustained "free men."

This hierarchical differentiation between the citizen and its subjugated other was globally reactivated during European colonialism and imperial rule. Introducing new geographical, religious, racial and ethnic divides through legal differentiation, the European colonial powers[1] established a global system of governance (James 2001), trade and organization of labor organized around the social category of race (Du Bois 2004; Robinson 1983; Quijano 2000), a colonial binary gender system (Lugones 2007) and the annexation of land and extraction of resources (Galeano 2004; Williams 1994). Capitalism, coupled with colonial difference, racism and cisheteropatriarchy, expanded globally, advancing to the dominant organizing social system of Eurocentric modern societies. At the center of this system is a gendered and racialized division of work, differentiating geographically between urban waged and unwaged workers and peasants and enslaved laborers. Gendered, racial and colonial differentiation systems operated along these lines, relegating women and the enslaved to the sphere of unpaid labor. The structural and epistemic violence of gendered colonial racial differentiation produced specific material realities and ontologies that have been challenged and opposed by specific forms of resistance to dispossession, extraction, colonization and dehumanization.

When Arendt differentiates between the spheres of work and labor, this historical specificity is either overlooked or, in the case of women, mentioned as a mere sidenote. Yet the gendered and racialized colonial division of work and the devaluation of enslaved and feminized labor were absolutely central to the configuration of modern social hierarchies. Though these social inequalities have transformed over time and through space, they remain constitutive for reflections on civil disobedience and political action.

Civil Disobedience and Political Action

In the essay "Civil Disobedience" (1972), Arendt elaborates upon her concept of political action. Arguing that civil disobedience emerges from "common conscience" (1972, 58), a shared moment of awareness, Arendt (ibid., 80) considers that civil disobedience

> arises when a significant number of citizens have become convinced either that the normal channels of change no longer function, and grievances will not be heard or acted upon, or that, on the contrary, the government is about to change and has embarked upon and persists in modes of action whose legality and constitutionality are open to grave doubt.

For Arendt, civil disobedience is political action representing citizens' concerns that have not been addressed by the state or considered in the constitution. Disrupting institutional consensus building and opening spaces for common deliberation, political action as civil disobedience is radically transformative, articulating a democratic commitment to social justice (Isaac 1998). Using the example of the US Civil Rights Movement of the 1950s and 1960s, she demonstrates how civil disobedience can change the normative legal structure of society. Thus, antidiscrimination laws are "always the result of extralegal action" (Arendt 1972). For Arendt, the Civil Rights Movement was the force heading this change and calling on the Supreme Court to act against laws that denied racial equality. Perceiving racial segregation as an "American Dilemma" (ibid., 81), Arendt refers to Tocqueville's observation of the exclusion of Black and Indigenous people in the US Constitution and the way this set the grounds for ongoing discrimination against these groups. The Civil Rights Movement denounced this constitutionally established racial injustice and demanded its abolition. In conclusion, Arendt defines the "evil of slavery" as the "original crime" that was not even remedied by the passing of the Fourteenth and Fifteenth Amendments to the Constitution. Her perception of the inherent racial inequality in the US Constitution and of civil disobedience as a motor for social justice indicates a general understanding of structural racism in her work. However, as different scholars (cf., Norton 1995; Benhabib 2003; Bernasconi 1996; Belle 2014) have noted, Arendt's analysis of racism needs to be set within the hermeneutical context of its emergence. As Joy James (2003, 253) argues, while Arendt has many observations about social racism, the constitutive character of anti-Black racism for the configuration of modern societies needs further elaboration. Belle (2014) demonstrates how this becomes apparent in two key interventions, *On*

Violence (first published in 1970), which discusses the student movement and the role of Black activism, and "Reflections on Little Rock" (Arendt 1959a, b). In the latter, Arendt introduces the idea of social racism in her analysis of school desegregation in Little Rock, Arkansas.

On Violence examines the rise of student movements on US university campuses at the beginning of the Vietnam War. Approaching the question of violence in the sense of Carl von Clausewitz's "war as the continuation of politics by other means," she expresses her dismay at what she perceives to be acts of "vandalism, [...] bad temper, and worse manners." Describing these instances as acts of violence, she discusses the ideological incoherence and democratic limitations of the students' movement. Further, voicing her disagreement with Jean-Paul Sartre and Frantz Fanon as the two public intellectuals spearheading the movement; in fact, she accuses them of lacking intellectual rigor. She even reads Fanon's discussion of violence as a glorification of armed militancy, thus distancing herself from what she considers an apologetic and undemocratic stance. However, her interpretation of Fanon's argument demonstrates a limited knowledge of his analysis of colonial violence (see Belle 2014).

In his study of French colonialism in Algeria, Fanon (1952, 1961) showed how violence is constitutive to colonial rule. Trained as a psychiatrist, Fanon was attentive to the symbolic, emotional, material and physical forms of violence structuring state and social institutions, constituting subjectivities and processes of subjectification—in short, determining colonial societies. Examining the violent psychosocial character of colonialism and racism, Fanon approaches questions of Black subjectivity formation, colonial and anticolonial consciousness and resistance. He addresses these phenomena in relation to both the construction and constitution of racialized subjectivity in *Black Skin, White Mask* (1952) and the formation of the colonial state as well as collective anticolonial resistance in *The Wretched of the Earth* (1961). With his psychosocial analytical approach, Fanon develops a methodology that implicitly echoes the analysis of the dialectic of enlightenment (Horkheimer and Adorno 1947) and the authoritarian personality (Adorno 2019) of the early Frankfurt School. He engages with critical theory by focusing on colonial power and the impact and effects of racism (Goldberg 2003). Outlining zones of being and zones of nonbeing (Wynter 2003), he uncovers the underside of modernity (Grossfoguel 2016): the construction, abjection and annihilation of the racialized other.

In the anticolonial Algerian Revolution, Fanon saw a path to liberation from colonial rule. His observations, preoccupations and analysis of violence are related to this historical conjuncture of colonial oppression but also anticolonial resistance. Arendt (1972, 162) oversees this detail when she summarizes

Fanon's work in three words: "irrational black rage." She also misreads the Black Power Movement as engulfed in a rhetoric of violence with no democratic political aim. Further, she devalues the academic credentials of the Black students in the movement by claiming that their access to education was enabled by "white guilt" (ibid., 121). In stark contrast, she (ibid., 121) describes the white students as "white rebels" whose claims she considers as "highly moral." Arendt's discussion on violence falls short of understanding colonial and anti-Black racism, as do her thoughts on the public debate about school desegregation in Little Rock in the late 1950s.

Racial segregation and anti-Black racism

In "Little Rock," Arendt attempts to understand the specificity of racial segregation in the US South. More than 90 percent of Little Rock's residents voted against racial desegregation, and a white mob tried to violently impede the access of Black students to Central High School. Arendt, who arrived in the United States as a Jewish refugee fleeing the Holocaust, felt an affinity to the struggles of the NAACP and the Civil Rights Movement against racial segregation. Although she expresses sympathy for the cause of Black people as a Jewish person (ibid., 46) who experienced antisemitic violence, she states that as a European she has little comprehension for the racial "prejudices of Americans." However, her argument evinces a gap between her analytical approach and her perception of reality (Kujala 2021). While some critiques have described this attitude toward the question of anti-Black racism in the US as ambivalent (James 2003; Johnson 2009; Belle 2009; 2014; Burroughs 2015; Owens 2017), others have drawn attention to her heuristic skepticism (Benhabib 2003) toward the realization of an antiracist society (Kujala 2021).

  While Arendt is critical of racial exclusion in a segregated school system, she also warns about the social impact racial desegregation might have on the individual Black student, fearing that Black students might not achieve full educational integration or that they may continue to experience discrimination. As James (2003) notes, her focus here is social racism, whereas she misjudges anti-Black racism as systemic structural violence. In "Racism in the Theory Canon: Hannah Arendt and 'the One Great Crime in Which America was Never Involved,'" Patricia Owens (2017) discusses the ambivalence and pitfalls of Arendt's work when it comes to Africa and the African diaspora. Referring to Arendt's *The Origins of Totalitarianism* (1951), Owens highlights the contributions of this outstanding political theorist to an otherwise exclusively white male canon. In this work that has introduced readers globally to the entanglement of imperialism (see Mantena 2010), racism and antisemitism, Arendt (1951, 206) notes that the partition of Africa was the "most fertile soil for the flowering of what later was to become the Nazi elite." Looking at how processes of racialization work by dividing populations and constructing them within racial hierarchies, Arendt examines the historical grounds and global formations of racism (see King 2004). Yet when it comes to "the nation-destroying and humanity-annihilating power of racism" of the US, her analysis seems driven by what Owens (2017, 405) describes as "horrific racial stereotypes about Africans." Arendt's distinction between the political and the social provokes a questioning of the relationship between her analytical framework and its point of empirical reference (Kujala 2021). Several scholars have discussed the inconsistency between concept and reality in Arendt's discussion of Little Rock. In fact, Arendt's observations on anti-Black racism and the political struggle against it demonstrate limited insight into this political conflict. For Owens (2017, 405), Arendt's misreading of civil disobedience as a "new form of post-totalitarian politics [...] relied on a distorted historical and political analysis of settler-colonialism, slavery, and racism in the United States" (ibid.). The struggle of Black families for equal education as articulated in the debates about desegregation in Little Rock addressed systemic racial exclusion. Though Arendt's argument could be read, as Kujala (2021) notes, as indicating the unpreparedness of US-American society to culturally accept this structural change, this argument obscures the fact that the Black population has the right to participate in this society on equal terms. As the Civil Rights Movement notes, access to civil rights and, in particular, education should be based on the political principle of equality, and not on differential treatment (Belle 2014).

Several critiques have drawn attention to Arendt's limited analysis of racial equality and social justice in the United States (cf., Bernasconi 1996; Johnson 2009; Benhabib 1993, 2002; Butler 2007; Burroughs 2015; Belle 2009, 2014). Johnson (2009, 80), for example, perceives Arendt's lack of understanding of the Black struggle for abolition democracy not just as a "blind spot," but as part and parcel of classical occidental philosophy's amnesia "surrounding the atrocities committed by white people against Native Americans and blacks."[2] Arendt's ambivalent approach to colonial violence seems, as Owens (2017, 420) observes, to be "deeply troubled by a notion of a continuum between colonial violence abroad and colonial violence 'at home,' when this 'home' was her own and so much of her post-totalitarian political theory was invested in its civic republican form of government."

Resigning the Political

Arendt's remarks on Fanon and the Black student movement did not provoke any public outcry among her readers in the 1960s and 1970s. It is this "tacit consensus universalism" (Buck-Morss 2009) or heuristic horizon (Benhabib

2002), widely represented among European intellectuals at this time and still today, that obfuscates the analysis of the entanglement of colonial violence and racism in European modernity. Thus, when Arendt (1972, 123) describes the anticolonial struggle of enslaved people and their uprising against slavery as the "mad fury" of "disinherited and downtrodden [...] that turned dreams into nightmares for everybody," the reader wonders what message she is trying to convey. It is unclear why she describes the anticolonial struggles of the African continent in these terms and for whom this is a "nightmare." Considering the heterogeneous anticolonial struggles active in Africa at the time of her writing *On Violence*, one might wonder which historical events Arendt is referring to. Is she referring to the Haitian Revolution[3] of 1791–1803 (James 2001; Trouillot 2015), or to the maroon uprisings against enslavement in Jamaica in the eighteenth and nineteenth centuries, or to the Underground Railroad, organized by Harriet Tubman and others, which guided enslaved people to freedom? Or to the Algerian War of Independence (1954–1962) or other anti-colonial struggles in the Asian and African continent in the 1950s and 1960s? All these struggles are linked to Europe's history of colonialism and racism. Acknowledging this requires that we admit the constitutive character of coloniality for the shaping of modernity. Hence, when Arendt claims that the "Third World is not a reality but an ideology" (1970, 21), one notices the omission of a political analysis of anti-colonial movements in the 1950s. If we recall the Bandung Conference in 1955,[4] where the concept of the so-called Third World was proclaimed as a political entity by anticolonial forces for decolonization headed by countries in Africa, Asia and Latin America, Arendt's assumption does not just reflect a heuristic discrepancy between concept and reality but an unawareness of the analysis deriving from anticolonial struggles and their theoretical proposals.

Thus, while Arendt has offered deep insights into the analysis of antisemitism and racism, authoritarian states and the aporia of Human Rights,[5] the misrecognition of anticolonial struggles in *On Violence* evinces a myopic understanding of the constitutive character of colonialism as the underside of European modernity. Her universalist approach reflects her own situatedness in Europe and the United States. As Owens (2017, 421) notes, "she was unable to extend her analysis to those who experienced themselves as stateless and rightless within an imperial nation-state purportedly founded on rights but built on settler colonialism and slave labor." Despite these limitations in her discussion of colonial violence and anti-Black racism, Arendt's conceptual framework of political action invites us to consider the field of practice—in other words, *doing* as a primordial axis.

Arendt's political action inspires my approach to decolonial mourning as political work. By situating political action within the context of anticolonial/

decolonial intersectional feminist struggles, I would like to draw our attention to a sphere of practices neglected by Arendt. The guarding, recreation and maintenance of life—the care and domestic work that sustain our lives—is the privileged site of political action. As I will further argue throughout my discussion on decolonial mourning, its connection to the life-dead continuum considers reproductive activities related to the social organization of our daily lives and relations as central elements of the political. "Reading Hannah Arendt against Hannah Arendt," following Benhabib (1993), I connect Arendt's political action to the labor of the oikos, the household and the microcosm of our daily lives. The political, in this sense, is mediated by the materiality of our lives and its connection to death, conveyed in the multiple activities and social relations related to decolonial mourning as grief work. It is in this regard that the intense work that goes into what Gillian Rose (1996) calls "inaugurated mourning" becomes political action.

Inaugurated Mourning

In *Mourning has Become the Law: Philosophy and Representation*, Rose (ibid) argues that the labor of mourning is an attempt to render justice to the lives lived. She relates space, feelings and practice to one another by exploring mourning in dialogue with architecture (the city), aesthetics (the soul) and the law (the sacred). Within these dynamics, practices of mourning articulate a normative matrix, while they are also transformative. Working through the trauma of Auschwitz and the loss of loved ones, Rose links mourning to the experience of tragedy and memory. Reflecting on the Shoah, she attempts to understand how utopian hope endures even when experiences of annihilation and genocide prevail. In other words, Rose focuses on the question of how to articulate justice in a context of injustice.

Proposing "inaugurated mourning" as an answer to this question, Rose works through memory and suffering, expressing the experiences of trauma and loss. Mourning engages with the paradox of both acknowledging the finitude of existence and the hope of endurance through remembrance. As Kate Schick (2012) notes, Rose's reflection of mourning emanates from a tradition of Jewish hermeneutical thought on being and acting in a broken world. In *The Broken Middle* (1992), she explores this fissure by setting up a dialogue between poststructuralism, metaphysics and law—all of which also inspire her writings published posthumously in the previously mentioned collection of essays *Mourning becomes the Law*. Focusing on mourning as dealing with the "broken middle"—the moment that interrupts the primordiality of the text in poststructuralism, existence in metaphysics and the normative framework of law—Rose argues that mourning speaks of matter, finitude, memory and feelings. For Rose, mourning is an act that expresses hope and engages with the belief that another world is possible, despite the fact that she concurs with Adorno (1997, 34) that "to write poetry after Auschwitz is barbaric." Mourning resides in the abyss of the "broken middle," marking the continuum of death-life. As such, it denotes less an ethical position than a material condition from which a metaphysical claim for representational justice derives. Inaugurated mourning challenges Jacques Derrida's (1995a, b) understanding of mourning as related to "aporetic ethics."

For Derrida the tension between finitude and endurance in mourning is an aporia. Considering that the act of mourning is meant to overcome the sentiment of loss, but mourning itself is a never-ending process, Derrida (1995a, 321) introduces mourning as a relational process between the griever and the object or subject of grief:

> Even before the death of the other, the inscription in me of her or his mortality constitutes me. I mourn therefore I am, I am—dead with the death of the other, my relation to myself is first of all plunged into mourning, a mourning that is moreover impossible. This is also what I call ex-appropriation, appropriation caught in a double-bind: I must and I must not take the other into myself, mourning is an unfaithful fidelity if it succeeds in interiorizing the other ideally in me, that is, in not respecting his or her infinite exteriority.

The task of mourning articulates Derrida's "aporetic ethics" (Zlomislić 2007, 120). Critiquing Heidegger's inability to listen to the voice of the other through his concentration on Being, Derrida argues that the Heideggerian model forecloses the possibility of mourning for the other. In contrast, Derrida conceives mourning as a relational act paying tribute to the memory of the other, though he sees tension between assimilation and alterity. In other words, mourners might work with their imagination of the other and risk assimilating them into their own projection and not respecting the other's alterity. For Derrida this tension leads to an "impossible mourning"[6] as it centers the pain of the mourner while disregarding mourning that is for the other's sake.

Rose (1996) critiques the self-referential logic of Derrida's claim that "I mourn, therefore I am." While Derrida focuses on the interdependency between the mourner and the loss of the loved one, Rose discusses Derrida's self-other dyad as self-confirming prophecy. Challenging Derrida's "aporetic ethics" (1996, 4) as a postmodern articulation, characterized by "postcolonial fragmentation of modern societies [that] has given rise to diverse 'ethnic' communities, based on 'race,' religion, language, and gender constituencies," Rose distances herself from what she perceives as "identity politics" (ibid.). Classifying this political stance as guided by individual interests, she (ibid.)

formulates that "politics begins not when you organize to defend individual or particular or local interests, but when you organise to further the 'general' interest within which your particular interest may be represented."[7] Rose's differentiation between "general" and "particular interest" does not interrogate what determines the general or the positionality that defines the general. Thus, to consider positionalities marked by processes of racialization and colonial difference as particular manifests a lack of analysis when it comes to racism and coloniality as two dimensions constituting contemporary societies. Nonetheless, Rose's insistence on metaphysical claims brings demands for justice to the fore. As we have seen through the example of Caminando Fronteras and as we will attend to in the following chapters, the political, communal labor of mourning of #NiUnaMenos, #SayHerName, Women in Exile, the NSU Komplex Auflösen and the Initiative 19. Februar and the claims of the family, relatives and friends of persons murdered in racist attacks elevate what might be perceived within a hegemonic normative setting as particular to a general level of speaking/ enacting justice. In other words, the communal political labor of mourning disrupts the normative order of representation. On this metaphysical level, the communal political labor of mourning resonates with Rose's notion of inaugurated mourning.

Rose allocates mourning not as an act voicing identity politics related to the self-other dynamic, but as one surfacing from a social historical moment. Thus, she differentiates between a political position that addresses metaphysical claims and a postmodern one guided by identity issues. Her focus lies on the potential of mourning to trespass the self-other tension. The act of mourning, for Rose (1996, 6), carries a transformative force; it intervenes in a normative matrix of speaking "objective truth" by committing to "objective reality" and goes beyond Derrida's reverence for the other. As a descendant of survivors of the Holocaust, Rose sees mourning as the work that enables the articulation of pain and the trauma that is transferred intergenerationally and experienced in bodily form. Identifying this experience as "objective reality," inaugurated mourning becomes an articulation related to "objective truth."

It is this predicament for political reasoning that she establishes as a point of departure for understanding inaugurated mourning. Defining "aberrated mourning"[8]—the inability but also refusal to mourn for the other, which leads to "incomplete mourning"—Rose opts for "inaugurated mourning," the intense practice of mourning that works through memory, pain, loss and tragedy. She (1996, 70) accentuates "the possibility of an ethics" that departs from "historical and political presuppositions." In this sense, Rose connects to Marx's critique of Hegel by addressing the concrete historical and societal conditions of life. More than representing an ethical responsibility to the other, mourning speaks about the material conditions in which death occurs and mourning emerges as practice. This situatedness of "speaking truth" invites us to follow Rose's aim to understand mourning as an utterance that goes beyond reverence for the other, while also returning the voice of the other to the sphere of "objective truth." The act of mourning inhabits both levels—the articulation of intersubjectivity and the stating of objective reality—as a practice of remembrance and affective connections in relationality. It is then that mourning as intense work becomes law.

Intense Work and Representational Justice

Analyzing Poussin's 1648 painting, *Landscape with the Ashes of Phocion collected by his Widow*, Rose interprets the activity of the women in the painting as disrupting the patriarchal stereotype of a woman's submissive devotion to her dead husband. For Rose, the women in the painting invent a new relationship between the city, the sacred and the soul through their intense work of grief. They inscribe a novel understanding of ethics and address objective truth by introducing their acts of speaking justice within a context of injustice. It is in this regard that inaugurated mourning intervenes in the normative matrix of justice by creating and enacting a new understanding of ethics and truth. As such, inaugurated mourning does not articulate a particular positionality, for example, that of a woman; rather, it signals a political intervention that produces a shift in the normative matrix of representation. Stating that the act of gathering the ashes by (presumably) Phocion's widow "is not solely one of infinite love: it is a finite act of political justice," Rose (ibid., 26) argues that the "gathering of the ashes is a protest against arbitrary power; it is not a protest against power and law as such."

In this painting[9] commissioned by the Paris silk merchant Jacques Serisier, Poussin granted his patron's wish for a secular but moralizing theme with a classical background (Sauerländer 2006). Art critics (Wollheim 1987; Sauerländer 2006) have discussed this painting as a political statement, demonstrating the illegibility of public favor and addressing the "moral contrast between the ceremony of official rites and unadorned private piety" (Sauerländer 2006, 105). The art historian Richard Wollheim (1987) adds an interesting aspect to the discussion by drawing attention to the woman gathering the ashes in the foreground and relating her to the painting's middle ground—the city—and its background—nature, mountain and forest. Arguing that the moral ground of this image lies in the woman's act of gathering the ashes, he (ibid., 241) comments that with the "stubborn act of piety the woman has placed herself beyond the world of custom and civic obligation." We do not know for certain if this woman is Phocion's widow; some critics (Wollheim 1987; Sauerländer 2006) have argued that she is the servant of the woman behind her, who is the actual widow, but there is no evidence to support either assumption. In Plutarch's (1919) *Parallel Lives*, the figure of the wife is mentioned in two paragraphs: In paragraph 19, Plutarch (ibid.) says that as "for his wives, nothing is told to us about the first, except that she was a sister of Cephisodotus, the sculptor; but the reputation which the second had among the Athenians for sobriety and simplicity was not less than that of Phocion for probity." This information might guide us in our interpretation of the painting, and we might consider that both women in the painting are wives: the woman standing is the sculptor's sister and the woman kneeling is the second wife.[10]

Rose's interpretation of this painting was inspired by the nun, Sister Wendy, who hosted a television program on art objects in Liverpool's Walker Art Gallery. Working with a "speculative interpretation" of the painting, Rose takes up Sister Wendy's observation that the widow expressed "pure love" for her dead husband by consuming his ashes to allow his soul to rest peacefully in her body. Rose (ibid., 25) challenges the moral implications of this assumption by describing "this presentation of the rational order in itself as unjust power." Depicting the widow in the "pathos of redeeming love" (ibid.), inserts the representation into a normative matrix, repeating the social order of things. In contrast, she argues that the women's actions in the painting produce a new relationship between knowledge and power, the soul and the city. Thus, the women's actions cannot be reduced to just an act of individual redeemed love; rather, they could be interpreted as a new form of speaking truth and exercising justice.

The women's act of mourning defies the political order and represents what Rose (ibid., 10) describes as a "reassessment of reason, gradually rediscovering its own moveable boundaries as it explores the boundaries of the soul, the city and the sacred [...]." According to Rose (ibid.), "completed mourning acknowledges the creative involvement of action in the configuration of power and law; it does not find itself unequivocally in a closed circuit which exclusively confers logic and power." In this vein, Rose introduces "inaugurated mourning" as a reversal logic crossing the imposed boundaries of the city and the boundaries of the soul, while the act of gathering the ashes represents "acts of justice, against the current will of the city" (ibid., 35–36). On these grounds, Rose (ibid.) concludes "women reinvent the political life of community" because by

insisting on the right and rites of mourning [...] the wife of Phocion carries out that intense work of the soul, that gradual rearrangement of its boundaries, which must occur when a loved one is lost—so as to let go, to allow the other fully to depart, and hence fully to be regained beyond sorrow. To acknowledge and to re-experience the justice and the injustice of the partner's life and death is to accept the law, it is not to transgress it—mourning becomes the law. Mourning draws on transcendent but representable justice, which makes the suffering of immediate experience visible and speakable. When completed, mourning returns the soul to the city, renewed and reinvigorated for participation, ready to take on the difficulties and injustices of the existing city. The mourner returns to negotiate and challenge the changing inner and outer boundaries of the soul and of the city; she returns to their perennial anxiety.

Mourning, for Rose, articulates an ethical claim to objective truth. Through inaugurated mourning, she foregrounds the practices and materiality shaping the rites and rights established in the relationship to the dead. Through the act of mourning, Phocion's widows intervene in the normative matrix: not only do they render justice to their loss, they also realize their rights to mourning on their own terms. They transform mourning into law.

Agonistic Mourning – Contested Grieving

The transformative force of the politics of mourning is also explored in Athanasiou's (2017) *Agonistic Mourning: Political Dissidence and the Women in Black* (ŽuC). Drawing on Butler's framework of precarity and vulnerability and Honig's agonistic politics, Athanasiou (2017, 289) interprets the political work of Women in Black (Žene u Crnom) in the former Yugoslavia as agonistic mourning, which she describes as

the performative power implicit in transforming mourning's impossibility into an incalculable and unquantifiable political potentiality, capable of deconstituting the interpellating terms of conventional mourning that are posed by state-nationalist authoritarianism.

Drawing as well upon Derridas's (1990; 2001) treatment of mourning as incomplete and (im)possible work, Athanasiou defines agonistic mourning as caught in an aporia. She utilizes Derrida's (1988; 1994) notion of mourning as a "spectral remainder" to interrogate it as a performative enactment, caught between the failure to represent what has been lost and the iteration of the presence of loss. For Athanasiou (ibid., 293), mourning is an act of resistance and speaks about the "critical agency [that] alludes to what resists and remains inappropriable in memory and thus infinitely challenges the established and iterable realms of memorability." Grievability, for Athanasiou, represents an agonistic act, entrenched in the ambivalence of an embodied/disembodied present. Evolving in "the contingent realm of agonism, conceived in its double valence agon and agony" (ibid.), mourning relates to memory and loss in its double function of absence and presence. Discussing the dimension of "agon" as the site of dispute and struggle, while agony marks suffering and tragedy, Athanasiou challenges Honig's perception of mourning as the sphere of lamentation—something exterior to the field of the political. For Honig (2013, 23), the relationship of humans to life and death is "suffused with hybrid combinations of virtue, pleasure, use." Responding to Butler's approach to mourning as an ethical condition, Honig focuses on its limitation by asserting the sociopolitical material conditions in which the relationship between human beings and death is established. Mourning is not just an articulation of agony, related to drama, tragedy and suffering, but also entrenched in agon—the experience of struggle against violence. Offering a different interpretation of Antigone that does not emphasize the maternal or suicidal force, Honig opts for the strategy of resistance. For her, Antigone is not just a sister in sorrow but a political actor. Her sole act of mourning, perceived by Honig as lamentation, cannot be understood as a political enactment. For Honig, it is the power struggles between the different political actors of the polis vying for power that determines the field of the political.

Yet as Athanasiou and Rose demonstrate, the act of mourning can turn into political action. As Rose indicates with the widows of Phocion, and Athanasiou with Women in Black's political work of mourning, these acts of political communal mourning disrupt the official normative matrix of injustice. Furthermore, for Athanasiou, the double valence of agony and agon resides in the political work of mourning. It is this agonistic mourning that represents for her not a "reconcilable contradiction but an interminable event temporality that involves calling the normalizing ordinariness of the past and the present into question" (ibid., 191–92). Mourning is entrenched in an entangled temporality, where the past informs the present and vice versa. From this angle, a critical enquiry of what is experienced as normality might surface. Mourning deals with the precarity of the self but also the uncertainty of time. It is a "precarious exercise of subjectivation and de-subjectivation," as Athanasiou (ibid., 193) argues in relation to the grief activism of Women in Black. In this way, Athanasiou (ibid., 289) engages with "the politics of contested grievability as a means to refigure agonistic political subjectivity beyond sovereign accounts of agency." Mourning destabilizes the assumption of a sovereign subject, while it recognizes the finitude of being and the inconceivability of nonbeing. Agency evolves here in the confrontation with the ruins of life, in the struggle against violence or, as we will see in the following chapters, in the defiance to necropolitics. In this sense, mourning can work as a politics of witnessing by listening, presenting and reconstructing the events, accounts and practices that speak of the experience of annihilation, while also combating it. Though, as Athanasiou (ibid., 192) asserts, mourning as a form of witnessing is not straightforward; it is not about producing authentic accounts of truth-telling or state-sponsored memoralization. The witnessing of political groups like ŽuC engages with what Rose calls the "broken middle"—the impossibility of witnessing. As Athanasiou (ibid.) observes, it "is the very breakdown of witnessing, and also the acknowledgement of this breakdown, that can produce a transformational archive—an archive open to new possibilities for change."

I will attend to this ambivalence between bearing witness and the impossibility of witnessing by evincing in the following chapters the political communal labor of mourning by the families, relatives and friends who have lost their loved ones to colonial racist cisheteropatriarchal intersectional violence. Producing a remembrance practice through the labor of mourning, these political actors contribute to the creation of transformational archives defining "the terms of inflicted violence but also the terms of remembering and witnessing" (ibid.).

Conclusion: Decolonial Mourning as Communal Political Action

Arendt, Rose and Athanasiou all approach the question of political action by addressing different levels of collective change. For Arendt, political action derives from intellectual critical exchange. Rose's inaugurated mourning and Athanasiou's agonistic mourning approach political action as expressed in the intense grief work that needs to be realized to disrupt the normative order of injustice and render justice to the lives lived. Decolonial mourning surfaces along these lines of inaugurated mourning (Rose) and contested grieving (Athanasiou) as political communal work. While resonating with inaugurated and agonistic mourning, decolonial mourning insists on the materiality of the labor of mourning and its historical and societal implications by relating to Rose's (1996) "objective truth" and "objective reality." It derives from the intense work related to the communal political (re)negotiation of the relationship between death and loss. Transforming the objective view of society by remembering the (post)colonial and diasporic composition of modern society, as well as the colonial entanglement of Europe's modernity, the objective truth spoken by decolonial mourning considers colonialism, settler colonialism and what Saidiya Hartman (1997) calls the afterlife of slavery to the understanding of objective reality.

Attending to the effects of migration-coloniality necropolitics and its resistance, decolonial mourning as political communal action addresses the injuries and losses produced by intersectional structural violence and the necropolitics of a colonial racial cisheteropatriarchal capitalist system of extractivism, accummulation and dispossession. As such, as I discuss in the next chapter, it relies on practices that involve the social reproduction of life at the juncture of bio- and necropolitics.

Notes

1 Through the construction of an exteriority to Europe (Spivak 1987; Dussel 1995) embodied by the woman and the racialized and colonized other, Europe was constituted as the cradle of culture, civilization, emancipation and Enlightenment in eighteenth and nineteenth centuries' Europe.

2 The eminent thinkers of the occidental canon of philosophy seem not to be aware of the enduring anticolonial struggles, for example, of the Túpac Katari Revolutionary Movement (Mamani 2019; Rivera Cusicanqui 2012) or of the Mapuche (Bengoa 2000; Garbe 2022) or the Maya Q'eqchi' (Tzul Tzul 2018a; 2019b)—of which women were key protagonists—in the resistance against the Spanish Crown. Later Indigenous resistance would be organized against the white criollo nations of Bolivia, Chile, Guatemala and Mexico and other nation-states in Abya Yala and the Caribbean. The struggles of the First Nations in Northern America, such as the Inuit, Cree, Anishinaabe, Sioux, Dakota, Navajo and Iroquois against white settler colonialism, among others, are also omitted from current official accounts about modern civilization, settler-colonial advancements and futurity.

3 The anticolonial struggles in Haiti between 1789 and 1801 were sparked by a group of military officers, among them the leader of the Revolution, Toussaint de L'Ouverture, who had fought in the ranks of the French Revolution and demanded for Haiti the abolition of slavery and the status of a republic where Black people would be citizens.

4 Patricia Owens (2017, 416) notes that the "Third World Project began as early as 1928 when anticolonial leaders met in Brussels to form the League Against Imperialism and was revived in Bandung, Indonesia in 1955 against violent and nonviolent subversion."

5 In my research project on the aporia of human rights in migrants and refugee movements in Germany and the United States I follow this aspect, see https://gepris.dfg.de/gepris/projekt/501116737.

6 As Michael Naas (2014) notes, Derrida discusses impossible mourning throughout his work. See *FORS*; *Limited Inc*; *Memoires for Paul de Man*; *Specters of Marx*; *The Gift of Death*; *By Force of Mourning* and *The Work of Mourning*.

7 Rose reiterates here some of the clichés that circulated in the polemic between postmodernity and critical theory on universality and particularity in the 1990s—claims that Stuart Hall (1994; 1996; 1997) problematized by discussing the historical entanglement between identity and society.

8 Rose (1996, 70) illustrates "aberrated mourning" using "the case of Heidegger, who never mourned, who never spoke about his Nazism or about the Nazi genocide of six million Jews."

9 Poussin's painting depicts mountains and a forest in the background with the city of Megara and people sitting in a meadow in the middle ground. In the foreground, we see a small wall and two women, one standing with her back to us and looking to her right in light colored, finely textured clothes, while the other one, dressed in white and wearing a blue scarf, is kneeling and gathering the ashes of Phocion. The painting is coupled with a series of Poussin's paintings related to Plutarch's accounts of Phocion in *Parallel Lives*. Plutarch tells the story of Phocion, an Athenian general of the fourth century B.C., who after a glorious life engaging in war and peace found himself in political disagreement with the rulers of Athens. This affront cost him his life, as he was condemned to death for treason and his funeral could not take place in Athenian territory.

10 In paragraph 37, Plutarch mentions one wife together with her "maidservant" collecting the bones of her husband and putting them in her bosom. As Plutarch (§34) writes, "[…] and carrying them by night to her dwelling, she buried them by the hearth, saying: 'To thee, dear Hearth, I entrust these remains of a noble man; but do thou restore them to the sepulchre of his fathers, when the Athenians shall have come to their senses.'" In *Gathering the Ashes*, Poussin creates an additional narrative. The painting shows, in the foreground, two women: one is dressed in thin fabric in light creamy colors with her back to the viewer, looking to her right; the other, is dressed in humble clothes in white with a blue scarf, kneeling on the ground as she gathers the ashes. Both women could represent the previously mentioned two wives: the sculptor's sister and the modest second wife. Some art historians have opted for the interpretative version of the wife and her servant, and others have just seen the widow in the figure of the woman gathering the ashes.

Chapter 4

COUNTERING NECROPOLITICAL SOCIAL REPRODUTION

Introduction

#NoEstamosTodas

Paramos porque nos faltan las víctimas de femicidio, voces que se apagan violentamente al ritmo escalofriante de una por día sólo en la Argentina.
Nos faltan las lesbianas y travestis asesinadas.
Nos faltan las presas políticas, las perseguidas, las asesinadas en nuestro territorio latinoamericano por defender la tierra y sus recursos.
Nos faltan las mujeres encarceladas por delitos menores que criminalizan formas de supervivencia, mientras los crímenes de las corporaciones y el narcotráfico quedan impunes porque benefician al capital.
Nos faltan las muertas y las presas por abortos inseguros.
Nos faltan las desaparecidas por las redes de trata; las víctimas de la explotación sexual.
Frente a los hogares que se convierten en infiernos, nos organizamos para defendernos y cuidarnos entre nosotras.
Frente al crimen machista y su pedagogía de la crueldad, frente al intento de los medios de comunicación de victimizarnos y aterrorizarnos, hacemos del duelo individual consuelo colectivo, y de la rabia lucha compartida. Frente a la crueldad, más feminismo.[1]
(Ni Una Menos 2017).

On International Women's Day, 8 March 2017, the Argentinean feminist movement #NiUnaMenos presented their manifest *#NosotrasParamos— #WeStrike*. In it they state:

Este 8 de marzo la tierra tiembla. Las mujeres del mundo nos unimos y organizamos una medida de fuerza y un grito común: Paro

Internacional de Mujeres. Nosotras Paramos. Hacemos huelga, nos
organizamos y nos encontramos entre nosotras. Ponemos en práctica el
mundo en el que queremos vivir.[2]

The feminist mobilization against feminicide represented "un grito común" (a
united outcry)—while also mourning the members it has lost to feminicide and
violence against LGBTIQA+. It is this act of mourning that articulated the
affective labor involved in the political manifestation against violence, voiced
by the feminist strike of #NiUnaMenos. Women of all occupations went on
strike for one hour in Argentina, initiating a social movement that went viral.
The manifesto of #NiUnaMenos *#NosotrasParamos—#WeStrike* was written
and signed by several political organizations, from grassroots groups to trade
unions. It offers an analysis of violence against women as a specific articulation
of contemporary neoliberal capitalism in Latin America and the women's
strike as its political counterforce. This movement manifests a new potentiality
of the political and resistance to structural cruelty (Gago 2020). Connecting
with the analysis of feminicide by Latin American feminists (Monarrez 2002,
Segato 2003, 2014; Lagarde 2006a,b), the movement addresses previous
feminist analyses of social reproduction, capitalist exploitation, precarious
work and reproductive rights. The struggle against sexual violence is
broadened by a social analysis that considers the interwovenness between
capitalism and patriarchy. Yet as Yuderkys Espinosa Miñoso (2019) notes, this
analysis, while it mobilizes a resistant force, it reproduces an absence. While
Black and Indigenous women are evoked, their analysis of how the gender
binary system and gender relations are entrenched in coloniality (Gunn Allen
1986; Anzaldúa 1978; Lugones 2007) and racial capitalism (Truth 1851; Wells
1892; Combahee River Collective 1977, Davis 1983) is disregarded. Thus,
as Espinosa Miñoso (2019) points out, a closer look at the epistemological
underpinning of these articulations reveals a Eurocentric feminist logic, and
traces of a hegemonic understanding of gender that requires a decolonial
examination. Evoking Frantz Fanon's *The Wretched of the Earth*, Miñoso argues
that Black, Indigenous and decolonial struggles have already decentered the
classical normative subject of feminism. According to her, these movements
have created a new narrative that sharpens the social analysis and proposes
other models of understanding social relations beyond Eurocentric reasoning[3]
(Espinosa Miñoso 2022b; Espinosa Miñoso and Sepúlveda 2022).

From this perspective, this chapter argues for understanding decolonial
mourning as an articulation of resistance to necropolitical social reproduction.
Though the concept of necropolitical social reproduction might sound
contradictory, it helps us to understand the negative dialectic constituting
social reproduction. Thus, as we will see, social reproduction does not just rely

on the production of life, but is deeply entrenched in the systemic allowing to die and killing of feminized, gendered, sexualized, disabled, racialized, migrantized, impoverished and abandoned populations. The politics of mourning, specifically decolonial mourning, as this chapter will argue, articulates the contradiction and continuum between life and death. As such, it speaks about necropolitical social reproduction. In this chapter, I will develop this argument in four steps. First, I will engage with the analysis of feminicide in the Argentinean movement #NiUnaMenos through its politics of mourning and relate it to a theoretical genealogy of Latin American feminist theory. Then I will approach necropolitical social reproduction and contrast it to Gladys Tzul Tzul's proposal of communal social relations as resistance to genocidal and extractivist capitalism. Following this argument, I will consider Leanne Betasamosake Simpson's understanding of ontological relationality. To conclude, I will discuss decolonial mourning as affective labor, surfacing at the juncture of biopolitics and necropolitics and propose decolonial mourning as supported by communal social relations and shaped by relational ontology.

A Cry of Rage: Feminicide and Rethinking Violence

The activist and social theorist Verónica Gago[4] describes in a 2019 documentary on the Argentinean women's movement in the TV channel ARTE the feminist movements against feminicide in Argentina as a *grito de rabia* (cry of rage). This cry of rage began on 11 May 2015 when 14-year-old Chiara Páez was murdered by her 16-year-old boyfriend. As the political theorist Natália Maria Félix de Souza (2019, 90) notes, Chiara's murder was only "one drop in a sea of similar cases throughout Argentina." On 3 June 2015, thousands of cisgender and trans-women/men and nonbinary people gathered in 80 cities in Argentina, chanting in protest "¡Ni una menos!" (Not one woman[5] less!) (Gago 2019, 2020; Félix de Souza and Rodrigues Selis 2022). Sharing a common sentiment of indignation and readiness, the Argentinean feminist movements designated the officially silenced violence against trans, queer, nonbinary persons, heterosexual and cis women and girls as trans-queer feminicide.

The cry of rage unleashed regional and global outrage: Long-standing protests against feminicide in countries such as Mexico (Segato 2008, 2019; Fregoso and Bejarano 2010), Guatemala (Cabnal 2019; Cumes 2019; Velásquez Nimatuj 2019), Colombia (Marquéz 2016; Marquéz and Salcedo 2012; Lozano Lerma 2019), Ecuador (Colectivo Miradas Críticas 2017; Sempértegui 2021, 2022), Brazil (Félix de Souza and Rodrigues Selis 2022) and Chile (Silva-Tapia and Fernández 2022) were reactivated, forming part of a broader social protest against neoliberalism (Gago and Sztulwark 2016;

Gago, Malo and Cavallero 2020), extractivism (García 2014; Hernández Castillo 2014; García-Torres, Vázquez, Cruz and Bayón 2020; Rodríguez Castro 2021) and state and police violence (Veillette 2021; Martínez-Andrade 2022). In other countries, such as Spain, France, the United States, Canada, India, Kenya, Uganda and South Africa, the protest against intersectional gendered violence (see also Crenshaw 2005; 2015a, b) also took to the streets, demanding legal and political measures against the systemic killing of women, trans and nonbinary persons, including racialized, Indigenous, other-abled and queer bodies. Some of these struggles were successful in partially achieving new legislation and political measures to combat femicide—in some Latin American countries, such as Mexico, Chile and Argentina, against "feminicide" (Carrigan and Dawson 2020; Schröttle et al. 2021). These struggles as we will see in the following have sharpened the analysis of violence by thinking through feminicide, gore capitalism and gendered necropolitics.

Feminicide

Rita Segato (2003; 2014; 2016) describes feminicide as a contemporary manifestation of the "war against women" rooted in colonialism in Latin America. In contrast to the term "femicide," feminicide addresses the intersectional character of gendered violence against women and racialized, Indigenous, gender nonbinary, trans and queer persons of all ages and social backgrounds. Following the notion of feminicide as systemic violence articulated by the feminist anthropologist, theorist and activist Marcela Lagarde (2006a,b; 2007; 2008) and sociologist Julia Monárrez (2002), Segato favors this term to underline gendered violence. Influenced by Jill Radford and Diana E. H. Russell's (1992) analysis of what they have coined "femicide" to address the systemic killing of women by the state (cited in Lagarde 2006b, 220), Lagarde instead opts for a definition that encompasses everyday forms and institutionalized pattern of misogynist violence:

> Feminicide is genocide against women and it happens when the historical conditions enable social practices that allow attacks against the integrity, health, freedom and lives of women.

Lagarde considers feminicide to include violent misogynistic acts such as harassment, physical violence and rape by known or unknown individuals and groups that may occur in an everyday or professional setting. Lagarde notes the absence of police investigations, prosecution and public condemnation of such crimes and argues that feminicide conditions modern societies in times of both war and peace, representing the thingification of feminized bodies and the dehumanization of women. Between 2003 and 2006, Lagarde pursued this matter at the parliamentary level. Heading the *Comisión Especial para Conocer y Dar Seguimiento a las Investigaciones Relacionadas con los Feminicidios en la República Mexicana* (Special Truth Commission for Investigations Related to Feminicide in Mexico), she helped compile official statistics about the cases of disappeared and murdered women, while getting the problem onto the agenda of the Mexican Parliament.

Segato broadens Lagarde's concept of feminicide by classifying it as a form of genocide. Referring to the United Nations Protocols of Minnesota (2016[1991]) and Istanbul[6] (2004 [1991]) that define sex crimes in war as crimes of torture, she (2008; 2019) suggests that we consider crimes against women as crimes against humanity that are related to histories of domination such as colonialism, imperialism and extractivist capitalism. For Segato, this understanding of feminicide challenges liberal perceptions of gendered violence that focus on individual and interpersonal expressions (2003; 2014; 2016). Instead, feminicide denotes a structural form of violence that is historically rooted and socially organized.

As Ruth Trinidad Galván (2016) argues, feminicide galvanizes the brutality and cruelty of colonialism, racism and misogyny. It shows how feminized bodies are used as territories of capital exploitation, resource extractivism and necropolitical conquest. Instantiating mechanisms of racialized and feminized subjugation, the systemic killing of women—particularly racialized, working-class and poor feminized subjects—reveals the public and administrative approach of a patriarchal racialized state and the complicity of its institutions such as the police, the court and the media that "turn a blind eye to female-targeted violence" (ibid., 346). The state—both local governments and federal institutions—when confronted with the demands of the relatives and friends of victims and the political organizations denouncing these crimes, often responds by portraying them as singularly exceptional crimes, contradicting the structural and systemic character of feminicide. Furthermore, state actors often utilize victim-blaming rhetoric that places responsibility for the murderous acts on the victim's own behavior and appearance. In the case of feminicide along the US-Mexico border, the media has contributed to a large extent to this racist, misogynist culture. Its depictions of autonomous, often financially independent, racialized and Indigenous women as not "respectable" and sexually immoral (Alcocer 2014) conform to white bourgeois ideals of femininity and monogamous heteronormativity (Alcocer 2016; 2020). Echoing Segato, feminicide constitutes not only an act of colonial subjugation but is also related to the goal of extermination. Capitalism is reproduced on the basis of this structural intersectional violence. Capitalism does not only evolve by expanding its biopolitical potential; rather, as Sayak

Valencia (2010; 2018) suggests with the term "gore capitalism," it operates through necropolitical destruction.

Gore capitalism and gendered necropolitics

Valencia has coined "gore capitalism" in her attempt to analytically grasp the structural violence of the US-Mexico border by describing the confluence of drug cartel activity, the state's cooperation, the production of disposable bodies, the destruction of territories and feminicide. "Gore capitalism," as Valencia notes, operates necropolitically: the systemic killing of people forms part of the productive character of capital, its circulation of people, drugs and money. Killing is not the exception; it is the modus operandi. Social reproduction under conditions of gore capitalism is not focused on the immediate productive and extractivist potential of capital. Rather, it derives from the commensurability of two apparently incommensurable phenomena: life and death. The capitalist logic implemented in the advent of European colonialism and enslavement, from the sixteenth century onward, and in an expanded form in the plantation economy of the Caribbean and in other settler-colonial territories, operated through the production of life and its destruction. Similarly, struggles against feminicide show the ambiguity of social reproduction as caught between biopolitics and necropolitics.

In her analysis of the exploitation and systemic violence against *maquiladora* (*maquila* to follow)—assembly plants of multinationals—women workers on the US-Mexico border, Melisa Wright (2006, 2011) analyzes femicide as gendered necropolitics. Drawing from a Foucaultian paradigm, she argues for a multi-situated analysis of gendered violence that takes into account the different mechanisms of direct, cultural and structural violence these women encounter in their everyday lives. As young women arriving from other parts of Mexico to the free trade zone near the US border, these maquila workers are internal migrants—often single mothers and heads of families. They are faced with mechanisms of feminized labor exploitation in the maquilas as well as sexualized and racialized violence. This is materially articulated in low wages, disqualification of their educational degrees and professional experiences, long working hours and the disavowal of their working rights by company management (Domínguez et al. 2010).[7] Since Wright conducted her study in the late 1990s and early 2000s, trade union organizing of maquila workers has increased (Prieto and Quintero 2004; Bacon 2019) and there has been some progress regarding the bargaining of contractual working conditions and fair wages (De la O and Zlolniski 2020). However, violent attacks against maquila workers, including their disappearances and murders, as well as against trade union organizers and activists, remain high in this border region of Mexico (Gaspar de Alba and Guzmán 2010; Segato 2014; Fracchia Figueiredo 2021).

Despite increasing awareness, political campaigning and the passing of a law in Mexico against feminicide (Michel 2020; Pasinato, Wania, and Ávila 2022), Lourdes Portillo's 2001 documentary *Señorita Extraviada* accurately depicts the brutal reality of feminicide on the US-Mexico border. Portillo shows how the disappearance and murder of women maquila workers are deliberately and systemically organized—their dead bodies dispersed and often mutilated in an attempt to destroy their personal identities. A vast network of police officers, local politicians and members of the judiciary and organized criminals are often behind these disappearances and murders. Their work often obscures, diverts and impedes the thorough and exhaustive police investigations and the corresponding prosecutions of these cases. Wright and Portillo's analysis resonates with the writings of Cynthia Bejarano and Rosa-Linda Fregoso (2010) and Julia Monárrez Fragoso's (2014, 2019). Concurring with Segato (2008; 2014; 2016), they examine feminicide as a systemic model of eradication of feminized subjects, shaped by specific historical legacies of destruction in Latin America, particular along the US-Mexico border.

Following these observations, Félix de Souza (2019) proposes understanding the systemic killing of women, girls, queer and non-binary persons as endemic to contemporary Latin America societies. As she (ibid., 97) observes, "the production of (normative) life in some places gives way to the daily reproduction of (non-normative) dead bodies as the normalized condition." In (post)colonial societies, necropolitics uncovers the logic of colonial rule, indicating the limits of sovereignty and exercising "the power and the capacity to dictate who may live and who must die" (Mbembe 2003, 11). The killing of migrantized, racialized and Indigenous women and girls, trans and nonbinary persons is embedded in this normative structure of killing and allowing death to occur. Based on this observation, Félix de Souza (ibid., 97) defines femicide as "a nomological—rather than exceptional—condition of democracy" coexisting with democracy and pushing it to its limits. Democracy performed under the circumstances of modern colonial racial feminicide becomes a "necropolitical regime which operates not privately, but through the systematic reproduction of feminised, racialised, minoritised, marginalised, imperialized dead—or killable—bodies" (ibid.). Feminicide as a social phenomenon articulates the configuration of contemporary forms of capitalist expansion and sociopolitical interdependencies. It surfaces at the juncture of neoliberal policies, transnational migration, the gendered and racialized division of work and borderland economies, reflecting a specific form and articulation of intersectional structural violence.

Intersectional structural violence

Johann Galtung introduces the concept of structural violence in his 1969 essay "Violence, Peace and Peace Research," differentiating between personal violence as a singular act or "with a clear subject-object relation" (ibid., 171), and structural violence as a repetitive, broad occurrence. Marked by vertical relations of power that are based on unequal value-exchange relations and asymmetrical interactions on the political, military, communication and cultural levels, structural violence refers to historically sedimented forms of power, control and domination (Galtung 1969). In his essays "A Structural Theory of Imperialism" (1971) and "Cultural Violence" (1990), he further develops this argument by defining violence as an intended physical or psychological act of infringement on a person or group. In his analysis of direct violence, he differentiates between the aggressor and the victim of violence, while he approaches structural violence by insisting on its twofold character as material formation (unequal distribution of resources) and symbolic articulation (patterns of inequality). Finally, Galtung synthesizes the multifaceted dimensions of violence in his concept of "cultural violence," reflecting feminist debates from the 1980s that are also represented in Pierre Bourdieu's analysis of symbolic violence (Galtung and Fischer 2013). Galtung developed this approach empirically through his analysis of imperialism, war and armed conflicts and his engagement with peace negotiations and processes. Structural violence refers to repressive forms of exercising power and domination. In concrete terms, this means the "power to decide over the distribution of resources" (ibid., 171), which Galtung defines as tools of material or immaterial support for the creation of livable lives, including a living wage, health, education, infrastructure, access to democratic participation and representation as well as basic human rights (Galtung 1994).

Other scholars (Dilts et al. 2012) have expanded upon Galtungs's argument by highlighting the symbolic, cultural and emotional dimensions of violence and examining the more fluid, subtle and ordinary character of violence. Feminist critiques (Confortini 2006; Dilts et al. 2012) have addressed the interdependent character of personal and structural violence when it comes to gendered and sexualized violence. Though this concept identifies causes, effects and symptoms produced by historical formations of global inequalities and their local impact, Yves Winter (2012) has pointed to its limitation, when it comes to the consideration of specific temporalities and configurations of violence. He (2012, 195) notes, "slavery, racism, sexism, colonialism, and class domination [...] are collapsed into a single category." How these systems of domination work on an invisible level cannot always be addressed if we only focus on structural violence as its common denominator. Instead, Winter (ibid., 225) suggests working with a notion of structural violence related to tragedy. Employing the Ancient Greek understanding of tragedy, he points to the "hidden violence in social relations and to the persistence of violence," capturing its relational moments. Joan Cocks (2012) approaches the same issue by relating structural violence to foundational violence: she complicates Galtung's normative conceptualization of structural violence by deconstructing its foundational grounds. Cocks (2012, 222) considers that the "concept of structural violence discloses injustices built into ongoing relations and practices that are not visibly coercive" but does not differentiate "between the potential and the actual realization of some consensually valued aspects of human life." With this observation, she draws our attention to foundational violence by observing two orders of analysis: the material and the symbolic. The "first order" implies the material realization of commonsensical meanings, while the "second order" relates to its "mystification." This focus on foundational violence enables us to understand the specific historical formations upon which universal claims are built and articulated. This view broadens an understanding of structural violence as a historical-societal entangled configuration.

Veena Das unpacks this perspective in her analysis of quotidian violence as structural, symbolic, cultural and interpersonal (Das et al. 2000). Studying the effects of the 1947 partitioning of India and the 1984 Sikh Massacre and their impact on ordinary lives—particularly women's lives (Das 2006)—Das conceptualizes ordinary violence as relational and formative of subjectivity. She addresses feminist theory debates on everyday violence, drawing attention to the somatic and emotional impact of violence on women's bodies, agency and resistance.[8] Kimberlé Crenshaw's (2015a,b) own concept of intersectional violence has some resonance with both Galtung's understanding of structural and cultural violence and Das's conceptualization of ordinary violence. These articulations of structural, ordinary and intersectional violence describe the multidimensional forms of violence addressed by feminist theory and activism in Latin America in relation to feminicide, bringing us to reconsider the struggle against genocide and extinction by focusing on the interstices of resistance in the life-death continuum (c.f., Rodríguez Aguilera 2021).

Countering Extinction: Communal Life as Resistance

Following Mbembe's observations about the relationship between sovereignty and the state of exception by addressing the parallel coexistence of biopolitics and necropolitics, Félix de Souza (2019) foregrounds the feminist protest against femicide[9] within contemporary social struggles. As Mbembe (2003, 14) shows through his discussion of the Holocaust, colonial rule and apartheid, the project of modern sovereignty has been historically tied to "the general-ized instrumentalization of human existence and the material destruction of human bodies." Sovereignty has been overshadowed by the "modern terror" (ibid., 21) of colonialism and slavery. Considering the latter "the first instance of biopolitical experimentation," Mbembe (ibid.) describes "the plantation system and its aftermath" as "the emblematic and paradoxical figure of the state of exception." It is within this system that the relationship between life and death is organized around "the politics of cruelty" (ibid., 22) that con-tours the colony and the apartheid regime. In conclusion, he (ibid., 25) notes that "the most original feature of this terror formation is its concatenation of biopower, the state of exception, and the state of siege" and their relationship to race. Inserting the sovereign's rule to kill in the colony lays bare a system relying on "the sovereign right to kill [...] at any time or any manner" (ibid.). Thus, while Western sovereign power reaffirms the will to peace, peace "is not necessarily the natural outcome of a colonial war" (ibid.). In the colonies, the principle governing life is that of necropolitics, which is not an exception but the rule of modern governance. As Mbembe (ibid., 39) writes, "contem-porary forms of subjugation of life to the power of death (necropolitics) pro-foundly reconfigure the relations among resistance, sacrifice, and terror."

Seeking an understanding of the relationship between life and death in the feminist protests against feminicide in Abya Yala, Souza reflects on Mbembe's observations, when she contemplates the banners and posters of the numer-ous marches against feminicide invoking the lost loved ones. Actualizing their presence through their calling out of their names by the protesters or shouting during the gatherings and marches "¡Ni una menos!" or "¡Ellas están entre nosotras!" (They are here with us!). This occurred, for example, when the movement against feminicide chanted in the streets of Argentina "¡Vivas nos queremos!" (We want to stay alive!) in 2017 or when the Brazilian movement mourned the death of Marielle Franco (2017), a Black Brazilian antiracist, queer, feminist politician and activist murdered by paramilitaries in Rio de Janeiro on 14 March 2018.[10] The crowd gathering in mourning shouted "pre-sente!" (here!), so that when the names of lost loved ones are called out, their living spirits, souls and minds are revived in the present, nourishing and sus-taining the struggle for justice. As a protester in the 3 June 2020 march against feminicide, transvesticide and transfeminicide in Viedma, Argentina,[11] stated on their banner, "Today I protest for you, for me, for all those who are alive and for all those taken away from us by violence."[12] This performative practice connects the presence of those lost with the utterance of the living. While the murders ended women's trans and queer lives, their presence lived on through different utterances and acts of resistance. The protests against feminicide, Félix de Souza (2019, 100) writes, "materialize political resistance through their daily entanglements and solidarities." Movements against feminicide confront political systems and actions that attempt to control and negate the lives of women by publicly mourning, bearing witness and demanding justice. In this sense, they resonate with Tzul Tzul's (2018a, b; 2019a,b) analysis of life as resistance.

Communal life as resistance

In her chapter "Rebuilding Communal Life: Ixil Women and the Desire for Life in Guatemala," Tzul Tzul (2018b) focuses on the creation of life in the presence of death and extractivism. After the Guatemalan genocide, in which over 200,000 people were killed or disappeared over a 36-year period, "communities returned to their lands, rebuilding their homes and systems of communal authority" (ibid., 404). In the 2000s, she notes, while women were searching for the remains of their community members and loved ones killed during the 1970–1996 genocide, they encountered miners digging for minerals and water in the land inhabited by the bodies of those killed (see also Pereira 2020). Thus, Ixil women "adjusted to a new rhythm of defense against the political regime of extractivism" (ibid.). This new rhythm is connected to what Tzul Tzul defines as "la voluntad de vida" (the desire to live), "which is to say the social energy Indigenous women produce that allows them to preserve their memory and defend the land where the dead rest and water is born. Ixil people often refer to *la voluntad de vida* as that which keeps them struggling and living despite all the problems they face" (ibid.). The voluntad de vida sustains their daily work and forms the backbone of their reproductive lives. Tzul Tzul further elaborates (ibid., 402):

> The process of searching for those who were killed in the war but whose bodies were never recovered is the backbone of these Indigenous women's political struggle in their communities. They look for the dead in order to continue to defend life and future generations. The dead are under the earth, which is why defending the land itself is so central. Within the Ixil communal lands, communitarian economies produce corn and more than 17 plant species are reproduced. And so, this struggle can be understood from the perspective of the defense and the recuperation of communal land.

This desire to live is articulated in the continuous and collective work of building communal lives, reflected in the corn and the 17 plant species grown by the community, the bonds between the women, the preservation of memories and the struggle for communal land (Tzul Tzul 2018a). "The region where they live," as Tzul Tzul (2018b, 404) writes, is shaped by the suffering of infinite massacres and losses in their own community. The search "for those who were killed in the war but whose bodies were never recovered" (ibid.) forms the "backbone" of the political struggle, connecting death with the continuous struggle for life. As Tzul Tzul (ibid.) notes in the above quote, the connection with the dead is at the root of their present and future, thus, the "dead are under the earth, which is why defending the land itself is so central." The connection between life and death drives the struggle for communal land but also, as Tzul Tzul (ibid.) argues, the struggle against the "expropriation of their weaving and textiles, the genetic modification of seeds, the police and military occupation of their lands," and against the establishment of heteropatriarchal settler-colonial entertainment industries, such as the sex industry, that contribute to gendered and sexualized violence in these communities. "Communitarian women," Tzul Tzul concedes, "have laid out political horizons that we call the desire to live, the desire to live communally" (ibid.), which drive the Ixil women's struggles for "the autonomous reconstruction of land-based communal systems, and also [...] the construction of truth and memory in Guatemala's genocide trials" (ibid.).

While recovering and rebuilding their communal land, Ixil women were also active in truth commissions and in the genocide trials against Efraín Ríos Montt and Mauricio Rodríguez Sánchez in 2013. There, they testified "that they were victims of sexual violence, and that the army burned their crops, massacred communities, and killed their families" (ibid. 405). These testimonies "demonstrated the connections between territorial dispossession, sexual violence, and forms of resistance and of organizing for life" (ibid.). Tzul Tzul concludes that the analysis and struggle of Ixil women uncovers the connection between genocide and sexual violence, serving "as a means of suppressing entire communities and weakening processes of social reproduction" (ibid.). Ixil women's struggles, therefore, represent "the sentiment [...] that never again shall there be sex slavery, never again shall there be violence against women's bodies, never again shall communities be destroyed and forced off their lands" (ibid.).

As Tzul Tzul (2018a, 2019a) notes, the connections between settler-colonial genocide, capitalism and modern colonial heteropatriarchy have formed Ixil women's political analysis and praxis. Necropolitics as an attempt to hinder their social reproduction is countered by their desire and struggle for communal life in the form of daily resistance. At the same time, the necropolitics produced by a colonial modern cisheteropatriarchal racial capitalist system threatening their lives and "the autonomous reconstruction of land-based communal systems" (2018b, 404) represents the ground on which the social reproduction of these communities evolves. Following Tzul Tzul's argument, while the social reproduction of Ixil women's communities is infused with their communal lives, energies and resistance against genocidal gendered violence and extractivism, the social reproduction of the agribusiness oligarchs, extractivist corporations and international financial and stock-market industries relies on the logic of necropolitics. This situation demands that the Marxist analysis of social reproduction be complicated and interrogated in relation to colonial modern racist cisheteropatriarchy necropolitics. Tzul Tzul's analysis adds a new element to the discussion of social reproduction or, as Schild (2019) argues regarding contemporary Latin American feminist struggles, brings the Marxist debate up to date. It also complicates Marxist feminist debates on social reproduction by foregrounding the communal labor of mourning.

Rethinking Social Reproduction: Life-Death Continuum

The analysis of social reproduction lies at the heart of Marxist feminist theory (Precarias a la Deriva 2004; Gutiérrez Rodríguez 2010; Pérez Orozco 2014; Bhattacharya 2017; Ferguson 2019; Gimenez 2019). Examining the dynamics between the spheres of production and reproduction, this perspective focuses on what Marx (2004) describes as the twofold character of the production of life. In *The German Ideology*, Marx (ibid., 50) writes that the "production of life" is determined by "one's own labor and 'fresh life in procreation.'" These social and generative dimensions of reproduction are characterized by what he defines as a "double relationship: on the one hand as a natural, on the other as a social relationship." What lies behind the labor force and its reproduction is the historically determined outcome of social relations. Thus, the conditions of existence and maintenance of human beings are socially organized; their basic needs such as sustenance and shelter comprise a "materialistic connection of men with one another" (ibid., 48).

Biopolitical reproduction

Feminist Marxist theory has sharpened Marx's original analysis of social reproduction: In the 1970s, Marxist feminism interrogated domestic work as the neuralgic axis of social reproduction (Dalla Costa and James 1972; International Feminist Collective 1972; Federici 1975). Addressing the naturalization of women's work as an outcome of a heteropatriarchal structure of domination (Lerner 1986; Federici 2004), Marxist feminists contested the divide between nature and society. This perspective has complicated Marx's (1990, 493) observation that the "conditions of production are also those of reproduction" by differentiating between generative reproduction (Mies

1986; Mies, Benholdt-Thomson and von Werlhof 1988) and the historical social formation of the feminization of labor (Federici 2004, 2012; Caffentzis 1999). Offering the possibility to think about the means of production in the broader sense of the production of life, this approach has directed its analysis to the historical entanglement between capital and patriarchy (cf. Mies 1986; Federici 2004). For example, Maria Mies focuses on feminized bodies to trace the historical development of women's procreational capacities as sources of extraction for capital production. Activities related to nourishment, care and domestic work, she states, are constitutive for the maintenance and reproduction of society. Mies develops a social historical analysis of women's activities to create and regenerate life by centering her focus on women's capacity to give birth. This argument, though it acknowledges the social historical character of procreation, carries a biological presumption when it comes to feminized bodies as procreative ones. From a similar, but also different angle, Silvia Federici draws our attention to the feminization of labor by focusing on women's reproductive capacities as socially learned and historically formed. This view of social reproduction as a social historical outcome is also foregrounded by the Madrid-based feminist collective Precarias a la Deriva (2004).

Precarias a la Deriva updates the discussion about social reproduction by exploring moments of coping, but also resistance in everyday life. Weaving stories, images and urban walks into their own experiences of precarious living and working conditions, Precarias' members dwell on the biopolitical dimension of feminized precarity in their book and video *Adrift through the Circuits of Feminized Precarious Work* (2004). The members of the collective interrogate the dynamics of the production-reproduction continuum in advanced capitalism in terms of domination and power relations but also subjectivity, belonging, collective rights and affects. Conceiving social reproduction as forged by multiple social relations, associations and pathways, Precarias emphasizes the cooperative character of current modes of (re)production by highlighting the recreation of social life on the levels of community and communal care (Vega Solís 2019). Their analysis has enriched the debate on social reproduction by interrogating the dynamics of the feminization of labor in Western European urban settings as an outcome of contemporary neoliberal politics and austerity measures organized around a binary gender system through which feminized bodies are produced. Identifying the intersections of bodies, spaces, desires and capitalist relationalities, Precarias determines social reproduction as the primordial constitutive site of the production and accumulation of capital.

Following Precarias' analysis, I look at affective labor as a site of social reproduction. In my work on migration, domestic work and affect (Gutiérrez Rodríguez 2010, 2014a), I have unpacked this argument by looking at the organization of care work, particularly outsourced domestic labor in Western Europe. Looking at the domestic sphere where household members share moments of affection and disaffection, I discuss affective relationships as relational. Established through ties of (dis)attachment to things, space and people, the household represents an affective assemblage. Activities serving the biopolitical reproduction of the household and its members are instilled with feelings and emotions. Working processes related to cleaning, cooking and caring evolve in webs of affective energies, intensities and sensations. Spaces, objects, people and their connections to each other and their environment are suffused with corporeal impulses and sensations, driving us to act or to pause. The physical and emotional well-being of the household and its members is accomplished through tangible reproductive (paid and unpaid) labor, but also through less tangible sensorial moments and affective layers circumventing our existence and placing us in relation to one another. Precarias's proposal of social reproduction as encompassing the production-reproduction continuum and my understanding of social reproduction as nested in affective social relations resonate with contemporary SRT debates.

Susan Ferguson's (2016) understanding of social reproduction that goes beyond labor power as the ultimate source of reproduction is inspired, though no references are given, by these new insights. Ferguson (ibid., 30) suggests that we look at social relations outside of labor relations in order to capture "the processes and institutions through which labor-power is (re)produced." Seeking to widen the perspective on social reproduction by considering "a wider sociality, integral to the very existence and operation of capitalism and class" (ibid., 29), she proposes an analysis of social reproduction that integrates unpaid or low-paid work, often disregarded in Marxist analyses of capital production. Ferguson takes up an argument made by scholars such as Heidi Hartmann (1979) and Christine Delphy (1980). Drawing attention to the intangible character of domestic work as unwaged or low-waged labor, these scholars note that the tasks related to this work, coined also as the three "C's"—cleaning, caring and cooking—remain largely invisible in society and are not accounted for in the Gross National Product (GNP). In this vein, Isabella Bakker (2007) and Nancy Folbre (2006) identify care work as the neuralgic node of social reproduction in a gendered political economy, while the feminist economist Amaia Pérez Orozco (2014) proposes that we shift the equation between capital and labor to that of capital and care. Further, the sociologists Matxalen Legarreta Iza (2013) and Karina Batthyány (2020) examine the value of care work by attending to a time metric that accounts for the intangible and tangible value produced by the numerous tasks of personal attention, support and maintenance on emotional, physical, psychological, social and relational levels. Centering on an analysis of the feminization of reproductive labor, these perspectives have broadened and complicated Marxist understandings of the relationship between production and reproduction.

The analysis of capitalism's absorption of life and its biopolitical dynamics is central to SRT (Bhattacharya 2017; Ferguson 2019). Queer, trans and decolonial SRT scholars have critiqued the heteronormative logic often reproduced in SRT (Gutiérrez Rodríguez 2014b; Klesse 2014; Aizura 2017, 2018; Malatino 2020; Carastathis and Tsilimpounidi 2020; Gleeson and O'Rourke 2021) and proposed an intersectional analysis of social reproduction (Gutiérrez Rodríguez 2010; Ferguson 2019; Arruza et al. 2019; Stewart 2021). Abbi Stewart (2021, 32) draws attention to the "totalizing systemic logic" performed in approaches such as *Feminism for the 99%: A Manifesto* by Tithi Bhattacharya, Nancy Fraser and Cinzia Arruza (2019). In this manifesto, 99% is invoked as a unifying category for political organization. Nevertheless, as Stewart (ibid) notes, this category does not acknowledge the differences, asymmetries and contradictions embedded in "intersectional resistance" (ibid, 33), through which "meaningful bonds of solidarity" (ibid, 32) are formed. Thus, "emancipatory practice" derives from concrete material conditions linked to "lived experience of multiple oppressions." For Stewart (ibid), the concept of intersectionality emerges within a Black feminist materialist tradition. However, the white feminist materialist tradition ignores Black feminist analysis and anti-oppression struggles which address racist, colonial, cisheteropatriarchal antagonisms, as it reproduces (ibid, 33) "a unitary explanatory frame for social oppressions in a certain Hegelian-Marxist fashion." This explanatory frame omits the constitutive character of racism and coloniality in the social reproduction of modern capitalist societies. Other scholars have broadened the SRT analysis through their focus on land resource (Federici 2004; Svampa 2019) or their critical inquiry of socio-ecological reproduction (Bakker and Gill 2019; Rispoli and Tola 2020; Dengler and Lang 2022; Mezzadri 2022). All these debates, while distinct in their approaches, share an interest in social reproduction as the site of the communal production of life (Vega Solís et al 2018; Cavallero and Gago 2020). Common to all is their engagement with the biopolitical dimension of social reproduction. Yet, as I will now argue, social reproduction needs to be thought alongside the tension between biopolitics—the production of life—and necropolitics—the extinction of life. In *Revolution at Point Zero*, Silvia Federici (2012) observes that capitalism engages not only in the production of life but in its exploitation and destruction. Social reproduction, then, takes place between these two poles: production and destruction.

Necropolitics: The underside of social reproduction

George Caffentzis (1999, 163) notes that social reproduction is "permanently vulnerable to the possibility of crises and catastrophe." He develops this argument by looking at the famines in Ethiopia (1983–1985) and Sudan (late 1980s) that took place while development policies oriented toward capital growth were conceptualized in the Global North. Indeed, the parallel between capital growth and destruction, as Wallerstein (1976; 2004; 2011a,b,c) has argued and our discussion on intersectional structural violence and the resistance to extinction has shown, is inherent in the logic of capitalism. War, political conflicts, state violence, and extractivist and austerity policies are geared toward destruction and social deprivation. Accordingly, the "possibility of crises" not only results from the immanent discrepancy between regimes of accumulation and modes of regulation (Wallerstein 2013), but through the paradox of growth and extinction inherent in capitalism as well. It is this contradiction that Quijano (2000a/b; 2008) captures in his concept of the "coloniality of power." He identifies this paradox by introducing an analytical framework that denotes the specific historical conditions that have shaped capitalist societies in Latin America through the prism of "historical-structural heterogeneity" (2020). Considering the uneven development created by historically determined forms of economic, political, cultural and social dependency in colonized territories, Quijano (1981; 1988; 1992) identifies the simultaneity of modernity and coloniality as the two poles shaping contemporary societies. As he notes (2000a, 549),

> [...] in the rest of the world, and in Latin America in particular, the most extended forms of labor control are nonwaged (although for the benefit of global capital), which implies that the relations of exploitation and domination have a colonial character. Political independence, at the beginning of the nineteenth century, is accompanied in the majority of the new countries by the stagnation and recession of the most advanced sectors of the capitalist economy and therefore by the strengthening of the colonial character of social and political domination under formally dependent states. The Eurocentrification of colonial/modern capitalism was in this sense decisive for the different destinies of the process of modernity between Europe and the rest of the world.

This unequal organization of labor, based on economic and political dependencies, articulates the coloniality of power. Within the coloniality of power, biopolitical forms of production coexist with necropolitical regimes of extinction. Capitalism thrives on the basis of creating life and on systemic forms of ending it. Marked by historical and contemporary regimes of production organized around exploitation, usurpation, incarceration, encampment and extinction, capitalism is shaped by racial cisheteropatriarchal necropolitical forms of violence. Racial capitalism scholars, such as W. E. B. Du Bois, Ida B. Wells, Eric Williams, C. L. R. James, Claudia Jones, Cedric Robinson and Neville Alexander have drawn attention to the historical formation of capitalism on the grounds of systemic racial extinction.[13] Structural gendered racial inequalities in the organization of "free" indentured and enslaved labor, unwaged and waged labor, the organization of ownership, distribution of wealth and the divide between the sphere of production and reproduction have been shaped by this exterminatory logic since European colonialism (Robinson 1983; Du Bois 2007b; Bhattacharyya 2018; Jenkins and Leroy 2021). For example, in *Capitalism and Slavery*, Eric Williams (1994) introduces the term "triangular trade" as a framework of analysis to understand the relationship between the slave trade, labor exploitation and global capitalist expansion. Modern industrial production was sustained by the introduction of coerced labor, constituting the development of "free" industrial work on the backs of subjugated unfree laborers. Racialized labor denoted this spectrum between the worker and the enslaved laborer that Williams examines through his analysis of the plantation economy system in Trinidad and Tobago. Looking at the colonial trade relations and organization of labor established by English colonial rulers in the Caribbean, Williams complicates Marx's Eurocentric approach by demonstrating the persistence of two coexisting temporalities in the organization of modern capitalist societies: those of industrialization and slavery. The enslavement and peonage systems in the Caribbean coexisted with industrial waged work in Northern England and the US Northeast in the nineteenth and first half of the twentieth centuries. C. L. R. James's (2001) study on the Haitian Revolution illustrates this entanglement between colonialism, slavery and modernity. Focusing on the colonial interests of France and the anticolonial struggle in Haiti, he traces the complexity of imperial governance and its contestation by the organized abolitionist revolt of the enslaved population. He painstakingly demonstrates the hegemonic struggles that shaped the Haitian Revolution by understanding how the racialization of society was mediated through access to property, creating the grounds for recognition as a liberal subject of politics or its rejection as Black racialized (former) enslaved subjects.

Following this path of complicating the Marxist analytical script of production-reproduction, Lloyd Best and Kari Polanyi Levitt (2009) argue that the plantation economy is the primordial locus of global capitalist exploitation. Inspired by Caribbean critical theory (Reddock 1994; 2014), Best and Polanyi Levitt, along with James Millette, David de Caires and Norman

Girvan, initiated the British West Indies plantation economy school in the 1960s, where they developed the plantation economy model (PEM). Best and Polanyi Levitt draw upon the Latin American dependentista school (Frank 1969; Cardoso and Faletto 1969, 1979; Grosfoguel 2000; Ruvituso 2020; Cárdenas Castro and Lana Seabra 2022) as well as Wallerstein's world system analysis to examine the plantation economy system as a globally integrated peripheral economy that functions as a microcosm of the global capitalist system. Marked by the paradox of existing on the economic periphery, while performing a core function within global capital production, the plantation economy system reveals the coexistence of precarious, low-waged or unwaged labor and industrial waged labor. Best and Polanyi Levitt draw attention to the different modes of engagement with global capitalism and its distributional effects by defining three historical phases of the plantation economy system: (1) the colony of conquest, (2) the colony of exploitation and (3) the colony of settlement. These systems are denoted by a logic of production based on coerced labor, settler colonialism and the exploitative extraction of resources operating within a logic of extinction or in other words, the co-existence of biopolitics and necropolitics.

Indigenous scholars (Tsosie 2012; Tuck and Yang 2012; Coulthard 2014; Simpson 2017; Estes and Dhillon 2019) on Turtle Island have introduced us and deepened the understanding of the dynamic between colonialism, racism and capitalism. Drawing on the analysis of contemporary forms of ecocide, land occupation and fossil fuel extraction as forms of production based on displacement, encampment, incarceration and the systematic killing of Indigenous communities as well as the disappearing and murder of Indigenous women, girls[14] and LGTBQIA2S+ people (Ficklin et al. 2022),[15] these analyses have sharpened the view on the entanglement between biopolitics and necropolitics. Also, Indigenous and anticolonial theories in Abya Yala have insisted on the persistent terracide, ecocide and genocide, the systemic killing of communities, rivers, plants, mountains and other species in the analysis of contemporary articulations of racial cisheteropartriarchal capitalism (see Tzul Tzul 2018a,b; Leyva Solano and Icaza 2019; Cariño Trujillo 2020, 2021; Rodríguez Aguilera 2021; Itzu 2022).[16] As Leyva Solano (2019) has argued, these "new forms of war" are systemically structured around racial and sexual violence, shaping the plurality of violence in its ordinary manifestation. The analysis of social reproduction, as I have argued throughout this chapter, is crossed by necropolitical dynamics evolving within what the Maya-Xinka theorist and activist Lorena Cabnal defines as the body-territory-land axis (Cabnal 2010, 2017, 2019; Cruz et al. 2020). The Binizaá (Zapotec) from the Isthmus of Tehuantepec scholar Isabel Altamirano-Jiménez (2020) refers also to Cabnal when she considers the specific historical embeddedness of Indigenous social reproduction, marked by the experience of colonial, settler state and resource extraction. As Altamirano-Jiménez notes in her study on the mine industry in Capulálpam de Méndez, Oaxaca (Mexico), Zapotec communities, particularly women, counter these extractivist projects through organized resistance. Opposing the attitude toward the land of mining corporations and the settler state, their social practices of reproduction and maintenance of life are connected to a Zapotec worldview. Altamirano-Jiménez (ibid., 162) draws upon Aquino Centeros to describe "water and forest" as "sacred forms of life on the ground," while "subsoil [...] represents the roots, the seeds that make possible the existence of mountains, water, plants and so on. Thus, the subsurface is part of the spiritual, symbolic, and material life of Indigenous communities." Social reproduction, then, is more than just the reproduction of human life; it includes the relationship between humans and nonhumans (Celemajer et al. 2020).

These approaches countering systemic extinction and intersectional structural violence complicate the analysis of social reproduction. We will attend to these complications next in our observations on decolonial mourning as communal affective labor.

Mourning as Communal Affective Labor

Tzul Tzul's (2018a,b; 2019a,b) discussion of communitarian bonds, creativity and production also draws on the specific historical embeddedness of social reproduction in the Maya Q'eqchi' context of Guatemala (Tzul Tzul 2019c). As we have seen previously, in her analysis of the social reproduction of the Ixil community and the relevance of women's work, she shows how the women of this community cultivate the land, negotiate peace and struggle for truth while working through grief (2018b). While not explicitly analyzing the labor of mourning, Tzul Tzul determines grief as articulating the bond between life and death. The labor of mourning is a constant reminder of the work members of the community realize. They pay tribute to their loved ones lost in the genocide while communally working the land. The labor of mourning is entrenched in the work on the land, in the household and in everyday activities. Searching for the dead, and working with the land where the dead are buried, connects with life. The creation of communal land and communitarian economies demonstrates the material and affective bonds of communal labor as la voluntad de vida. This implies working with and through the pulses of life while dealing with the atrocities of the genocide and the loss of loved ones who remain in the soil that will give life again. In other words, the cycle of life is not interrupted by death. Rather, the women's labor in the presence of their ancestors is honored, while they reconnect with the lives lived through their practices of communal living. The communal labor of mourning is thus intertwined with what Tzul Tzul defines as "cycles of life", connected to the dead through the organization of common lives and the futures of their communities.

The struggle against feminicide foregrounds the communal labor of mourning, which derives from a matrix of social reproduction traversed by necropolitics. Following Tzul Tzul (2018b), we have seen that the feminist movements against feminicide reestablish a new understanding of the connection between death and life by insisting on the presence of and their connection to those lost. The acts of remembering, presenting, bearing witness and demanding justice constitute the labor of mourning carried out through moments of life and struggle, redeemed through caring for the loss of loved ones, actualizing their presence and working through the grief of those left behind. The political is conceived here through the immediate connection of life with death, shaped by the intense work of grief delivered daily. One of the banners of the protest marches against feminicide reads "Nos tocan a una, nos tocan a todas" (When you lay a hand on one of us, you lay a hand on all of us). The feelings of those lost are transferred to those who can still voice their pain, which endures in the protesters' chants. A collective form of resistance, strengthened by evoking those lost as actively participating in the forging of a communal rebellion, culminates in utterances such as "¡Vivas y muertas estamos presente!" (We are present, both in life and in death!). The communal labor of mourning in the protests against feminicide in Argentina, Mexico and other countries in Abya Yala denounces the systemic killing of feminized, racialized and Indigenous bodies and connects to a long history of affective politics linked to public mourning. In Argentina, the act of public mourning was initiated by the Madres de la Plaza de Mayo.[17] Today, the Madres (mothers) and the Abuelas (grandmothers) de la Plaza de Mayo as well as the children's organization HIJOS[18]— daughters and sons searching for their parents who were disappeared by the military dictatorship in power during the 1970s—have politicized affective relationships by making their personal grief public in their struggle for justice (Amado 2003; Piasek 2015, 2016). Searching for their disappeared parents, (grand)daughters and (grand)sons, participants gather in the central public square, Plaza de Mayo in Buenos Aires, holding their pictures. Their work against oblivion and for a politics of memory that calls for justice while acknowledging their loss and grief continues today. This public daily grieving enacts what I call here the communal political labor of mourning. It is in these daily acts of forging connections and solidarity that the affective labor of mourning is realized.

Affective labor and relational ontology

Mourning is care work oriented toward loss and is a form of affective labor that is relational and spatially contingent and speaks about the impact of feelings and emotions at work—but also about how the quality and conditions of work impact affectively. Fostered by specific feelings, sensations and intensities related to the experience of loss, and to memories as well, the affective labor of communal mourning works through the layers of our being and its connection to death and loss. In the case of the political struggle against necroborders, feminicide, genocide, extractivism, ecocide and the necropolitics of the coloniality of migration, mourning as affective labor counters the social, political, historical and economic conditions responsible for the systemic killing of our loved ones and the planet we live on. In this sense, decolonial communal mourning as affective labor is driven by the search for truth, the quest for reparative justice, the preservation of memories and bearing witness to the lives lived. As affective labor, mourning is an ongoing process and speaks about collective interdependent lives, in other word: ontological relationality.

Inspired[19] by the Michi Saagiig Nishnaabeg[20] scholar and artist Leanne Betasamosake Simpson's[21] (2014) reflections on the creation of Nishnaabeg intelligence in her essay "Land as pedagogy: Nishnaabeg intelligence and rebellious transformation," I approach the affective labor of mourning as entrenched in and resurfacing from communal living relations and knowledge practices. My view that mourning is relational acknowledges the specific history of Nishnaabeg intelligence and critically examines my own positionality as a white Southern European, situated at the juncture of the European coloniality-migration entanglement. Thus, my listening and learning entails addressing responsibility and accountability for past and present murderous acts of Europe—particularly Spain and Germany—and its settler colonialism, coloniality of migration and politics of extinction. My thinking through decolonial mourning as communal political work attempts to engage with this task. I am attentive to Eve Tuck and K. Wayne Yang's (2014) argument that "decolonization is not a metaphor." This is a matter of land rights, Indigenous jurisprudence and autonomy. Although Simpson does not speak about mourning in her reflections on Nishnaabeg intelligence, she invites us to think along relational ontology. Rooted in the specific history and social context of Nishnaabeg intelligence, relational ontology carries a universal and transcendental meaning that offers some insight into other forms and expressions of communal living. Nishnaabeg intelligence surfaces from a relational communitarian process of sharing, respect and reciprocity. Related to "wisdom within a Michi Saagiig Nishnaabeg epistemology […]—it takes place in the context of family, community and relations" (ibid., 7) and is about "consensual engagement" (ibid.).[22] But Nishnaabeg intelligence is also formed through resistance to settler-colonial domination and necropolitics (ibid., 13):

> Nishnaabeg intelligence has been violently under attack since the beginning days of colonialism through processes that remove Indigenous peoples from our homelands, whether those processes are residential and other forms of state-run schools, outright dispossession, the destruction of land through resource extraction and environmental contamination, imposed poverty, or heteropatriarchal and colonial gendered violence. Our peoples have always resisted this destruction by engaging in Nishnaabewin, whenever and wherever they could.

Nishnaabeg intelligence is also materially rooted and entangled with the question of land. As Simpson writes (ibid., 7),

> [land] is both context and process. The process of coming to know is learner-led and profoundly spiritual in nature. Coming to know is the pursuit of whole body intelligence practiced in the context of freedom, and when realized collectively it generates generations of loving, creative, innovative, self-determining, inter-dependent and self-regulating community minded individuals. It creates communities of individuals with the capacity to uphold and move forward our political traditions and systems of governance.

Simpson unfolds these reflections through the traditional Michi Saagiig Nishnaabeg story[23] of the young woman Kwezens, which she (ibid.) argues is a "theoretical anchor" articulating "individual and collective Nishnaabeg consciousness." Kwezens learns how to ask the tree for juice by watching the squirrel harvesting sweet water from the trees (ibid., 2). The squirrel sucks on the tree, and Kwezens copies the squirrel and drinks from the tree with a contraption she has devised. She then shares this knowledge with her mother and her elders and asks them to join her the next day. But when she arrives the next day with her family and friends, no syrup comes out of the tree. Her community then works together to learn how to extract syrup from the tree. During this process, different actors engage with one another, cherishing a common knowledge in relation to the tree, respecting its vulnerability and connecting to its readiness to share its fruit with them. Kwezens and her community are grateful for this gift and celebrate the tree's generosity. From this experience, Kwezens "learned both *from* the land, and *with* the land [...]

learned what it felt like to be recognized, seen and appreciated by her community" (ibid., 6).

In comparison to the Western myth of knowledge as the product of a single white affluent man or woman, Kwezens is neither the central nor the sole producer of knowledge, Simpson tells us. Her understanding of her environment comes about through observing and communicating with other inhabitants of the planet. With this story, Simpson contrasts settler-colonial values in Canada with the Nishnaabeg intelligence of relational planetary living. Kwezens's practice is based on mutual learning with the tree; she offers tobacco to it in order to show her "mutual respect, reciprocity, and caring."[24] Thus, Kwezens's story invites us to consider how relational planetary living has been destroyed by the settler colonialists who occupied the territory and abused the generosity of its inhabitants, treating them as sources of plunder and capital accumulation. From the settler-colonial perspective, living with the tree is overturned in favor of a master-servant hierarchy. By subjugating the tree and the squirrel to settler-colonial interests, needs and values, a social relationship based on the liberal framework of individualism, private property and sole capital gain is established. In contrast, Nishnaabeg intelligence traces a very different path, which departs from the conviction that

> coming to know is the pursuit of whole body intelligence, practiced in the context of freedom, and, when realized collectively, it generated generations of loving, creative, innovative, self-determining, interdependent and self-regulating community minded individuals. (ibid., 7)

Knowledge practices in this sense are interwoven and connected to common practices of living together by respecting what each member brings to the community and to common living (see also Tzul Tzul 2019a,b). Nishnaabeg intelligence is based on a relationship with the land that is not determined by ownership; rather, it is a mutual relationship of respect and care between the land and the Nishnaabeg community. When land is treated as individual property and the people, plants, rivers, mountain and air as resources to be exploited and extracted, social reproduction is coupled with extinction and destruction. This leads Simpson to ask, "What if Kwezens lived in a world where no one listened to girls? Or where she had been missing and murdered before she ever made it to the sugar bush?" (ibid., 9). As Simpson observes, the white settler-colonial attempt to negate and devalue Indigenous women's lives articulates the extractivist principle of settler epistemology, capitalist production and the settler state. Kwezens's story, however, reminds us of the ongoing resistance to settler-colonial oppression.

If we consider decolonial mourning as political affective labor through the prism of Nishnaabeg intelligence and Kwenzens's allegory, Freud's grief work (Trauerarbeit) is shifted from an individual act to a communal and relational one. Furthermore, if we follow Tzul Tzul in her understanding of grief as entrenched in social reproduction based on communal relations, social reproduction evolves within the life-death continuum (Rodríguez Aguilera 2021). This brings us to consider social reproduction at the juncture of biopolitics and necropolitics. Finally, situating communal mourning at the juncture of epistemology, ontology and cosmology, grief work carries the historical traits of its moment of emergence, as it speaks about facing the pain of loss and the struggle against settler colonialism and racial cisheteropatriarchy capitalism.

Conclusion: Relational Mourning as Resistance

Thinking through Nishnaabeg intelligence, decolonial mourning, as we have seen in this chapter, takes place at the intersection of biopolitics and necropolitics. It is an articulation of affective labor, emanating from the struggles against feminicide, extractivism, terracide and ecocide. Decolonial mourning as communal affective labor speaks about the relational character in which this work is realized. It also makes us aware of the cultural predication and societal imbrication accompanying the feelings, emotions and sensations resulting from Trauerarbeit or grief work. Set in (e)motions, touching and being touched, affecting and being affected, decolonial mourning addresses the lives and the well-being of those mourning and calling for justice for their communities, children, siblings, parents, grandparents, uncles, aunts, friends and neighbors. It engages with the everyday work of cleaning, cooking and caring while grieving and sharing mourning in protest. Grief work is about dealing with loss and trauma, coping with despair, pain, sadness and anger, while looking after the well-being of oneself, others and the planet. As such it is an expression of communal labor, grounded on relational ontology. It is about mutual respect and love for the lives lived and the reactivation of their energies, practices and knowledge. The affective labor of mourning reflects the relationality of our being and thinking. It speaks to what Tzul Tzul (2018a, b) refers to as social reproduction and Simpson as Nishnaabeg intelligence.

Addressing the societal conditions of exploitation, abuse, degradation and dehumanization in which loss and mourning occur, decolonial mourning is composed of acts of resistance. As such, the resistance against the politics of death as relational affective labor evolves as a transformative "social energy"[25] in "rhizomatic arenas of political entanglements" (Félix de Souza 2019, 91). This connects different struggles against racial capitalism, cisheteropatriarchy and settler colonialism while articulating intertwined temporalities and addressing and delineating the potential of possible common futures. As the discussion on the necropolitical dimension of social reproduction through the filter of the movement against feminicide has shown, political actions deriving from decolonial mourning turn lament into outcry—against the state, police, politicians, organized crime and other perpetrators of colonial racial gender ableist violence—and public condemnation and calls for the prosecution of these crimes. In this vein, I argue here and in the next chapters that the political articulation of decolonial mourning derives from the relational affective labor of communities in struggle. Resisting necropolitical intersectional violence, these communities convert their communal grief work into new meanings of relationality. Not only the relationship between life and death is reconsidered but also that of human and nonhuman, deriving from a multispecies understanding of political grief. For the analysis of social reproduction, this perspective offers new theoretical insights into the historical complexity and its present manifestations of understanding the reproduction of society along the death-life continuum and the resistance to necropolitical social reproduction. We will explore this argument further in the next chapter, when we bear witness to the political communal labor of mourning of the mothers, daughters and sisters of #SayHerName and Women in Exile. Listening to them, we engage with their theoretical analysis of misogynoir state and police violence and the necropolitics of the coloniality of migration.

Notes

1 Translation by author: #We Are Not All Here. We strike because we are missing the victims of femicide, voices that are violently extinguished to the chilling rhythm of one per day only in Argentina. We are missing the murdered lesbians and transvestites. We are missing the political prisoners, the persecuted, the murdered in our Latin American territory for defending the land and its resources. We are missing women imprisoned for minor crimes that criminalise forms of survival, while the crimes of corporations and drug trafficking go unpunished because they benefit capital. We are missing the dead and those imprisoned for unsafe abortions. We are missing those disappeared by trafficking networks; the victims of sexual exploitation. In front of homes that have become hell, we organise to defend ourselves and take care of each other. In the face of sexist crime and its pedagogy of cruelty, in the face of the media's attempt to victimise and terrorise us, we make of individual mourning a collective consolation, and of rage a shared struggle. Face with cruelty, more feminism. See: https://m.facebook.com/nt/screen/?params=%7B%22note_id%22 %3A2733343383648814%7D&path=%2Fnotes%2Fnote%2F

2 Translation by the author: On this 8th of March, the earth trembles. Women of the world unite and organize a measure of strength and a common cry: International Women's Strike. We Stop. We strike, we organize and we meet among ourselves. We put into practice the world we want to live in.

3 Please see Anti-Futurismo Cimarron, curated by Yuderkys Espinosa-Miñoso and Katia Sepúlveda, La Virreina – Centre de la Imatge, Barcelona, 16.10.2021 – 15.10.2022. https://ajuntament.barcelona.cat/lavirreina/es/recursos/lecciones-de -lumbung-uno-en-torno-la-conocida-documenta-quince/674 (accessed April 2023)

4 ARTE Documentary, *Argentina: The Women's Revolt (2019)* and Verónica Gago, 2018, "#We Strike: Notes toward a Political Theory of the Feminist Strike," *The South Atlantic Quarterly* 117: 3, 660–69.

5 The use of woman includes here self-identified, trans and nonbinary gender positionalities.

6 See also Istanbul Convention. Action against Violence against Women and Domestic Violence. Council of Europe. https://www.coe.int/en/web/istanbul-convention/text -of-the-convention

7 For a critical discussion on the maquila industry in Mexico, see Bendesky et al., 2004.

8 For further discussion of the symbolic and ordinary character of violence, see the study of Çiçek Tanlı "Daily Struggles as Everyday Violence: Narratives of Divorced Mothers with Migration Biographies from Turkey in Germany," PhD submitted at the Faculty of Cultural and Social Studies, Justus-Liebig-University Giessen, Germany, 2023.

9 Félix de Souza opts to speak of femicide instead of feminicide without further elaboration. However, the use of femicide refers to Segato's analysis of feminicide.

10 See short portrait, global initiative: https://assassination.globalinitiative.net/wp -content/uploads/2020/06/GI_Faces_2020-06-10_HI_website-profiles-Marielle -Franco.pdf.

11 See https://www.nodal.am/2020/06/a-5-anos-del-grito-de-ni-una-menos-en-argen- tina-protesta-virtual-y-marchas-en-las-provincias-contra-la-violencia-machista/.

12 In original: "Hoy protesto por vos, por mí, por todas las que viven y por todas las que la violencia nos arrebató."

13 See the discussion in Du Bois *The Philadelphia Negro* (1989); *Black Reconstruction in America 1860–1880* (1935); and *Africa and the World*. For Ida B. Wells, see *The Red Record* (1895); for Claudia Jones see *Beyond Containment* (2016) and Carole Boyce Davies' *Left of Karl Marx* (2008). For the other mentioned authors, see previous references.

14 Women and girls include all individuals who identify as women or girls.

15 Reclaiming Power and Place: The Final Report of the National Inquiry into Missing and Murdered Indigenous Women and Girls. https://www.mmiwg-ffada.ca/final -report/ and further information on national action plan: https://www.mmiwg -ffada.ca.

16 See the special issue on femicide and everyday violence in Latin America in the jour- nal *Iberoamérica Social* (2020), https://iberoamericasocial.com/ojs/index.php/IS/issue /view/17.

17 See https://madres.org.

18 See https://www.hijos-capital.org.ar/nuestra-historia/.

19 I came across Simpson's text and Kwenzens's story during my tenure as a visiting pro- fessor at the University of Alberta, Canada. Together with my students, we read this text in my undergraduate class on anticolonial/decolonial feminisms. I am grateful to them for the communal process of learning that we pursued together. Simpson's text introduced and taught us about Nishnaabeg intelligence, anticolonial struggle and land as pedagogy.

20 Simpson uses the term Nishnaabeg "to refer to Ojibwe, Odawa, Bodawadami, Mississauga/Michi Saagiig, Sauteaux, Chippewa, Nipissing, our relatives Omawinini and all the various groups of peoples that make up our nation," in Simpson, Leanne Betasamoka (2014) "Land as pedagogy: Nishnaabeg intelligence and rebellious transformation," *Decolonization: Indigeneity, Education & Society* 3 (3): 6.

21 This thinking, as Simpson (ibid., 1) writes, "[...] was generated inside a community of intellectuals, artists, Elders and cultural producers to whom I am both influenced by and accountable to. Previous drafts were peer-reviewed outside of the standard academic peer-review process and within a community of practitioners and Nishnaabeg thinkers including Doug Williams, John Borrows, Tara Williamson, and Niigaanwewidam Sinclair. *Mahsi/Mahalo* to Glen Coulthard, Erin Freeland Ballantyne and Manulani Meyer for on-going discussions and comments on earlier drafts, and *miigwech* to Toby Rollo, Matthew Wildcat and the editorial team for their helpful comments."

22 Simpson (2004, 7) notes that communal practices of knowing require "complex, committed, *consensual* engagement. Relationships within Nishnaabewin are based upon the consent –the informed (honest) consent—of all beings involved. The word consensual here is key because if children learn to normalize dominance and non-consent within the context of education, then non-consent becomes a normalized part of the 'tool kit' of those who have and wield power. Within the context of settler colonialism, Indigenous peoples are not seen as worthy recipients of consent, informed or otherwise, and part of being colonized is having to engage in all kinds of processes on a daily basis that, given a choice, we likely wouldn't consent to. In my experiences with the state-run education system, my informed consent was never required –learning was forced on me using the threat of emotional and physical violence."

23 Simpson (ibid., 1) writes: "I learned from Washkigaamagki (Curve Lake First Nation) Elder Gidigaa Migizi (Doug Williams). This is my own re-telling of it, and it is one of the ways I tell it in March, when my family and I are in the sugar bush, making maple syrup. I have chosen to gender the main character as a girl because I identify as a woman, but the story can be and should be told using all genders. Michi Saagiig Nishnaabeg refers to Mississauga Ojibwe people, and our territory is the north shore of Lake Huron in what is now known as Ontario, Canada. We are part of the larger Anishinaabeg nation."

24 Reflecting on her own experience with settler education, Simpson (ibid., 12) comments on the lack of relational thinking beyond the recreation of persons as the center of agency, transformation and history. Thus, the agent of knowledge tends to be marked by the categories defining the hegemonic group, often prescribed by whiteness and masculinity. Consequently, the knowledge practices rooted in her genealogical background as a *metis* person were absent from settler colonial education. The education she received in school was centered around books and not communal practices resulting from common experiences of planetary living. Her experience with the colonial institution of knowledge was not that of Kwezens, who was "immersed in a nest of Nishnaabeg intelligence" based on "the importance of observation and learning from [...] animal teachers."

25 I refer here to Tzul Tzul's commitment to the struggle of Ixil women as "social energy" (2018b).

Chapter 5

ACCOUNTABLE MOURNING: BEARING WITNESS

Introduction: (Con)Dolence and Accountability

We walked everyday with literally amputated hearts, every single day. And it hurts—every single day and for people to even expect that you get over it or that your grieving pattern or grieving stage, wherever you are in a grief that somehow there is a blueprint to navigate it—that we should be at a certain point. It comes to you unaware, it comes to you at the most unpredictable moments, because we don't give a chance to our sisters to rest, there is going to be someone else killed. And it starts it over again, the festering wounds, the acid is poured again. It starts it over and over again and yet our daughters are still erased.

(Gina Best, mother of India Kager, AAPF, Pt. 11[1])

Gina Best describes the unintelligible pain of losing her 27-year-old daughter **India Kager** in the webinar "Under the Blacklight: Say Her Name—Telling Stories of State Violence & Public Silence" (Pt. 11) on 17 June 2020, organized by the #SayHerName[2] campaign, Kimberlé Crenshaw, the African American Policy Forum (AAPF), and the Center for Intersectionality and Social Policy at the Columbia Law School. I listen at home while Best recalls that India and her partner **Angelo Perry** visited his family 5 September 2015 to introduce Roman, their four-month-old baby, to them. After the visit, they were sitting in a Walmart parking lot when police officers fired 50 bullets into their car. Angelo and India were killed immediately; Roman was left disabled and now lives with his grandmother, Gina.

The police failed to immediately inform Kager's family about her killing, leaving her body on the ground of the parking lot overnight. In a statement, the police admitted that India and Angelo were killed because they mistook the latter for a wanted offender (Pt. 11). In the webinar, Best raises questions about the police's responsibility for the murder of her daughter, the failure to care for her dead body and the negligence displayed in dealing with the

families' grief and need for information, clarification and a thorough investigation. India "was in her own car with her own baby, going about her life"
(ibid.); thus the question of why her life was violently ended by police brutality
remains unanswered.

Listening to the accounts of loss of the members of the #SayHerName
campaign and following their analysis of intersectional violence and practices of
daily resistance, this chapter engages with bearing witness through accountable
listening as a double-bind. I address the limitations of rhetorical solidarity by
focusing on the need for radical material change and thinking through (con)
dolence as affective connections traversed by the structural abyss of a colonial
modern cisheteropatriarchal racial capitalist system. Attending to unbridgeable
disparities, this chapter engages in imagining points of encounter upon which to
build partial connections (Strathern 2004; Cadena 2015; Sempértegui 2021b)
working toward intersectional justice. It introduces the communal political
labor of outraged mourning (Rocha 2020) of #SayHerName in the United
States and its analysis of state and police misogynoir[3] (Noble and Palmer 2022)
violence, while it also looks at the practices of countering the coloniality of
migration in Germany proposed by Women in Exile e.V. (WiE). The chapter
concludes with some thoughts on abolitionist mourning.

Accountable Listening as (Con)Dolence: #SayHerName

I am moved as I listen to the words of Gina Best. Her grief touches me, though
as Luciane de Oliveira Rocha (2014; 2020) notes in her study on Black mothers'
suffering in the context of Black genocide in Brazil, there are contextual and
relational limits to the translatability of Black suffering. Drawing on the work
of Saidiya Hartman (1997), Rocha argues that Black sentience is inconceivable
to bodies not subjected to the afterlife of slavery. For my accountable
listening this means that the impact of Best's words on my body encounters
my positionality as a white Southern European cisgendered queer lesbian,
marked by my parents' *Gastarbeiter* history. My experience of being treated as
an *Ausländerin* in my childhood and youth in Germany is—historically and
socially—differently located. Thus, while my parents dealt with a specific
geographically and historically rooted form of racism in Fordist Germany,
as their daughter I am structurally embedded and situated within the context
of the European Union. It is this intersubjective witnessing (Lugones 2010)
that sets me in relation to the accounts of the members of #SayHerName and
shapes my accountable listening. My position as an accountable listener is set
within an interlocking system of oppression and power relations. Accountable
listening means that thinking and writing process in academic work is in
a dialogic relationship. This decenters the hegemonic notion of academic

work as linked to a single author or theorist. At the same time, it reveals the communal fabric of knowledge production by tracing the collective process of analysis, reflection and conceptualization. The communal labor behind thinking is laid open, which challenges academic neoliberal, capitalist strategies of knowledge branding and extractivist appropriation. Knowledge belongs to everyone, not just to those few authorized by academic institutions. However, the accountable listening process is also marked here by my position within the university. Structural asymmetries and hierarchies between academia and community/activism organize the field of intellectual encounter and exchange. While based on accountable listening, the writing of this book is shaped by antagonistic relationships of (re-)production between academia and activism. A critical analysis of these contradictions cannot dissolve their structural existence. This realization pushes us to formulate claims and initiate structural changes. Demands for equal distribution of research funds between everyone included in the research process or practices of devolution need to be at the center of institutional research funding. Accountable listening is just one step in this process and represents one device in a community- and activism-oriented research process of joint knowledge production. As such, it derives from the co-labor (Sempertégui 2021a) emanating from the dialogue between academia and communities, social movements and activism. Accountable listening contests the extractivist stand in academic knowledge production and pushes the listener to take responsibility and engage in political action. As Mack and Na'puti (2019) point out, this constitutes a heuristic decolonial approach that opens up the possibility to conceive and build forms of communal analysis and theory. This requires that we be attentive to the different historical genealogies, sociopolitical and cultural configurations in which our listening and speaking take place. The continuation of terror and structural violence Best speaks about is related to the geography of inequality, knowledge and governance brought about by European colonialism, the Maafa and the global expansion of cisheteropatriarchal racial capitalism.

(Con-)dolence as double-bind

My bearing witness to Best and the other stories of the #SayHerName campaign is guided by my active listening as (con)dolence, marked by my positionality of accountability as a white European citizen. The Merriam-Webster dictionary defines condolence as "sympathy with another in sorrow."[4] I am using it here in this way but also in the morphological sense. The prefix "con" stands for the communal character of condolence, while "dolence" refers to pain. It is this sharing of pain felt as an affective moment that nourishes my accountable listening. This communal affective sensation is shaped by the incommensurability of two temporalities: proximity and distance. While the sensation of pain might be felt individually, the pre- fix "con" indicates that proximity is experienced through the sharing of this pain. Distance, however, is structurally given through the relation- ship between the person who experiences the pain and the one who shares it. Condolence expresses an antagonistic relational practice of communal sharing.

In the concrete moment of (con)dolence that I have shared, while lis- tening to the members of the #SayHerName movement, this antagonism determines our diametrical structural positionalities and potential for par- tial connections.[5] The affective politics of (con)dolence make us aware of the structural inequalities in which our common working toward an end to injustice unfold—setting us apart, while bringing us together. Though our positionalities might partially overlap, when it comes to systems of oppres- sion such as cisheteropatriarchy and racial capitalism, the constitution of our subjectivities are determined by specific historical geographical-political con- junctures and societal contingency. It is this simultaneity of societal structural convergence and divergence that configures the asymmetrical relationship between my listening and the accounting of #SayHerName. My (con)dolence is determined by this double-bind: it results from the historical and societal embeddedness of our interdependent subjective agency as well as its struc- tural limitations reflected in our diametrical positionalities. It is within this affective scope that (con)dolence defines the connection and the abyss in the communal sensing and practice of mourning.

As Gayatri C. Spivak (2012) argues in *An Aesthetic Education in the Era of Globalization*, the structural divides that guarantee capitalist profit for some through a systemic dispossession of others cannot be dismantled solely through gestures of solidarity, campaigns or programs. Solidarity work, while socially necessary, is always trapped in the matrix of its own emergence within a colonial modern cisheteropatriarchal racial capitalist global unjust system. Our struggles for change are embedded in this system of oppression that requires us to address interdependent asymmetries, where the good life for some is based on the exploitation of others. Our practices of solidarity—here, (con)dolence—evolves within this immanent systemic contradiction. Nonetheless, as Spivak (ibid.) reminds us, practice, or doing, can be a force of change. Understanding (con)dolence as *doing* engages with Spivak's (1994, 44) notion of "responsibility-as-accountability," a listening that is a concrete response and accountable to working against structural injustice. (Con)dolence in this case represents a response to a common struggle for social justice—concretely, intersectional abolitionist justice. As I bear witness to Best's account and to Kimberlé Crenshaw and the mothers and sisters of

#SayHerName, I feel their sorrow. It is at this point that my mourning for my parents traverses their mourning, and my journey of bearing witness to their stories of sorrow begins.

Bearing witness

We bear witness to their and their families' losses. We bear witness to their stories. We mind the possibilities and conditions that led to their tragedy. We examine the possible policy changes that would have made a difference.

(Kimberlé Crenshaw, AAPF, Pt. 11,
introductory remarks)

I listen to Crenshaw's words in her introduction to Installment 11 of the webinar "Under the Blacklight" dedicated to all, but focusing on some of the mothers, daughters and sisters who died at the hands of state and police racial violence: **Sandra Bland**, **Michelle Cusseaux**, **Shelly Frey**, **Korryn Gaines**, **India Kager** and **Kayla Moore**. As I sit at my kitchen table, Crenshaw's words reach out to me. The words of the mothers and sisters circulate—their thoughts, memories and feelings impact me, affect me. Separated by geographical distances and time zones, I become part of a virtual encounter with Kimberlé Crenshaw, Gina Best, Rhanda Dormeus (mother of Korryn Gaines), Fran Garrett (mother of Michelle Cusseaux), Maria Moore (sister of Kayla Moore), Sharon Cooper (sister of Sandra Bland) and Sharon Wilkerson (mother of Shelly Frey). As a remote listener, I am not visible to the speakers sharing their feelings and thoughts with me. Nonetheless, their words move me, make me pause and think about the political consequences and work that needs to follow. It is this affective encounter that transforms my listening to a form of remote sharing, while bearing witness to their suffering and resistance. I learn from their analysis of state and police racial violence and their insights on abolitionist democracy (Davis 2005; Gilmore 2007; Cullors 2019). Attending to their wisdom, I witness their work of grief.

Seeing the pain, the stress, the trauma, the violence, the lack of justice and the economic precarity of these mothers and sisters, I must ask what my listening and bearing witness to their stories means. Their stories draw me close to them; I am introduced into the reality of intersectional violence against Black women, girls and "femmes."[6] Their stories transmit their sorrow but also their perseverance as they search for justice. As Fran Garrett says, "they need the audience's help in making things happen, in moving forward."[7] We, the audience, are called upon to engage in "active listening," to commit to listening that moves us toward "responsibility-as-accountability" and collective change. Affective bonds of mourning are forged remotely, binding our lives with potentially transformative political energy. Accountable listening requires that we place ourselves in dialogue and allow ourselves to be moved by the words of the other. Although Sharon Wilkerson (ibid.) remarks that the loss of daughters and sisters cannot be felt by anyone who has not been "truly through it," their pain might resonate with our own experiences of loss.

My accountable listening is intertwined with my personal loss: my mourning for my parents. Remembering my parents means speaking up about the injustice they experienced as Gastarbeiter in Germany, but also situating this experience within a broader context of intersectional violence and cisheteropatriarchal racial capitalism. While my mourning for my parents resonates with the sorrow of the mothers and sisters of "Under the Blacklight," I can only catch glimpses of their pain. I do not know what it is like to lose a daughter or sister to state and police racial violence because they are Black. My geopolitical, historical racial positionality and my active listening situate me in a space that addresses accountability and responsibility. Understanding this outraged mourning (Rocha 2020) as communal political labor, my accountable listening engages with the reflections and attempts of Black mothers to put into words that which is inconceivable. In other words, drawing on Crenshaw (2015a,b; 2016) and Rocha (2020), the mothers and sisters create their own analysis and understanding of intersectional violence. Their accounts call upon me as a potential ally in their abolitionist struggle against state and police racial violence. Listening, though remotely, I accept the invitation extended by Crenshaw and #SayHerName to march together for #AllBlackLivesMatter. Their words call on me to act, to mourn collectively, to bear justice to the lives lived and to honor them in memory.

Sentient listening and partial connections

Accounting for their truth, the stories of the mothers and sisters touch me deeply and affectively, while moving me to act. It is this interdependent relationship between mind and action that Spinoza (1994) describes as affect: the potential to turn feelings and emotions into action. Feelings of sorrow, but also of joy and love, circulate in these gatherings, impacting me, affecting me as well as my potential for action. This virtual gathering, "Under the Blacklight," has probably moved other members of the audience too, inspiring and influencing their forms of reflection, intervention and resistance to state and police violence against Black women, girls and femmes. The labor of mourning displayed by Crenshaw and the mothers and sisters may be continued by their listeners in regard to their social positionalities by different ways and degrees. Responding to the stories of #SayHerName and repeating the names of the mothers, daughters and sisters killed by state and police violence has strengthened the attempt of the organizers of the webinar to break the silence and counter disinformation. Through this event and other activities,[8] #SayHerName and the AAPF create a group of members, affiliates and allies committed to the goal of advancing the fight for intersectional "gender sensitive social justice" theoretically, politically and pragmatically (Crenshaw 2016).

I partake in this communal labor of mourning through collective accountable listening that engages in witnessing, while reflecting on my own experiences and complicity with state and police brutality. In this sense, active accountable listening establishes a bridge to a community of struggle and may contribute to the forging of a political assembly based on what Sempértegui (2021b) defines as "partial connections"—borrowing a term from Marilyn Strathern (2004) and Marisol de la Cadena (2015)—in her analysis of alliances between ecofeminists and Indigenous women of the Ecuadorian Amazon. With "partial connections," Sempértegui (2021b, 204) accentuates the political navigations and negotiations between these parties that "are partially, asymmetrically, and ambiguously connected" in their cosmological struggles for planetary futures. Similarly, the political assembly remotely created by #SayHerName is forged by allies, asymmetrically positioned in relation to one another, while being partially affectively connected through the circulation of stories of sorrow and practices of resistance against state and police racial violence. Crenshaw and the mothers and sisters of #SayHerName create a practice imbued by and constructing an epistemology of resistance, making visible and intelligible the affective and material dimensions of the loss of their daughters and sisters to state and police violence. To quote Crenshaw's remarks in her introduction to "Under the Blacklight": "narrating the story of the loss of your loved ones and also of the killing of Black women, girls and femmes is to speak justice." In this vein, the AAPF together with #SayHerName contribute to establishing a new framework of analysis of state and police violence as well as to formulating demands for intersectional justice (see also Crenshaw 2015a,b; 2016).

Enacting Intersectional Justice

I echo the analysis of racial gendered necropolitics articulated by Kimberlé Crenshaw and the mothers as they memorialize their daughters and sisters. Bearing witness to their demands for intersectional justice, I attend to their rites and rituals of speaking justice. I am reminded of Gillian Rose's (1996) interpretation of Phocion's wives' acts of mourning. Though their grief work is set in abolitionist and intersectional feminist struggles in the United States, like Phocion's widows in Ancient Greece, their acts of mourning interrupt the hegemonic matrix of political representation. They produce a crack in the official discourse of commemoration, where their loss remains unnamed and ungrieved. Shifting the normative epistemic realm of speaking justice, they confront its limitations and failures when it comes to Black women's lives. As Crenshaw notes in her introductory remarks in the webinar, the killing of Black lives has a long history both in the United States and globally (Taylor 2016). Walking together with the activists and supporters of the Black Lives Matter movement, #SayHerName realizes its "campaign to advance a gender inclusive narrative in the movement for our lives" by centering the "stories and perspectives of Black women, girls and femmes" (Pt. 11).

In 2013, the hashtag #BlackLivesMatter (BLM) went viral as a response to the acquittal of George Zimmerman, a neighborhood watch member who killed 17-year-old **Trayvon Benjamin Martin** on 26 February 2012 in Sanford, Florida, while he was visiting his father. BLM became the primary actor in denouncing the racist treatment of this case by the police and courts. Following his arrest after the protest, Zimmermann was released due to Florida's "stand your ground" law, which permits the use of weapons to defend private property. The broad social support for the BLM protest meant Zimmermann was again charged, but the jury acquitted him of second-degree murder and manslaughter in July 2013. As a nonviolent civil disobedience movement, BLM has broken the silence on racist state and police violence by addressing mass incarceration, violent policing, a biased criminal justice system and the criminalization of Black, but also People of Color and poor population (Davis 2003; Gilmore 2007; Alexander 2012; Hinton 2016). It has placed abolitionist democracy (Davis 2005; Gilmore 2011; Garza 2020) on the political agenda (Hooker 2017), calling for the defunding of the police in favor of investing in Black, but also People of Color and poor communities (Movement for Black Lives 2016; Cullors 2019; Simon 2021). In an interview with Mia Birdsong for a TED[9] event on 20 December 2016, the three cofounders of BLM—Patrisse Cullors, Alicia Garza and Ayọ (former Opal) Tometi—defined BLM as a "call for action" and a "tool for reimagining the world, where Black people are free to exist, free to live" (ibid.). As Cullors further elaborates, "it is a tool for our allies to show up differently for us" to fight against the daily "stop and frisk by law enforcement" (ibid.), raiding of homes and control of neighborhoods by heavily armed police. Furthermore, as Tometi (ibid.) affirms, BLM addresses the dehumanization of Black people on the social, economic, political and cultural levels (Hesse and Thompson 2022). It offers an analysis of anti-Black racism and calls for global action that understands the connection between racism and other social issues like heteropatriarchy, poverty, homelessness, climate change and migration. For the analysis of race and racism, as Garza (ibid.) notes, it means that inequality cannot be addressed as a racially unmarked matter (see also Garza 2020). It needs to be approached at its roots by establishing the analysis of racism as its point of departure. Thus, a broader understanding of inequality requires an intersectional analysis of structural violence. Accordingly, BLM for Tometi is a "human rights movement that challenges systemic racism in every single context." Black Lives Matter, Cullors (ibid.) concludes, is a "new vision for young Black girls around the world that we deserve to be fought for, that we deserve to call on local government to show up for us."

Resonating with this ontological wisdom and planetary vision, the mothers and sisters of #SayHerName send "the powerful message that indeed All Black Lives Matter" (Pt. 11). Resisting institutionalized forms of mourning by mobilizing diachronic ways of understanding and living with death, their accounts and memories are demands for justice. Inscribed into a genealogy of struggle against racism, colonialism, ableism, heteropatriarchy and capitalism, they connect with a long tradition of abolitionist struggles. Their stories, as Crenshaw (ibid.) affirms, resonate with the

> work songs, spirituals of enslaved African American people to the post-emancipation work from writers like Ida B. Wells, Zora Neale Hurston; political demands of civil rights leaders like Rosa Parks and Martin Luther King Junior, to the center of workers' demands we see today. Their narratives have been deployed as tools of radical resistance, rebellious protest and re-imagined community building.

#SayHerName follows this path by breaking the silence and making their unheard truth known.

Sisterhood of sorrow

In "Under the Blacklight," Crenshaw, the AAPF and #SayHerName open up a space to relate stories of state and police violence against Black women, girls and femmes. The audience is invited to listen to Fran Garrett's[10] stories about her daughter, **Michelle Cusseaux**. Moderating the webinar, Crenshaw recalls that her mentor and friend Barbara Arnwein sent her a link about the action organized by Michelle's mother back in summer 2014 (Pt. 11). With several local activists, Garrett organized the carrying of a casket to Phoenix City Hall in Arizona. They called out "Justice for Michelle!" demanding an exhaustive investigation of her shooting by the local government as well as racial justice and health parity. On 14 August 2014, police killed Michelle, who had just graduated at the top of her class, on her own doorstep, after responding to an emergency call about a mental health crisis she was experiencing. When the police arrived, she refused to open the door as she felt she could manage the situation on her own. However, the police forced their way in and killed her. This happened just five days after the police killing of Mike Brown,[11] which was denounced by BLM. Three months later, as Crenshaw recalls, #SayHerName was initiated, holding the banner of Michelle Cusseaux and other Black women, girls and femmes killed by police in the Justice for All and Million March against police brutality in New York City on 14 December 2014. It was Garrett's courage that sparked the #SayHerName campaign and, as Crenshaw states, established the "foundational dimension" (Pt. 11) for its creation. In the words of the AAPF, it "was this brave act that drew the attention of the African American Policy Forum, which catalyzed the #SayHerName campaign" (ibid.).

In the spirit of collective struggle, mothers, daughters and sisters have shared their stories denouncing police violence and spoken publicly about stress, trauma, economic precarity and emotional exhaustion as situations defining their daily lives. As Best describes it in the quote that begins this chapter, the trauma restarts every time "someone else" is killed. For the mothers, daughters and sisters, the grieving never ends; as Best observes: "we don't give a chance to our sisters to rest" (Pt. 11). Thus, every time a wound is reopened in "the most unpredictable moments," "festering" and pouring "acid" once again (ibid.). Feeling abandoned by the state, their claims seem to have been ignored, while the police are protected and their funding increased. As most of the mothers and sisters recount, the police entered the homes of their daughters and sisters without warrants, knocking down the door and shooting randomly. On 13 March 2020, **Breonna Taylor**,[12] a 27-year-old emergency room technician from Louisville, was murdered by police at midnight while lying in bed. The police suspected she had drugs in her apartment and were operating based on a "no-knock warrant," allowing them to forcibly enter a private home without warning or identification (ibid.). While none of the four suspects have been condemned for Breonna's killing, on 4 August 2022, the Justice Department charged them[13] with federal civil rights violations, including accessing her apartment by obtaining a search warrant on false grounds.

In the case of **Kayla Moore**, a 41-year-old trans woman from Berkeley, California, killed by police during a nonviolent mental health crisis (Pt. 11), her sister Maria Moore recalls a similar situation. On 12 February 2013, her roommate called 911 hoping for an ambulance, but instead the police answered the call. They "mistook" Kayla for a man 20 years her senior, and when she ran to the bathroom to take refuge, the officers assaulted her, choking her to death. Her last words, "I can't breathe" (ibid.) resonate with

George Floyd's cry for help while he was being suffocated by the police on 25 May 2020 (Samuels and Olorunnipa 2022). As her sister (ibid.) affirms, Kayla needed help—needed the care and the resources that the state could have provided—but instead was confronted with police brutality. The police, she noticed, do not have any expertise in mental health care (see Thompson 2021a). For her, this raises the question of how the first response infrastructure is organized in the United States and the implications this has on Black lives (Pt. 11).

#SayHerName, a "sisterhood of sorrow" (ibid.) as the mothers and sisters define themselves, works through this injustice, the pain and the grief. As Cassandra Johnson, mother of **Tanisha Johnson**, tells us, she joins her daughter in the struggle against police violence by giving her a voice: living through her speech enables a collective performative act of resistance. Johnson explains it like this (ibid.): "she is not coming back, how can I live on through her speaking, how can she live on through speech?" Tanisha was murdered by police on 13 November 2014 in Cleveland, Ohio. She was 27 years old when her family called 911 while she was having a mental health breakdown. Here, too, instead of medical assistance, the police arrived. In their attempt to control Tanisha, the situation escalated. As the police officer tried to force her to the ground by kneeling on her, he pointed a gun at the family. Tanisha's last words were a cry of help to her mother. Crenshaw notes that the horror Tanisha and her family experienced—Tanisha was murdered right in front of her family—shows the "familiar disrespect" (ibid.) of police officers toward family bonds. Bringing her voice into the center of the fight against misogynoir's necropolitics, Johnson uncovers the intense work of mothers, daughters and sisters to render justice to them. As Cassandra (ibid.), asserts, her daughter lives on "through her speaking" (ibid.).

Acts of speaking, remembering, telling stories, sharing sorrow, supporting and embracing one another by grieving with families and friends form the political labor of mourning that #SayHerName and the AAPF collectively enact. Working with and continuing the legacies of their daughters and sisters, as Sharon Wilkerson, the mother of **Shelly Fry**, shares, they are voicing what their daughters would have liked them to: "we are a voice now, we're gonna break the silence [...], because I am doing what she would want me to do" (ibid.). Shelly was 27 years old when police shot her on 6 December 2012 in a Walmart parking lot in Houston. An off-duty policeman/security guard at Walmart who suspected she and her friend of shoplifting followed them. When Shelly returned to her car, he shot her twice through the window with her friend's two children sitting right behind her. As Crenshaw stated in a TedxWomen talk on 1 October 2016,[14]

Black girls as young as seven, great-grandmothers as old as ninety-five, have been killed by the police. They have been shot to death, they have been stomped to death, they have been suffocated to death, they have been manhandled to death, they have been tasered to death. They have been killed shopping while Black, having a mental disability while Black, having a domestic disturbance while Black, they have even been killed being homeless while Black. Why don't we know these stories?

The stories of these mothers, daughters and sisters, Crenshaw concedes, need to be told. In her introductory remarks in "Under the Blacklight" (Pt. 11), she notes:

> without stories there is hardly space for a movement at all. This truth simultaneously holds that if your story doesn't exist than that movement isn't entirely for you. Without your story, any benefit for social change or trickle down is flattened and is limited. Centering the stories and perspectives of Black Women, girls and femmes in the discourse around police violence sends the powerful message that indeed All Black Lives Matter. Our collective outrage around cases of police violence is meant to serve as a warning to police that officers cannot kill without consequences. Now, silence around cases of Black Women and girls sends the message that perhaps certain crimes do not merit significant repercussions. #SayHerName is a campaign to advance a gender inclusive narrative in the movement for our lives.

Concluding, Crenshaw notes that these stories are "integrated into calls for justice, policy proposals, and media representations of police brutality" (ibid.), while they also represent insights into the communal political labor of mourning.

Outraged mourning

The mothers, daughters and sisters of #SayHerName, as Rocha (2020) concurs, reflecting on the struggle of Black mothers in Brazil, are giving voice to their outraged mourning. In her dissertation "Outraged Mothering: Black Women, Racial Violence, and the Power of Emotions in Rio de Janeiro's African Diaspora" (2014), Rocha looks at the emotional and political work of Black mothers who have lost their sons to anti-Black state and police violence in Rio de Janeiro. Conceptualizing these "Black women's love and *luta* (struggle)" as "outraged mothering," Rocha challenges normative notions of motherhood through her analysis of racism, particularly in the form of Black

genocide. In this context, she argues for an approach to the African diaspora that considers the "creating, nurturing, resisting, and recuperative acts"
(ibid., 43) of these women as practices of resistance. They represent "an alternative to genocidal practices," imbued with what Rocha (ibid., 149) defines as
"deep-diaspora death," carrying the feelings of "scared joy, nurturing warning, worried reality, and sad acceptance." When we listen to the mothers and
sisters of #SayHerName, we are attending to this mélange of feelings structuring their lives. Their communal labor of mourning reminds us of Rocha's
outraged motherhood, and their accounts of utterances of outraged mourning. This form of mourning is intertwined with their analysis and attempts to
put into words and theory what remains inconceivable, while conceiving of
an alternative present and future.

The words of mothers, daughters and sisters resonate with Crenshaw and
Rocha; they create their own analysis and theoretical understanding of intersectional violence by offering an epistemology of intersectional justice. They
perform their outraged mourning in the series of webinars and events organized by Crenshaw and the AAPF and contribute to developing an intelligible
framework of representation, while revealing the complexity of an intersectional analysis of state and police violence and working toward intersectional
justice. In Crenshaw's words, "narrating the story of the loss of your loved
ones and also of the killing of Black women, girls and femmes is to speak
justice."[15] The stories of mothers, daughters and sisters reflect the labor of
mourning that goes into organizing their daily lives, while resisting intersectional violence.

Pluriversal Grief: Building Communities of Rexistence

Considering the labor of mourning as going beyond lamentation, as I argue
throughout this book, we see how it is attached to the rhythms and rites of life
connected to death. The communal political labor of mourning performed
by #SayHerName is an expression of pluriversal grief work. It faces the
injuries of the past and the wounds of the present, while it paves a new path
to a visionary practice of reparative justice. It is, as Christina Sharpe (2016)
argues, wake work. Resonating with what Andrea Sempértegui (2021a)
calls rexistencia—life as resistance—decolonial mourning—concretely the
political grief work of #SayHerName and the AAPF—emerges from the
daily organization of life in the wake of necropolitics. Sempértegui (2021b)
comes across the notion of rexistence in her ethnographic fieldwork with the
Achuar, Shuar, Sapara, Kichwa, Shiwiar, Andoa and Waorani communities
in Ecuador. In conversations with Zoila Castillo, Nancy Santi, Elvia Dagua,
Rosa Gualinga and Salomé Aranda, Sempértegui delves into the practices

and texture of communal living. Inspired by the handicraft *Weaving Spider* of the Amazonian Kichwa leader Elvia Dagua, Sempértegui[16] describes rexistence as a series of relations and events that create a web to sustain communal life while resisting exploitative practices and the politics of dispossession and dehumanization.

When it comes to the communities in struggle against misogynoir necropolitics in the United States, the accounts of the mothers, daughters, sisters and friends of #SayHerName reveal how they cope with the pain of loss while also being affected by processes of dispossession and dehumanization. Their lives are marked by grieving acts of resistance inserted into their everyday practices of guaranteeing the lives of their loved ones, their communities and their own lives. In this manner, the political communal labor of mourning becomes a site of social reproduction, instilled in what Félix de Souza defines as "rhizomatic arenas of political entanglements."[17]

The stories of the mothers, daughters and sisters of #SayHerName represent collective practices of living, analysis and interrogation of the established social order. Resisting institutionalized forms of mourning by mobilizing diachronic ways of understanding and living with death, their accounts, memories, analyses and theoretical proposals are demands for justice. In Chapter 2, I discussed C. Nadia Seremetakis's notion of mourning as a practice of contestation when she observes how women's laments in the Greek Peloponnese region of Mani serve to interrupt the social order. Similarly, #SayHerName creates rituals and performances that preserve the dignity of mothers, daughters and sisters while demanding state and police accountability. Reflecting on their social lives as shaped by racial, gender, social and economic inequalities, they remind the audience of the structural intersectional violence they encounter daily. At the same time, they also speak about their coping strategies and moments of resistance. Through their accounts, they provoke a "defamiliarization" (ibid., 14) of the established social order by introducing a critique of intersectional violence and an analysis of misogynoir as racial gendered necropolitics (Noble and Palmer 2022).

Political entanglements: Countering intersectional violence

As I listen to the stories of the members of #SayHerName, I find myself in this rhizomatic political entanglement. I remotely yet affectively connect to the collective project of a "refusal to accept a loss of memory" (Pt. 11). The organizers of the webinar—Kimberlé Crenshaw, Julia Sharpe-Levine and G'Ra Asim—and the mothers and sisters invite the audience to show solidarity by committing to loyalty and political friendship. Pronouncing an inclusive "we," Crenshaw invites the audience to become part of the tribute paid to the daughters, mothers and sisters by addressing the audience with the words "we bear witness to their and their families losses. We bear witness to their stories" (ibid.). As I discussed earlier, bearing witness is about active and committed listening, that is, accountable listening. It asks the audience to join the communal labor of mourning. Bearing witness means, in Crenshaw's words, that "we mind the possibilities and conditions that lead to their tragedy. We examine the possible policy changes that would have made a difference" (ibid.). The audience is asked "to help interrupt what has been an ongoing invisibility" (ibid.). Fran Garrett addresses the audience directly by saying, "now, they know that these are things that we can't do on our own that we need their help, we need the audience's help in making things happen, in moving forward" (ibid.). The question of the responsibility and accountability of the audience is raised in this context.

In one of the webinar conversations, Crenshaw raises a series of questions about the economic, material, social and emotional support that the mothers and sisters have received from state institutions. All the women confirm that they received no support for the children their daughters or sisters left behind. They have all experienced health problems. They have faced unexpected financial burdens—for example, funerals and/or property damage or lawyers' fees. They have suffered losses of income and custody issues. They were exposed to inaccurate media coverage about the loss of their loved ones and never saw any of the police perpetrators indicted or convicted. When Crenshaw asks the mothers and sisters if they experienced "just us instead of justice" in the pursuit of public, legal, political and ethical accountability for the crimes committed, they unanimously respond "just us" (ibid.). The pursuit of justice carries further economic burdens, traumatic exposure, a lack of ethical recognition and no social support. In other words, the political communal labor of mourning of #SayHerName carries the affective burden and loneliness that the loss of a loved one entails, while working through and opposing the racial systemic injustice the mothers and sisters face daily.

Intelligible justice

Turning their pain into a transformative collective force for change, they build a "sisterhood of sorrow" organizing communal strategies and responses to the persistent intersectional violence shaping their lives. #SayHerName connects to centuries of struggle against racism and misogyny, offering a sustained space of connection and forging communal relationships of trust and support. In an Open Letter (2020)[18] to the mothers who lost their daughters, the members answer the question, "What would you all say to the next mother who finds herself entering this sisterhood of sorrow?" (ibid.) Initiating the conversation, Gina Best answers, "Sister, I want you to know, I see you" (ibid.), while Fran Garrett says, "I hate to meet you under these circumstances" (ibid.). Best remarks, "Now, you are facing something, you are dealing with something that you never could begin to plan or account for and this is the murder of your beautiful daughter" (ibid.). Maria Moore continues, "It is important that they know that when they are ready, there will be people that will help, they will support them, because what they are going through is incredibly lonely" (ibid.). Sharon Wilkerson concludes: "We are caring for all. Still trying to be strong for everybody else" (ibid.). As Garrett summarizes, #SayHerName has created an organization "that supports each other. We are supporting each other and we extend our arms or extend the olive branch to you to let you know that we are here for you and your family in your time of need" (ibid.). Thus, as Wilkerson says, "You don't know which way to turn; family members don't understand, because they never been truly through it" (ibid.). This is because, as Best says, the labor of mourning is an ongoing process where the feeling of loss is "never gonna go away" (ibid.). Yet the love for the daughter will keep their struggle going as, in Best's words, "you birth that baby, you birth your daughter and you'll birth her continued legacy as well" (ibid.).

Paying tribute to this legacy is accomplished by the political communal labor of mourning. The mothers and sisters fight against state and police violence: they institute what Rose (1996, 35) considers "rights and rites of mourning" and describes as "intense work of the soul, that gradual arrangement of its boundaries, which must occur when a loved one is lost—so as to let go, to allow the other fully to depart, and hence fully to be regained beyond sorrow." Inscribing a new understanding of mourning as communal resistance, they alter the normative script. They rewrite the meaning of justice and injustice, while their communal political labor of mourning mirrors attempts of rexistence. Through their voicing of their practices of mourning, they intervene into the hegemonic matrix of representation. Their experiences become intelligible through the theoretical framing of their grieving practices. In other words, they interrupt the normative matrix by inserting their social life of mourning. According to Rose (1996), their "mourning has become the law." Like Phocion's widow, the mothers and sisters of #SayHerName open a space, create a vocabulary and rewrite the normative script in order to make their experiences readable, understandable and graspable. Their suffering and struggle are elevated to the sphere of the speakable and the visible, introduced into the normative script of representation. The labor of mourning transformed into political work voices a communal sentiment and frames a new vocabulary in the struggle for intersectional social justice.

The political subjectivity deriving from the activities of #SayHerName challenges Bonnie Honig's (2013) reduction of mourning to a sentimental moment, an act of lamentation depleted of concrete political demands. Rather, mourning as political communal labor derives from historical sociopolitical material conditions and forges what we will discuss in the last chapter as conviviality infrastructure, based on mutual material and affective support. As the AAPF and #SayHerName demonstrate, the moment of sorrow conveyed in mourning is one of political awakening. It is conditioned by the experience of social injustice, inequality, and state and police brutality. Confronting these conditions of existence and their misogynoir necropolitical effects drives these actors to act. Working through grief turns affect into politics. Political communal mourning is a force of collective existence and resistance, while it contributes to social (re)production and communal living. Crenshaw underlines the fact that

> today's space is one that holds grief, but also love. It holds tears, but also joy. And it holds rage, but also resolve. It's grounded in irreversible loss, but also is grounded in a refusal to accept a loss of memory. We are here this evening to help interrupt what has been an ongoing invisibility. We are here to find, to see, to shout, and to sit with the stories of Black women who have been killed by police.

Bearing witness to this political communal labor of mourning, to the pain and the consequences of losing a loved one to state and police racial violence, prompts me to reflect upon my mourning for my parents but also mourning as accountability. As a white Southern European, my structural positionality is one of privilege. When it comes to racially motivated police violence, I would never be randomly stopped on the street and asked for identification because of my skin color. I am unlikely to be treated or perceived as a potential threat to others as long as I do not become a political dissident or "unwanted migrant." However, as the daughter of Gastarbeiter, my structural whiteness is overlaid by the anti-migrant racism that my parents and I experienced in Germany. It is from this dual positionality of whiteness and working-class migration within Germany that I have listened and borne witness to the stories of the mothers and sisters of #SayHerName. Going back to the location of my situated accountable listening, I next approach the accounts of contesting the coloniality of migration of the organization Women in Exile e.V. in Germany.

Contesting the Coloniality of Migration

Women in Exile e.V.

The advocacy group Women in Exile e.V. (WiE)[19] was established as an initiative for refugee women in Brandenburg in 2002 (Women in Exile 2022). Elizabeth Ngari, a 56-year-old woman born in Kenya, cofounded this initiative to publicly denounce and combat intersectional violence against refugee women. Together with her two daughters, Ngari arrived in Germany in 1996 and was placed in a *Lager* or refugee camp. There, she told a journalist,[20] she experienced the poor living conditions endured by those seeking asylum in Germany while they wait for their request to be processed. In the Lager, Ngari recounts, one often shares a bedroom and the bathrooms and kitchens are always communal. No private or safe spaces are provided, exposing women in the Lager to potential sexual harassment or physical attacks by security personnel and other residents.

Refugee Lager are usually established on the outskirts of villages, towns and cities, in abandoned military barracks or housing facilities provided by sponsoring companies. They represent Marc Augé's (1992) notion of "nonplaces." Augé's reference here is to Michel de Certeau's (1984) differentiation between "place" as a sedimented unit and "non-place" as a provisional, "never completed" space. For Augé (1992, 77), nonplace is a site of supermodernity; challenging the modern notion of place as "relational, historical and concerned with identity," the nonplace is defined by its opposite. Accordingly, "supermodernity produces non-places, meaning spaces which are not themselves anthropological places" (ibid., 78). Referring to Baudelaire's notion of modernity, Augé conceives places as imbricated and related to history. Places are sites of agency, but nonplaces are artificial entities, depleted of any historical agency and identity production. They are "transit points and temporary abodes [...] proliferating under luxurious or inhumane conditions" (ibid.). Among those places marked by inhumane conditions, Augé lists refugee camps. Refugee camps as nonplaces, Ngari makes us aware, are shaped by their transitory character, the legal suspension of privacy and the enforcement of shared spaces of intimacy. The Lager as a nonplace is organized through the creation of an imposed identity—"refugee"—under which all inhabitants are subsumed regardless of their personal biographies and individual needs (Dustin and Held 2021; Held 2022). The category of refugee determines the governmental regulation of the lives and mobility of Lager inhabitants (Gutiérrez Rodríguez 2016). The liberal notion of freedom characterized by the right to individuality and entitlement to privacy is revoked. These rights do not exist and are not applied, as Ngari observes, to people seeking asylum who fall under this legal category. Furthermore, the Lager as a nonplace goes beyond Augé's "supermodernity"; rather, it articulates the underside of modernity, its coloniality. As such, it emerges from a history of encampment, incarceration and confinement related to modes of colonial ruling (Peters 2018). As Michel Agier (2002, 320) argues in a study on refugee camps, they are shaped by "the coupling of war with humanitarian action," where life is "kept at a distance from the ordinary social and political world." They represent, as such, laboratories of "large-scale segregation" (ibid.) of human beings.

In the United States, the Indian Removal Act of 1830 (ibid., 1166) forcibly removed Cherokees from their land, forcing them to live on reservations—a North American manifestation of this colonial tradition of encampment and incarceration. As Jeremy Sarkin (2009) has noted in his analysis of the Herero genocide (1904–1908) in German South West Africa (today Namibia), five concentration camps were established where survivors of the genocide were enslaved. Benjamin Madley (2005) has also observed how the Herero genocide and these concentration camps provided the Nazis with a historical precedent for the establishments of Lagers as exterminations camps during Nationalsocialism. As administered confinements, the refugee camps or Lager resonate with this history of colonial imprisonment and incarceration, constructing racialized and colonized populations as "savages," "unruly" and "criminals" (Malkki 1994). While the enforced allocation of persons seeking asylum in refugee camps does not indicate per se regulation within the sphere of crime control, the status of "asylum seeker" is embedded in a set of rules monitoring and controlling this subject's rights to movement and autonomy. As such, refugee camps articulate what Simon Turner and Zachary Whyte (2022) define as a "carceral junction": a space determined by the paradox of mobility and coerced immobility. Thus, they forcibly confine people under carceral conditions, while refugee camps are also governed by the multiple movements of their residents and their institutional transitory character.

As Ngari identifies in her analysis of intercommunity gendered violence in the Lager, life inside is shaped by the experience of being held in a state of constant uncertainty (Women in Exile 2022). Ngari supports this observation with her own experiences: When she arrived as a refugee in Germany, she was provisionally placed in a Lager. At first, she thought this would only be for a few months, but her stay in the refugee camp in Prenzlau lasted five long years. Most members of WiE had a similar experience when they arrived in Germany—the struggle against dehumanizing conditions in the Lager and the call for its abolition forms the core of their political work. Critiquing the Lager and the legal administration of people through asylum policies, WiE addresses the subjugation of people in situations of vulnerability, as they seek refuge from war, political conflicts and persecution. In this case, access to the labor market, education, money and healthcare is regulated and restricted by the state. WiE denounces these circumstances that constrain and curtail individual mobility and autonomy. They have campaigned against the *Gutscheinsystem*, a food-stamp voucher system that precludes persons who have applied for asylum from buying and cooking the food they desire and require. Furthermore, WiE has decried the imposition of a *Residenzpflicht* that dictates the radius of movement for a person who seeks asylum, confining them within close proximity to the Lager to which they have been assigned. For example, if they decide to go shopping in a nearby city, this is considered a breach of the Residenzpflicht and constitutes a criminal act. Connecting these issues to the specific situation of women and girls, WiE together with advocacy groups have successfully denounced Residenzpflicht measures (International Refugee Tribunal 2013).[21]

The categories of refugee or asylum seeker not only objectify people by reducing them to administrative units of control but also serve as devices of exclusion, discrimination and punishment (Dosthossein and Narges 2020; Gutiérrez Rodríguez 2024). Contesting this logic of subjugation, the refugee strike[22] in the last decade has denounced terms such as refugee and asylum seeker as devices of domination and oppression (International Refugee Tribunal 2013; Women in Exile and Gürsel 2013; Bendix 2018; The Voice 2014; Ünsal 2015; Mokre 2015; Odugbesan and Schwiertz 2018; Women in Exile 2022; Caravan 2023). Ashkan Khorasani (Ulu 2013; Doppler 2021), a member of a Bavarian politically active group of persons who arrived as refugees in Germany, argues that the term refugee does not entail a critique of a racial capitalist system that produces subjects excluded from the cycle of production, distribution and reproduction. In order to capture this status, Khorasani and other members of the Bavarian group have opted to call themselves "noncitizens." In her book on the relevance of Herbert Marcuse's critical theory to the refugee movement, Lisa Doppler (2021) relates that some organic intellectuals involved in the refugee strike consider that the term refugee is too vague and does not define the conditions under which people seeking asylum in Germany live. As a term subsuming different legal positionalities in the process of acquiring a legal status as such, it does not differentiate between precarious legal situations administered by the state, such as *Duldung*, which grants provisional residency based on health or other life-threatening issues to a person whose asylum application has been rejected.

Returning to the Lager as a site of administered confinement—as a nonplace in Augé's sense—the refugee camp is more than a nonplace; it is a site of communal living and at times also of resistance. The lives of Lager residents do not end when they enter this place: they continue to pursue their desires, dreams, plans and aspirations of building alliances, affective communities, communal strategies for survival and self-determination (Women in Exile et al. 2013; The Voice 2014; International Women Space 2015; Women in Exile 2022). Although within the walls of the Lager the arrangement of living spaces is not organized by prioritizing residents' basic needs for privacy and intimacy, the residents themselves organize safe spaces, particularly for women and children (Ngari 2020). WiE has initiated and supported these networks in the Lager.[23] As Vanessa E. Thompson (2022) notes in conversation with WiE, "their work draws on the feminist practices and alternatives that are lived in many contexts of the African continent, such as the collectivization of funds and resources on the basis of 'Tontines,' as well as community accountability when harm is committed." Further, Céline Barry (2021) discusses the two political organizations, Women in Exile and International Women Space, a politically self-organized group of migrant and refugee women and LGBTIQ+ in Berlin, as Black and African diasporic border feminism in Europe. Denouncing the inhumane living conditions and the likelihood of gendered violence due to spatial arrangements, for example, WiE has raised awareness about sexual assaults and the lack of safety for women and children in the Lager. In particular, they have addressed the failure of these places to sustain well-being by providing decent living conditions.[24] Analyzing the intersections of racism, misogyny and asylum control policies and considering global economic and political interdependencies and inequalities (Ngari 2020), WiE has drawn our attention to what I define as the coloniality of migration (Gutiérrez Rodríguez 2018a).

The internment of people in sealed administrative confinement and their subjection to categories and mechanisms of differential segregation are reminiscent of a colonial logic of ruling. Migration and asylum policies represent modern colonial forms of population governance through which the divide between human and nonhuman is reactivated and redefined. Though no racial vocabulary is explicitly and administratively used in the legal classification and differentiation of migrants and refugees, the public perception, media representation, political definition and popular rhetoric around these groups in Europe follow a colonial logic of differentiation restricting their material living and working conditions. Reflecting on the case of **Oury Jalloh**,[25] killed in a prison cell in Dessau on 7 January 2005 (The Voice et al. 2007), Thompson (2018, 208) extends this analysis to the coloniality of policing. Drawing on Fanon and Loomba (ibid.), she outlines forms of racial control and incarceration constructing the racial other as an object of threat, unruliness and violent suspicion. In the colonies, the police represented one of the colonial forces actively discerning and enacting the racial borders between the colonized population as object of control, confinement and imprisonment and the colonial rulers as the representatives of law and order. This is materialized in political debates, administrative measures and the passing of laws targeting and disciplining bodies marked as refugees or migrants. Populations subjected to racial violence and the logic of abjection of asylum and migration control policies are a main target in the logic of colonial modern policing in Europe (International Refugee Tribunal 2013; Bruce-Jones 2015, Thompson 2021a).

While WiE does not explicitly work with the analytical framework of the coloniality of migration, its examination of the impact of the asylum regime on persons seeking asylum resonates with it. Breaking the silence on violence against women in the Lager by creating networks of support, WiE engages with a gendered analysis of racism that considers their own historical, geographical and sociopolitical specific experiences (Women in Exile 2022). They take into account global histories of oppression and contemporary entanglements, organizing solidarity events and disseminating information about intersectional gendered violence on social media and other media outlets. Their work of communal mourning resurfaces from this political organizing. Every year on 7 April, WiE pays tribute to **Rita Awour Ojungé**, a 32-year-old Kenyan mother of two who disappeared from the Hohenleipisch Lager on that day in 2019.

Paying tribute

In April 2019, the residents of the Lager in Hohenleipisch, a municipality in the Elbe-Elster district of Brandenburg, Germany, reported to the camp's management that Rita Awour Ojungé had gone missing.[26] Ojungé had arrived in Germany in 2012 to work as an au pair and applied for asylum shortly after. Then, she met her partner and they had two children together. At the time of her disappearance, she had been living in the country for seven years with a precarious residency status, or Duldung, which can end in deportation. For Ojungé, this meant that she had no guarantees for long-term settlement or protection from deportation. She found herself in a legal limbo without citizenship or refugee legal status. Most of the residents of Hohenleipisch had the Duldung status, preventing them from working or studying.

When Rita Ojungé disappeared for more than three days in April 2019, leaving her children alone in the Lager, other inhabitants became concerned that something might have happened to her. They immediately contacted the police and asked them to investigate. After two weeks, the police published a search notice and two weeks later pressed criminal charges. On 25 June 2019,[27] her remains were found in the woods bordering the Lager.[28] The investigation yielded few results and is still ongoing. Along with WiE, International Women* Space (IWS), Initiative Schwarze Menschen in Deutschland (ISD) and Opferperspektive (Victim's Perspective) have demanded an extensive reconstruction of the case and a thorough investigation by the state public prosecutor, as the police investigation has revealed inconsistencies and missing links.[29] As the International Independent Commission on the Death of Oury Jalloh[30] notes, this pattern of police "active inaction," negligence and deliberate non-prosecution (Thomspon 2021c, 208) is symptomatic of systemic racism in the police force (cf., Browne 2015; Thompson 2021b; Plümecke, Wilopo and Naguib 2022). After more than 13 years of investigation, the evidence presented by the police and legal prosecutor in Jalloh's case has been incomplete and misleading.

In the case of Rita Ojungé, her mother, Felista Adhiambo Onyango, has spoken publicly about seeking justice for her daughter.[31] For her and WiE, IWS and ISD, this failure to follow up on the police investigation and the lack of current state prosecution evince the systemic neglect by state authorities for the pursuit of justice for refugees, particularly women, in Germany. These organizations have made these circumstances public and denounced the anti-Black racism of the police (Barry 2021; Women in Exile 2022). Organizing vigils and events commemorating Ojungé together with Opferperspektive, the Flüchtlingsrat (Refugee Council) Brandenburg, and family, friends and residents of the refugee camp, they have honored Ojungé's life and paid tribute to her memory. They also laid her body to rest on 14 December 2019, after police finally released it. During Black Lives Matter protests in Germany, WiE carried banners reading "Justice for Rita." In their *Newsletter Campaign #19*[32] from July 2020, they write:

> We will keep going to the streets and making all sorts of actions to demand from the authorities to give us answers to the questions on: why did it take the police so long to find Rita's remains? Who murdered her? How safe are the Lagers for women* and children if reported sexual harassment has no consequences? Why has the Hohenleipisch Lager which is situated in the woods near Hohenleipisch not been closed, although the residents wrote an open letter to the authorities demand-ing its closure?
>
> It is now over one year since Rita died and so far, the only report known to us is that the files for Rita's case were released to the lawyers a few

weeks ago. For us what we need are answers to the above questions. Rita repeatedly reported sexual harassment in the Hohenleipisch refugee Lager, but no steps were taken. How many more femicides does it take for preventive measures to be taken? The segregation and isolation of refugees massively increases the vulnerability of refugee women and queers.

Framing the dehumanizing conditions in the Lager within an antiracist intersectional analysis of systemic violence, WiE breaks the silence about the entanglement of femicide and anti-Black racism in the context of asylum. Their public acts of mourning are constant reminders of abolitionist calls for an end to policing and police violence (El Tayeb and Thompson 2019; Loick and Thompson 2022; Thompson 2021b,c, 2022). Addressing the intersecting of the Lager and the misogynoir and feminicide necropolitics of asylum policies, WiE's political claims and demands for an end to the coloniality of migration, state and police violence resonate with #SayHerName's, Crenshaw's and AAPF's demands for justice and struggle against the violence of state and police misogynoir violence. Both, WiE and #SayHerName, call for and enact abolitionist mourning.

Conclusion: Abolitionist Mourning

Kimberlé Crenshaw, Gina Best, Rhanda Dormeus, Fran Garrett, Maria Moore, Sharon Cooper, Sharon Wilkerson and other members of #SayHerName have formulated demands for the defunding of the police and investment in poor racialized and migrantized communities while advocating for gender-sensitive intersectional justice. Likewise, Elizabeth Ngari, Women in Exile and International Women Space join these demands by fighting against the incarceration of persons seeking asylum, particularly women in German refugee Lager, while also asking for ending refugees' exclusion from human and citizen rights. This chapter concluded with some thoughts on abolitionist mourning by drawing on #SayHerName's abolitionist intersectional Black feminism and the anticolonial and antiracist struggles of Women in Exile. In the next chapter, we will continue our discussion of decolonial mourning by bearing witness to the affective labor of communal mourning of family members, relatives and friends who lost their loved ones to racist murders in Germany from the 1980s to today.

Notes

1 The eleventh installment of "Under the Black Light: Say Her Name—Telling Stories of State Violence & Public Silence," organized by the mothers and sisters of the

#SayHerName campaign, supported by Professor Kimberlé Crenshaw, cofounder and executive director of the African American Policy Forum of the Center for Intersectionality and Social Policy at Columbia Law School, Columbia University and screened on 17 June 2020; https://www.youtube.com/watch?v=S2MfJOJaeGA. Forthcoming publication: Kimberlé Crenshaw (ed.), *#SayHerName: Black Women's Stories of State Violence and Public Silence*, Haymarket Books.

2 For further information, see https://aapf.org/sayhername.

3 Mobilizing a decolonial Black feminist analytical framework, Noble and Palmer (2022) discuss gendered anti-Black racism in their essay "Misogynoir: Anti-Blackness, Patriarchy, and Refusing the Wrongness of Black Women." Their analysis draws on the work of Sylvia Wynter (1984; 1994; 1995), Hortense Spillers (2003) and Cristina Sharpe (2016) and is inspired by Moya Bailey's (2010; 2013) discussion on misogynoir as gendered anti-Blackness and misogyny in US hip-hop culture, and Trudy's (2013; 2014) definition of misogynoir as racist gendered violence toward Black cis women or anyone identifying as a woman.

4 https://www.merriam-webster.com/dictionary/condolence.

5 Sempértegui (2021b) discusses partial connections in her analysis of the alliance between environmental feminist activists, activist scholars and Amazonian Women.

6 This term is used by the mothers and sisters, https://www.youtube.com/watch?v=S2MfJOJaeGA.

7 https://www.youtube.com/watch?v=S2MfJOJaeGA.

8 See endnote 2.

9 https://www.ted.com/talks/alicia_garza_patrisse_cullors_and_opal_tometi_an_interview_with_the_founders_of_black_lives_matter?language=en.

10 Fran Garrett's action is discussed in the podcast "Intersectionality Matters with Kimberlé Crenshaw, 8: When They See Her—The Story of Michelle Cusseaux," https://soundcloud.com/intersectionality-matters/when-they-see-her.

11 See https://www.facebook.com/JuticeForMikeBrown/ and interview with Michael Brown's parents, CNN, 21 August 2014, https://www.youtube.com/watch?v=PYmbXPqBmmY.

12 Richard A. Oppel Jr., Derrick Bryson Taylor and Nicholas Boge-Burroughs, "What to Know About Breonna Taylor's Death," *New York Times*, 23 August 2022, https://www.nytimes.com/article/breonna-taylor-police.html?smid=url-share.

13 One of the four, a retired detective, pleaded guilty; another was fired by the Louisville Police. The third officer faces state charges, while the fourth was acquitted. The Justice Department confirms that the apartment search was poorly planned and recklessly executed by the police; see endnote 11.

14 TED Talks: Kimberlé Crenshaw: "The Urgency of Intersectionality," October 2016, San Francisco: https://www.ted.com/talks/kimberle_crenshaw_the_urgency_of_intersectionality?language=en.

15 Crenshaw in her introduction to Pt. 11, https://www.youtube.com/watch?v=S2MfJOJaeGA.

16 Sempertegui (ibid., 39).

17 Félix de Souza 2019, 91.

18 On 20 May 2015, the African American Policy Forum hosted "#SayHerName: A Vigil in Memory of Black Women and Girls Killed by the Police," https://www.youtube.com/watch?v=OapJHPcoMFE.

19 https://www.women-in-exile.net/wp-content/uploads/2020/08/newsletter19.pdf.

20 See Mareike Barmeyer, 2022, "Ich bin eine Kämpferin," *Taz*, https://taz.de/Women-in-Exile/!140673/.

21 See concluding statement of the International Refugee Tribunal against Germany 2013, by Women in Exile, The Caravan for the Rights of Refugees and Migrants/ KARAWANE für die Rechte der Flüchtlinge, the Voice, International Women Space and other refugee organisations, http://thecaravan.org/node/3857.

22 The refugee strike in Germany was organized by different refugee organizations fighting for legalization and the right to remain in Germany, see Doppler 2021.

23 See documentary *Women in Exile e.V.* 20 November 2016, https://www.youtube.com/watch?v=N7RTNli1wrU.

24 Pia Stendera, "Flucht vor Gewalt in Gewalt, "1 December 2020," *Taz*, https://taz.de/Gefluechtete-Frauen-in-Erstaufnahmelagern/!5728919&s=Rita+Ojunge/.

25 See The Voice Refugee Forum, the Refugee Initiative Brandenburg (FIB), Initiative Schwarzer Menschen in Deutschland (ISD) and the African Refugee Initiative in Dessau: Oury Jalloh Family Campaign in Dessau 2007, http://thevoiceforum.org/ouryJalloh_Family_Campaign; see also The International Independent Commission on the Death of Oury Jalloh: https://www.ouryjallohcommission.com/welcome.

26 Gareth Joswig, "Zu wenig, zu spät," 25 November 2020, https://taz.de/Der-unaufgeklaerte-Tod-von-Rita-Ojunge/!5727453/.

27 Marlene Gürgen, "Tod im Dschungelheim," 7 August 2019, *Taz*, https://taz.de/Aufklaerung-eines-Mordes/!5610674/.

28 Alexander Fröhlich, "Brandenburgs Polizei in der Kritik," 4 July 2019, *Tagesspiegel*, https://www.tagesspiegel.de/berlin/brandenburgs-polizei-in-der-kritik-erst-kaum-ermittlungen-dann-leichenteile-von-kenianerin-im-wald/24522046.html.

29 See statement by International Women* Space, Berlin, 6 August 2019, https://iwspace.de/2019/08/iws-report-on-the-murder-of-rita-awour-ojunge/ and Women in Exile e.V., https://www.women-in-exile.net/en/im-gedenken-an-rita-ojunge/.

30 International Independent Commission on the Death of Oury Jalloh, https://www.ouryjallohcommission.com.

31 See International Women*s Space documentary, 16 October 2019, https://www.youtube.com/watch?v=JuwVJEV4zsQ.

32 See endnote 19.

Chapter 6

COMMUNAL MOURNING: BECOMING-WITH

Introduction

This chapter focuses on the communal labor of mourning as political work against racist violence in Germany between the 1980s and the beginning of the millennium by naming, remembering and unraveling moments of anti-racist resistance. Reconstructing some of the numerous acts of racist violence that have occurred in East and West Germany before and after the fall of the Berlin Wall in 1989, I listen to accounts of grief and resistance and bear witness to the communal political labor of mourning of the families, relatives and friends of those who lost their lives, and of those of the activist network NSU Komplex auflösen (Unraveling the NSU Complex).

Initiating Memory

Until recently, the memory of racist attacks and murders that occurred in East and West Germany in the early 1980s had faded into oblivion. In the aftermath of the creation of the Tribunal NSU Komplex auflösen / Unraveling the NSU Complex (2017), initiatives memorializing racialized and migrantized persons who lost their lives in racist attacks were formed. These initiatives join other projects of remembrance of the victims of racist attacks in the 1990s and early 2000s. To follow, we will attend to their communal political labor of mourning.

Naming racist attacks: 1980s Western Germany

Postwar Western German society has been characterized by different migratory movements, from German refugees arriving immediately after WWII in Western Germany, fleeing from formally occupied territories in Eastern Europe to the systematic recruitment of Gastarbeiter from Turkey, Italy, Greece, Spain, Yugoslavia, Morocco, Tunisia and Portugal between 1955 and 1973 as well as miners and nurses from South Korea from the late 1950s onwards. During this time, the number of migrant workers from these countries increased from 280,000 in 1960 to 2.6 million in 1973.[1] In the 1980s and 1990s, refugees, particularly from the former Yugoslavia, Afghanistan, Iran, Iraq and other countries of the Middle East, also arrived in Germany. The moderate increase of migrant workers in relation to the German population in the early 1980s was perceived as a threat to German society in public political debates. Fueling what came to be known as *Ausländerfeindlichkeit* (hostility to foreigners), the dominant political parties proposed curbing migration by restricting family reunification for migrant families. To this end, a reward scheme (*Rückkehrprämien*)[2] was proposed for Gastarbeiter to hasten their return to their countries of origin in exchange for a lump sum of money (Thym 2018). When the Christian Democratic Party (CDU) headed by Helmut Kohl assumed power in 1982, *Ausländerpolitik* (policy on foreigners) became a core topic of the government agenda, and the reward scheme was implemented, targeting migrant workers from Turkey in particular. This was followed by negotiations with the Turkish government in 1983 to promote the repatriation of these workers (Dreß 2018). The conservative government's focus on Ausländerpolitik was reflected in media representations and the popularization of racist sentiments against migrant workers, particularly those from Turkey. In their analysis of the lethal arson attack on the Satır family's home on the 26th of August 1984, the Initiative Duisburg 1984[3] draws attention to the racist climate, particularly against citizens from Turkey in Germany at that time (Türkmen 2018, 2020; Kocatürk-Schuster and Türkmen 2021). It was in this context that, in the Wanheimerort district of Duisburg, an industrial hub of North Rhine-Westphalia, the Satır family fell victim to a murderous act of racist violence.

Recalling how the Satır family was awakened by flames on the night of 26 August 1984, the Initiative Duisburg 1984[4] commemorates **Döndü Satır** (40 years old), **Zeliha Turhan** (18 years old), **Rasim Turhan** (15 years old), **Çiğdem Satır** (7 years old), **Ümit Satır** (5 years old), **Songül Satır** (4 years old) and **Tarık Turhan** (less than 2 months old). Only Rukiye and Aynur Satır survived, jumping from a window to escape the flames. Reconstructing the events of that night through the accounts of the surviving family members and neighbors, the Initiative Duisburg 1984 demands that the German state officially acknowledge the racist nature of this crime. Working on the reconstruction of the murderous events of 26 August 1984 and documenting it on their homepage,[5] the Initiative recalls that at the moment of the attacks, the scant media coverage of this multiple murder referred to the family members without mentioning their names as "Turkish people" who had died in an arson attack. A police investigation was hesitantly initiated but soon discontinued. Even when, in 1994, a German woman detained by police for setting fire to a refugee camp in Hamborn admitted responsibility for the attack on the Satır's home, police failed to investigate. Instead, as the Initiative Duisburg 1984 states, the family became a target of defamation and accusations by the media and authorities. They experienced what is referred to in the literature as victim blaming (Tribunal 2017). As noted in the previous chapter, the family members, relatives and friends who have lost a loved one to intersectional racial violence often report experiencing police negligence and deliberate accusations (Amnesty International 2016). In the case of the Satır family, this was expressed by a flagrant disregard for their suffering and the absence of public mourning or a lack of financial, legal, psychological and emotional support. Today, surviving and extended family members are still waiting for an official apology from state and local authorities. It was not until the publication of the Initiative Duisburg 1984 in 2019 that the racist murders in Duisburg were even publicly made known.[6] Organizing vigils and public gatherings to accompany the Satır family in their remembering, the Initiative supports demands for the legal prosecution of this crime and reparations for the family members. As the Initiative notes, these activities are understood as acts of political mourning (Kocatürk-Schuster and Türkmen 2021).

In this spirit, the Initiative also mourns for other victims of racist violence by recalling their names. Remembering **Semra Ertan** (Cana Bilir-Meier 2013, 2017; Zühal Bilir-Meier 2019; Cana Bilir-Meier and Zühal Bilir-Meier 2020; Yildirim 2021), the migrant worker, poet and writer from Turkey introduced in Chapter 1, the Initiative joins her sister, Zühal Bilir-Meier, her niece, Cana Bilir-Meier, and her nephew Can-Peter Meier in their public mourning. Cana Bilir-Meier,[7] a curator and filmmaker, dedicated a short film to her aunt, recounting her life and celebrating her poetry.[8] Along with the Initiative in Gedenken an Đỗ Anh Lân and Nguyễn Ngọc Châu, the Initiative Duisburg 1984 commemorates the lives of the 18-year-old student **Đỗ Anh Lân** and the 22-year-old teacher **Nguyễn Ngọc Châu**, both of whom arrived in Hamburg from Saigon as part of humanitarian rescue actions.[9] They were murdered in a racist arson attack, committed by a known Nazi group, against a refugee camp in the Billbrook district of Hamburg on the night of 21–22 August 1980 (see podcast *Rice and Shine*, 2021). These were the first documented racist murders in West Germany. Each year, the Initiative organizes a commemoration event on the day these crimes were committed. In 2020, when the tombs of Châu and Lân were removed from the Öjendorf cemetery due to their plots' expiration,[10] the initiative set up a memorial there to commemorate every year of their lives.

Mehmet Kaymakçı and **Ramazan Avcı**[11] are also remembered. **Mehmet Kaymakçı**, a 29-year-old construction worker married to a German woman, was attacked by three neo-Nazis at Kiwittsmoor Park in the Langenhorn district of Hamburg on 24 July 1985. All three attackers were eventually arrested, found guilty of manslaughter and jailed for between five and six years. The 26-year-old **Ramazan Avcı** was awaiting the birth of his child when he was brutally assaulted by a group of neo-Nazis on 21 December 1985. He died of his injuries four days later. The five offenders were found guilty of manslaughter, but the public prosecutor played down the evidence showing racist intent. The Ramazan Avcı Initiative, launched by Gülistan Ayaz, his partner and the mother of his child born shortly after his murder, publicly commemorates Ramazan Avcı and Mehmet Kaymakçı. On 24 July 2021, a plaque with Mehmet Kaymakçı's name was inaugurated at the site of the crime. His nephew, Yener Kaymakçı, has thanked the Initiative for providing his uncle with a dignified remembrance after decades of official oblivion. The Ramazan Avcı Initiative, along with Faruk Arslan (whose story is narrated below) and NSU Komplex auflösen successfully lobbied for the renaming of the square near the crime scene at the S-Bahnhof Landwehr in Hamburg[12] as Ramazan-Avci-Platz.

Recalling their Names: 1980s Eastern Germany

Between 1967 and 1986, East Germany implemented training and employment programs, recruiting contract workers from Algeria, Angola, China, Cuba, Mongolia, Mozambique, Poland, Hungary and Vietnam (Ha 2012; Heyden et al. 2014; Poutros 2019). After German reunification, the industrial and agricultural sectors of the GDR were primarily taken over by West German companies operating competitively on a global scale. Most GDR companies were considered economically inefficient, leading to their closure or restructuring. As a result, the majority of the 90,000 contract workers (Dennis 2007; Schwenkel 2014)[13] employed by these companies in 1989 lost their jobs. Angolan, Mozambican (Schenck 2016; Burton et al. 2021), Cuban (Unfrid 2022) and Vietnamese (Hillmann 2005) workers who had arrived in the late 1970s in the GDR faced unemployment and racism (Panayi 1994).[14] In November 1989, 192,000 registered migrants were living in the GDR (Poutrus 2005; Dennis 2007; Glorius 2020).

As Ibraimo Alberto (2014) illustrates in the autobiography narrating his life as a Mozambican contract worker and professional boxer in the GDR between the 1980s and the 1990s, *Ich wollte leben wie die Götter* (I Wanted to Live Like the Gods), racist verbal and physical attacks were common during that time (see also Alberto and Schenck 2021). Contract workers' homes and dormitories were frequently attacked by groups of neo-Nazis and their followers with firebombs. The police were often absent or observed the events from a distance (Poutrus 2022). When faced with this violence and economic deprivation after 1989, most contract workers opted to return to their countries of origin. Some, however, remained in the former East Germany, where in the early 1990s, racist attacks and murders by organized right-wing groups rapidly increased (Perinelli and Lierke 2020). Panikos Panayi (1994, 266) notes in 1991 a "dramatic increase in racial violence in the newly unified Germany, from 270 to 1,438 right-wing offenses—attacks against people or their property." These were the offenses registered by the Verfassungsschutz (federal domestic intelligence service).

On 24 November 1990, three Angolan workers including **Amadeu Antonio Kiowa**—a 28-year-old Angolan contract worker who had come to the GDR to study engineering but was working in a meat processing plant in Eberswalde—were attacked on their way home by a racist mob of approximately 26 young people (Partridge 2012; Florvil 2017). Kiowa and his German girlfriend were expecting a baby when he died of his injuries in the hospital on 6 December 1990. Three policemen had been sitting in their car, observing without intervening, as the racist mob ambushed him. Earlier that day, the police had been informed that a group of approximately 40 young people had met at a youth center and were planning to "hunt foreigners" (*Jagd auf Ausländer*). Only five of the attackers were prosecuted and sentenced to a maximum of four years for manslaughter. Twenty-one of the attackers were not prosecuted due to insufficient evidence. In 2011, a group of citizens in Eberswalde formed the initiative Light me Amadeu in solidarity with Kiowa's family and proposed that a street be named after him as an act of official commemoration. The proposal was vetoed by conservative and right-wing members of the local parliament. In 1998, the independent nongovernmental organization Amadeu Antonio Foundation was founded to fight "neo-Nazism, right-wing extremism, antisemitism, racism and other forms of bigotry and hate in Germany."[15]

Less than one year later, on the night of 31 March 1991, **Jorge Gomondai** was attacked on a tram by a group of neo-Nazis; he was either ejected or jumped from the tram to escape his attackers.[16] Gomondai had arrived in East Berlin on 10 July 1981, at the age of 18, with a group of 70 young men from Mozambique recruited as contract workers by the meat factory VEB Fleischkombinat in Dresden. On 6 April 1991, he died of his injuries in a hospital. Recently, the initiative Gegen Uns (Against Us),[17] which compiles victims' accounts of antisemitism, fascism and racism in East Germany in the 1980s and 1990s, has made a documentary about **Gomondai's** life. Besides tracing Gomondai's migration story, the documentary also reconstructs the events of his racist murder and portrays the politics of his family's mourning. His brother Pita Gomondai, his mother Luisa Nhandima Gomondai and his father organized his body's transfer from Dresden to Chimoio, Mozambique, shortly after his murder. His family and friends are still demanding a thorough investigation of the events of that night.

The early 1990s was marked by the aftermath of the fall of the Berlin Wall. While Germany was celebrating unification, Black people, people of color, migrants, refugees, homeless people and antiracists were assaulted and, in some cases, murdered by organized Nazi groups and racist mobs (Hügel et al. 1993; Ayim 1996; Ünsal et al 2018; Piesche 2020). Thus, the attacks in Eastern Germany were not regionally limited, on 19 September 1991 in the town of Saarlouis, for example, 25-year-old **Samuel Kofi Yeboah** from Ghana died in an arson attack on a refugee home.[18] Those responsible for this attack have been recently identified.[19] Instead of reporting on the racist murders and attacks, media and political discourses at that moment fostered nationalistic racial sentiments by mobilizing a rhetoric of biological filiation. This rhetoric imagined Germany as a culturally, ethnically and racially homogeneous white Christian nation, while migrants and refugees were vilified and denigrated in media representations and political discourses as "invaders" and a "threat" to Western civilization (Jäger and Link 1993; Gutiérrez Rodríguez 1999). In everyday life, this rhetoric would often violently manifest as racist attacks and arson against homes inhabited by Vietnamese, Angolan and Mozambican contract workers—and newly arrived refugees and Roma and Sinti people. Yet these groups would also fight back and organize themselves in order to find ways to elude this racist violence.

Countering Racism

In East Germany, racist attacks were organized in the early 1990s as mass gatherings and riots that blocked buses transporting refugees, attacked refugee camps, set fire to houses inhabited by refugee and/or migrant families or attacked people identified as refugees/migrants. In September 1991, it became apparent that neo-Nazis and their supporters were openly organizing these attacks.

Opposing politics of oblivion: Hoyerswerda 1991

Between 17 and 23 September, contract workers and refugees were systematically attacked by a racist mob in Hoyerswerda. The mob first assaulted Vietnamese workers on the street, who then sheltered in a nearby contract workers' house. From there, the mob went on to an apartment building inhabited by refugees, where the attacks continued for four more days. The police initially failed to intervene at the crime scene and stood by as spectators,[20] while approximately 1,000 bystanders applauded the throwing of stones and petrol bombs. After a few days, the local municipality finally reacted by evacuating the building and transferring the workers to other contract worker or refugee compounds in the East.

However, some victims refused to stay there; for example, one group of Vietnamese contract workers made their way to Hanover, where their asylum request was approved.[21] In Berlin, a group of 48 Mozambican workers, together with church asylum groups and antiracist activists, occupied a Protestant church in the neighborhood of Kreuzberg,[22] demanding permanent residence and welfare support for the refugees. The church reacted by offering them a provisional solution in a villa, provoking a group of "concerned residents" to organize a signature campaign against them. Three weeks later, the Berlin Senate agreed to a transitional residence permit for two months in Berlin, where they were allocated to country-of-origin-specific refugee dorms. A month later, a group of refugees and their advocates occupied the third floor of the Technical University of Berlin (TU) between 24 October 1991 and March 1992. This gave rise to the creation of the first antiracist centers in Berlin (Kleffner 2014). Demanding an end to the *Residenzpflicht*—the imposition of a mobility restriction within the immediate zone of residence—the occupiers went on hunger strike (Ünsal et al. 2018). When the struggle ended in March 1992, some families decided to accept the state's offer of relocation within West Germany. Most of the 48 refugees from Hoyerswerda, as well as the refugees occupying the TU Berlin, partially succeeded in keeping control over their own lives. Some of them settled down in Germany or other parts of Europe, while others went elsewhere. As was later pointed out, the Hoyerswerda refugees' struggle for self-determination and autonomy helped initiate the political articulation of the refugee strike that in 2014 became a strong force in the struggle against racism in Germany (The Voice 2014; Caravan 2023; see also Doppler 2021).

Only 19 of the attackers in Hoyerswerda were found guilty, and most of them received minor or suspended sentences due to being underage or because the statute of limitations on criminal proceedings had expired. In the years following the racist attacks, however, a group of antifascist and antiracist citizens organized shows of solidarity in the form of *Lichterketten* (candlelight vigils). Other groups, such as Progrom91, began to work against the official politics of oblivion of these racist attacks by challenging the city's commemoration practices. With the website www.hoyerswerda-1991.de, Progrom91 established a digital living archive of the Hoyerswerda attacks. The archive consists of video documentaries, photographs, journal articles and other materials, and the events are reconstructed by acknowledging the different actors, the complex societal dimensions and their historical situatedness. Additions are regularly made to the archive to support victims' recollections of the events and the memory of antiracist resistance in the area. In 2011, Progrom91 called upon the local municipality to launch a competition for a memorial, as part of the group's efforts to oppose the official historiography and politics of memory of local politicians. Progrom91 suggested that the memorial be called "In Memory of the Racist Pogroms of Hoyerswerda," to additionally acknowledge the neo-Nazi murders of **Waltraud Scheffler**, who worked in a leftist center in Geierswalde (1992); **Mike Zerna**, a member of a leftist music band, and **Bernd Schmidt**, a homeless man, in Hoyerswerda (1993). However, the city opted for a memorial with the words "Open Door, Open Gate" and the motto "Autumn 1991: Hoyerswerda Does Not Forget, We Remember." Despite the government's refusal to call the events by their name—racist pogroms—Programs91's establishment of a living archive demonstrates a politics of communal mourning that bears witness to racist necropolitics and speaks justice to the demands for reparation for the victims of racism. Collecting the stories of Angolan, Mozambican, Vietnamese and Cuban contract workers or refugees, this work uncovers the circumstances surrounding the crimes that were inflicted upon them, while commemorating their lives. The racist pogroms of Hoyerswerda were followed, less than one year later, in the summer of 1992, by another week of racist violence—this time in Rostock.

Allyship and feeling-with: Lichtenhagen, Rostock, 1992

Between 19 and 21 August 1992, a racist mob gathered in front of the Sonnenblumenhaus, a refugee reception center and accommodation hub in the Lichtenhagen district of Rostock, a city in northern Germany. Stones and firebombs targeting the residents hit the 13-story building. The police present at the crime scene stood by and did nothing until media images—showing mostly Vietnamese and Roma families and a television crew from a primetime media outlet trying to break open an exit door to escape the flames—reached a global audience (Ha 2012b; Nguyen and Lorenz 2022). Trapped in the building with no possibility of escape as the mob outside was preventing the fire brigade from extinguishing the flames, the residents immediately understood that what they were experiencing were lethal racist attacks. Only after three days did police reinforcements with water cannons and tear gas arrive on the scene. The racist mob was held back as residents were escorted out by the police. Yet the attacks con-tinued, even while residents were sitting in the buses that would evacu-ate them. Between 1993 and 1994, 257 criminal investigations followed by 43 prosecutions related to disorderly conduct and arson were undertaken against the perpetrators of these racist attacks. However, most sentences were suspended due to the statute of limitations. Only three attackers were prosecuted and sentenced in 2002, receiving suspended sentences of between 12 and 18 months.

In 2012, an alliance of antiracist advocacy groups and self-organized migrant and refugee groups convened in the rally "Twenty Years after the Racist Pogroms" in Rostock on the 27th of August. The academic, author and activist Kien Nghi Ha was invited to speak and addressed the audience by sharing his feelings and thoughts. The 2019 documentary film made by Nadiye Ünsal, Zerrin Güneş and Tijana Vukmirović, *Without Community, There is No Liberation*, captures Kien Nghi Ha's keynote speech on that day "Ich bin hier, weil ihr hier seid" (I Am Here, Because You Are Here). Facing the audience, he says (see also, Ha 2012c):

> I used to think I would never come to Rostock-Lichtenhagen and sit here, in front of the Sonnenblumenhaus, where 20 years ago this s* happened, where 20 years ago, white Germans tried to burn human beings: Roma and Vietnamese people. And I never thought I would be here, but here I am. Because I am no longer afraid; we are no longer afraid. Never again, for me, for us—this will never happen again. It is important to have a historical reappraisal of Rostock-Lichtenhagen, not only from the dominant German perspective, by breaking the silence about it, but to recover our own history—to reappropriate this history. Also, here there was resistance. In the Sonnenblumenhaus, the Vietnamese people tried to arm themselves in order to defend themselves. They tried to prepare themselves for the Nazi terror.

After these touching words, Ha raises his voice, asking the mainly white German audience,

> Why did you attend the rally today? To celebrate yourself? Or, because you would like to know how people like me feel? How Asian looking people are coping with this racist violence? So look at me now. The Nazis you can gawk at later; they are here the whole night.

Sanchita Basu, a member of the Coalition against Racism and the Migration Council of Berlin e.V., who was present at the rally, comments on Ha's words in the 2018 documentary. Moved by the speech, she felt that Ha articulated her own feelings and positionality by expressing the bodily, emotional and psychological injuries inflicted by racist violence. Basu notes how becoming a target of this violence makes you look at racism from a specific angle—this experience shapes your life regardless of your will or choice. To confront and combat racism is not an option but a necessity for survival. People directly affected by racism, Basu remarks, are dealing with historically produced societal structures, and their fight against racism is thus connected to their lives because racism as a societal structure interferes in one way or another with their very existence (ibid.). They cannot choose to deny the presence of racism or the racialization of their bodies or existence, as it configures their social being. Antiracist struggles, Basu concludes, include people with different social positionalities set in relation to one another within a racialized hierarchical system. Awareness around these differences is key to understanding the effects and the implications of racism for subjectivity formation and social configurations. For Basu, antiracist struggles that are organized with an acknowledgment of these social hierarchies and differences constitute the potential of working together in allyship.

Ha and Basu's reflections voice the potential of (com)passion, a communal affective moment of emotional connection that does not attempt to appropriate the other's feelings but rather to feel, as we discussed in Chapter 2 drawing on Mariana Ortega (2019), a "becoming-with." Ortega (ibid., 125), drawing on Esteban Muñoz's (1999, 74) discussion of mourning as a communal practice, emphasizes that mourning within the context of racist misogynistic homophobic and intersectional violence becomes an "integral part of everyday lives" when we take the experienced injuries and loss "with us to the various battles we must wage in their names—and in our names." Mourning under these conditions speaks about the material site of pain and sorrow that migrantized and racialized bodies experience through the violence inflicted by "histories of injustice and practices of racism and xenophobia" (ibid.). Working through sorrow and communal forms of mourning can be fortified, as Ortega (2019) emphasizes, by "resistant sorrow," practices of resistance sustained by a coalitional politics of transformation striving toward racial and social justice.

While Ha und Basu are not referring to a politics of mourning, their observations on the corporeal, affective dimension of the intelligibility of racial violence brings us back to consider grief work as an instance of the political communal labor of mourning. Relating to the pain and suffering of the inhabitants of the Sonnenblumenhaus, Ha (2012c) confronts the white German antiracist audience with the limits of (com)passion. Their inability to "feel with" the inhabitants of the Sonnenblumenhaus is flagged as a moment of affective ineptitude, which hinders the potential of a political commons that cares for all in Ortega's sense of "becoming-with." It is in this regard that Ha and Basu draw our attention to the lack of "feeling-with," which I discuss in the following as dis(com)passion.

Resisting Dis(com)passion

The Vietnamese and Roma inhabitants of the Sonnenblumenhaus experienced a second racist assault after their evacuation from the house. Mai

Phương Kollath, a survivor of the attacks, recalls in the documentary *The Second Attack* (Reinhardt 2018) how white Germans made her feel she did not belong to this country. Also, in an interview with Manuela Pfohl on 1 October 2008 in the German weekly magazine *Stern*,[23] Kollath speaks about how living in Germany meant constant confrontations with a semi-official expectation that she would return to Vietnam. As a young woman, Kollath arrived in the GDR in 1981 as a contract worker. In 1980, 2,482 Vietnamese people were already living in the GDR, and by 1989 this number had grown to 59,053 (Hillmann 2005, 90). During her first years in Rostock, Kollath lived in the Sonnenblumenhaus. After marrying a German citizen, she moved out but frequently visited her friends who still lived there. When the racist pogroms occurred in 1992, she feared for the lives of her friends. She comments on the lack of compassion she encountered at this time in her everyday life. People seemed to ignore the racist assaults, and no gestures or words of compassion were offered by her work colleagues or neighbors. As Kollath (Reinhardt 2018) recalls, the chants *Deutschland den Deutschen* (Germany for Germans) and *Ausländer Raus!* (Foreigners Go Home!) could often be heard in the streets. But no one mentioned this in the media or in political discourse, nor did anyone offer any immediate support or solidarity. Instead, the fabricated fears of "concerned" white German citizens objecting to small groups of refugees seeking shelter were dealt with as a serious matter that needed to be addressed by severely curtailing and restricting the right to asylum.

In Pagoris Pagonakis's 2013 documentary *Alle sind noch da, nur die Toten fehlen—20 Jahre nach dem Brandanschlag in Solingen* (Everyone is Still There, Only the Dead Are Missing: 20 Years after the Arson Attack in Solingen; see also Odabaşı 2013) the minister of internal affairs of Mecklenburg-Vorpommern, Lothar Kupfer, a member of the conservative CDU party, describes the racist attacks in Rostock as a reaction to an "uncontrolled influx" (*unkontrollierten Zustrom*) that needed to be immediately stopped (*den Riegel vorschieben müssen*). Kupfer added that it was particularly difficult to send the police against their "compatriots" (*Landsleute*) to "protect foreigners" (*um Ausländer zu schützen*). The divide between "compatriots" and "foreigners" seems to legitimize the lack of empathy and mourning for the people that have experienced the cruelty committed by these racist attackers, those whom Kupfer identifies as *Landsleute*. When asked for his analysis of the racist pogroms in Rostock, the minister identifies the quantity of foreigners arriving as the problem that has triggered the "compatriots" reaction. His focus on the number of refugees as the problem, instead of the racist violence itself, represents the typical reaction of most politicians in Germany at this time (Prenzel 2005). This kind of xenophobic—and racist—argument served to legitimate the restriction of the right to asylum (Poutros 2019).

Thus, instead of publicly condemning racist violence and protecting its victims, the state restricted migrants and refugees' access to the national territory. Ha, Basu and Kollath draw attention to this societal reality. As they note, the lack of public outrage, indignation and compassion in regard to racist violence, in particular against Sinti and Roma people, Black people and people of color and refugees and migrant workers, uncovers the deliberate ignorance of the dominant society for the lives, suffering and ultimately death of these human beings. It is this inability to feel with the victims of racist violence that Ha addressed in his speech when he spoke about the lack of (com)passion of the audience to "feel with" the inhabitants of the Sonnenblumenhaus. It is this act of disaffection that articulates the inability of (con)dolence—the limit of feeling-with. Thus, as Ha's intervention suggests, an antiracist struggle that prioritizes "fighting the enemy" while ignoring that they are directly facing the persons who are attacked, wounded and mourning the loss of loved ones indulges in a self-referential politics of alleviation and elevation. Communal mourning under these circumstances is impossible. Yet, as Ha and Basu reiterate, antiracist alliances speak to each other when the moment of feeling-with is a practice forging the everyday communal struggles toward intersectional justice.

Ha, Basu and Kollath's observations point toward an acknowledgment of relational affective practices in antiracist work. Their acknowledgment of the need to "feel-with" echoes Muñoz's (1999, 74) assertion that "we do not mourn just one lost object or another, but we also mourn as a 'whole' by feeling that we are losing a part of ourselves." Through this perspective, Basu and Ha establish an understanding of antiracist solidarity and allyship grounded on the possibility for mutual grief and communal mourning.

Mutual grief: Mölln 1992

In the West Germany of the 1990s, the necessity of grieving mutually and countering racist attacks and murders became a life-saving matter. In 1991, there were 500 attacks against refugees and migrants and 100 arson attacks in West Germany (Panayi 1994). Migrant families from Turkey who had lived in Germany for decades were also targeted.

On the night of 23 November 1992, two houses were set on fire by neo-Nazis in the town of Mölln in Lower Saxony, 30 minutes by car from Hamburg. Two phone calls were received by the fire brigade 30 minutes apart, announcing that houses on Ratzeburger Straße and Mühlenstraße were on fire; both phone calls ended with a Nazi greeting. The Turkish families living there experienced the worst nightmare of their lives (Reinhardt 2018). They tried to escape the flames by jumping out of windows and climbing down curtains—breaking legs and fracturing skulls in the process. As Ibrahim Arslan, one of the survivors of the attacks, recalled, both his mother and aunt broke their hips after jumping from the window (Nobrega and Arslan 2021b; Arslan and Ünsal 2022). Ibrahim survived the arson attacks as a seven-year-old boy. Today an educator and media speaker, he is often invited to speak about this night in schools and on television talk shows.[24] He recounts how his grandmother, **Bahide Arslan**, came into his room, wrapped him in wet towels and took him to the kitchen. According to his vague recollections of that night, he believes that he had been sleeping in the room with his sister, **Yeliz Arslan**, and his cousin, **Ayşe Yilmaz**, visiting from Turkey. The grandmother then tried to rescue the other two children, but all three became trapped by the fire. Yeliz was 10 years old, Ayşe was 14 and Bahide was 51 when they died. Nine other people were injured in the attack. The two persons responsible for these crimes were prosecuted: one of them was tried for numerous murders and given a life sentence, while the other perpetrator received a reduced ten-year sentence as a minor (ibid.). However, both were released between 2000 and 2007 after serving shorter sentences. The police and media initially targeted the Arslan family as prime suspects—particularly Ibrahim's father, Faruk Arslan, who lost his mother, daughter and niece in the attack (Berlin 2012). These acts of defamation and disinformation deeply harmed his reputation, while also exacerbating the grief and irreparable human loss he and his family suffered.

In a 2012 documentary by Malou Berlin entitled *Mölln—20 Jahre nach dem Brand* (Mölln: Twenty Years after the Fire),[25] Faruk tells how the loss of his loved ones has "planted a small black stone inside me that I cannot get rid of, and this makes me very sad" (ibid.). Reflecting on the traumatic effects of these racist events, he shares how one of the attackers used to frequent their house as a child. But it is not only this realization that weights heavily on him. As he reveals in this interview, the media, the police and public prosecutors focused their interest on him as a prime suspect. Blaming and defaming him and his family, the media would be decisive in prolonging the racist attacks. The racist murders of his mother, daughter and niece have left scars that will not heal, causing Faruk to suffer from clinical depression that has made it impossible for him to have a normal professional or social life. Yet, along with his son, he has found strength by connecting with other families, relatives and friends who have lost loved ones to racist attacks. For example, Ibrahim Arslan[26] took part in the launch of the Tribunal of the People in Cologne, Germany, between 17 and 21 May 2017.[27] I will address the Tribunal project—initiated by the network of political organizations and allies of NSU Komplex auflösen—dealing with the 10 murders committed by the Nazi trio of the NSU between 2001 and 2007, later on in this chapter.

The work of the Tribunal has empowered Faruk and Ibrahim Arslan's struggle for justice as they have identified parallels between their own experience and that of the NSU victims, defamed and misrepresented by the media as perpetrators of the murders of their fathers, uncles, brothers and cousins. This secondary display of racism in the police investigation, the media coverage and the legal system is not an exception; it is the rule. After losing their loved ones to racist murders, these families endured public denigration, false accusations, disinformation, distortion of the facts by the media, character assassination, deliberate neglect, oblivion and mainstream society's failure to acknowledge systemic racism among state authorities and the police and in the media. Under these circumstances, the Arslan family, and the other families, relatives and friends, experienced social abandonment while mourning for their losses.

Despite this cruel reality, the families, relatives and friends of the Arslan family continue their struggle for justice. Speaking out publicly, they have shared their analysis of the causes and confluences that led to these racist murders. Challenging the commemorative events[28] organized by the city of Mölln, the Arslan family has countered the official narrative by organizing the annual Möllner Speech in Exile since 2012.[29] The mayor of Mölln is regularly invited as a guest to this public vigil. The families present their current political demands during these public vigils. For example, the Arslan family has called for the renaming of a street near the site of the crime as Bahide-Arslan-Gang (Bahide Arslan Way) and proposed adding the sentence "ermordet bei einem rassistischen Brandanschlag" (murdered in a racist arson attack) to the street sign. As Faruk Arslan noted in an interview with the international German news broadcaster Deutsche Welle on 23 November 2017,[30] "they [the city administration] have refused for a long time to record how my mother died." All these acts articulate an "epistemology of resistance" (Medina 2012) deriving from the experiences and wisdom of the family members in dealing with the losses of their loved one to racist violence.

Trauer – die reinste Form des Erinnerns[31]

Both Faruk and Ibrahim are indebted to the fighting spirit and resilience of their mother and grandmother, **Bahide Arslan**. As they publicly acknowledge, they owe their antiracist convictions to her struggle against fascism. Bahide arrived alone in Germany as a Gastarbeiterin in 1967; her husband joined her in 1970. For Ibrahim, his political engagement as an educator and media speaker is intertwined with his desire to speak justice for his grandmother who saved his life. In a talk show[32] on 28 April 2020, Ibrahim related this work to the labor of mourning, describing mourning as the "reinste Form des Erinnern" (the purest form of remembrance). In his words:

> One remembers the person who is no longer with us. [...] Therefore, mourning is a tool for those affected by the loss of their loved ones. Through mourning we bring back those who died and we remain connected to them by keeping them in our memories.

Bahide's memory is revived every time Ibrahim tells the story of how he survived in 1992; thus, she remains an active part of her grandson's life. Though she rests in peace in the ground, her memory and her experiences continue to shape the lives of her son and grandson. Listening to Ibrahim's words, I am reminded of Gladys Tzul Tzul's (2018b) observation about the cycles of life connected to death and life. It also brings me back to consider Benjamin's notion of *Eingedenken*: remembering as a practice actualizing memory in the situated present. Memories surface in concrete spaces.

It is this temporal-spatial entanglement that Benjamin attempts to capture with the term Eingedenken. Drawing on Jewish religious thought, he defines Eingedenken as a theological and ritual practice of remembering, describing the notion of *Bundesschluss* (Schatzker 1995). The Bundesschluss is the relationship between God and the people established through practices of mutual remembering. As Benjamin notes—this kind of remembering, actualizing the past in the present—opens up the possibility of forefeeling the future. Eingedenken appears rather late in Benjamin's (2010) work, when he introduces the term in his reflections on historical philosophy and literary criticism (see also Schwepenhäuser 1999). Benjamin's Eingedenken connects memory with a moment of the *Jetzt* (the now). The Italian philosopher Stefano Marchesoni (2016, 162) summarizes this term as follows: "The space takes the position of time, the instance that of the course of time, and the steadiness that of a river."[33] In the act of Eingedenken, unsorted memories, images and instances of different time frames are reshuffled and reordered within a spatial contemporaneity. Gaps, discontinuities and tortuous paths appearing during the attempt to remember are weaved into a situated awareness of the present. A topography of memories is produced in the entanglement between remembrance and space. Collective practices of remembering are inserted into a present awareness of our being in time. As Marchesoni (ibid.) describes it, "[when] something is now remembered, that means it is memorable: each memory presupposes something like a 'memorable now.' Focusing on this, forces us to realize the social relations of its emergence."[34]

The Arslan family's political communal labor of mourning articulates a current analysis of racism through their memory of the loss of their family members in 1992. As Ibrahim notes, the relationship with death is set within a circular temporality. Working through the past, the experience of loss and injustice carries the potential for resistance. While this connection of existence and resistance is set within the specific context of migration and racist murders in Germany, it resonates with the analysis of Tzul Tzul's (2018b) cycles of life and Rodríguez Aguilera's (2021) life-death continuum. The Arslan's communal labor of mourning is shaped by this rebellious ontology resurfacing from "resistant sorrow" (Ortega 2019). Faruk and Ibrahim share this ontological moment of resistance with other relatives in the struggles against racist violence in Germany (Ünsal et al 2018). It is this "becoming-with" with other acts of communal mourning that forges the political work of mourning by expressing resistance at the juncture of the "death-life continuum." Despite this ongoing struggle against racism, the official politics of commemoration failed to bear witness, perform accountable listening or give justice to the families. The state did not publicly acknowledge the societal rootedness of this racist violence, nor did it act on it. A few months later, Solingen became the next site of racist violence. Here, too, affected families used their grief work to confront the state and German society's politics of oblivion.

Confronting denial: Solingen 1993

On the night of 29 May 1993, three days after the Asylkompromiss[35] was passed and few days before the start of the Muslim festivity *Kurban Bayramı* (Demirtaş et al. 2023), a group of neo-Nazis set fire to the home of a Turkish family in Solingen. Mevlüde Genç and her husband, Durmus, were awakened by flames enveloping the home they had inhabited since their arrival to Germany in 1970. Their daughter, 27-year-old **Gürsün Ince,** lost her life when she escaped by jumping from the window. Their 18-year-old daughter, **Hatice Genç**, 12-year-old niece, **Gülüstan Öztürk**, and granddaughters, **Hülya Genç** (9 years old) and **Saime Genç** (4 years old), all suffocated to death (ibid; Hatice Genç and Demirtaş 2023; Kâmil Genç and Demirtaş 2023; Cihat Genç and Schmitz 2023). Fourteen additional family members suffered life-threatening injuries. Immediately afterward, four neo-Nazis between the ages of 16 and 23 were arrested and tried for five murders, 14 attempted murders, and arson. They were given sentences of between 10 and 15 years each in October 1995.[36] The court judgment acknowledged that racism was the motivation for these crimes.

In her first media statement, Mevlüde Genç asserted the need for solidarity, which she continued to reiterate until her death on 30 October 2022. Her spirit continues on in the struggle against racist violence and her relatives', friends' and advocates' search for reparative justice (ibid). In April 2023 the edited collection *Solingen, 30 Jahre nach dem Brand-Anschlag. Rassismus, extrem rechte Gewalt und die Narben einer vernachlässigen Aufarbeitung*, edited by Birgül Demirtaş, Adelheid Schmitz, Derya Gür-Şeker and Çağrı Kahveci, was published. This volume engages with a politics of remembrance, establishing a dialogue with the family members of the Solingen racist attacks. It also gives voice to the analysis of other family members, relatives and friends who lost their loved ones to racist attacks in Germany. The authors combine what I call here a political labor of mourning with engaged community-oriented research and the reconstruction of memories, filling the gaps, but also marking them in the nation-state narration and historiography of these events. Sustained by the immediate support the Genç family received from their multicultural neighborhood in Solingen, Mevlüde and her husband, Durmus, voiced their hope for cross-cultural understanding following the racist arsons. Drawing on the potential of affective connections based on communal grief, the Gençs evoked the sentiment of unity. The German media, however, interpreted their words as a gesture of reconciliation. Mevlüde and Durmus Genç soon became the media patrons of multicultural reconciliation politics. German officials also reacted along these lines by publicly praising Mevlüde as a peace ambassador. In 1996, she received the Bundesverdienstkreuz am Bande (The Order of Merit of the Federal Republic of Germany)—the highest German honor awarded by the German state. Mevlüde also received other honors, such as the Verdienstorden der Landesregierung (OM of the regional government) from North Rhine-Westphalia in 2015 (Nobrega 2014). Since 2018, North Rhine-Westphalia has awarded the Mevlüde Genç medal for special contributions to tolerance and living together. At first glance, the treatment of the Genç family by the media and state officials in the 1990s seems to contrast with the Arslan family's experiences.

Yet, the normalization of racial crimes was met with multitudinal and loud protests by the immigrant community from Turkey. The arson perpetrated on the Genç family's house was not a singular fleeting act. It was a symptom of the everyday and institutional racism migrant communities suffered (Neşe/Fatma et al. 2023). The communities from Turkey, but also other migrant communities and antiracist groups, organized public vigils and mourning commemoration events several weeks and months after the racist attacks (Kahvaci 2017; Kocatürk-Schuster and Yurtseven 2023). Also other forms of protest such as assemblies and strikes—for example, not sending children to school in protest, or the cancelling of bank accounts in Solingen, and the blocking of motorways—took place immediately after the attacks (Demirtaş et al. 2023). The trial against the four perpetrators in Solingen lasted 18 months and revealed a series of investigative errors, such as missing fingerprints, interrogation records and a failure to thoroughly inspect the crime scene. As in other cases of systemic racist crimes, a so-called *V-Mann* (informant), the manager of a martial arts school in Solingen frequented by right-wingers, played a significant role (ibid).[37]

The official commemoration politics of the city of Solingen reflect the contestation about and uneven accounts of the racist murders in Solingen in 1993 (ibid). Propelled by some concerned citizens who collaborated with the family to establish a site of commemoration, the Monument to the Arson Attack of 29 May 1993 (Das Mahnmal des Brandanschlags vom 29. Mai 1993) was placed just outside the city center, close to the Mildred Scheel Vocational School, where Hatice Genç was a student. As Eray Çaylı (2021) notes, this location was chosen by local authorities aiming to neutralize the social tensions that they assume existed on the outskirts of the city. The monument has become the site of official commemorations organized annually by the city of Solingen and DİTİB, an organization affiliated with the current Turkish government. At Untere Wernerstraße 81, where the house once stood, the Genç family planted five trees in remembrance of the five murdered women in 1994 (Çaylı 2021; Demirtaş et al. 2023). A square near the house has also been renamed Mercimek Square in 2012, in honor of the Genç family's hometown in Turkey. After Mevlüde Genç's death in October 2022, the family members demanded that a central street in Solingen be named after her. On the 28th of Mai 2023 Mercimek-Square was renamed to Mevlüde Genç Square. This was the option offered by the city council, which refused to name a central street after the lost members of the Genç family (ibid.). Accordingly, despite all the political and media attention the Solingen case received, the Genç family and their supporters have not succeeded in realizing their wish to establish a memorial in a central square in Solingen.

During her life, Mevlüde Genç voiced the horror and trauma that shapes the lives of her family members. In the media, she expressed her refusal to reconcile with the perpetrators, who have shown no remorse and denied their responsibility for the racist murders. The family has also addressed the absence of any reparative justice, like investing in structural changes against racism. Between April 1994 and October 1995, the Genç family attended the trial daily because they felt the need to confront the offenders' lack of remorse for their murderous acts. For Mevlüde and Durmus Genç, the trial was like a reenactment of their trauma. Little attention was given to the racist motivation behind this violence; although the jury condemned the murderers, no societal reparation was enacted. The accused were treated as isolated neo-Nazis behaving irrationally.

This distortion denied the systemic and organized political dimension of extreme right-wing factions and disregarded racism as part of the dominant societal structure (Demirtaş et al. 2023; Kahveci 2023). For the Genç family, this outcome meant that they must continue their labor of mourning as political action.

In a 2018 interview,[38] Mevlüde, then 75 years old, and Durmus, 74 years old, introduced their 18-year-old granddaughter Özlem as representative of the new generation. Pursuing studies in nutritional science, she personifies her grandmother's insistence that Germany is their home—immediately after the racist arson in 1993, Mevlüde had declared, "We are staying here."[39] Transforming her lasting grief into political remembrance and combating racism, on 21 February 2020, Mevlüde expressed her condolences to the families who lost loved ones to the Hanau racist murders of 19 February 2020.[40] Sharing her experience of losing a child to racism, she affirms,[41] "this is our country. Our children will stay here forever." In *Alle sind noch da*,[42] one of Mevlüde's granddaughters, Güldane Inci, the daughter of **Gürsün Inci** and Ahmet Inci, shares a different experience from that of her cousin Özlem. She jumped out of the window with her mother and survived but still has scars and pain in her leg. Despite efforts by her grandmother and her father to protect her from this pain by not talking about that night, it still marks her life. Both Özlem and Güldane still carry the trauma and scars of the events of 1993 (see also, Demirtaş 2023b; Gün 2023). Appearing in the media, they continue the political labor of mourning their grandparents initiated by bearing witness and speaking justice for the loss of their loved ones. This intense grief work is intergenerationally approached in the Genç family by taking care of and demanding accountability and responsibility from the state. As Mevlüde summarizes it,

> We are all human. I carry the love of my lost ones inside me. Otherwise there is no hope. The dead ones will not return and I live on, carrying their love inside of me.

Mevlüde's intense work of grief has embraced love, respect and living together, relating the labor of mourning to a process of transformative justice through practices of mutual understanding. Her dialogic approach of building bridges has required the state's political commitment to combating structural racism. Within their rhetoric of reconciliation, German and Turkish political parties have instrumentalized Solingen as an exceptional case. Yet, as would become apparent over a decade later, racist attacks on migrant and refugee homes were not merely aberrations exclusive to the 1980s and 1990s.

Uniting, Archiving, Resisting: NSU Komplex Auflösen

Between 2000 and 2007, nine Kurdish, Turkish and Greek small business owners and employees—**Enver Şimşek, Abdurrahim Özüdoğru, Süleyman Taşköprü, Habil Kılıç, Mehmet Turgut, İsmail Yaşar, Theodoros Boulgarides, Mehmet Kubaşık, Halit Yozgat**, and a German policewoman, **Michèle Kiesewetter**—were murdered by the NSU (National Socialist Underground).[43] These murders occurred across Germany. Images of the murders only began to circulate in the media, following the investigation of a bank robbery on 4 November 2011 in Eisenach by two men, who fled from the police and committed suicide that same day. The woman they shared an apartment with in Zwickau set the apartment on fire after receiving news of the suicides. Later that day, she sent confessional DVDs made with her two companions to media outlets and to cultural, religious and political organizations before turning herself in to the police in Jena. The videos contained images of their victims at the moment of their execution. During the trials for the NSU murders in Munich from 2013 to 2018, the public learned that the woman was the head of the neo-Nazi trio and that all three had been known to the Verfassungsschutz as members of militant right-wing groups since 1998 (Funke 2015; Tribunale 2021).

The Şimşek family had watched their father and husband fight for his life for two days after the attack; being subjected to images of their bleeding father circulating in the media over a decade later only reiterated the cruelty and blatant racist violence they had endured. After **Enver Şimşek**'s death on 11 September 2000, the police and media treated his family like suspects (Şimşek 2013). The events of 2011 confirmed what the Şimşek family had known all along: Enver was murdered by politically organized racists. As was the case for the Arslan and Satır families, during the crime investigation and the legal prosecution, the Şimşeks were subjected to a second racist attack. Only two days after Enver's death, the police investigating the case in Hamburg wrote in a memo, without any supporting evidence, that they were dealing with a drug case. They fabricated a string of lies, portraying Enver as a member of a drug-dealing ring, leading a double life with a second wife and two additional children (Tribunale 2021). Adile Şimşek, Enver's widow, was shown pictures of the fictitious blond wife and children meant to provoke her to reveal information about her husband. Telling this story to the filmmaker Aysun Bademsoy in the 2019 documentary *Spuren—Die Opfer des NSU* (Traces: The Victims of the NSU), Adile speaks calmly, never losing her composure as she presents the facts surrounding the circumstances of her husband's murder. Her account repeats some of the observations other families affected by racist murders have reported and what the political network NSU Komplex auflösen (2017; 2021) has classified as racist police investigations (Hielscher 2016; Pichl 2018). The racist bias in the investigation and media reporting was reflected in the police's naming of special investigation units in orientalist ways as "Bosphorus" or "Halbmond" (crescent)—as if the NSU murders had occurred outside of a white German context (Schmincke and Siri 2013; Güleç 2015; Güleç and Hielscher 2015). In the German regional court in Munich where the NSU trial took place, it was shown that the police investigations were extremely extensive (Tribunale 2021). Police operated on the assumption that the crimes were linked to the so-called Turkish drug scene. Over 11 years, hundreds of investigators were deployed, interviews were conducted in Turkey, fake Döner stores were opened and undercover agents were employed as journalists (Behrens 2017). These police investigations were guided by racist stereotypes revealing the predominant institutional racism of police investigations (Dengler and Faroutan 2017); evidence for this was provided by a commission to investigate the background of the NSU set up by the German Bundestag (Parliament) on 26 January 2012 (Kleffner and Feser 2013).[44] In their final report presented to the parliament 19 months later, on 22 August 2013, 47 recommendations were formulated, some of them addressing structural racism in the police.[45] The mobilization of racist stereotypes reflected not only the racist assumptions of the police and the media, which dubbed the racist murders "Döner Morde" (kebab murders) (Figge and Michaelsen 2017), but also what the Tribunal identified as "the practice of victim-perpetrator role reversal" (Tribunal 2017). That is, blaming the victims for the racist violence they have endured.

In Bademsoy's 2019 documentary, Adile and Semiya Şimşek reflect on this racist violence. They recount how, during the 11 years that followed Enver's death, they were unable to just be victims. Semiya (2013) also recounts this experience in her book *Schmerzliche Heimat. Deutschland und den Mord an meinem Vater* (Painful Homeland: Germany and the Murder of My Father). In her book, she narrates her family story and her father's entrepreneurial career, from selling flowers to becoming a flower wholesaler working with different flower shops in Schlüchtern and the surrounding area. On the day of his murder, Enver was selling flowers at his stall at the exit of Highway A9 in Nuremberg. Semiya, who was 14 years old at the time, recalls how she received a phone call saying that her father was in the hospital in a coma. She recalls that in her first encounter with the police, they interrogated her. They had wanted to know if her father owned a weapon and if he had enemies in the drug and gambling mafias. For Adile and Semiya, all these suspicions were unfounded, and being treated like suspects made the police investigation unbearable. In fact, Semiya would later find out as a plaintiff during the trial that the police had tapped her mother's phone (Liebscher 2017).[46] The persecution of their family after Enver's death has filled Adile and Semiya with shame—an ambiguous feeling related to the trauma, intimidation and denigration they experienced during these years. The other family members who lost loved ones to the NSU terror recount similar stories of being turned into objects of public defamation and criminalization by the police, in other words: encountering the practice of victim-perpetrator role reversal (Kubaşık 2014; Özüdoğru 2014; John 2014; Friedrich et al. 2015; Funke 2015; Tribunale 2021). However, Adile and Semiya, along with family members of other victims, managed to deflect the blame and become politically active.

Public vigils and political reconstruction: *"Kein 10. Opfer"*

Following the racist murder of 21-year-old **Halit Yozgat** in his family's internet café in Kassel on 6 April 2006, his family, along with the families of **Enver Şimşek** and **Mehmet Kubaşık**—the latter a Kurdish refugee who arrived in Germany in 1991 and was murdered at the age of 39 on the 4 April 2006 in his Dortmund kiosk, just two days before Halit—organized public vigils in Kassel and Dortmund under the slogan "Kein 10. Opfer"[47] (No Tenth Victim) (Güleç 2018a,b). Halit's father, Ismael Yozgat, and Semiya Şimşek gave speeches, addressing the failures of the police investigations. Presenting some observations and conclusions—why these murders might be racist crimes committed by organized neo-Nazis—they asked the state authorities to take responsibility for these racist crimes. The participants of the rallies demanded an exhaustive police investigation and subsequent prosecution of the perpetrators. Ismael Yozgat (see also 2014) addressed the rally with these words ("Kein 10. Opfer" 2006):

> My son was killed a month ago by two gunshots. There should be no further killings of innocent people in this way. What has occurred cannot be reversed. Between September 2000 and April 2006, nine vendors were killed with the same murder weapon. The perpetrator(s) are still around. How many executions need to take place before the murderers are caught? Why was the investigation not intensified prior to the nine murders?
>
> Dear Ministry of the Interior, open your eyes so you can see this bitter reality. Listen to the mourning of the relatives. Please place yourself in our position. Try to realize what losing a child in the prime of his life means for my family and me. Once you do this, you will understand the desperate situation we find ourselves in. We are grieving for our son and do not want others to be in a situation of grief due to similar murderous acts. There should be no further vicious gunshots. Make sure of it!

In these rallies, the families, relatives and friends publicly demonstrated their communal mourning by wearing T-shirts with pictures of their lost loved ones and carrying black banners (Güleç and Schaffer 2017).

"Kein 10. Opfer" also remembered the other five victims of the NSU. **Abdurrahim Özüdoğru**, a 49-year-old resident of Germany since 1980, was killed by the same weapon (a Česká 83) used in Enver Şimşek's murder. He was gunned down while working in his clothing and alterations shop in Nuremberg on 13 June 2001. Two weeks later, on 27 June 2001, **Süleyman Taşköprü**, 31 years old, was killed by three shots from a Česká 83 in his father's fruit and vegetable shop in Hamburg. On 29 August 2001, **Habil Kılıç** was murdered in his fruit and vegetable shop in Munich. Two years later, on 25 February 2004, **Mehmet Turgut**, a 25-year-old resident of Hamburg, was shot in a friend's *Döner-Imbiss* (kebab stand) while visiting him in Rostock. One year later, **İsmail Yaşar**, the 50-year-old owner of a kebab stand, was shot dead with the same weapon in Nuremberg on 9 June 2005. Here, too, the police initiated their investigation by looking for suspects among "Turkish drug dealers," while ignoring the descriptions of two white men provided by eyewitnesses at the crime scene. The description of one of these men matched the description of a man who had left a woman's bike with a travel case in front of the Yildirim brothers' barbershop on Keupstraße in Cologne on 9 June 2004 (Maus 2016). A few minutes later, a nail bomb with 700 nails detonated on this street in the multicultural neighborhood of Mülheim and 22 people were injured.[48] On 15 June 2005, the NSU killed **Theodoros Boulgaridis**, the 41-year-old co-owner of a locksmith store who had relocated from Greece to Munich in 1973.

The NSU was also responsible for a series of bomb attacks between 2000 and 2001, such as those targeting a family-run store in Cologne and a bar in Munich. In both cases, the owners of these establishments had Iranian or Turkish names. Investigative journalists and political initiatives have reconstructed the events around these attacks, and yet the state has failed to fully prosecute those responsible for the crimes (Tribunale 2021).

Speaking Truth: "We accuse!"

During the 2013–2018 trial in Munich, the families, relatives and friends of the NSU victims raised the following questions (Tribunale 2021):

How was the infrastructure organized in the preparation and carrying out of these killings? Who observed the victims and their working environment and passed this information on to the executioners?

Gamze Kubaşık[49] faced the judges and public prosecutors and asked,[50]

Who helped the NSU perpetrators to carry out their crimes in Dortmund? Who spied on her father and the kiosk and passed this information on to the NSU? And if the Verfassungsschutz was aware of the NSU, why did they not prevent these murders?

In the search of answers to these questions, families, friends and allies have created a series of local initiatives and worked with political organizations engaged in combating antisemitism and racism. Between 17 and 21 May 2017, the first Tribunal—NSU Komplex Auflösen (Unraveling the NSU Complex Tribunal) took place in Cologne with the slogan "Wir klagen an!" (We accuse!). Since then, three more public tribunals in Mannheim (2018), Chemnitz/Zwickau (2019) and Nürnberg (2022) have been organized.[51] As stated on its website, in the Tribunal there is "no jury, no judges and thus no judgment" (Tribunal 2017). In comparison to other public tribunals, such as the Russell Tribunal conceptualized as a people's tribunal in the wake of the Vietnam War and headed by a group of concerned citizens and intellectuals, or the Truth and Reconciliation commissions in Colombia, South Africa and Canada, which have sought an acknowledgment of wrongdoings while establishing dialogue between opposing parties, the Unraveling the NSU Complex Tribunal is not interested in a politics of reconciliation where crimes might not be prosecuted (ibid.). Rather, it aims to make the process of investigation transparent by archiving material and making it accessible to a wider public. Most importantly, it establishes the experiences and perspectives of the relatives, families and friends as a point of entry for the examination and understanding of the sequence of events. As members of the Tribunal insist (ibid.),

The trial will unmistakably represent a migrant perspective. We insist that an understanding of the workings of racism in all its dimensions has to rest on the knowledge of those targeted by this racism. We want to strengthen this knowledge, spread it and transfer it into new alliances of solidarity in order to show ways to overcome racist realities.

This moment of solidarity speaks to what I am discussing here as the political communal labor of mourning, nourished by the wisdom and the epistemology of resistance of the family members, their relatives and friends. Their knowledge of the events, analysis and interpretations guide their itinerary in the process of searching for truth and seeking justice.

The Society of Friends of Halit Yozgat (initiated by Ayşe Güleç), Initiative 6. April and other allies of the Yozgat family in Kassel work in a similar way. Departing from the question raised in particular by the Yozgat family, The Society of Friends of Halit was invited to the international art exhibition documenta 14 in Kassel in 2017, where they collaborated with the London-based research collective Forensic Architecture (FA), among others, to digitally reconstruct the movements and distances between persons and objects at the crime scenes and the trajectory of the Verfassungsschutz (Marschall and Simke 2022). This reconstruction revealed that a member of the secret service was present at the crime scene and likely saw the dead body on the ground, which raises questions about the connection between the NSU and the Verfassungsschutz (Kleffner and Feser 2013, 2021; Funke 2015; Pichl 2015). In 2011, a few days after the media revelation of the NSU murders, the Verfassungsschutz offices in Berlin, Thuringia, Saxony and Saxony-Anhalt shredded documents relevant to Halit Yozgat's case. Additionally, in May 2021 the conservative government of Hessen implemented a 30-year embargo of the secret files on the Verfassungsschutz's handling of Halit's case. The Society thus addresses the Yozgat family's questions as well as the inconsistencies in the state prosecutor's case against the NSU—paying tribute to the memory of the victims and bearing witness to their families' accounts and analyses of the series of events leading to the racist killing. Citing the Yozgat family's "situated migrant knowledge," Güleç (2018a,b) draws attention to the active downplaying, ignoring and negating practices performed by state authorities. From very early on, the families had unanimously expressed their concern that they were dealing with racist attacks, likely inflicted by politically organized Nazis and other fascist groups (Tribunal 2021). However, it was not until the surviving member of the NSU trio confessed to the nine murders that the families' suspicions were finally investigated. Güleç (2018b) describes the families' intervention as articulations of "affirmative sabotage": attempts to destabilize and undermine the dominant accounts and reconstruction of the crimes by state authorities such as the police, the state prosecutor and the court. During the trial in Munich, İsmail Yozgat showed photographs of his son's dead body lying behind the reception desk in the internet café, confronting the court with a different interpretation of the events, which addressed the presence of a Verfassungschutz agent at the scene of the crime. This fact remains unexplained, as the relevant files that might provide some insight into these circumstances have been barred from public view for 30 years.[52]

Güleç (ibid.) describes the media, police and legal system's silencing of the families' accounts as an act of "Nicht-Hören-Wollen" (not-wanting-to-listen). Families, relatives and friends react to this negation of their embodied knowledge by interrupting the official matrix of representation. Through the example of the public vigils in Kassel in 2006, depicted in Sefa Defterli's 2006 video documentation of "Kein 10. Opfer," Güleç and Johanna Schaffer draw attention to how the families succeed in conveying their message by using images, body politics, and different vocabularies and knowledge traditions "to develop new ways to turn societal attention to their accounts and experiences." (Güleç and Schaffer 2017, 65) Through these public acts of mourning, the families intervene in the official rhetoric and representation, debunking the account of a lone perpetrator.

Demystifying the lone perpetrator

In 2018, the woman who had headed the NSU trio was sentenced to life imprisonment for numerous crimes including first-degree murder and arson. Four of their supporters, all Nazis known to the police, were charged with helping the trio plan and carry out the racist attacks. However, two of the offenders were immediately released due to the statute of limitations. During the trial in Munich, only one of the offenders expressed any remorse; the others showed no sign of repentance. The charges against the offenders included membership in and support of a terrorist organization, perpetrating and being accessories to murders and attacks and participating in at least 15 robberies, acts of arson and attempted murders. The perpetrators were prosecuted as individuals, not as members of a broader systematically organized extreme right-wing national network associated with other neo-Nazi networks internationally. Thus, the questions that Gamze Kubaşık (2017) and other family members, relatives and friends have raised regarding the infrastructure, personnel and financial support of the NSU remain at the center of the investigation.

As Güleç[53] insists, the NSU cannot be reduced to a group of three individuals. Rather, as revealed by investigations conducted by numerous independent committees and initiatives—NSU Watch, Keupstrasse ist überall, the Initiative 7. April and NSU Komplex auflösen, among others—the NSU is a complex formation composed of a variety of organizations and institutions across different sectors of society (Tribunal 2021). Its reduction to the murderous trio disregards the probability that these three individuals were executioners working on behalf of a potentially broader right-wing network. The family members, relatives and friends concur in their summary of the main elements of the NSU complex (Tribunal 2017):

> The NSU complex is given a concrete form in the practice of victim-perpetrator role reversal, in the racist reporting in the German media, the collaboration between Germany's secret services and the neo-Nazi underground, the attempted cover-ups, the deliberate disappearance of evidence, the unexplainable deaths of witnesses and the persistent obstruction of attempts to clarify the background and details of the crimes.

As previously mentioned, until 4 November 2011 the police had concentrated their investigation on the communities and families of the victims of the NSU. The Tribunal (ibid.) noted,

> In their state of suffering, the victims and their families were categorized as suspects and subjected to massive repression. Intensive interviews, house searches, DNA tests, secret investigations, deliberately spread rumors of failed marriages, implications of involvement in drug dealing and organized crime—victims of the NSU's crimes were subjected to all of this over a period of many years.

These different levels of racist violence illustrate the complexity of the NSU, which came into existence not only through its militant branch but also through the actions of the police, the media and the attitudes of some politicians toward the families and the racist crimes committed. These invasive acts expose the structural racism of German society, which is expressed on three levels: (a) the lack of (com)passion for the families' loss and respect for their grief, (b) the noncompliance with democratic procedures in the handling of the police investigation and prosecution and (c) the media distortion of the crimes and the victim-blaming narratives (Hielscher 2016; Karakayali et al. 2017; Nobrega et al. 2021a).

During the Munich trial, the plaintiffs, their lawyers and supporters consistently drew attention to the magnitude and sophisticated matrix of the NSU complex. Arguing that the NSU was not a one-off organization or a small group of disturbed individuals, they focused on the entanglement of structural, institutional and symbolic forms of racial violence. Racism, they argued, is never a singular incident in contemporary German society. Rather, it is constitutive of the very functioning of that society. This has raised questions and demands about how to combat systemic racism and how to make society accountable. As Kutlu Yurtsever, a survivor of the nail bomb attacks, has warned, "if the true connections are not named and laid open, the events can repeat themselves."[54]

Until today, the police have not publicly accounted for the intimidation and harassment of the families, nor have the families received any official apology or offer of reparation for the material, physical and emotional harm this caused. The political and cultural event organized by Aysun Bademsoy and Ayşe Güleç in the Haus der Kulturen der Welt (House of World Cultures) in Berlin, "It's not over: The joint plaintiffs speak out one year after the NSU trial" (6–9 November 2019),[55] performed a statement by Mehmet Kubaşık's daughter, Gamze Kubaşık (ibid.), released one day before the NSU trial verdicts were announced:[56]

Mehmet Kubaşık was my father. He was the most important man to me. He was the most wonderful human being that I knew. The pain and the loss will follow my family and me for the rest of our lives. It is not easy to live with this destiny. We miss him just as much now as we did 10 years ago. The NSU murdered my father. The investigators destroyed his honor. In this way, they have killed him a second time. [...] The five years of trial have been a disappointment. [...] I want to know how my father was chosen as a target. I want the Verfassungsschutz to finally tell us what it knew.

After attending the NSU trial for five and a half years, the family members felt let down. Although the remaining member of the NSU trio was sentenced to life imprisonment, two of the four accomplices were set free. One of their defense lawyers insisted that jail time would deprive his client's children of a father and stressed the difficult circumstances the family was going through. In "It's not over," Semiya Şimşek wonders why the feelings of the families that lost loved ones to the NSU murders were not represented at the trial. No one seemed to consider how the families of the victims have survived this situation of mistrust, defamation, denigration and humiliation. The murders of their loved ones, followed by police and media accusations, have left incurable wounds. Recalling her age when her father was murdered, Semiya (ibid.) states,

My childhood was taken. My son needs to live now without a grandfather. When I go with him to his grave, I feel an incredible pain. No one is interested in this. This still hurts me.

Annette Ramelsberger, the trial reporter of the German newspaper *Süddeutsche Zeitung*, comments in Bademsoy's (ibid.) documentary about how the families maintained their composure and discipline throughout the trial (see also Ramelsberger 2020). The judge did not show any gesture of condolence or acknowledgment regarding their loss and suffering, and neo-Nazis were allowed to break into a round of celebratory applause after the announcement of the verdict, which exculpated two of their members. The "complete clarification" of the case promised by the then German chancellor Angela Merkel to the families during the state's official mourning event in 2012 is still to come.[57] Gamze Kubaşık, for example, expressed her loss of faith in politicians in a statement she made in court after the verdict was handed down. Addressing the court, she stated, "You have broken your promise."[58] For Güleç, as she says in "Spuren—Die Opfer des NSU," the trial obfuscated the entanglement of politics, the police and the Verfassungsschutz. It focused instead on the fabricated narrative that the murders were the acts of individuals and not connected to an organized racist network. The statement by Enver Şimşek's son, Abdul Karim Şimşek, performed at the event "It's not over," challenges this narrative by remembering the pain his father might have suffered:

> I often wonder what my father might have felt and thought when they shot him. I often wonder how he felt while he was severely injured and lying defenseless on the ground. I often wonder if he suffered a lot of pain. I often wonder why they precisely chose him. [...] I cannot find any closure, because I have the feeling that not everything has been done to clarify his death. I cannot find any closure because I am certain that there are still confidants and helpers out there. I cannot find any closure because I cannot understand how in a country like Germany files are shredded and no one is made accountable for it.

Endless Mourning

As we have seen in the cases of racist violence throughout the 1980s, 1990s and early 2000s, families, relatives and friends are fighting for commemoration politics that render justice to the lives lost. Most of them have requested that cities rename the streets where their family members were murdered. Political initiatives, such as the Initiative 6. April in Kassel or Keupstrasse ist Überall in Cologne, have been organized. For example, Ismael and Ayşe Yozgat, together with the Initiative 6. April, are fighting for the renaming of Holländische Straße, where their internet café was located, as Halitstrasse. For Ismael, this would be a gesture that the city is embracing the idea of a truly democratic society:[59]

> I thought for a while how we could protect future generations from fascist ideas and their consequences. It should be something that enables us to never forget these cruel murders and keep them in the present, and always keep an attentive eye open [...]. Halit was born on Holländische Straße; he lived and was brutally murdered there. [...] By renaming the street Halitstraße, I am convinced that there will be a lot of questions about where this name comes from. In this way, these cruel murders would never be forgotten and our attentive eye will be further strengthened.

After the NSU trial in Munich, Ismael repeated this demand addressing the German state:

Either you give us our 21-year-old son Halit back or you rename
Holländische Straße as Halitstraße.

Ayşen Taşköprü, Süleyman Taşköprü's sister, addressed the question of
reparative justice in her response to an invitation by President Joachim Gauck
to the official reception for the relatives of the NSU victims held at Schloss
Bellevue in 2013 (see also Taşköprü 2014). In a letter dated 15 February of
that year, she states the reasons for her refusal (Tribunal 2017):

> Something has been broken inside of me. [...] In summer 2001, neo-
> Nazis murdered my brother. In late summer 2011, the criminal investi-
> gation police rang my bell. They brought my brother's personal items. I
> asked the officers why now; they said they forgot to bring them earlier.
> [...] The confessional video of the NSU was then screened. I started to
> shout. My brother was lying in his own blood on the red-white tiles. I saw
> his delicate hands; I recognized his watch. There was no smile on his lips.
> He was murdered. On that day, my brother died a second time and some-
> thing broke inside of me. [...] And now, Mr. Gauck, my brother might
> also be important to you, because the NSU has become a political issue.
> But what would you like to do to change our suffering? [...] Empathic
> invitations do not help. Only actions will help. Can you help me?

Amid this situation of failure, as we have seen, families, relatives and friends
of the victims have found ways to pay tribute to their loved ones. Their political communal labor of mourning continues. In Bademsoy's documentary, this
intense work of grief becomes tangible in the words of Adile and Semiya Şimşek.

After years of suffering and struggling in Germany, they moved to Turkey.
Their house is near the cemetery where their father and husband rests. Showing
the audience the trees that she planted after her husband's death, Adile tells
the audience: she is here with him now; his spirit and energy surrounds her.
Mourning is an endless process. It is the reminder of the connection of our life
with death. For the other families, this affective connection between life and
death is also realized in the acts, gestures and words transmitted through the
organization of vigils, rallies, political events, publications and the daily coalition
work with other political initiatives. Bearing witness, telling truth and standing
for reparative justice, the political communal labor of mourning is endless.

Conclusion: Reparative Mourning

In this chapter, I have engaged with the political communal labor of mourning
of the relatives, families and friends of the victims of racism in Germany from

the 1980s to the early 2000s. I have looked at three dimensions of these politics by addressing the work of naming, remembering and unraveling the cases of racist murders during this period. Focusing on cases where family members, relatives and friends have played a decisive role in confronting the German public with structural racism as the root cause behind the murders of their loved ones, I have discussed this work as a political communal labor of mourning. Accordingly, I have engaged with the grief work of families, relatives and friends, listening to their pain and bearing witness to their accounts. I have followed their words and connected with their feelings. This affective engagement allows us to consider their work in the sense of Benjamin's Eingedenken: a reconstruction of memories in a spatial present guided by our contemporary perceptions, ideas and knowledge. These two spatial dimensions—past and present—overlap and produce a vision of demands for a prospective present-future. It is this circular temporality that enables us to consider the political communal labor of mourning as a perennial resistance connected to what Tzul Tzul (2019a,b) defines as *trama comunitaria*—a communal fabric. We have seen this communal labor of mourning branching out in numerous ways to build antiracist alliances and practices of resistance, sustained by coalitional politics demanding reparative justice. These forms of speaking justice are part of a collective political process as the Unraveling the NSU Complex Tribunals (2017; 2021) demonstrates. In this sense, the political communal labor of mourning evolves in Ortega's (2019) sense of "becoming-with," forging connections through the sharing of a collective "resistant sorrow" that becomes, following Muñoz (2006, 125), an "integral part of everyday lives." In this context, demands for reparative justice and a caring commons are central, as we will see in the concluding chapter.

Notes

1 See https://www.bpb.de/politik/hintergrund-aktuell/68921/erstes-gastarbeiter-abkommen-20-12-2010.
2 See the law "Gesetz zur Förderung der Rückkehrbereitschaft von Ausländern," 28 November 1983 (BGBl. 1983 I 1377).
3 See https://www.inidu84.de/ and Facebook page: https://de-de.facebook.com/IniDu1984/.
4 Ibid.
5 Ibid.
6 Ibid.
7 Cana Bilir-Meier interviewed by Nina Prader: "Poetry as Survival Ritual: An Interview with Cana Bilir-Meier about Semra Ertan," 6 April 2021, *Berlinartlink*, https://www.berlinartlink.com/2021/04/06/cana-bilir-meier-interview-semra-ertan-poet-activist/.
8 See a short film entitled *Semra Ertan*, 2013, by her niece, Cana Bilir-Meier, https://vimeo.com/90241760; see also Cana Bilir-Meier reading Semra Ertan: https://www

.youtube.com/watch?v=IRqPNfrldvk; and remembrance by her sister Zühal Bilir-Meier "[…] sonder nauch das Recht haben, wie Menschen behandelt zu werden," *Malmoe*, 6 December 2019, https://www.malmoe.org/2019/12/06/sondern-auch-das-recht-haben-wie-menschen-behandelt-zu-werden/. See also Sultan Doughan's (2022) discussion of Cana Bilir-Meier's work and Semra Ertan's poem.

9 Initiative in Memory of Đỗ Anh Lân and Nguyễn Ngọc Châu, https://inihal-skestrasse.blackblogs.org/; see also podcast *Rice and Shine* by Minh Thu Tran und Vanessa Vu, 27 December 2021: "Hamburg 1980: Als der rechte Terror wieder auf-flammte," https://www.ardaudiothek.de/episode/rice-and-shine/hamburg-1980-als-der-rechte-terror-wieder-aufflammte-archiv/cosmo/10569269/.

10 This is a practice in some European cemeteries, where plots are rented for a specific period of time and need to be renewed or the remains moved to a different site.

11 See Facebook group Zu Gedenken an Ramazan Avci (In Memory of Ramazan Avci), https://www.facebook.com/groups/211618055586474/.

12 http://netzwerk-erinnerungsarbeit.de/?p=429

13 DoMiD; https://domid.org/en/news/contractwork-in-the-gdr/.

14 A digital chronicle of the racist events can be accessed here: https://www.hoyerswerda-1991.de/1991/vertragsarbeit.html. "Blindspot Rassismus in der DDR," 12 June 2019, The Initiative 12. August on racist attacks against Cuban contract workers in East Germany: https://www.malmoe.org/2019/12/06/blindspot-rassismus-in-der-ddr/.

15 https://www.amadeu-antonio-stiftung.de/en/about-us/.

16 As this case has not resulted in any prosecution, state authorities have not recon-structed evidence for each possibility.

17 See "Gegen uns. Betroffene im Gespräch über rechte Gewalt nach 1990 und die Verteidigung der solidarischen Gesellschaft," https://gegenuns.de/.

18 "Mehr als 30 Jahre nach Anschlag auf Asylbewerberheim: Generalbundesanwaltschaft erhebt Anklage," 3 August 2022, *Süddeutsche Zeitung*, https://www.sueddeutsche.de/politik/samuel-yeboah-saarlouis-brandanschlag-1.5632876; See also the flyer of the advocacy group Aktion 3.Welt Saar for a demonstration to honor Samuel Kofi Yeboah's memory: https://a3wsaar.de/neuigkeiten/demonstration-zum-20-todestag-von-samuel-yeboah.

19 In April 2022, Peter Werner S. was sentenced for committing the arson attack on the refugee camp on the 19th of September 1991 in Saarlouis, see: https://taz.de/Rechter-Mordanschlag-in-Saarlouis-1991/!5936113/. On the 27th of February 2024, Stefan St. was accused of having been the ideological spearhead behind the arson attack in Saarlouis, see https://taz.de/Rassistischer-Brandanschlag-in-Saarlouis/!5995238/.

20 The digital documentation of events by Initiative Pogrom 91 can be accessed here: https://www.hoyerswerda-1991.de/start.html.

21 Ibid.

22 https://www.hoyerswerda-1991.de/1991/vertreibung.html.

23 Manuel Pfohl, "Phuong Traum," 1 October 2008, *Stern*, https://www.stern.de/pano-rama/vietnamesen-in-deutschland-phuongs-traum-3757186.html.

24 Johannes Kulms, "Wenn Opfer nicht mehr schweigen wollen," 6 November 2017, *Deutschlandfunk Kultur*, https://www.deutschlandfunkkultur.de/moelln-25-jahre-nach-dem-brandanschlag-wenn-opfer-nicht-100.html.

25 See *ZDF info* feature: *Mölln - 20 Jahre nach dem Brand*, 23 December, 2012, https://www.youtube.com/watch?v=nWhM6LZEsc8.

26 Ibrahim Arslan interviewed for *Deutschlandfunk* by Matthias Dell, 31 October 2021, "Mölln, NSU, Hanau—Ibrahim Arslan über rechte Gewalt und Erinnerungskultur,"

https://www.deutschlandfunk.de/moelln-nsu-hanau-ibrahim-arslan-ueber-rechte -gewalt-und-erinnerungskultur-dlf-925b6033-100.html. Interview of Ibrahim Arslan by NSU Watch, 20 December 2020, "They deprived us of solidarity by archiving it for 27 years." https://www.nsu-watch.info/2020/12/they-deprived-us-of-solidarity -by-archiving-it-for-27-years-interview-with-ibrahim-arslan/.

27 NSU Tribunal: https://www.nsu-tribunal.de/en/.

28 Johannes Kulms interviews Ibrahim Arslan for *Deutschlandfunk*, 22 November 2017, https://www.deutschlandfunk.de/25-jahre-nach-dem-brandanschlag-in-moelln -gedenken-mit-100.html.

29 Möllner Rede im Exil / Mölln Speech in Exile, 28 January 2015, *Mölln 1992. Reclaim and Remember.* https://gedenkenmoelln1992.wordpress.com/2015/01/28/moellner -rede-im-exil-speech-of-moelln-in-exile-adetoun-kueppers-adebisi-in-memoriam-der -opfer-des-rassismus-in-deutschland-in-memoriam-victims-of-racism-germany/.

30 Deutsche Welle "Brandanschlag von Mölln: 'Meine Tochter hat noch einmal Papa gesagt'", see https://www.dw.com/de/brandanschlag-von-m%C3%B6lln-meine-tochter-hat-noch-einmal-papa-gesagt/a-41488181.

31 Mourning as the purest form of remembrance (all translations by author).

32 SWR, "Programm Nachtcafe, Mölln Überlebender Ibrahim Arslan," 28 April 2020, https://scontent-frt3-2.xx.fbcdn.net/v/t1.6435-9/94717750_4103507653023319 _8947450800750198784_n.jpg?stp=cp0_dst-jpg_e15_fr_q65&_nc_cat=109&ccb =1-7&_nc_sid=8024bb&_nc_ohc=iBp-7Am3mCgAX_befei&_nc_ht=scontent-frt3 -2.xx&oh=00_AT_weHEEqgK7jUPeLn91IpaqYlfaTMTt_QzE4x8m1i4TFA&oe =634D6325.

33 The German original reads: "Der Raum tritt an die Stelle der Zeit, der Augenblick an die Stelle des Ablaufs und das Unstetige an die Stelle eines Flußes." (Marchesoni 2016, 162).

34 In German: "etwas gerade jetzt erinnert wird, heißt das, dass es errinnerbar ist: Jede Erinnerung setzt so etwas wie ein 'Jetzt der Erinnerbarkeit' voraus, dessen Thematisierung zu einer Selbstbesinnung über die jeweils aktuellen Verhältnisse zwingt." (ibid).

35 The Asylkompromiss was unanimously passed on 26 May 1993 by the German Parliament, restricting the fundamental right to asylum anchored in the 1948/49 German Constitution from an individual right to one regulated by state agreed country protection status (cf., Poutrus 2019; Prenzel 2005).

36 https://www.deutschlandfunk.de/vor-25-jahren-der-brandanschlag-in-solingen-100 .html.

37 "Kanzler Kohl weigert sich zur Trauerfeier zu gehen," 29 May 2013, *Süddeutsche Zeitung*, https://www.sueddeutsche.de/politik/brandanschlag-von-solingen-1993-rech tsextremismus-1.1683458-2.

38 See Peter Maxwill, 29 May 2018, "Ich spüre den Schmerz wie am ersten Tag," *Der Spiegel*, https://www.spiegel.de/panorama/gesellschaft/solingen-anschlagsopfer -spricht-ueber-den-brandanschlag-von-1993-a-1207379.html.

39 Interview with Pagonis Pagonakis, WDR-Archiv, 2015, https://www1.wdr.de/archiv /solingen/jahrestagbrandanschlagsolingen101.html.

40 See Mevlüde Genç's twitter condolences to the families that have lost their loved ones in the racist murders in Hanau, 19 February 2020: https://twitter.com/aktuelle _stunde/status/1230903363275018243?lang=en.

41 Ibid.

42 Interview with Pagonis Pagonakis: https://www1.wdr.de/archiv/solingen/jahrest agbrandanschlagsolingen101.html.

43 The NSU is also believed to have caused life-threatening injuries to a police officer and committed three bomb attacks in which approximately 20 people were injured, some of them severely. It is also suspected of 15 bank robberies (http://www.nsu -tribunal.de/en). See also accounts of family members in Barbara John (ed.), *Unsere Wunden kann die Zeit nicht heilen* (Bonn: Herder, 2014).

44 See minutes in the special issue of the *Bundeszentrale für politische Bildung* (bdp), 12 March 2014, https://www.bpb.de/themen/rechtsextremismus/dossier-rechtsextremismus /180528/protokolle-des-nsu-untersuchungsausschusses-im-bundestag/.

45 See Deutscher Bundestag, Drucksache 17/14600 (11 August 2013), Beschlus sempfehlung und Bericht des 2. Untersuchungsausschusses nach Artikel 44 des Grund gesetzes: https://dserver.bundestag.de/btd/17/146/1714600.pdf.

46 Matthias Bölinger, Deutsche Welle, 09 March 2013, "Eine Jugend unter Verdacht," https://www.dw.com/de/eine-jugend-unter-verdacht/a-16659331.

47 Sefa Defterli, video documentation of the demonstration "Kein 10. Opfer in Kassel" on 6 May 2006: https://pad.ma/CTC/editor/00:00:00,00:05:43.321#?embed=true.

48 The archive of the Initiative Keupstraße ist Überall! can be seen here: http://keup-strasse-ist-ueberall.de.

49 Newspaper interview with Gamze Kubaşık in *Zeit*, 27 October 2017, "Ich glaube nicht mehr an den Rechtsstaat," https://blog.zeit.de/nsu-prozess-blog/2017/10/27/ ich-glaube-nicht-mehr-an-den-rechtsstaat/?wt_ref=https%3A%2F%2Fwww.google .de%2F&wt_t=1663801221418.

50 Conversations: "It's not over. The joint plaintiffs speak out one year after the NSU trial," with Adile and Semiya Şimşek, Elif Kubaşık, and curators Aysun Bademsoy and Ayşe Güleç, moderated by Azadê Peşmen, 6 September 2019, Haus der Kulturen der Welt, Berlin: https://www.hkw.de/en/app/mediathek/video/75492.

51 Tribunal NSU-Komplex auflösen: https://www.nsu-tribunal.de/tribunal/.

52 Konrad Litschko, "Die geheime Akte," *Taz*, 4 November 2021, https://taz.de/ Verschlusssache-NSU/!5809436/.

53 See opening talk with Hito Steyerl, Ayşe Güleç and Amelie Deuflhard, 13 April 2021, on the occasion of the exhibition "Kein 'Einzelfall'. Rechtsradikale Realitäten in Deutschland," Kampnagel, Hamburg: https://www.youtube.com/watch?v =WFoaKbV8Nbo (accessed September 2022).

54 Kutlu Yurtsever in a 2016 documentary by Andreas Maus, "Der Kuaför aus der Keupstraße," https://www.youtube.com/watch?v=R8PnnuOUlwc.

55 See endnote 47.

56 The statements of the family members during the Munich trial were performed by theater artists following the tradition of verbatim theater such as *Die NSU Monologue*, directed by Michael Ruf and the theater collective Bühne für Menschenrechte, see https://buehne-fuer-menschenrechte.org/en/nsu-monologues/.

57 Deutsche Welle "Germany pays tribute to neo-Nazi victims," https://www.dw.com/ en/germany-pays-tribute-to-neo-nazi-victims/a-15760217.

58 See Bayern Rundfunk (BR), "NSU-Prozess. 390. Verhandlungtag," (Day 390 of the hearings: 22 November 2017): https://www.br.de/nachricht/nsu-prozess/171122 -tagebuch-gerichtsreporter-100.html.

59 "Halitstraße Jetzt!" *Malmoe* 90, https://www.malmoe.org/2019/12/06/halitstrasse -jetzt/.

Chapter 7

MOURNING'S JUSTICE: CONVIVIALITY INFRASTRUCTURE OF A CARING COMMONS

Introduction: No Time to Mourn

Also ich bin mir hundert Prozent sicher, solange wir keine Aufklärung bekommen und solange wir keine Gerechtigkeit bekommen, werden die Menschen nicht in ihren Gräbern ruhen.[1]

Gamze Kubaşık and Elif Kubaşık in conversation with Onur Suzan Nobrega. (2021c, 76)

Das Kämpfen hat mich daran gehindert zu trauern.[2]

(ibid., 62)

The words of Gamze Kubaşık above are from a conversation she and her mother, Elif Kubaşık, had with Onur Suzan Nobrega in April 2021. Gamze's father, **Mehmet Kubaşık**, was murdered by the NSU (Nationalist Socialist Underground) on 4 April 2006. Commemorating their loss, Gamze and Elif Kubaşık reaffirm their constant search for justice. Echoing other family members, relatives and friends of the victims of racist violence, they recount how they experienced a second racist attack after the loss of their loved one. The families of the victims could not withdraw and mourn on their own time and in their own way, as they were confronted with police investigations that treated them and their lost loved ones as prime suspects (Tribunale 2021). Additionally, access to the dead bodies of their loved ones was restricted and they were unable to mourn in accordance with their personal wishes and religious customs.

While the families mourned the loss of their loved ones, the German public remained mostly silent (Michaelsen 2015). There was no nationwide public mourning at the moment these racist crimes were revealed, nor did crowds gather in public squares to grieve for the loss of these members of

German society. Despite their insistence on creating their own representation, vocabulary and analysis concerning the origin and nature of the murders and communicating this to the public, the families received no response or gesture of shared grief from the wider political and civil society (Utlu 2013). This environment has led to what Gamze Kubaşık defines as the impossibility to have time to mourn or what Çiğdem Inan (2022) describes as "dispossessed mourning", defining the inability of a politics of grief under circumstances of racist violence. Yet, as I have shown throughout this book, the families, relatives and friends have continued to raise their voices and make their views known notwithstanding the hurdles and barriers confronting them. In 2006, as we have seen in the previous chapter, the families in Kassel and Dortmund organized public vigils, where they mobilized their situated migrant knowledge to address the reconstruction of facts and the racist nature of these crimes (Güleç 2018a,b).

It is this tenacious labor of telling their story, bearing witness and articulating claims of justice that I have discussed here as the political communal labor of mourning. In spite of the attempted silencing (ibid.) and "systemic oblivion" (Nobrega et al. 2021a) the families have faced from state authorities and society as a whole, the grief that has entered their lives has yielded feelings, corporeal responses, actions and words. The families of the NSU victims share this with other accounts of mourning we have been listening and witnessing throughout this book. The mothers and sisters of #SayHerName, the members of the Arslan and Genç families, Women in Exile and others have repeatedly borne witness and spoken justice, despite the emotional, physical and material exhaustion they have experienced throughout their grieving journey. This communal political labor of mourning has traversed my own personal grief for my parents. Through them, I am constantly reminded of the *Gastarbeiter* history of Germany. With them, I have tried to understand how mourning has entered and shaped my life.

Through my bearing witness and accountable listening, I have followed the words and actions of this communal labor of mourning transformed into political action. I have understood how mourning as *Trauerarbeit* is entrenched in the cycles of life (Tzul Tzul 2018a,b) and how it articulates the "death-life continuum" (Rodríguez Aguilera 2021). Listening to Leanne Betasamosake Simpson (2014), we have understood how these practices embody and sustain knowledge based on relational ontology, and we have been attentive to Güleç's (2018a,b) analysis of "situated migrant knowledge." We have discussed disaffection in relation to Kien Nghi Ha and Sanchita Basu's observations on the absence of public mourning and engaged with Mariana Ortega's (2019) "becoming-with" to trace the communal labor behind these political articulations. The struggles against the EU necroborders; the movements against feminicide; the resistance of #SayHerName to misogy-noir state and police violence; Women in Exile's abolitionist labor against the *Lager* and the coloniality of migration; and the families, relatives and friends who tirelessly seek truth and justice for the racist murders committed in Germany over decades are all sustained by a continuous and intense grief work that speaks to the communal labor of decolonial mourning. This grief work uncovers a political practice of contestation and resistance, engaging with the pain of loss but also with communal ethics of reciprocity, respect, trust and emotional and material support. In this way, the political labor of mourning articulates practices of common justice. It speaks of accountability and reparation by addressing representational, distributive and restorative justice. Looking at these dimensions of justice, this chapter concludes with some thoughts on the caring commons and the infrastructure of conviviality. We will enter this discussion by bearing witness to the accounts of my neighbors in Hanau.

My Neighbors: Hanau 2020

Say their names!

We are mourning.
We are angry.
We are calling the problem by its name.
It is racism.
We do not want a society that discriminates people in everyday life
due to their skin color, their name, their religion, their gender or their
sexual orientation.
Racism kills.

#Hanau[3]

On 19 February 2020, nine of my neighbors—**Ferhat Unvar, Gökhan Gültekin, Hamza Kurtović, Said Nesar Hashemi, Mercedes Kierpacz, Sedat Gürbüz, Kalojan Velkov, Vili Viorel Păun** and **Fatih Saraçoğlu**—were murdered by a Nazi in Hanau, a city in southern Hessen, Germany. Afterward, the shooter executed his 72-year-old mother, **Gabriele Rathjen**, and committed suicide. I was not in Germany at the time. When I heard the news, my body began to tremble and I felt both petrified and restless. Hanau is just one metro stop away from Offenbach, where I live. The populations of these two multicultural cities, Hanau and Offenbach, are multifaith, agnostic or atheist and comprise people with diverse geographical backgrounds. Some arrived in the 1950s and 1960s as Gastarbeiter from

Italy, Turkey, Greece, ex-Yugoslavia, Morocco, Spain and Portugal to work in the growing industrial, cleaning, gastronomy and hospitality sectors; others came in the 1970s as family members and still others arrived in the 1980s as migrants from the EU or refugees from Eastern Europe and conflict zones in Turkey, Africa, Asia and Latin America. This immigration has continued during the last few decades with newcomers finding work in mostly low-paid and middle-range jobs such as in the airline industry and financial sectors. Yet, this region, in particular Frankfurt am Main, is also known for its international recruitment of highly paid employees for the financial, IT and engineering sectors. Over 50 percent of Hanau and Offenbach's populations have migration, exile or diaspora biographies. Over 60 percent of schoolchildren have grandparents or parents who were born abroad. Multilingualism is a reality in everyday life, as is cultural mixing. In this region, I feel sheltered—with no need to explain my name or identity. These are places where a creolized convivial culture (Gutiérrez Rodríguez and Tate 2015) has developed over recent decades and where cosmopolitan Jewish culture once thrived and is still present (Gelbin 2017). Today, Muslims, Jews, Christians, agnostics and people of other faiths coexist in Hanau, Offenbach and Frankfurt, in this place my Andalusian transculturalized self feels at home.

Ferhat Unvar, Gökhan Gültekin, Hamza Kurtović, Said Nesar Hashemi, Mercedes Kierpacz, Sedat Gürbüz, Kalojan Velkov, Vili Viorel Păun and *Fatih Saraçoğlu waren auch Zuhause in Hanau und einige auch in Dietzenbach und Erlensee. Einige von ihnen waren in Hanau geboren, ihre Eltern oder Großeltern waren immigriert. Sie waren Hanauer*innen. Sie wurden in ihrem Zuhause ermordet.* I automatically wrote these sentences in German. They were at home in Hanau; some of them at home in Dietzenbach or Erlensee. Those places were home, places where they felt sheltered, far away from racist harassment and attacks. In Kesselstadt, the neighborhood in Hanau where most of them lived, they felt ordinary. There, the color of their hair or skin or their names were not exceptional. On 19 February 2020, this assumption was shattered. Yet, as the families, relatives, friends and advocates keep reminding the German and international public, Kesselstadt and Hanau are still their homes.

Both places reacted immediately and intensely to the killings, publicly and politically demonstrating their readiness to deal with these murderous acts and demanding justice.[4] Public gatherings took place all over Germany, and the Hanau families were immediately connected to other families, relatives and friends who had lost their loved ones to antisemitic and racist intersectional violence. Solidarity networks were quickly built, and Hanau has taken a significant leading political role in condensing the demands for justice of these collectives into four words: (1) remembrance, (2) justice, (3) investigation and (4) consequences (see Initiative 19. Februar,[5] Unvar 2023). With these cornerstones, Initiative 19. Februar Hanau, formed by the family members, relatives and friends immediately after the attacks (Initiative 19. Februar Hanau 2021; Cholia and Jänicke 2021),[6] has demanded an exhaustive investigation of the cases and full-scale legal prosecution. It is in this regard that I consider their political work to be an expression of the political communal labor of mourning. These acts of communal mourning were instant, supportive and resourceful. Numerous marches, vigils and events linked to their demands for adequate remembrance, social justice, a thorough investigation and political consequences were organized. Initiative 19. Februar Hanau has not allowed anyone the opportunity to distort the facts around the murderous events, and has stopped any attempt at disinformation and victim blaming. For the vigils held on the first anniversary of the murders, they prepared public screenings of the current state of the police investigation and legal proceedings. They kept their supporters informed about their own investigations and kept demanding an independent legal prosecution. The initiative has also addressed the material, symbolic and emotional challenges the family members encountered in their lives after the racist murders of their loved ones. Initiative 19. Februar Hanau has, then, committed to negotiating with authorities about reparations for the relatives by suggesting a fund for victims of right-wing terror. In July 2021, the state of Hessen approved the fund. Some of the family members were no longer able to continue living in the same neighborhood due to proximity to the murderer's home and are still unable to work due to emotional and psychological trauma (Saciak 2021).

Nonetheless, like the political organizations and actors discussed in previous chapters, they continue the affective labor and politics of communal mourning by bearing witness and speaking out on—as well as demanding—intersectional justice. Initiative 19. Februar Hanau demands (i) adequate remembrance of migrant, refugee, People of Color[7] and Black Lives; (ii) social justice for the victims; (iii) an exhaustive investigation of the course of events of the crime and the actors implicated in it, and the prosecution and indictment of the perpetrators and (iv) political consequences for the perpetrators of racist attacks and for systemic racism in the police, media and politics.[8] In what follows, I discuss these demands in more detail, in order to explore the relationship between the political communal labor of mourning and demands for justice.

Adequate Remembrance

The labor of mourning goes on—traversing my family's history, the loss of my parents, the killing of refugees attempting to reach the European Union, the murders of migrants, refugees, Black people and People of Color in Germany, the NSU and Hanau. As I was abroad, I could not go to my neighbors and mourn with them. I could not be part of the mourning marches organized in the months immediately following the murders. When I returned to Offenbach a few weeks later, a six-month anniversary commemoration with relatives and friends took place in Hanau. The city had announced that the rally organized by Initiative 19. Februar Hanau could not take place due to the Covid-19 pandemic,[9] so there was an assembly at Freiheitsplatz, Hanau's main square, instead. Initiative 19. Februar Hanau, together with the relatives and friends of the victims, invited us to the vigil and rally to mourn, remember and bear justice. I listened to relatives and friends remembering their loved ones.[10]

Nesrîn Unvar, the sister of **Ferhat Unvar**, echoes his words when she states that one is only dead when forgotten. Ferhat was 23 years old and had just completed his training as a heating and gas system installer when he was shot at the Arena Bar in the Kesselstadt neighborhood of Hanau. The son of Serpil Temiz Unvar and Metin Unvar was born in Hanau. Along with Nesrîn, he had two younger brothers, Mirkan Can and Mirza. Much of Unvar's extended family—uncles, aunts and cousins—all lived in Hanau. He was at home in Hanau, where he felt safe and planned to open a gas and heating installation store. At the assembly, his mother, Serpil, tells the audience that she never would have thought that a man who lived just a few blocks away would one day murder her son in his own hometown. She speaks about the institutional racism her son experienced in school—how, for example, a teacher told her that he would leave if her son remained in the school. She tells us how she would tell her son to be twice as good in school as German children, otherwise he would have little chance of finding a job. She wonders why she even needed to give her children this advice. In an interview by Carolina Torres for the weekly magazine *Bento*,[11] Serpil Temiz Unvar shares the paradox her son was forced to deal with: although he had a German passport, he was not treated in school as a German. Ferhat grew up with the paradox of feeling at home in Germany while often being marked as an *Ausländer*, a foreigner, in his everyday life. The murderer acted on the grounds of this last assumption. As Serpil tells Torres (ibid.), she suspects that her son was killed because of the color of his hair, his name or his religion.

In the interview with Torres (2020), Serpil Temiz Unvar describes her mourning as subsisting between life and death: "I cannot die and I cannot live. I am somewhere in between. But I need to move on. I draw force from my pain." Serpil Unvar together with her family and supporters have initiated the Bildungsinitiative Ferhat Unvar on the date of his birth, the 24th of November, in 2020.[12] The Bildungsinitiative together with the Initiative 19. Februar Hanau have demanded for clarifications, why the police did not immediately act upon the statement published on social media by the murderer just two weeks before he committed the crimes. Serpil also remembers the moment the names were read aloud by the police, without any gesture of compassion and how the families felt the heartlessness of this situation.

Social Justice

At the assembly commemorating the Hanau victims at Freiheitsplatz on 22 August 2020, Armin Kurtović, the father of **Hamza Kenan Kurtović**, spoke about how the families waited in a hall for almost 10 hours on the night of the shootings. Hamza was 22 years old, and his family had come to Germany from Bosnia and Herzegovina. He had just finished his apprenticeship as a warehouse specialist and was celebrating a new job he had started three weeks earlier. Hamza was born in Hanau and lived with his brothers, Aziz and Karim, and his sister Ajla. His father tells the assembly how the death of their children was announced without any official gesture of sympathy extended to the family members. Furthermore, no acknowledgment or cultural sensitivity was displayed in relation to the families' mourning, particularly the rituals associated with their Muslim faith. Due to the lengthy autopsy process, family members were not given the opportunity to say goodbye to their dead children and brothers. Armin Kurtović felt they were treated as second-class citizens, and wondered if the treatment would have been different had their names been regular German ones.

Operating on a racist matrix, the shooter chose his targets by their physical appearances and the places they frequented. On that day in February 2020, he began his rampage at the Midnight shisha lounge in the city center, where he murdered one of the co-owners, **Sedat Gürbüz,** and injured several guests. **Kalojan Velkov**, who was working in the vicinity of Midnight, was also gunned down. From there, the assassin headed to Kesselstadt, a multicultural neighborhood where he himself and most of his victims lived. There, he entered a kiosk and then the Arena Bar, where the emergency exit door happened to be locked, and murdered **Ferhat Unvar, Gökhan Gültekin, Hamza Kurtović, Said Nesar Hashemi** and **Mercedes Kierpacz**. **Fatih Saraçoğlu,** who was in the area of the bar, was also fatally shot. Nearby, the police also discovered **Vili Viorel Păun** dead in his car. It is believed that **Păun** followed the murderer to Kesselstadt after seeing him in the center of Hanau. Before he was killed, he called the police emergency number in Hanau at least three times, but no one picked up; nor was his call transferred to another police station, due to outdated technical infrastructure. Initiative

19. Februar Hanau has raised questions about the police's failure to answer the emergency call and the locked exit door at Arena Bar.[13] In summer 2021, the police investigation concluded that these two situations could not be linked to police negligence or deliberate action. Still, the initiative continues to question these suspicious circumstances by linking them to demands for social justice.

Armin Kurtović relates to how racism has permeated their institutional encounters and social lives. In an interview with Franziska Bulban on 21 August 2020,[14] Armin and his wife, Dijana Kurtović, comment on their bewilderment when the police described their son as "oriental." Their son was blonde, and people were often surprised when they learned his name, Hazan, and that he was Muslim. Armin Kurtović feels also abandoned by the state authorities. Though he holds a German citizenship, his son still became a target of lethal racist violence. The question remains unanswered of why the shooter, who had been diagnosed with severe mental health issues, was even allowed to own a gun. The political communal labor of mourning of the family members addresses the unexplained circumstances, mistakes and failures of the police and state authorities. Organized as Initiative 19. Februar Hanau, they voice their analysis, observations, questions and demands, calling for accountability of the state and the police and asking for social justice, material support and an end to antisemitism and racism. They have demanded an exhaustive police investigation from the very start.

Exhaustive Investigation

For Çetin Gültekin, sharing his grief means remembering his only brother, **Gökhan Gültekin**, by bearing witness and rendering justice to the life he lived. Born in Hanau, Gökhan was 37 years old and ran his own moving company. He sometimes earned additional money by working in the kiosk that became a target of the racist attacks in Kesselstadt. He was planning to get married soon and he took care of his parents, particularly his father, who was suffering from cancer. After the death of Gökhan, their father died too, Çetin tells the participants in the rally.[15] For his mother, the loss of both her son and her husband has been unbearable. Unable to continue living in their apartment so close to the crime scene, she has moved to Turkey. Çetin is relentless in his search for justice for his brother and the other Hanau victims. As one of Initiative 19. Februar Hanau's most public actors, he is attentive to an accurate and critical analysis of the events and circumstances that led to the murder of his brother and neighbors.

Raising questions about the police investigation and the work of the public prosecutor, Çetin publicly denounces the investigation's lack of diligence.[16] He is still waiting for answers to his questions: Why did the ambulance arrive at the crime scene earlier than the police, even though the police department was just a few blocks away? How could it be that the murderer's social media manifesto preceding his crimes went undetected by cyber investigation units? How could the murderer be permitted to own a weapon when he had been diagnosed with mental health issues? Why were his numerous rants and complaints, revealing his potential to commit harm, ignored by the public prosecutor's office? Çetin wonders how the same public prosecutor's office would have reacted if the person in question had had a Kurdish, Turkish or Arabic name. Would it have been possible for somebody with such a name to own a weapon after writing letters to the attorney general in Hessen in 2019 voicing violent conspiratorial views?[17] For Çetin, these questions have not been answered. Nor, as he remarks, have the inconsistencies in the investigation of the deaths of his brother and the other victims been resolved. Questions regarding the managing of the crime scenes by the police still remain unanswered. Even an official apology or gesture of sympathy at this moment would have meant a lot to the families, but no such gestures were made. Nor have authorities made any public commitment to combat racism.[18] During the commemoration on 22 August 2020, Çetin concludes, "Hanau should not be one stop. It should be the final stop. Hanau needs to be a turning point. Hanau should be a crossroads—from now on we take a new path."[19]

Political Consequences

In the interview with Franziska Bulban, **Mercedes Kierpacz's** mother, Sofia Kierpacz, and her son, Colorado Kierpacz, share their grief and demands for social justice.[20] Mercedes, a 35- year-old Romnja, was born and raised in Offenbach with her three sisters; her family had emigrated from Poland. Her 16-year-old son and her 9-year-old daughter, Lorena-Génevière, grieve for their mom. She was a single mother and worked daily in the kiosk next to the Arena Bar, where she was shot. That day she went to the kiosk to buy pizza for her family, when the perpetrator appeared. Her father, Filip Goman, tells Bulban that he has been unable to sleep, as his medication is no longer working. On the evening of the murders, he waited for almost 20 hours until he was allowed to access the scene of the attack. He immediately recognized the body of his daughter. The fact that the murderer had made public that he was planning to kill racialized people still spins in his head. He raises similar questions to those posed by Çetin Gültekin: how was it possible that the perpetrator had a weapon, even though he had communicated on social media as well as to authorities his intent to kill? Filip Goman indignantly states that the crimes cannot be undone. Asking for reparations for the families, he demands more safety and financial support for his grandchildren, who have lost a mother that can never be replaced.

The father and sister of **Said Nesar Hashemi**, Mir Salam and Saida Hashemi, tell Torres[21] about the need for antiracist memorials commemorating the victims. Said Nesar was born in Hanau and had four siblings: his older sister Saida, his older brother Said Etris and his two younger brothers. Said Etris Hashemi was also in the Arena Bar where his brother was killed but survived the racist attack after several weeks in intensive care. Said Nesar was 21 years old; having completed an apprenticeship in machine and installation management in the company where his father worked, he was training to become a state-approved technician. Hanau was his home and he enjoyed living in Kesselstadt. The family recalls how they were not allowed access to Nesar's body for more than a week after his death, with no official explanation given. No one seemed to care about their feelings or their cultural bereavement customs. As Etris says to Torres, they are still waiting for an apology from the authorities. Advocating for a differentiated analysis, he draws attention to how anti-Muslim racism works by constructing a whole community as perpetrators and a threat to society; this systemic racism directly led to the deaths of his brother and the other victims in Hanau (ibid). For Etris, the media and politicians who mobilize anti-Muslim racism need to also be held accountable for these murderous actions.

Niculescu and Iulia Păun, the parents of **Vili Viorel Păun**, make similar comments regarding the loss of their son. In an interview with Franziska Bulban,[22] they wonder if their son might have seen the murderer in Heumarkt, a square located in the city center. Vili Viorel, a Romanian Rom, was on his way home after delivering the last parcels of the day, when he might have seen the shooter and decided to follow him to Kesselstadt. His body was found in his car in front of the building where the crime was committed. His father told the media that he was almost home when he decided to follow the shooter in order to prevent further killings. As Niculescu tells the reporter, "My son tried to stop the shooter. He is a hero—for Hanau, for Germany. But we are waiting in vain for the authorities to react, and we have only heard empty promises. We still do not know what happened: we need an exhaustive investigation of the course of the crime, and the people in charge need to be made accountable for the failures that led to this crime" (Torres 2020). Iulia and Niculescu Păun only learned of their son's death after contacting the police. It is not clear why the police did not contact them immediately after the shooting. "We are calling for political consequences" (ibid.), they repeat every time they speak to the public. Like the other family members of the victims of Hanau, they have been waiting for further signs of investigation and clarification by the public prosecutor's office.[23] However, in July 2021 it was determined that the police station Südosthessen was technically not equipped to handle parallel calls—phone calls could therefore not be diverted to other police stations.²⁴ In September 2020, a memorial dedicated to Vili Viorel Păun and the other victims of the Hanau murders was erected in the Kesselstadt parking lot. However, the family members of the victims of Hanau are calling for a monument to be built in the center of Hanau, in Kurt-Schumacher-Platz, where Vili Viorel confronted the shooter. On 18 June 2021, Vili Viorel posthumously received the Medal for Civil Courage of the state of Hessen. Vili Viorel was the only child of Iulia and Niculescu; today, they feel depleted of any life energy.

Born in Iskilip, Turkey, **Fatih Saraçoğlu** was 34 years old and had moved from Regensburg to Hanau three years prior to his murder. He was very close to his parents and his partner, Diana. He was taking a friend to a hotel when the shooter killed him in Heumarkt. Hayrettin, his brother, and Derya Saraçoğlu, his sister-in-law, remember him in an interview with Bulban.²⁵ Fatih had opened a pest control business in Hanau. His murder has destroyed Derya and Hayrretin's lives. Derya Saraçoğlu speaks about her husband's depression; he has withdrawn from family life and it is up to her to keep the family going. Her husband is thinking of leaving Germany, but for Derya, Germany is her home. As Derya tells Bulban: "I was born here, German is the language I think and speak in. I don't see why I shouldn't belong to this country" (Bulban 2020). As is the case for the other families, they are demanding accountability and reparation for the families.

Vaska Zlateva, the cousin of **Kaloyan Velkov**, speaks to Torres²⁶ about how her cousin arrived in Germany two years ago from Bulgaria. They both lived near Hanau, in Erlensee, and Kaloyan was planning to bring his wife and 8-year-old son to Germany. A 33-year-old Bulgarian Rom, Kaloyan Velkov was employed as a truck driver. He was working temporally at La Votre Bar, near the Midnight shisha lounge in Heumarkt, where he was murdered. Vaska Zlateva supported her cousin when he arrived in Germany. On the day of the crime, she took a taxi and went to the bar to ask the police if her cousin was there. No answers were given; a week later the police and representatives of the *Ausländeramt* (immigration office) came to ask her if she needed any help. Vaska has moved out of her apartment: she could no longer bear to live there and has been struggling emotionally. Like the other family members, she too raised the question of why the police did not arrive immediately at the crime scene and how the murderer could publish his hate on the internet without being flagged.

Emiş und Selahattin Gürbüz, the parents of **Sedat Gürbüz,** tell Torres²⁷ how their 29-year-old son was planning his wedding. Born in Langen, he lived in Dietzenbach, where a memorial in his name was inaugurated in August 2021. Sedat worked in logistics and co-owned the Midnight shisha lounge where he was murdered. They recalled how much he loved summers.

During the 2020 assembly, his mother tells the audience how she still waits every night for him to come back home. Emiş Gürbüz arrived in Germany 50 years ago, her husband 32 years ago; Dietzenbach is their home. As Emiş tells the reporter, the victims of Hanau are not only nine, they are hundreds: the "families, the friends, the grandparents are still alive" but they are "living corpses" (Torres 2020). Like the other relatives, Emiş und Selahattin Gürbüz are calling for an exhaustive investigation and for the file to remain open until it is clear how this crime could have occurred.

In December 2021, an independent investigative commission (UNA 20/2), which completed its work by summer 2023, was set up by the Landtag (the parliament of Hessen).[28] Comprising 15 elected politicians, this commission invited various witnesses to address the failures observed and experienced by the family members during the investigation of the murders, as well as the treatment of the family members by the police and the federal state prosecutor investigation. The Initiative 19. Februar collated these observations in a report entitled "Kette des Versagens"[29] (Catalogue of Failures, 2021). As Oscar Herzog Astaburuaga (2023) notes, the dossier contains information and an analysis of 10 aspects of the reconstruction of the prosecution process: (1) police deployment on the night, raising concerns that it took five hours "between the identification of the killer and the storming of the house" (ibid., 3), even though the address of the killer was known to the police; especially concerning is that "thirteen of the special forces officers on duty" that night were members of fascist police WhatsApp groups (ibid.); (2) the blocking of the emergency exit at Arena Bar; (3) the treatment of witnesses who were victims of the attack, but were approached by some politicians and the media as suspects (ibid., 5); (4) the emergency phone line; (5) the negligence, denial and disrespect shown toward the families and survivors on the night of the massacre by the police and the media (ibid., 6); (6) victims' family members were confronted with racist stereotypes and attitudes by the police and media (ibid., 7); (7) the failure to heed early warnings and thus forestall the attack; in 2018 the murderer had already been seen armed with an assault rifle by neighbors in the vicinity of the places where the attacks later occurred in 2020; (8) online posts by the offender were already available in August 2019, including a racist manifesto, video and other materials; (9) mental health, criminal record and ordnance licensing: despite the killer's mental illness record (he was forcibly detained in a psychiatric hospital in 2002), he was still able to procure a weapon license (ibid., 8); and (10) flaws in the investigations defending state actions. In the independent investigative commission, 10 points are further examined: (1) the perpetrator and his father, (2) the perpetrator's access to the murder weapon, (3) the emergency number's failure to respond, (4) the bolted up emergency exit in Arena

Bar, (5) police investigations at the crime scene, (6) the police's operational structure, (7) confirmation and recognition by the police that this was a racist crime, (8) the circumstances and the delayed raid on the perpetrator's apartment, (9) the treatment of the family members and relatives by the police and (10) the violent attack on a youth center (JUZ Kesselstadt) by the perpetrator in 2017. The family members, the Initiative 19. Februar and the Bildungsinitiative Ferhat Unvar hope that some of these questions regarding the police, the perpetrator and his father will finally be answered.

In this section, we have listened to the memories of relatives and friends. We have borne witness to their pain and demands for justice. We have attended to their stories and their analysis of the events. We have seen that the question of common justice is reflected in the different accounts and demands of the family members, relatives and friends who form part of Initiative 19. Februar Hanau and the Bildungsinitiative Ferhat Unvar. Bringing us back to decolonial mourning as an expression of common justice, this political grief work speaks to questions of accountability, representation and reparation.

Common Justice: Accountability, Representation and Reparation

As we have seen throughout the previous chapters, decolonial mourning as affective labor and political action speaks about enacting intersectional justice (Crenshaw 2017). It engages with the pain caused by loss and its transformation into a political force. Following the accounts of the families, friends and relatives, we have witnessed their communal struggles and collective organizing of campaigns and tribunals, the creation of multisited archives and the publication of their investigations and analysis of these situations. As political action, the labor of mourning mobilizes and materializes a collective urge for social justice and radical change. It is in this regard that the communal political labor of mourning addresses common justice on three levels: (1) representational, (2) distributive and (3) transformative.

Representational justice: Epistemic justice

In my discussion of Gillian Rose's concept of inaugural mourning in Chapter 3, I looked at how communal grief work makes the suffering and pain of loss "visible" and "speakable." It creates a representation and, as Liz Stanley (2002, 2) further develops, it reinvents the "political life of the community." The unfolding of mourning as a material act makes us realize "with what consequences 'lives' are written about, and the complex and ultimately unknowable relationship that 'written lives' have to 'lives lived'" (ibid., 3). Stanley formulates this observation in regard to working with archival materials (written lives) and attempting to reconstruct the lives lived. It is through this work that she approaches "representable justice" (ibid.) by giving voice to the experiences of justice and injustice in the process of mourning. Acknowledging the presence of the "lives lived" and their connection to the living, representable justice is realized through the work that goes into allowing "the other fully to depart, and hence fully to be regained beyond sorrow" (Rose 1996, 35).

I have engaged with this labor of mourning and the lives lived of those lost to colonial modern structural intersectional violence through the accounts of the family members, relatives and friend. I have listened to numerous stories and engaged with Kimberlé Crenshaw's (African American Policy Forum, Pt. 11, 2020) storytelling as the radical political work of remembering and speaking justice. In a similar manner, the relatives, friends and supporters organized around Initiative 19. Februar Hanau, the Bildungsinitiative Ferhat Unvar, the Tribunal NSU-Komplex Auflösen, the Arslan family, Women in Exile, the #NiUnaMenos movement, the NGO Cruzando Fronteras and other organizations are developing a new language and practice of bearing witness, demanding accountability and reparations and, ultimately, acting and speaking justice. Furthermore, they are expanding the epistemological framework of representation in regard to colonial entanglements and spatial connections, while also contributing to an epistemology of resistance (Medina 2012). Their analysis of racism challenges and interrogates monoethnic, monocultural and monolingual accounts of national history. As Initiative 19. Februar Hanau asserts, the attacks in Hanau and their victims belong to German society.[30] Hanau represents a landmark in the series of racist attacks during the last five decades in Germany. As the initiative reminds its German audience, it "is the duty of our society to not forget this" (ibid.). This acknowledgement refers to both the right to counter and create a new framework of representation and the need to change the material conditions of entangled global inequalities as well (Gutiérrez Rodríguez and Reddock 2021). In other words: remembrance works toward distributive justice.

Distributive justice: Reparations

Within the context of emancipatory politics, the communal labor of mourning binds disparate social groups together in their yearning and struggle for social justice. Thus, as Judith Butler (2015, 26) notes in regard to the political subjectivity emanating from the assembly, "when bodies gather as they do to express their indignation and to enact their plural existence in public space, they are also making broader demands; they are demanding to be recognized, to be valued, they are exercising a right to appear, to exercise freedom, and they are demanding a livable life" (ibid., 43). The demand for "livable" lives has been put forth in the previous chapters of this book. This demand involves legal recognition but also material-infrastructural support.

As we have seen, with their statement "there is no justice, there is just us," the members of #SayHerName rely on their own infrastructure of support. Like other actors in this book, such as Women in Exile, Initiative 19. Februar Hanau and the Tribunal NSU-Komplex auflösen, their demands address concrete material claims in terms of financial and social support and access to adequate housing, healthcare and education. The experience of structural inequalities coupled with intersectional violence shapes the everyday lives of these actors. Some of the families lack the financial means to cover the costs related to bereavement, the funeral, legal representation and the need for individual and community care. Some were forced to move away from the neighborhood or the home where they had experienced the violence. Others were so affected by the traumatic impact of these crimes that they could no longer continue working, lost their jobs or had to interrupt their studies. This is why the question of reparations is so vital. In recent years, political movements in the form of anticolonial (Beckles 2013) and abolitionist (Davis 2005; Gilmore 2007; Cullors 2019) struggles have demanded reparations.

A grouping of 20 countries of the Caribbean Community[31] (CARICOM) promotes anticolonial reparation campaigns directed at the former colonial European powers. Haiti, for example, requested reparations from France in 2014.[32] In 2019, the University of the West Indies and the University of Glasgow signed the first-ever agreement for slavery reparations in Kingston, Jamaica.[33] Pointing to the fact that Britain paid compensation to plantation owners in 1834, Hilary McDonald Beckles (2013) notes that no reparations have been paid to amend for the genocide of Indigenous people and the enslavement of African people, nor for the extraction of resources and the exploitation of lands in the Caribbean and the American continent. As he (ibid., 43) notes "between 1492 and 1730, the native population of the Lesser Antilles fell by as much as 90 per cent," while the British financial and insurance sectors prospered.

The case for reparations made by the US-based movements against racial cisheteropatriarchal capitalism draws on this analysis in relation to the structural violence endured by Black, Latine and other communities of color in contemporary society. Connecting to abolitionist praxis and thought, this debate engages with reparatory ways of reciprocal communal care and healing practices through arts, culture and new ways of living together (Cullors 2019; Loick and Thompson 2022). By uncovering how coloniality shapes contemporary societies through racist violence and the subordination of racialized, feminized, trans, queer, nonbinary and crip communities in the Global North, abolitionist claims address the global-local entanglement of economic and social inequalities. Campaigns for reparations in the Global North are intricately connected to struggles against extractivism and dispossession in the Global South as well as to demands for financial restitution, land redistribution, Indigenous jurisprudence, political self-determination, language recuperation and the cultural autonomy of Indigenous communities in settler colonial societies (Amadahy and Lawrence 2009; LASA Forum 2019; Tate forthcoming). The question of reparations voiced by Black Lives Matter, while entrenched in anti-Black racism struggles for racial justice, also calls for an analysis of intersectional violence (Garza 2014) and demands defunding the police and the penitentiary judicial system, investing instead in precarious racialized communities (Cullors 2019; Oliver 2021). These goals inform the BLM movement and outline an abolitionist praxis that Patrisse Cullors summarizes in nine "principles: people's power; love, healing, and transformative justice; Black liberation; internationalism; anti-imperialism; dismantling structures; and practice, practice, practice." In the words of Cullors (2019), "abolition calls on us not only to destabilize, deconstruct, and demolish oppressive systems, institutions, and practices, but also to repair histories of harm […]."

In sum, the demands for reparations voice an analysis of contemporary societies marked by coloniality and the afterlife of slavery. Set within the context of modern colonial structural intersectional violence, demands for material reparations in the form of financial support for the families that have lost loved ones stand at the forefront of the political communal labor of mourning. This is reflected in the Initiative 19. Februar Hanau campaigning for funds for victims of racist violence in the state of Hessen. Although they have been successful in accessing funds for victims of right-wing violence, they demand the establishment of a fund that specifically addresses racist violence. As previously mentioned, funds are often not made available to the families of the victims in a timely manner, forcing families, relatives and friends to organize campaigns and crowdfunding activities in order to cover immediate costs (bereavement, funerals and legal representation). These activities occur in the context of trauma, where the families are navigating a rollercoaster of emotions, pain and grief. Emotional and psychological support is just as necessary in this situation as material and political support. Continuing paid work under these circumstances is challenging as well and often leads to long periods of sick leave or loss of employment. Often the families that have encountered racist intersectional violence were already living under economically precarious circumstances, which are only aggravated by the murderous attacks (Saciak 2021). Hence, the question of distributive justice stands at the core of the demands for common justice and is closely tied to claims for transformative justice.

Transformative justice: Restoring and speaking truth

The discussion about transformative justice is related to debates on transitional justice in the context of peacebuilding, truth and reconciliation processes, and postwar/post-conflict societies (Gready and Robins 2014; Lambourne 2014). Western Europe has not been subjected to these considerations, as it is perceived by international relations standards as a relatively peaceful region. The aims of transformative justice, Paul Gready and Simon Robins (2014, 314) note, are to emphasize local agency and resources, to prioritize processes of transformation and to challenge "unequal and intersecting power relationships and structures of exclusion at both the local and global level." As Wendy Lambourne (2014) argues, the project of transformative justice is committed to social, economic and political justice. Thus, suggesting that we speak about transformative justice in relation to European legacies of colonialism, slavery and imperialism and their impact on EU asylum and migration control policies requires us to address processes of rendering justice to the victims of these systems of violence. It is on these grounds that decolonial mourning delineates one of the paths toward transformative justice.

Regarding the potential for speaking justice, the actors discussed in this book share the hard truth that the legal system cannot bring back their lost loved ones. Accordingly, demands for representative, distributive and transformative justice are limited and represent only one path in the political struggle for reparation and healing. When they demand accountability, most family members are aiming for an end to racist violence, while striving for a dignified life, political recognition, legal and political representation and economic autonomy. As Brian Stevenson notes,[34] in a concrete case of legal prosecution, restorative justice requires that the truth be told and that the perpetrator acknowledge this truth. Asking for accountability involves a process of encountering, listening, telling the truth, recognizing the wounds and supporting the healing process. It requires the commitment and attention of both parties: the perpetrator and those affected by the violence. However, the legal setting can only approach this process in a fixed temporal institutional framework. Such a process can only unfold without limits and achieve permanence if both parties are committed to the creation of a restorative environment and some approximation to reparative healing. Thus, the ultimate goal, as Angela Davis (2020) remarks in a conversation with the San Francisco District Attorney Chesa Bodin and legal prosecutor Ruth Marshall,[35] is not punishment but liberation from a system of oppression. For Davis (2003), mass incarceration in the United States reveals the failure of the state to confront the historical inequalities produced by racial cisheteropatriarchal capitalism.

In the process of transformative justice, the acts of truth telling and accountability enable the family members, relatives and friends to find words for their thoughts, analysis, feelings and impressions. Working through the multiple layers of their experience and accessing them through different pathways in the short, medium and long term, they create political campaigns, public gatherings and an infrastructure of communal care (Gutiérrez Rodríguez 2020). Increasing their personal and collective strength, these actors' political communal labor of mourning resonates with Escobar's (2018) *sentipensar*—the entanglement between intellect and affect, analysis and feeling. In the accounts of the mothers and sisters of the #SayHerName campaign, we have witnessed this thinking. Also, in the NSU Monologues[36] performed on different stages in Germany, the audience could listen to the family members' profound and moving analysis of their experiences of structural racism with police, prosecutors, politicians or journalists. Their battle for truth performatively evokes a form of transformative justice outlining the potential for restorative healing, while acknowledging the trauma.

Danielle Sered,[37] the founder and executive director of the New York City-based organization Common Justice,[38] emphasizes that the healing process of transformative justice goes beyond the legal procedural system. In a similar way, the Tribunal NSU-Komplex auflösen (Tribunal 2021) has publicly demonstrated the limits of the legal system by addressing the unexplained circumstances, loopholes and errors committed in the police investigation, prosecution and trial. In parallel, they have opened public spaces to enact their own sense of speaking justice, where the family members, relatives and friends have collectively interrogated, assessed and tried to discover what happened and why. For the participants in the Tribunals (ibid.), finding answers collectively has meant working around a survivor-centered perspective by (a) producing a coherent narrative of the events, (b) unleashing a process of healing by working with the pain of loss, (c) working toward gaining a sense of control over the situation, (d) participating actively in the process and (e) influencing the terms and scope of accountability for the harm caused. Political, legal and material support to restore the trust and the creation of an infrastructure of shelter, a safety net and the perspective of prospective closure are indispensable for the realization of these steps.

Throughout the chapters of this book, we have seen how the family members, relatives, friends, political movements and campaigns have set out on this path to create much-needed emotional, social and financial sustenance. These structures of support have enabled them to face the experiences of re-traumatization caused by the police and judicial system. They have told their stories to a jury of strangers; they have undergone cross-examinations by police; often experiencing racist criminalization of their lost loved ones and themselves; they have encountered incongruence in the reconstruction of evidence and have been placed under scrutiny themselves by prosecutors, judges and juries. Nonetheless, through their political communal labor of mourning, partially staged in public vigils, political marches, performances and intimate gatherings—and last, but not least, by finding ways to stage their own tribunals of transformative justice (ibid.)—they have addressed the wounds and harm experienced and demanded a path toward reparations. This requires that society and the state acknowledge the violence enacted and the harm committed by apologizing publicly, putting an end to racist inter-sectional violence, paying restitution, and actively contributing to community safety by supporting these actors' conviviality infrastructure and their vision of a caring commons. However, in the long run, the path to transformative justice calls for distributive reparative social justice. This entails a radical transformation of society and an end to the racist ableist cisheteropatriarchal logic of capital accumulation and extractrivism.

Conviviality Infrastructure and a Caring Commons

This chapter has discussed decolonial mourning as political communal labor by considering networks, discourses and practices supporting demands for representational, distributive and transformative justice—in sum, common justice. Focusing on the collective power of the family members, relatives and friends who have lost their loved ones to colonial modern racial cisheteropatriarchal capitalist forms of violence, I have attended to their experiences, analysis and strategies. Outlining their political communal labor of mourning, I have traced their practices of interrogation, contestation and naming. This has constituted the specific epistemology of resistance of organizations such as Cruzando Fronteras, #NiUnaMenos, the African American Policy Forum, #SayHerName, Women in Exile e.V. and the numerous initiatives for the remembrance of victims of intersectional racist violence in Germany, the Arslan and Genç families, the Tribunal NSU Auflösen, Initiative 19. Februar Hanau and Bildungsinitiative Ferhat Unvar. Through their political communal labor of mourning, these actors have enabled what AbdouMaliq Simone (2004; 2021) describes as "people as infrastructure."

Simone (ibid.) suggests understanding urban collective life in African cities as sustained by the communal organization of support structures. As he notes in his (2021) reflections on this proposal, the term emerged rather playfully from his ethnographic work in the inner city of Johannesburg (2004). Moving away from an analysis focusing on individuals, households, communities and institutions, people as infrastructure concentrates on "the ability of residents to engage with complex combinations of objects, spaces, persons and practices" (ibid., 408). In this interplay, people act and interact through relationships of reciprocity, exchange and transaction, sustaining the creation and maintenance of common livelihoods. People as infrastructure attends to how these "conjunctions become an infrastructure—a platform providing for and reproducing life in the city" (ibid.). Simone's concept of people as infrastructure resonates with my own work on creolized conviviality networks (Gutiérrez Rodríguez 2015; 2020; 2021). Drawing on Ivan Illich's (1973) convivial tools, I have approached conviviality as an expression of sociality, created by people's activities in forging relationships of common support. Considering people's affective and material interdependencies, I have defined this mode of connection as a "Being-in-Relation" (Gutiérrez Rodríguez 2018b; 2020). Conviviality considers that our lives evolve in a set of interdependent relations, guided by affective and material needs and desires. Relating conviviality to Simone's people as infrastructure opens up the possibility to be attentive to the assemblages, configured by people, objects, spaces and practices, but also by affect and desire. Infrastructure, as Simone argues, is not just about the creation of technical support such as water, transport or sewage systems; it is as I propose here about creating a platform through affective labor and building relationships of communal living.

The political communal labor of mourning of the families, relatives and friends that we have witnessed in this book has materialized as a collective structure of support. It is within this structure, sustained by financial, physical, emotional and affective nurturance, that a conviviality infrastructure of decolonial mourning, demanding and enacting reparative, distributive and representational justice emerges. Through people's activities, affective connections and political commitments, a caring commons is articulated and set into practice, which acknowledges the pain of the other as its own pain, mourning for the lives lost and the injustice experienced. Mourning here is not just individual, it is communal. It has to do with communal social relations (Tzul Tzul 2019a) and affective interdependencies. It is inserted in Tzul Tzul's cycles of life and Rodríguez Aguilera's life-death continuum. Mourning's conviviality infrastructure counters and challenges the everyday suffering of coloniality-migration necropolitics while also mobilizing Ortega's (2019) resistant sorrow. Organizing material, symbolic and affective support structures, these actors are guaranteeing the survival and sustainability of their communities and politically organizing against the daily cruelty and dehumanizing—the lethal violence of a colonial modern system of racial cisheteropatriarchal ableist capitalism. The families, relatives and friends have shared their common grief and opened up mourning as the potential to build relational affective connections. They have constructed possibilities for living together by transforming mourning into political action and instilling their affective labor of grief into the making of a conviviality infrastructure. Suffused with the affective dimensions of (con)dolence and (com)passion, the political communal labor of mourning has forged a multisited platform for communal caring, healing and reparations. Decolonial mourning relates to coalitional politics of transformation that interacts on a local, regional and international level in analogue and digital form. In this vein, I have attended to the networks of families, relatives and friends organizing ways of living together while striving for common justice. It is here that a conviviality infrastructure, mobilized by decolonial mourning and enacted by a caring commons, has surfaced.

As we have seen throughout this book, the political communal labor of mourning is carried out through affective relationships. Manifested in different practices of care, healing and collective sustainability, the organizations and collectives whose mourning labor we have borne witness to, remind us of an ethics of care that works on three levels. While decolonial mourning speaks about an ethical condition (Butler 2004), when it comes to thinking about ourselves as interconnected, it is also about ontological relationality, mutual material well-being, reciprocity and sustainability. Decolonial mourning, thus, addresses the ontological, material and moral dimension of our communal living (Sander-Staudt 2006). These observations bring us to consider Joan Tronto's (1994; 2006; 2011; 2013; 2015) argument, further developed by other ethics of care feminist theorists (Bowden 1997; Held 2006; Keller and Kittay 2017) that a democratic society based on solidarity needs to share the common understanding that care and love—and I would add mourning—are fundamental to communal life.

Decolonial mourning as communal affective labor and political action articulates and manifests a caring commons, arising from material conditions of global locally manifested entangled inequalities (Gutiérrez Rodríguez and Reddock 2021) and institutional forms of injustice deriving from historically formed intersectional structural violence. It addresses contemporary manifestations of the detrimental, annihilating and dehumanizing effects of colonial modern racist cisheteropatriarchal capitalism. In this sense, decolonial mourning as political affective labor addresses the social inequalities that Tronto (2013) analyzes in care work and her understanding of care as a fundamental ethical principle for democracy, while resonating with Patricia Hill Collins's (Collins 1990) insights on the "ethics of caring" as deriving from Black women's knowledge and practices in dealing with racial and gendered injustice. Furthermore, decolonial mourning draws on the proposals of Virginia Held (2006) and the collective Precarias a la Deriva (2004) to treat care as a political project as well as María Puig de la Bellacasa's (2017) understanding of care as based on human and nonhuman relationships. It speaks to Dean Spade's (2020) "radical collective care" by thinking about communal political mourning as practices connecting to what Melanie Yazzie and Cutcha Risling Baldy (2018) see as a form of "radical rationality" sustaining the relationship between human and nonhuman life. Echoing, as well, Christopher Paul Harris's (2021, 905) reflection on Tronto's analysis, decolonial mourning allies to a project in which "we ought to care for and go about undoing the world," as it is. Committed decolonial mourning, as we have learned by listening to the political work of mourning of #SayHerName, Crenshaw and the AAPF, as well as the protests against necroborders, feminicide and the coloniality of migration, "calls for abolition and decolonization, which have become staples of Black and Brown-led organizing and activism in the years following the emergence of #BlackLivesMatter" (ibid.).

Conclusion: Mourning's Reparative Justice

Throughout this book, and particularly in this chapter, we have reflected on the communal political labor of mourning of communities resisting colonial racist intersectional violence. We have acknowledged claims for representational, transformative, restorative, distributive and reparative justice. Connecting to Tzul Tzul, Simpson and Rodríguez Aguilera, we have also attended to Maimuna Touray's (2021) reflection on the implication of reparations as a radical care practice that "envisions the commons as a form of reparations for the atrocities of slavery, settler colonialism and their legacies of continued exploitation, violence and destruction of our earth's animate and inanimate communities." (ibid.). Along these lines, we have echoed Tzul Tzul's (2019a,b) analysis of *trama comunitaria*, or communal fabric, in which the question of care involves communal responsibility for and social reproduction of body-land-territory (Cabnal 2010) as a form of rexistence (Sempértegui 2021). This highlights the relational and interdependent nature of decolonial mourning as communal care, while it also apprehends Harris's (2021, 908) notion of an ethics of care that responds to and acts upon the (re)production of injustice by acknowledging "the death and source of the injury as experienced by the injured." As an outcome of affective, corporeal, multispecies and planetary connections, decolonial mourning is related to the immediacy of our past-present lives and futures. It reverberates with Audre Lorde's understanding of care as a source of survival and with Christina Sharpe's (2016) wake work as well. It is in this regard that I argue here for decolonial mourning as communal political affective labor articulating social reproduction crossed by migration-coloniality necropolitics. Set within the context of decolonial/anticolonial, antiracist, intersectional, feminist politics of liberation, the political communal labor of decolonial mourning becomes the affective glue through which caring practices attending to a relational, reciprocal living together unfold. As such, it connects to claims for reparative justice in transformative, distributive and representational ways.

Ferhat Unvar's sister, Nesrîn, reminds us of this when she speaks about the necessity of memory as social change in the assembly on 22 August 2020 in Hanau.[39] Serpil Temiz Unvar, Ferhat's mother, translates this observation into demands for distributive, representational and transformative justice. Reflecting on the limitation of financial compensation, when the emotional, physical and psychological harm persists, Serpil concedes that remembrance politics cannot be the sole answer to the struggle against systemic racism. Pursuing her son's vision of establishing an antiracist educational project, she has founded the Bildungsinitiative Ferhat Unvar,[40] turning her grief into a political claim that derives from her son's analysis of and demands for antiracist education. As she says, she cannot undo the racism her son endured at school, but she hopes to prevent it for future generations. Calling for a thorough police investigation and the prosecution of systemic racist, misogynistic, homophobic and transphobic necropolitics, all the actors in this book demand an end to the intersectional violence produced by modern colonial racial cisheteropatriarchal ableist capitalism.

I would like to end with a tribute to the lives of my neighbors: **Ferhat Unvar**, **Gökhan Gültekin**, **Hamza Kurtović**, **Said Nesar Hashemi**, **Mercedes Kierpacz**, **Sedat Gürbüz**, **Kalojan Velkov**, **Vili Viorel Păun** and **Fatih Saraçoğlu.** The lives they lived are entrenched within my own, and the mourning of their families, relatives and friends resonates with my mourning for my parents, **Juan José Gutiérrez Cabello** and **Josefa Rodríguez Santana**, Andalusian Gastarbeiter in Germany. Listening to the words of the family members and relatives, I share with them their grief, their tears, their hopes and their demands for intersectional common justice. This is my path through decolonial mourning.

Notes

1 Translation by author: I am 100 percent certain that as long as there is no investigation and as long as we don't get justice, the people will not rest in their graves. (All translations mine.)

2 The struggle has prevented me from grieving (ibid., 62).

3 From the notes I took while attending the rally in Hanau "Sechs Monate nach dem 19. Februar: Erinnerung – Gerechtigkeit – Aufklärung – Konsequenzen" (Six Months after February 19: Remembrance, Justice, Clarification, Consequences) on 22 August

2020. Video documentation can be seen here: https://19feb-hanau.org/2020/08/14/video/.

4 See Website of Initiative 19. Februar Hanau: https://19feb-hanau.org.

5 Ibid.

6 Ibid.

7 This is a political category, used to describe the positionality of people with a diasporic, exile or migrant biography that experience a specific form of racism in Germany.

8 See endnote 4.

9 Statement on this decision: https://medibuero.de/sechs-monate-nach-dem-19-februar-erinnerung-gerechtigkeit-aufklaerung-konsequenzen/.

10 All the accounts of the family members I refer to in the following are based on my personal notes, taken during my attendance of the assembly in Hanau on 22nd of August 2020.

11 Interview with Serpil Temiz Unvar by Carolina Torres, "Ich erschrecke immer noch, wenn ich seinen Namen unter denen der Verstorbenen sehe," 24 August 2020, https://www.bento.de/politik/hanau-19-2-serpil-temiz-unvar-ueber-ihren-sohn-ferhat-unvar-a-87bec47d-939b-4fbc-8ffa-616f21717874.

12 https://www.bildungsinitiative-ferhatunvar.de/

13 The reconstruction of events and the failures of the police investigation, in particular why the exit door of the Arena bar was locked are documented here: https://19feb-hanau.org/untersuchungsausschuss/.

14 Interview with Armin and Dijana Kurtović by Franziska Bulban, "Ich glaube, dass vieles anders gelaufen wäre, wenn die Opfer andere Namen hätten," 21 September 2020, https://www.bento.de/politik/ich-glaube-dass-vieles-anders-gelaufen-waere-wenn-die-opfer-andere-namen-haetten-a-ab0a8b5f-a84e-4de5-8c3f-6110a87e69cb.

15 From my notes; see endnotes 3 and 8.

16 Peter Hille, "How will Hanau's victims of far-right terror be remembered?" 21 August 2020, Deutsche Welle, https://www.dw.com/en/how-will-hanaus-victims-of-far-right-terror-be-remembered/a-54644557; and Çetin Gültekin interviewed by Franziska Bulban, "In der Hand hielt er das Herz meines Bruders," 26 August 2020, Der Spiegel, https://www.spiegel.de/panorama/hanau-19-02-cetin-gueltekin-hat-bei-dem-attentat-von-hanau-seinen-bruder-verloren-a-0570227b-fa05-46f0-8ee3-5d925c36e952.

17 Antwort der Bundesregierung. Deutscher Bundestag. Drucksache 19/19679. 19 Wahlperiode. 20.05.2020. https://dserver.bundestag.de/btd/19/196/1919678.pdf.

18 Webinar Heinrich-Böll-Stiftung Hessen, Erinnerung, Aufklärung, Gerechtigkeit, Konsequenzen, 23 March 2021, https://www.youtube.com/watch?v=WB15qwJPg6g.

19 From my notes; see endnotes 3 and 8.

20 Iulia and Niculescu Păun interviewed by Franziska Bulban, "Manchmal denke ich, es ist meine Schuld. Ich habe gesagt, dass es in Deutschland gut ist," 27 September 2020, Der Spiegel, https://www.bento.de/politik/hanau-19-02-iulia-und-niculescu-paun-haben-bei-dem-attentat-von-hanau-ihren-sohn-verloren-a-8f731ebb-c4d8-4237-822d-a436b5c076bf.

21 Interview with Saida, Said Etris and Mir Salam Hashemi by Carolina Torres, "Ich war froh, als er begraben wurde. Ich wollte, dass seine Leiche nicht mehr herumgereicht wird" 23 August 2020, Der Spiegel, https://www.spiegel.de/panorama/hanau-19-2-saida-said-etris-und-mir-salam-hashemi-ueber-said-nesar-a-aea067b2-4b24-4ae9-936c-2da7ac2ac217.

22 See endnote 14.
23 Chronicle of the Untersuchungsausschuss (Investigating Committee) of Hessen in Initiative 19. Februar Hanau: https://19feb-hanau.org/?s=vili+viorel+paun.
24 Konrad Litschko, "Mein Sohn könnte noch leben," 6 July 2021 *Taz*, https://taz.de/Keine-Ermittlungen-zu-Notruf-in-Hanau/!5780632/#.
25 Hayrettin Saraçoğlu interviewed by Franziska Bulban, "Warum sollte hinter dem Vorhang nicht jemand sein, der mich töten will?" 25 August 2020, *Der Spiegel*, https://www.bento.de/politik/hanau-19-02-hayrettin-saracoglu-hat-bei-dem-attentat-von-hanau-seinen-bruder-verloren-a-144d2414-8b27-45bc-8c35-35d5b8f165d9.
26 Interview with Vaska Zlateva by Carolina Torres, "Auf ein Tier schießt du einmal, vielleicht zweimal. Tobias R. hat sechs Mal auf meinen Cousin geschossen," 22 August 2022, *Der Spiegel*, https://www.bento.de/politik/hanau-19-2-kaloyan-velkovs-cousine-vaska-zlateva-ueber-ihren-cousin-a-cc52d8bc-1558-49a6-9c44-60d94a05f1a5.
27 Interview with Emiş and Selahattin Gürbüz by Carolina Torres, "Wenn ich an seinem Grab stehe, möchte ich die Erde weggraben und den Jungen da rausholen," 20 August 2020, https://www.bento.de/politik/hanau-sedat-guerbuez-eltern-emis-und-selahattin-ueber-ihren-sohn-a-19bd29eb-b859-4be3-a814-9e44e91fb4d5.
28 Newsletters: https://19feb-hanau.org/2021/09/18/saytheirnames-newsletter-04/; https://19feb-hanau.org/2021/11/10/1216/; https://19feb-hanau.org/wp-content/uploads/2022/01/Newsletter_06.pdf; https://19feb-hanau.org/2023/02/15/15-monate-una/ and https://19feb-hanau.org.
29 See https://19feb-hanau.org/wp-content/uploads/2021/02/Kette-des-Versagens-17-02-2021.pdf.
30 Initiative 19. Februar Hanau: https://19feb-hanau.org.
31 CARICOM Reparations Commission: http://caricomreparations.org/about-us/.
32 Alcenat Westenley, "The Case for Haitian Reparations," 14 January 2017, *Jacobin*, https://jacobin.com/2017/01/haiti-reparations-france-slavery-colonialism-debt/.
33 Severin Carrell, "Glasgow University to pay £20m in slave trade reparations," 23 August 2019, *The Guardian*, https://www.theguardian.com/uk-news/2019/aug/23/glasgow-university-slave-trade-reparations.
34 Podcast "Redemptive Justice with Bryan Stevenson," 2020, *Chasing Justice*, organized by San Francisco District Attorney Chesa Boudin and Rachel Marshall, season 2, episode 1, https://www.chasingjusticepodcast.com/episodes/season-2-episode-1-redemptive-justice-with-bryan-stevenson.
35 Podcast, "The Modern Civil Rights Movement with Angela Davis," 2020, *Chasing Justice*, organized by San Francisco District Attorney Chesa Boudin and Rachel Marshall, season 2, https://www.chasingjusticepodcast.com/episodes/episode-2-the-modern-civil-rights-movement.
36 See, for example, Bühne für Menschenrechte: Die NSU-Monologe, https://buehne-fuer-menschenrechte.org/nsu-monologe/.
37 Podcast "Restorative Justice with Danielle Sered," 2020, *Chasing Justice*, organized by San Francisco District Attorney Chesa Boudin and Rachel Marshall, season 2, episode 8, https://www.chasingjusticepodcast.com/episodes/season-2-episode-8-restorative-justice-with-danielle-sered.
38 Common Justice: https://www.commonjustice.org.
39 See endnotes 3 and 8.
40 Bildungsinitiative Ferhat Unvar: https://www.bildungsinitiative-ferhatunvar.de.

NOTES ON AUTHOR

Encarnación Gutiérrez Rodríguez is Professor in Sociology with a focus on Culture and Migration at the Goethe University, Frankfurt am Main. Previously to this position, she was Professor in General Sociology at the Justus-Liebig-University Giessen. Moreover, she is Adjunct Professor in Sociology at the University of Alberta, Canada, and Visiting Professor in CRISHET – Chair for Critical Studies in Higher Education Transformation, Nelson Mandela University, South Africa. In 2020/21, she was a Digital Senior Fellow in Maria Sibylla Merian Centre: Conviviality-Inequality in Latin America (Mecila), São Paulo. Currently, she is conducting research on human rights discourses in migrant and refugee protest in Germany and the United States as part of the German Research Agency—DFG—research network Human Rights Discourses in the Migration Society (MeDiMi). Among her many publications is the book *Migration, Domestic Work and Affect* (2010) and her co-edited collection with Manuela Boatcă and Sérgio Costa *Decolonizing European Sociology* (2010). More recently she has published with Shirley Anne Tate the *Palgrave Handbook in Critical Race and Gender* (2022), with Rhoda Reddock *Decolonial Perspectives on Entangled Inequalities: Europe and the Caribbean* (2021) and with Pınar Tuzcu *Migratischer Feminismus in der deutschen Frauenbewegung, 1985-2000* (2021). Her work engages with affective labor, care and domestic work, decolonial care ethics, materialities, institutional racism, racial cisheteropatriarchal capitalism and the coloniality of migration.

REFERENCES

Adorno, Theodor W. 2019 [1950]. *The Authoritarian Personality.* London: Verso.

Adorno, Theodor W. 1997 [1981]. *Prisms: Cultural Criticism and Society.* Translated by Shierry Samuel and Shierry Weber. Cambridge, MA: MIT Press.

African American Policy Forum (AAPF). 2020. 11th instalment of "under the black light: Say her name: Telling stories of state violence and public silence", organized by #SayHerName campaign and supported by Kimberlé Crenshaw. Centre for Intersectionality and Social Policy at the Columbia Law School, Columbia University, Screened 17 June 2020. https://www.youtube.com/watch?v=S2MfJOJaeGA (accessed September 2022).

Agier, Michel. 2002. Between war and city: Towards an urban anthropology of refugee camps. *Ethnography* 3, no. 3: 317–41.

Ahn, Yonson. 2020. Nursing care in contact zones: Korean healthcare 'guest workers' in Germany. In *Transnational Mobility In and Out of Korea*, edited by Yonson Ahn. Lanham: Lexington Books.

Aizura, Aren Z. 2017. Communizing care in the left hand of darkness. *Ada: A Journal of Gender, New Media, and Technology* 12(October).

Aizura, Aren Z. 2018. *Mobile Subjects: Transnational Imaginaries of Gender Reassignment.* Durham, NC: Duke University Press.

Albahari, Maurizio. 2016. After the shipwreck: Mourning and in the mediterranean, our sea. *Social Research* 83, no. 2: 275–94.

Alberto, Ibraimo. 2014. *Ich wollte leben wie die Götter. Was in Deutschland aus meinen afrikanischen Träume wurde.* Köln: Kiepenheuer & Witsch.

Alberto, Ibraimo, and Marcia C. Schenck. 2021. Path are made by walking: Memories of being a Mozambican contract worker in the GDR. In *Navigating Socialist Encounters*, edited by Eric Burton, Anne Dietrich, Immanuel R. Harisch, and Marcia Schenck, 247–64. Oldenbourg: De Gruyter.

Alcocer Perulero, Marisol. 2014. Prostitutas, infieles y drogadictas. Juicios y PreJuicios de género en la Prensa sobre las víctimas de feminicidio: El caso de guerrero, méxico. *Antipoda. Revista de Antropología y Arqueología* 20: 97–118.

Alcocer Perulero, Marisol. 2016. Ciudadanas de primera y segunda clase. acercamiento al femicidio en guerrero y la jerarquización en el acceso a la justicia. *Revista Inclusiones. Revista de Humanidades y Ciencias Sociales* 3: 38–58.

Alcocer Perulero, Marisol. 2020. ¿Feminicidio de afrodescendientes en México? Lo que no se nombra no existe. *Abya-Yala. Revista sobre acesso a justiça e direitos nas Americas* 1: 163–93.

Alexander, Michelle. 2012. *The New Jim Crow.* New York: The New Press.

Alexander, Neville. 2023. *Against Racial Capitalism. Selected Writings.* London: Pluto Press.

Altamirano-Jiménez, Isabel. 2020. Possessing land, wind and water in the Isthmus of Tehuantepec, Oaxaca. *Australian Feminist Studies* 35, no. 106: 321–335.

Altamirano-Jiménez, Isabel. 2013. *Indigenous Encounters With Neoliberalism: Place, Women, and the Environment in Canada and Mexico*. University of British Colombia.

Amadahy, Zainab, and Bonita Lawrence. 2009. Indigenous peoples and black people in Canada: Settlers or allies? In *Breaching the Colonial Contract: Anti-Colonialism*, edited by Arlo Kempf, 105–36. Springer.

Amado, Ana Maria. 2003. Herencias. Generaciones y Duelo en las Politicas de la Memoria. *Revista Iberoamericana* LXIX, no. 202: 137–53.

Amnesty International. 2016. *Living in Insecurity: How Germany is Failing Victims of Racist Violence*. London: Amnesty International. https://www.amnesty.be/IMG/pdf/hate_crimes_in_germany_english_combined_web_v2.pdf (accessed September 2022).

Anzaldúa, Gloria. 1987. *Borderlands/La Frontera: The New Mestiza*. San Francisco: Aunt Lute Books.

Arenas, Carlos. 2015. *Poder, economía y sociedad en el sur: Historia e instituciones del capitalismo andaluz*. Sevilla: Fundación Pública Andaluza Centro de Estudios.

Arendt, Hannah. 1959a. Reflection on little rock. *Dissent* 6, no. 1: 45–56.

Arendt, Hannah. 1959b. A reply to critics. *Dissent* 6, no. 2: 179–81.

Arendt, Hannah. 1970. *On Violence*. New York: Harcourt Brace Yovanovich.

Arendt, Hannah. 1972. On disobedience. In *Crisis of the Republic*, 51–102. Orlando: Harcourt.

Arendt, Hannah. 2018 [1958]. *The Human Condition*. Chicago: University of Chicago Press.

Arendt, Hannah. 2019 [1951]. *The Origins of Totalitarianism*. London: Penguin.

Arendt, Hannah. 2021 [1957]. *Rahel Varnhagen: Lebensgeschichte einer deutschen Jüdin Aus der Romantik*. München: Piper.

Ariès, Philippe. 1975. *Western Attitudes Toward Death*. Baltimore: John Hopkins University Press.

Arribas, Marta, and Ana Pérez. 2006. *Documentary: El Tren de la Memoria*. Produced by Santiago Gárcia de Leániz. (with the protagonists: Josefina Cembrero Marcilla, Leonor Mediavilla, Victoria Toro, Álvaro Rengifo, Heinz Saidel, Hans-Peter Sieber, Josefa Pérez, José Luis Leal, Alberto Torga, Pedro Serrano Molina, Virginia Sánchez Benítez, Victor Ganto, Heidi Strinski, Antonio Fernández, Juan Chacón, Fernandon Reinlein).

Arruza, Cinzia, Tithi Bhattacharya, and Nancy Fraser. 2019. *Feminism for the 99%: A Manifesto*. New York: Verso.

Arslan, Ibrahim. In inteview with NSU Watch. 20.12.2020. *They deprived us of solidarity by archiving it for 27 years*. https://www.nsu-watch.info/2020/12/they-deprived-us-of-solidarity-by-archiving-it-for-27-years-interview-with-ibrahim-arslan/ (accessed September 2022).

Arslan, Ibrahim. In interview with Matthias Dell. 31.10.2021. *Mölln, NSU, Hanau – Ibrahim Arslan über rechte Gewalt und Erinnerungskultur. Public German Radio Channel Deutschlandfunk Kultur*. https://www.deutschlandfunk.de/moelln-nsu-hanau-ibrahim-arslan-ueber-rechte-gewalt-und-erinnerungskultur-dlf-925b6033-100.html (accessed September 2022)

Arslan, Ibrahim, and Nadiye Ünsal (in conversation). 2022. Wenn der Verlust zum Urteil wird und Gerechtigkeite eine Utopie. In *Die extreme Rechte in der sozialen Arbeit*, edited by Christoph Gille, Birgit Jagutsch, and Yasmine Chehata, 20–36. Weinheim: Beltz Juventa.

ARTE Reports 2019. Argentina: The Women's Revolt. 26.10.2019. https://www.arte.tv/ en/videos/091749-000-A/arte-reportage/

Ataç, Ilker, Kim Rygiel, Maurice Stierl. 2021. Building transversal solidarities in european cities: Open harbours, safe communities, home. *Critical Sociology* 47, no. 6: 923–39.

Athanasiou, Athena. 2017. *Agonistic Mourning: Political Dissidence and the Women in Black*. Edinburgh: Edinburgh University Press.

Augé, Marc. 1992. *Non-Places. Introduction to an Anthropology of Supermodernity*, translated by John Howe. London, New York: Verso.

Ayim, May. 1996. *Grenzenlos und Unverschämt*. Berlin: Orlanda Verlag.

Bachir Diagne, Souleymane. 2020. Traduire en présence de toutes les langues du monde. In *Archipels Glissant*, edited by François Noudelmann, Françoise Simasotchi-Bronès, and Yann Toma, 31–39. Saint-Denis: Presses universitaires de Vincennes.

Bacon, David. 2019. In Mexico, a new dawn for independent unions? *NACLA* 51, no. 3: 268–75.

Bade, Klaus J. (ed.). 1987. *Population, Labour and Migration in 19th and 20th Century Germany*. Leamington Spa: Berg.

Bademsoy, Aysun. 2019. *Documentary: Spuren – Die Opfer des NSU*. Germany. https://www .bpb.de/mediathek/video/311574/spuren-die-opfer-des-nsu/?fbclid=IwAR2YD JGmeQ3M3O2j96vgiehgULA0W3edDJzOQzPcm4J0P3lB2dpiDB4Un64 (accessed September 2022).

Bailey, Moya. 2010. They aren't talking about me. *Crunk Feminist Collective Blog*, 14. March 14, 2010. http://www.crunkfeministcollective.com/2010/03/14/they-arent -talkingabout-me (accessed September 2022).

Bailey, Moya. 2013. Homolatent masculinity & hip hop culture. *Palimpsest* 2, no. 2: 187–99.

Baizán, Pau, and Amparo González-Ferrer. 2016. What drives senegalese migration to Europe? The role of economic restructuring, labor demand, and the multiplier effect of networks. *Demographic Research* 35: 339–80.

Bakker, Isabel, and Stephen Gill. 2019. Rethinking power, production, and social reproduction: Toward variegated social reproduction. *Capital & Class* 43, no. 4: 503–23.

Bakker, Isabellla. 2007. Social reproduction and the constitution of a gendered political economy. *New Political Economy* 12, no. 4: 541–56.

Barad, Karen. 2003. Posthumanist performativity: Toward an understanding of how matter comes to matter. *Sign* 28, no. 3: 801–31.

Barad, Karen. 2007. *Meeting the Universe Halfway: Quantum Physics and the Entanglement of Matter and Meaning*. Durham: Duke University Press.

Barmeyer, Mareike. 2022. Ich bin eine Kämpferin. *Taz*. https://taz.de/Women-in-Exile/ !140673/.

Barry, Céline. 2021. Schwarzer Feminismus der Grenze. Die Refugee-Frauenbewegung und das Schwarze Mittelmeer. *Femina Politica. Zeitschrift für feministische Politikwissenschaft* 3, no. 30: 36–48.

Batthyány, Karina (ed.). 2020. *Miradas latinoamericanas a los cuidados*. Ciudad Autónoma de Buenos Aires: CLACSO; México DF: Siglo XXI.

Beckles, Hilary McD. 2013. *Britain's Black Debt: Reparations for Caribbean Slavery and Native Genocide. University Press of the West Indies; Rodney, Walter (2018): How Europe Underdeveloped Africa*. London: Verso.

Behrens, Antonia von der. 2017. Kontrolle als Gestaltung: Der Verfassungsschutz und der NSU-Komplex. *Kritische Justiz* 50, no. 1: 38–50.

Bella, Casa, and María Puig de la. 2017. *Matters of Care: Speculative Ethics in More Than Human Worlds.* Minneapolis: University of Minnesota Press.

Bendesky, León, Enrique de la Garza, Javier Melgoza, and Carlos Salas. 2004. La Industria Maquiladora de Exportación En México: Mitos, Realidades y Crisis. *Estudios Sociológicos* 22, no. 65: 283–314.

Bendix, Daniel. 2018. *Jenseits von Externalisierung und Integration. Refugee-Aktivismus und postkoloniale Dezentrierung der Kritik globaler Ungleichheit.* Jena: DFG-Kollegforscher_innengruppe Postwachstumsgesellschaften).

Bengoa, José. 2000. *Historia del Pueblo Mapuche. Siglo XIX y XX.* Santiago: Lom.

Benhabib, Seyla. 1992. *Situating the Self: Gender, Community and Postmodernism in Contemporary Ethics.* Cambridge: Polity Press.

Benhabib, Seyla. 1993. Feminist theory and Arendt's concept of public space. *History of the Human Sciences* 6, no. 2: 97–114.

Benhabib, Seyla. 1995. The Pariah and her shadow: Hannah Arendt's biography of Rahael Varnhagen. *Political Theory* 23, no. 1: 5–24.

Benhabib, Seyla. 2002. *The Claims of Culture: Equality and Diversity in the Global Era.* Princeton: Princeton University Press.

Benhabib, Seyla. 2003 [1996]. *The Reluctant Modernism of Hannah Arendt.* Oxford: Rowman & Littlefield.

Benhabib, Seyla, and Bernard E. Harcourt. 2020. How to read Hannah Arendt's the human condition (1958)? *Critique* 13/13, 9/13, Maison Française at Colombia University, January 29. https://blogs.law.columbia.edu/critique1313/9-13/ (accessed August 2022).

Benjamin, Walter. 1965. Geschichtsphilosophische Thesen. In *Zur Kritik der Gewalt und andere Aufsätze*, 78–94. Frankfurt am Main: Suhrkamp.

Benjamin, Walter. 1982. *Das Passagen-Werk.* Frankfurt am Main: Suhrkamp.

Benjamin, Walter. 2010. *Über den Begriff der Geschichte. Werke und Nachlaß. Kritische Gesamtausgabe*, Vol. 19. Frankfurt am Main: Suhrkamp.

Benjamin, Walter. 2017. *Charles Baudelaire. Tableaux Parisiens. Werke und Nachlaß. Kritische Gesamtausgabe*, Vol. 7. Frankfurt am Main: Suhrkamp.

Berlin, Malou. 2012. *Mölln – 20 Jahre nach dem Brand.* Credo-Film Berlin: NDR.

Bernasconi, Robert. 1996. The double face of the political and social: Hannah Arendt and America's racial divisions. *Research in Phenomenology* 2, no. 6: 3–24.

Best, Lloyd, and Kari Polanyi Levitt. 2009. *Essays on the Theory of Plantation Economy: A Historical and Institutional Approach to Caribbean Economic Approach to Caribbean Economic Development.* Mona: University of the West Indies.

Bhagwati, Jagdisch N., Klaus-Werner Schatz, and Kar-yin Wong. 1984. The west German gastarbeiter system of immigration. *European Economic Review* 26: 277–94.

Bhattacharya, Tithi (ed.). 2017. *Social Reproduction Theory: Remapping Class, Recentering Oppression.* London: Pluto Press.

Bhattacharyya, Gargi. 2018. *Rethinking Racial Capitalism: Questions of Reproduction and Survival.* London: Rowman and Littlefield.

Bilir-Meier, Cana. 2013. *Contemplating the Archive – Notes on Semra Ertan.*

Bilir-Meier, Cana. 2017. *Semra Ertan. Her Own Voice. Kendi Sesi. Ihre eigene Stimme.* Wien: Kunsthalle Wien.

Bilir-Meier, Zühal. 2019. „(…) sondern auch das Recht haben, wie Menschen behandelt zu werden". *Malmoe*, special issue: NSU Komplex. https://www.malmoe.org/2019/12 /06/sondern-auch-das-recht-haben-wie-menschen-behandelt-zu-werden/ (accessed April 2023).

Bilir-Meier, Zühal, and Cana Bilir-Meier. 2020. *Semra Ertan. Mein Name ist Ausländer/Benim Adım Yabancı. Gedichte\Şiirler*. Münster: edition assemblage.

Biondi, Franco. 1979. *Nicht nur Gastarbeiterdeutsch: Gedichte*. Köln: Klein Winternheim.

Biondi, Franco, Gino Chiellino, and Habib Bektas (eds.). 1983. *Das Unsichtbare sagen!* Kiel: Südwind-Literatur.

Biondi, Franco, Jusuf Naoum, and Rafik Schami (eds.). 1981. *Zwischen Fabrik und Bahnhof. Prosa, Lyrik und Grafiken aus dem Gastarbeiteralltag*. Bremen: Südwindgastarbeiterdeutch.

Biondi, Franco, Jusuf Nauom, and Rafik Schami (eds.). 1982. *Annäherungen. Prosa, Lyrik und Fotographen aus dem Gastarbeiteralltag*. Bremen: Südwindgastarbeiterdeutsch.

Biondi, Franco, Jusuf Naoum, Rafik Schami, and Suleman Taufiq (eds.). 1980. *Im neuen Land*. Bremen: Südwindgastarbeiterdeutsch.

Bledsoe, Caroline H., and Papa Sow. 2013. Back to Africa: Second chances for the children of West African migrants. In *The International Handbook on Gender, Migration and Transnationalism*, edited by Laura Oso and Natalia Ribas-Mateos, 185–207. Cheltenham: Edward Elgar.

Bleicher-Nagelsmann, Heinrich. 2020. Zeitgenosse Walter Benjamin – Erinnern und Eingedenken. In *Conference: Erinnerns und Eigendenken*. 23.10.2020. Cologne: Hans-Mayer-Gesellschaft. https://www.hans-mayer-gesellschaft.de/dokumentation/ and https://nrw.rosalux.de/dokumentation/id/43262/walter-benjamin-erinnerung-und -eingedenken (accessed August 2022).

Bloch, Ersnst. 1989. *Thomas Münzer als Theologe der Revolution*. Leipzig: Reclam.

Bloch, Ernst. 2018 [1918]. *Geist der Utopie*. Frankfurt am Main: Suhrkamp.

Blumi, Isa. 2010. *Rethinking the Late Ottoman Empire: A Comparative Social and Political History of Albania and Yemen, 1878–1918*. Piscataway: Gorgias Press.

Bohn, Charlotte Odilia. 2019. Historiography and remembrance: On Walter Benjamin's concept of Eingedenken. *Religions* 10, no. 1: 40. https://www.mdpi.com/2077-1444 /10/1/40 (accessed April 2023).

Bojadžijev, Manuela. 2012. *Die windege Internationale: Rassismus und Kämpfe der Migration*. Münster: Westfälisches Dampfboot.

Bora, Renu. 1997. Outing texture. In *Novel Gazing*, edited by Eve Kosofsky Sedgwick, 94–127. Durham: Duke University Press.

Bowden, Patricia. 1997. *Caring: Gender-sensitive ethics*. London: Routledge.

Braudel, Fernand. 1949. *La Méditerranée à l'époque de Philippe II*. Paris: Editorial Armand Colin.

Brennan, Teresa. 2004. *The Transmission of Affect*. Ithaca: Cornell University Press.

Bröckling, Ulrich, Susanne Krasmann, and Thomas Lemke (eds.). 2010. *Governmentality: Current Issues and Future Challenges* (1st ed.). London: Routledge.

Brown, Jennifer E. 1987. News photographs and the pornography of grief. *Journal of Mass Media Ethics* 2, no. 2: 75–81.

Browne, Simone. 2015. *Dark Matters: On the Surveillance of Blackness*. Durham: Duke University Press.

Bruce-Jones, Eddie. 2015. *Race in the Shadow: State Violence in Contemporary Europe*. Abingdon, UK: Routledge.

Brunnett, Regina. 2009. *Die Hegemonie symbolischer Gesundheit*. Bielefeld: Transcript.

Buck-Morss, Susan. 2009. *Hegel, Haiti, and Universal History*. Pittsburgh: University of Pittsburgh Press.

Burton, Eric, Anne Dietrich, Immanuel R. Harisch, and Marcia Schenck (eds.). 2021. *Navigating Socialist Encounters*. Oldenbourg: De Gruyter.

Burrough, Elaine, and Kira Williams. 2018. *Contemporary Boat Migration: Data, Geopolitics and Discourses*. London/New York: Rowman & Littlefield.

Burroughs, Michael D. 2015. Hannah Arendt, 'Reflections on Little Rock,' and white ignorance. *Critical Philosophy of Race* 3, no. 1: 52–78.

Butler, Judith. 1997. *The Psychic Life of Power: Theories in Subjection*. Stanford: Stanford University Press.

Butler, Judith. 2004. *Precarious Life: The Power of Mourning and Violence*. Brooklyn: Verso.

Butler, Judith. 2005. *Giving an Account of Oneself.* New York: Fordham University Press.

Butler, Judith. 2007. I merely belong to them. *London Review of Books* 29, no. 9, 10 May. https://www.lrb.co.uk/the-paper/v29/n09/judith-butler/i-merely-belong-to-them (accessed April 2023).

Butler, Judith. 2009. *Frames of War: When is Life Grievable?* Brooklyn: Verso.

Butler, Judith. 2015. *Notes Toward a Performative Theory of Assembly*. Cambridge: Harvard University Press.

Butler, Judith. 2020. *The Force of Non-Violence: An Ethico-Political Bind*. London: Verso.

Cabnal, Lorena. 2017. Tzk'at, Red de Sanadoras Ancestrales del Feminismo Comunitario desde Iximulew-Guatemala. *Ecología Política* 54: 98–102. http://www.jstor.org/stable /44645644 (accessed August 2022).

Cabnal, Lorena. 2019. El relato de las violencias desde mi territorio cuerpo-tierra. In *En tiempos de muerte: Cuerpos, Rebeldias, Resistencias,* edited by Xochitl Leyva Solano and Rosalba Icaza, 113–23. Buenos Aires, Chiapas, La Haya: Cooperative Editorial Retos. CLACSO. Institute of Social Studies-Erasmus University Rotterdam.

Cabnal, Lorena, and Acsur-Las Segovias. 2010. *Feminismos diversos: El feminismo comunitario*. Madrid: ACSUR-Las Segovias.

Cadena, Marisol de la. 2015. *Earth Beings*. Duke University Press.

Caffentzis, George. 1999. On the notion of a crisis of social reproduction: A theoretical review. In *Women, Development and Labor of Reproduction: Struggles and Movements*, edited by Mariarosa dalla Costa and Giovanna F. dalla Costa, 153–87. Trento/Asmara: Africa World Press. https://www.academia.edu/27680943/On_the_Notion_of_a _Crisis_of_Social_Reproduction_A_Theoretical_Review (accessed August 2022).

Calderwood, Eric. 2018. *Colonial al-Andalus. Spain and the Making of Modern Moroccan Culture*. London/Cambridge: The Belknap Press of Harvard University Press.

Campesi, Giuseppe. 2018. Seeking Asylum in times of crisis: Reception, confinement, and detention at Europe's southern border. *Refugee Survey Quarterly* 37, no. 1: 44–70.

Carastathis, Anna, and Myrto Tsilimpounidi. 2020. *Reproducing Refugees: Photographìa of a Crisis*. Lanham: Rowman & Littlefield.

Caravan for the Rigsts of Refugees and Migrants. 2023. http://thecaravan.org/node /4773 (accessed April 2023).

Cárdenas Castro, Juan Cristóbal, and Raphael Lana Seabra (eds.). 2022. *El giro dependentista latinoamericano*. Los orígenes de la teoría marxista de la Dependencia, Santiago de Chile: Ariadna Ediciones.

Cardoso, Fernando Henrique, and Enzo Faletto. 1969. *Dependencia y desarrollo en América Latina*. Mexico City: Siglo XXI.

Cardoso, Fernando Henrique, and Enzo Faletto. 1979. *Dependency and Development in Latin America*. Berkeley: University of California Press.

Cariño Trujillo, Carmen. 2019. Colonialidad del poder y colonialidad del género: Sentipensar las luchas de mujeres indígenas en Abya Yala desde los mundos en relación. *Revista De Sociología* 28: 27–48.

Cariño Trujillo, Carmen. 2020. Feminicidio, una reflexión desde la imbricación de opresiones. *Iberoamérica Social* XIV: 13–15.

Cariño Trujillo, Carmen. 2021. Mujeres indígenas y campesinas en defensa de la tierra-territorio. Resistencia y r-existencias desde mundos en relación. In *Conflictos territoriales y territorialidades en disputa*, edited by Pabel López and Milson Betancourt, 195–220. Buenos Aires: CLACSO.

Cariño, Carmen, and Alejandro Montelongo González. 2022. Coloniality of power and coloniality of gender: Sentipensar the struggles of indigenous women in Abya Yala from worlds in relation. *Hypatia* 3, no. 3: 544–558.

Carrigan, Michelle, and Myrna Dawson. 2020. Problem representations of femicide/feminicide legislation in Latin America. *International Journal for Crime, Justice and Social Democracy* 9, no. 2: 1–19.

Cavallero, Luci, and Verónica Gago. 2020. 10 Theses on feminist economics (or the antagonism between the strike and finance). *CLCWeb: Comparative Literature and Culture* 22, no. 2. https://docs.lib.purdue.edu/clcweb/vol22/iss2/10/ (accessed September 2022).

Çaylı, Eray. 2021. The aesthetics and publics of testimony: Participation and ageny in architectural memorilizations of the 1993 Solingen Arson attack. *The Cambridge Journal of Anthropology* 39, no. 1: 72–92.

Ceceña, Ana Esther. 2004. Los desafíos del mundo donde en que caben todos los mundos y la subversión del saber histórico de la lucha. *Revista Chiapas* 16. https://chiapas.iiec .unam.mx/No16/ch16cecena.html (accessed August 2022).

Celermajer, Danielle, Astrida Neimanis, Susan Reid, David Schlosberg, Anik Waldow, Sria Chatterjee, Alasdair Cochrane, Stefanie Fishel, Anne O'Brien, and Krithika Srinivasan. 2020. Justice through a multispecies lens. *Contemporary Political Theory* 19: 475–512.

Certeau, Michel de. 1984. *The Practice of Everyday Life*. Berkeley: University of California Press.

Césaire, Aimé. 2001 [1950]. *Discours on Colonialism*. New York: Monthly Review Press.

Chakraborty, Debadrita. 2021. The 'living dead' within 'death-worlds': Gender crisis and covid-19 in India. *Gender, Work & Organization* 28, Supplement 2: 330–39.

Chaves Palacios, Julián. 2019. Consecuencias del franquismo a la España democrática: Legislación, exhumaciones de fossa y memoria. *Historia Contemporánea* 60: 509–38.

Cheng, Anne Anlin. 2000. *The Melancholy of Race: Psychoanalysis, Assimilation, and Hidden Grief*. Oxford: Oxford University Press.

Chin, Rita. 2009. *The Guest Worker Question in Postwar Germany*. Cambridge: Cambridge University Press.

Chiellino, Gino. 1995. *Fremde: A Discourse of the Foreign*. Translated by Luise von Flotow. Toronto: Guernica.

Cholia, Harpreet Kaur, and Christin Jänicke (eds.). 2021. *Unentbehrlich. Solidarität mit Betroffenen rechter, rassistischer und antisemitischer Gewalt*. Münster: Edition assemblage.

Cipolletta, Sabrina, Lorenza Entilli, and Sara Filisetti. 2022. Uncertainty, shock and anger: Recent loss experiences of first-wave COVID-19 pandemic in Italy. *Journal of Community & Applied Social Psychology.*

Clewell, Tammy. 2004. Mourning beyond Melancholia: Freud's psychoanalysis of loss. *Journal of the American Psychoanalytic Association* 52, no. 1: 43–67.

Cocks, Joan. 2012. The violence of structures and the violence of foundings. *New Political Science* 34, no. 2: 221–7.

Colatrella, Steven. 2013. Collective housekeeping and the revenge of the Oikos against Hannah Arendt on democracy, work and the welfare state. *International Critical Thought* 3, no. 4: 444–467.

Colectivo Miradas Críticas del Territorio desde el Feminismo. 2017. (Re)Patriarcalización de Los Territorios. La Lucha de Las Mujeres y Los Megaproyectos Extractivos. *Ecología Política* 54: 65–69.

Collins, Patricia Hill. 1990. *Black Feminist Thought: Knowledge, Consciousness and the Politics of Empowerment.* London/New York: Routledge.

Comas d'Argemir, Dolors, and Sílvia Bofill-Poch (eds.). 2021. *El cuidado de mayores y dependientes. Avanzando hacia la igualdad de género y la justicia social.* Barcelona: Icaria.

Combahee River Collective. 1977. *The Combahee river collective statement*, edited by Zillah Eisenstein. https://www.blackpast.org/african-american-history/combahee-river-collective-statement-1977/ (accessed March 2023).

Comité Clandestino Revolucionario Indigena, Enlace Zapatista. https://enlacezapatista.ezln.org.mx/2018/01/01/palabras-del-comite-clandestino-revolucionario-indigena-comandancia-general-del-ejercito-zapatista-de-liberacion-nacional-el-1-de-enero-del-2018-24-aniversario-del-inicio-de-la-guerra-contra-el-olvi/ (accessed August 2022).

Confortini, Catia. 2006. Galtung, violence, and gender: The case for a peace studies/feminism alliance. *Peace & Change* 31, no. 3: 333–67.

Coulthard, Glen Sean. 2014. *Red Skin, White Masks: Rejecting the Colonial Politics of Recognition.* Minneapolis: University of Minnesota Press.

Crenshaw, Kimberlé W. 2016. *The Urgency of Intersectionality.* San Francisco, CA:TED Talk, October 2016. https://www.youtube.com/watch?v=akOe5-UsQ2o (accessed September 2022).

Crenshaw, Kimberlé W. 2017. *On Intersectionality.* New York: The New Press.

Crenshaw, Kimberlé W., Andrea J. Ritchie, Rachel Anspach, Rachel Gilmer, and Luke Harris. 2015a. Say her name: Resisting police brutality against black women. https://scholarship.law.columbia.edu/faculty_scholarship/3226 (accessed August 2022).

Crenshaw, Kimberlé Williams, and Oristelle Bonis. 2005. Mapping the margins: Intersectionality, identity politics, and violence against women of color. *Cahiers du Genre* 39, no. 2: 51–82.

Crenshaw, Kimberlé W., Priscilla Ocen, and Jyoti Nanda. 2015b. Black girls matter: Pushed out, overpoliced and underprotected. https://scholarship.law.columbia.edu/faculty_scholarship/3227 (accessed August 2022).

Croce, Benardino di, Verein Migration und Integration in der Bundesrepublik. 2017. *Das Land, das nicht unser Land war. Erzählungen, Erlebnisse, Erfahrungen aus 50 Jahren Migration nach Deutschland.* Karlsruhe: von Loeper Literaturverlag.

Cruz, Hernández, Delmy Tania, and Manuel Bayón Jiménez from the Colectivo Miradas Críticas del Territorio desde el Feminismo (eds.). 2020. *Cuerpos, Territorios, Feminismos. Compilación latinoamericana de teorías, metodologías y practicas políticas.* Quito: Ediciones Abya Yala.

Çubukçu, Ayça. 2021. Of rebels and disobedients: Reflections on Arendt, race, lawbreaking. *Law Critique* 32: 33–50.

Cullors, Patrisse. 2019. Abolition and reparations: Histories of resistance, transformative justice, and accountability. *Harvard Law Review* 132, no. 6: 1684–729.

Cumes, Aura, and Médicos del Mundo. 2019. *Con nuestra fuerza hemos defendido la vida: Violencias patriarcales y coloniales desde la vivencia de mujeres y hombres Maya Q'eqchi' y Poqomchi'*. Cobán, Guatemala.

Cuttita, Paolo. 2018. Delocalization, humanitarianism, and human rights: The Mediterranean border between exclusion and inclusion. *Antipode* 50, no. 3: 783–803.

Dalla Costa, Mariarosa, and Selma James. 1972. *The Power of Women and the Subversion of the Community*. Bristol: Falling Wall Press.

Danewid, Ida. 2017. White innocence in the black mediterranean: Hospitality and the erasure of history. *Third World Quartely* 38, no. 2: 1–16.

Danisi, Carmelo, Moira Dustin, Nino Ferreira, and Nina Held. 2021. *Queering Asylum in Europe: Legal and Social Experiences of Seeking International Protection on grounds of Sexual Orientation and Gender Identity*. (IMISCOE Research Series). Cham: Springer Nature.

Das, Veena. 2006. *Life and Words: Violence and the Descent into the Ordinary*. Berkeley: University of California Press.

Das, Veena, Arthur Kleinman, Mamphela Ramphele, and Pamela Reynolds (eds.). 2000. *Violence and Subjectivity*. Berkeley: University of California Press.

Das, Veena, and Clara Han. 2015. *Living and Dying in the Contemporary World*. Berkeley: University of California Press.

Davies, Carole Boyce. 2008. *Left of Karl Marx – The Political Life of Black Communist Claudia Jones*. Durham: Duke University Press.

Davis, Angela Y. 1983. *Women, Race, and Class*. New York: Vintage Books.

Davis, Angela Y. 2003. *Are Prisons Obsolete?* New York: Seven Stories Press.

Davis, Angela Y. 2005. *Abolition Democracy: Beyond Empire, Prisons, and Torture*. Chico: AK Press.

Davis, Benjamin P. 2019. The politics of Édouard Glissant's right to opacity. *The CLR James Journal* 25, nos. 1–2: 59–70.

De Genova, Nicholas. 2018. The 'migrant crisis' as racial crisis: Do BlackLivesMatter in Europe? *Ethnic and Racial Studies* 41, no. 10: 1765–1782.

De la, O., María Eugenia, and Christian Zlolniski. 2020. At the crossroads: Challenges and opportunities of union organizing in the Mexico-US border. *Dialectical Anthropology* 44: 187–204.

DeBerry-Spence, Benét, and Lez Trujillo-Torres. 2022. 'Don't give us death like this!' Commemorating death in the age of COVID-19. *Journal of the Association for Consumer Research* 7, no. 1: 27–35.

Defterli, Sefa. 2006. *Kein 10. Opfer/No 10th Victim*. Video Documentation in Kassel on May 6, 2006, Digital Video, Color, Sound, 90 min.

Delphy, Christine, and Diana Leonard. 1980. A materialist feminism is possible. *Feminist Review* 4, no. 1: 79–105.

Demirtaş, Birgül, Adelheid Schmitz, Derya Gür-Şeker, and Çağrı Kahveci (eds.). 2023. *Solingen, 30 Jahre nach dem Brandanschlag*. Bielefeld: transcript.

Dengler, Corina, and Miriam Lang. 2022. Commoning care: Feminist degrowth visions for a socio-ecological transformation. *Feminist Economics* 28, no. 1: 1–28.

Dengler, Pascal, and Naika Foroutan. 2017. Die Aufarbeitung des NSU als deutscher Stephen-Lawrence-Moment? – Thematisierung von institutionellen Rassismus in

Deutschland und Großbritannien. In *Rassismuskritik und Widerstandsformen*, edited by Karim Fereidooni and Meral El, 429–46. Wiesbaden: Springer VS.

Dennis, Mike. 2007. Working under hammer and sickle: Vietnamese workers in the German democratic republic, 1980–89. *German Politics* 16, no. 3: 339–57.

Demirtaş, Birgül. 2023a. Der Solinger Brandanschlag – eine biografische und gesellschaftspolitische Annäherung aus der Perspektive einer deutsch-türkischen Solingerin. In *Solingen, 30 Jahre nach dem Brandanschlag*, edited by Birgül Demirtaş, Adelheid Schmitz, Derya Gür-Şeker, and Çağrı Kahveci, 197–210. Bielefeld: transcript.

Demirtaş, Birgül. 2023b. Der Brandanschlag hat unser Leben starkt geprägt, wir hätten alle sterben können. In *Solingen, 30 Jahre nach dem Brandanschlag*, edited by Birgül Demirtaş, Adelheid Schmitz, Derya Gür-Şeker, and Çağrı Kahveci, 67–80. Bielefeld: transcript.

Derrida, Jacques. 1977. FORS. *The Georgia Review* 31, no. 1: 64–116.

Derrida, Jacques. 1988. *Limited Inc*. Evanston: Northwestern University Press.

Derrida, Jacques. 1990. *Memoires for Paul de Man*. New York: Columbia University Press.

Derrida, Jacques. 1994. *Specters of Marx*. New York: Routledge.

Derrida, Jacques. 1995a. *The Gift of Death*, translated by David Wills. Chicago: University of Chicago Press.

Derrida, Jacques. 1995b. *Points … Interviews, 1974–1994*, edited by Elisabeth Weber and translated by Peggy Kamuf. Stanford: Stanford University Press.

Derrida, Jacques. 2001. *The Work of Mourning*, translated by Pascale-Anne Brault and Michael Naas. Chicago: Chicago University Press.

Derrida, Jacques, Pascale-Anne Brault, and Michael Naas. 1996. By force of mourning. *Critical Inquiry* 22, no. 2: 171–92.

Desprét, Vinciane. 2011. Acabando com o luto, pensando com os mortos. *Fractal: Revista de Psicologia* 23, no. 1: 73–82.

Di Maio, Alessandra. 2013. The mediterranean, or where Africa does (not) meet Italy. In *The Narratives*, edited by Sabine Schrader and Daniel Winkler, 41–52. Newcastle: Cambridge Scholars Publishing.

Dilts, Andrew, Yves Winter, Thomas Biebricher, Eric Vance Johnson, Antonio Y. Vázquez-Arroyo, and Joan Cocks. 2012. Revisiting Johan Galtung's concept of structural violence. *New Political Science* 34, no. 2: 191–4.

Domínguez, Edmé, Rosalba Icaza, Cirila Quintero, Silvia López, and Åsa Stenman. 2010. Women workers in the maquiladoras and the debate on global labor standards. *Feminist Economics* 16, no. 4: 185–209.

Doppler, Lisa. 2021. *Widerständiges Wissen. Herbert Marcuses Protesttheorie in Diskussion mit Intellektuellen der Refugee Bewegung in den 2010er Jahren*. Bielefeld: Transcript.

Dosthossein, Arash, and Narges Nasimi. 2020. Zur Position ›Asylsuchender‹ und ihren Kämpfen in modernen Gesellschaften. In *Der Begriff des Flüchtlings. Rechtliche, moralische und politische Kontroversen*, edited by Daniel Kersting and Marcus Leuoth, 247–56. Berlin: J.B. Metzler.

Doughan, Sultan. 2022. Memory meetings: Semra Ertan's *Ausländer* and the practice of the migrant archive. *Transit* 13, no. 2: 61–82.

Dreß, Matte. 2018. *Die politischen Parteien in der deutschen Islamdebatte. Konfliktlinien, Entwicklungen und Empfehlungen*. Berlin: Springer VS.

Du Bois, W. E. B. 1998 [1935]. *Black Reconstruction in America, 1860–1880*. New York: The Free Press.

Du Bois, W. E. B. 2004 [1903]. *Souls of Black Folk*, edited by Manning Marable. New York: Routledge.

Du Bois, W. E. B. 2007a [1899]. *The Philadelphia Negro: A Social Study*, edited by Henry Louis Gate. Oxford: Oxford University Press.

Du Bois, W. E. B. 2007b. *The World and Africa/Color and Democracy*, edited by Henry Louis Gate. Oxford: Oxford University Press.

Durkheim, Émile. 2001 [1912]. *The Elementary Forms of the Religious Life*, translated by Carol Cosman. Oxford: Oxford University Press.

Dussel, Enrique. 1995. *The Invention of the Américas: Eclipse of "the Other" and the Myth of Modernity*, translated by Michael D. Barber. New York: Continuum.

Dustin, Moira, and Nina Held. 2021. 'They sent me to the mountain': The role of space, faith and support groups for LGBTIQ+ asylum claimants. In *Queer Migration and Asylum in Europe*, edited by Richard Mole, 184–215. London: UCL Press.

El Tayeb, Fatima. 2001. *Schwarze Deutsche: Der Diskurs um »Rasse« und nationale Identität 1890–1933*. Frankfurt am Main: Campus.

El Tayeb, Fatima, and Vanessa Eileen Thompson. 2019. Alltagsrassismus, staatliche Gewalt und koloniale Tradition. Ein Gespräch über Racial Profiling und intersektionale Widerstände in Europa. In *Racial Profiling. Struktureller Rassismus und antirassistischer Widerstand*, edited by Mohamed Wa Baile, Serena O. Dankwa, Tarek Naguib, Patricia Purtschert, and Sarah Schilliger, 311–28. Bielefeld: Transcript Verlag.

Eng, David L., and David Kazanjian. 2003. *Loss: The Politics of Mourning*. Los Angeles: University of California Press.

Eng, David L., and Shinhee Han. 2019. *Racial Melancholia, Racial Dissociation: On the Social and Psychic Lives of Asian Americans*. Durham: Duke University Press.

Erel, Umut. 2009. *Migrant Women Transforming Citizenship. Life-Stories from Britain and Germany*. London: Routledge.

Escobar, Arturo. 2018. *Otro posible es posible: Caminando hacia las transiciones desde Abya Yala/ Afro/Latino-América*. Bogota: Ediciones desde Abajo.

Escobar, Arturo. 2020. *Pluriversal Politics: The Real and the Possible*, translated by David Frye. Durham: Duke University Press.

Espinosa Miñoso, Yuderkys. 2014. Una crítica descolonial a la epistemología feminista crítica. *El Cotidiano* 184: 7–12.

Espinosa Miñoso, Yuderkys (ed.). 2018. *Feminismo decolonial: Nuevos aportes teóricos-metodológicos a más de una década*. Quito: Ediciones Abya Yala.

Espinosa Miñoso, Yuderkys. 2019. Hacer genealogía de la experiencia: El método hacia una crítica a la colonialidad de la Razón feminista desde la experiencia histórica en América Latina. *Revista Direito e Praxis* 10, no. 3: 2007–32.

Espinosa Miñoso, Yuderkys. 2022a. *De por qué es necesario un feminismo decolonial*. Barcelona: Icaria

Espinosa Miñoso, Yuderkys, and Katia Sepúlveda. 2022a. El futuro ya fue. Exhibition Museum La Virreina, Barcelona. https://ajuntament.barcelona.cat/lavirreina/es/investigacion/el-futuro-ya-fue-antifuturismo-cimarron/550.

Espinosa Miñoso, Yuderkys. 2022b. The future already was: A critique of the idea of progress in sex-gendered and queer identitarian liberation narratives on Abya Yala. In *The Palgrave Handbook in Critical Race and Gender*, edited by Shirley Anne Tate and Encarnación Gutiérrez Rodríguez, 209–225. London: Palgrave.

Espinosa Miñoso, Yuderkys, Diana Gómez Correal, and Karina Ochoa Muñoz (eds.). 2014. *Tejiendo de otro modo: Feminismo, epistemología y apuestas descoloniales en Abya Yala*. Popayán: Editorial Universidad del Cauca.

Espinosa Miñoso, Yuderkys, María Lugones, and Nelson Maldonado Torres (eds.). 2022. *Decolonial Feminism in Abya Yala: Caribbean, Meso, and South American Contributions*. Lanham: Rowman & Littlefield Publishing.

Estes, Nick, and Jaskiran Dhillon. 2019. *Standing With Standing Rock: Voices From the #NoDAPL Movement*. Minneapolis: University of Minnesota Press.

Fals Borda, Orlando. 2015. *Una sociología sentipensante para América Latina/Orlando Fals Borda; antología y presentación*, edited by Víctor Manuel Moncayo. México, D. F.: Siglo XXI Editores; Buenos Aires: CLACSO.

Fanon, Frantz. 2002 [1961]. *Les damnés de la terre*. Paris: La Découverte.

Fanon, Frantz. 2008 [1952]. Peau noire, masques blancs. Seuil. In *Black Skin, White Masks*, translated by Richard Philcox. New York: Grove Books.

Fassin, Didier. 2012. *Humanitarian Reason: A Moral History of the Present*. Berkeley: University of California Press.

Fassin, Didier. 2020. *De l'inégalité des vies. (Leçon Inaugurale Collège de France 16.01.2020)*. Paris: Collège de France.

Fatma und Neşe im Gespräch mit B. Demirtaş. 2023. Wir waren geschockt, tieftraurig und wütend!. In *Solingen, 30 Jahre nach dem Brandanschlag*, edited by Birgül Demirtaş, Adelheid Schmitz, Derya Gür-Şeker, and Çağrı Kahveci, 127–47. Bielefeld: Transcript.

Federici, Silvia. 2004. *Caliban and the Witch: Women, the Body and Primitive Accumulation*. New York: Autonomedia.

Fedirici, Silvia. 1975. *Wages Against Housework*. Bristol: The Power of Women Collective and Falling Wall Press. https://caringlabor.wordpress.com/2010/09/15/silvia-federici-wages-against-housework/ (accessed August 2022).

Fedirici, Silvia. 2012. *Revolution at Point Zero: Housework, Reproduction, and Feminist Struggle*. PM Press.

FeMigra (Feministische Migrantinnen, Frankfurt). 1994. Wir, die Seiltänzerinnen: Politische Strategien von Migrantinnen gegen Ethnisierung und Assimilation. In *Gender Killer: Texte zu Feminismus und Politik*, edited by Cornelia Eichhorn and Sabine Grimm, 48–63. Berlin, Amsterdam: ID-Archiv.

Ferguson, Susan. 2016. Intersectionality and social-reproduction feminisms. *Historical Materialism* 24, no. 2: 38–60.

Ferguson, Susan. 2019. *Women and Work: Feminism, Labour, and Social Reproduction*. Toronto: Between the Lines.

Ferrándiz, Francisco. 2009. Fosas comunes, paisajes del terror. *Disparidades. Revista De Antropología* 64, no. 1: 61–94.

Ficklin, Erica, Melissa Tehee, Racheal M. Killgore, Devon Isaacs, Sallie Mack, and Tammie Ellington. 2022. Fighting for our sisters: Community advocacy and action for missing and murdered Indigenous women and girls. *Journal of Social Issues* 78, no. 1: 53–78.

Figge, Maja, and Anja Michaelsen. 2015. Das "rassifizierte Feld des Sichtbaren". Deutungen des NSU-Terrors 2004–2011. *Zeitschrift für Medienwissenschaften* 13: 107–17.

Florvil, Tiffany N. 2017. Transnational feminist solidarity: Black German women and the politics of belonging. In *Gendering Knowledge in Africa and the African Diaspora: Contesting History and Power*, edited by Toyin Falola and Olajumoke Yacob-Haliso, 87–109. New York: Routledge.

Folbre, Nancy. 2006. Measuring care: Gender, empowerment, and the care economy. *Journal of Human Development* 7, no. 2: 183–99.

Foucault, Michel. 1979. *Naissance de la biopolitique. Cours au Collège de France (1978–1979)*. Paris: Le Seuil.

Foucualt, Michel. 1984. *Histoire de la sexualité 3: Le souci de soi*. Paris: Gallimard.

Fracchia, Figueiredo Myriam. 2021. El proceso de exterminio selective de los activistas sociales en México (enero 2017–abril 2019). *Revista de Cultura de Paz* 5: 123–39.

Franco, Marielle. 2017. A emergência da vida para superar o anestesiamento social frente à retirada de direitos: o momento pós-golpe pelo olhar de uma feminista, negra e favelada. In *Tem Saída? Ensaios críticos sobre o Brasil*, edited by Winnie Bueno, Joanna Burigo, Rosana Pinheiro-Machado, and Esther Solano. Porto Alegre: Editora Zouk - Casa da Mãe Joanna.

Frank, André Gunder. 1969. *Latin America: Underdevelopment or Revolution*. New York: Monthly Review Press.

Fregoso, Rosa-Linda. 2020. Stolen lives: What the dead teach us. *Death Studies* 44, no. 11: 736–45.

Fregoso, Rosa-Linda, and Cynthia Bejarano. 2010. *Terrorizing Women: Feminicide in the Americas*. Durham: Duke University Press.

Freud, Sigmund. 1949 [1915] (8th Edition 1991). *Gesammelte Werke: Volume 10: Werke aus den Jahren 1913–1917*. Frankfurt am Main: S. Fischer.

Freud, Sigmund. 2018 [1915]. *Zeitgemäßes über Krieg und Tod*. Bremen: Inktank Publishing.

Freud, Sigmund. 2020 [1917]. Sigmund Freud. *Gesamtausgabe (SFG)*. Volume 16*: 1917–1920*. Gießen: Psychosozial Verlag.

Friedrich, Sebastian, Regina Wamper, and Jens Zimmermann (eds.). 2015. *Der NSU in bester Gesellschaft. Zwischen Neonazismus, Rassismus und Staat*. Duisburg: DISS.

Friedrichsmeyer, Sara, Sara Lennox, and Susanne Zantop. 1998. *The Imperial Imagination: German Colonialism and Its Legacies*. Ann Arbor: University of Michigan Press.

Friese, Heidrun. 2018. *Flüchtlinge: Opfer – Bedrohung – Helden: Zur politischen Imagination des Fremden*. Bielefeld:Transcript.

Funke, Hajo. 2015. *Staatsaffäre NSU. Eine offene Untersuchung*. Münster: Kontur-Verlag

Gago, Verónica. 2018. #We strike: Notes toward a political theory of the feminist strike. *The South Atlantic Quarterly* 117, no. 3: 660–69.

Gago, Verónica. 2019. *La potencia feminista o el deseo de cambiarlo todo*. Madrid: Traficantes de Sueños.

Gago, Verónica. 2020. *Feminism International: How to Change Everything*, translated by Liz Mason-Deese. London: Verso.

Gago, Verónica, and Diego Sztulwark. 2016. The temporality of social struggle at the end of the 'progressive' cycle in Latin America, translated by Liz Mason-Deese. *South Atlantic Quartely* 115, no. 3: 606–14.

Gago, Verónica, Marta Malo de Molina, and Luci Cavallero (eds.). 2020. *La Internacional Feminista. Luchas en los Territorios y contra el Neoliberalismo*. Madrid: Traficantes de Sueños.

Galeano, Eduardo. 2004 [1971]. *Las venas abiertas de América Latina*. Mexico, D.F.: Siglo XXI.

Galindo, María. 2021. *Feminismo Bastardo*. Bogota: Editorial Mujeres Creando.

Gallardo Saborido, Emilio. 2010. *Gitana tenias que ser. Las andalucias imaginadas por las coproducciones fílmicas España-Latinoamérica*. Sevilla: Consejo de Estudios Andaluces – Consejeria de la Presidencia.

Galtung, Johan. 1969. Violence, peace and peace research. *Journal of Peace Research* 6, no. 3: 167–91.

Galtung, Johan. 1971. A structural theory of imperialism. *Journal of Peace Research* 8, no. 2: 87–117.

Galtung, Johan. 1990. Cultural violence. *Journal of Peace Research* 27: 291–305.

Galtung, Johan. 1994. *Human Rights in Another Key*. Oxford: Polity Press.

Galtung, Johan, and Dietrich Fischer (eds.). 2013. Violence: Direct, structural and cultural. In *Pioneer of Peace Research*, edited by Johan Galtung, 35–40. Berlin, Heidelberg: Springer.

Garbe, Sebastian. 2022. *Weaving Solidarity: Decolonial Perspectives on Transnational Advocacy of and With the Mapuche*. Bielefeld: Transcript.

Garcés, Hellos F. 2016. El racismo antirom/anti-gitano y la opción decolonial. *Tabula Rasa* 25. http://www.scielo.org.co/scielo.php?pid=S1794-24892016000200225 &script=sci_arttext&tlng=es (accessed August 2022).

García-Fernández, Javier. 2021. Descolonización del conocimiento y pensamiento andaluz decolonial. *ANDULI* 20: 289–312. http://10.12795/anduli.2021.i20.16 (accessed August 2022).

Garcia-Sainz, Cristina, and Matxalen Legarreta. 2021. Working conditions on the care sector: Care homes after the tsunami caused by the covid-19 pandemic. In *33rd Annual Meeting*, SASE, 2021.

García Sanz, Carolina. 2018. 'Disciplinando al Gitano' en el siglo XX: Regulación y Parapenalidad en España desde una perspectiva europea. *Historia y Política* 40: 115–46.

García-Torres, Miriam. 2014. El feminismo reactiva la lucha contra extractivista en América Latina. *Periódico la marea*. https://www.lamarea.com/2014/02/17/ecuador -extractivismo-mujeres/ (accessed August 2022).

García-Torres, Miriam, Eva Vázquez, Delmy Tania Cruz, and Manuel Bayón. 2020. Extractivismo y (re)patriarcalización de los territorios. In *Cuerpos, territorios y feminismos. Compilación latinoamericana de teorías, metodologías y prácticas políticas*, edited by Delmy Tania Cruz Hernández and Manuel Bayón Jiménez from Colectivo Miradas Críticas del Territorio desde el Feminismo, 23–43. Quito: Ediciones Abya-Yala.

Gargallo Celentani, Francesca. 2014. *Feminismos desde Abya Yala. Ideas y Proposiciones de las mujeres de 607 pueblos en Nuestra América*. Mexico D.F.: Editorial Corte y Confección.

Garza, Alicia. 2014. A Herstory of the #BlackLivesMatter movement. *The Feminist Wire* (Blog), October 7. www.thefeministwire.com/2014/10/blacklivesmatter-2 (accessed September 2022).

Garza, Alicia. 2020. *The Purpose of Power: How We Come Together When We Fall Apart*. New York: Random House.

Gaspar de Alba, Alicia and Georgina Guzmán. 2010. *Making a Killing: Femicide, Free Trade, and La Frontera*. Austin: University of Texas Press.

Gatti, Gabriel. 2020. The social disappeared: Genealogy, global circulations, and (possible) uses of a category for the *bad life*. *Public Culture* 32, no. 1: 25–43.

Gatti, Gabriel, and Jaume Peris Blanes. 2020. The leftovers: The dead in life and social disappearance. *Death Studies* 44, no. 11: 681–9.

Gatti, Gabriel, and María Martínez. 2020. Dead in life: Lives pierced by death. *Death Studies* 44, no. 11: 677–80.

Gay, Peter. 1988. *Freud: A Life for Our Time*. New York: W.W. Norton & Company.

Gelbin, Cathy. 2010. *The Golem Returns: From German Romantic Literature to Global Jewish Culture, 1808–2008*. Ann Arbor: University of Michigan Press.

Gelbin, Cathy. 2017. *Cosmpolitanisms and the Jews*. Ann Arbor: University of Michigan Press.

Genç, Hatice im Gespäch mit B. Demirtaş. 2023. Keine Sprache der Welt kann unsere Verluste und die Folgen der rassistischen und extrem rechten Brandanschlags von Solingen 1993 beschreiben. In *Solingen, 30 Jahre nach dem Brandanschlag*, edited by Birgül Demirtaş, Adelheid Schmitz, Derya Gür-Şeker, and Çağrı Kahveci, 37–52. Bielefeld: transcript.

Genç, Kâmil im Gespräch mit B. Demirtaş. 2023. Der Brandanschlag hat unser Leben stark geprägt, wir hätten alle sterben können. In *Solingen, 30 Jahre nach dem Brandanschlag*, edited by Birgül Demirtaş, Adelheid Schmitz, Derya Gür-Şeker, and Çağrı Kahveci, 67–80. Bielefeld: transcript.

Genç, Cihat im Gesprächt mit Adelheid Schmitz. 2023. Meine Schwestern lernte ich nicht kennen. In *Solingen, 30 Jahre nach dem Brandanschlag*, edited by Birgül Demirtaş, Adelheid Schmitz, Derya Gür-Şeker, and Çağrı Kahveci, 93–106. Bielefeld: transcript.

Gibbs Hunt, Ida. 1923. Letter from Ida Gibbs Hunt to W. E. B. Du Bois, October 1, 1923. W.E.B. Du Bois Papers 2. Series 1A. Genereal Correspondence. Roberts S. Cox Special Collections and University Archives Research Center, University of Massachusetts Amherst. https://credo.library.umass.edu/view/full/mums312-b021-i313 (accessed April 2023).

Gilmore, Ruth Wilson. 2007. *Golden Gulag. Prison, Surplus Crisis, and Opposition in Globalizing California*. Berkeley: University of California Press.

Gilmore, Ruth Wilson. 2011. What is to be done? *American Quarterly* 63, no. 2: 245–65.

Gilroy, Paul. 1993. *The Black Atlantic: Modernity and Double Consciousness*. Cambridge: Harvard University Press.

Gilroy, Paul. 2000. *Against Race: Imagining Political Culture Beyond the Color Line*. Cambridge: Harvard University Press.

Gimenez, Martha E. 2019. *Marx, Women, and Capitalist Social Reproduction*. Leiden: Brill.

Gines, Kathryn T. 2009. Hannah Arendt: Liberalism, and racism: Controversies concerning violence, segregation, and education. *The Southern Journal of Philosophy* 47: 53–76.

Gines, Kathryn T. 2014. *Hannah Arendt and the Negro Question*. Bloomington: Indiana University Press.

Gleeson, Joanne Jules, and Elle O'Rourke (eds.). 2021. *Transgender Marxism*. London: Pluto Press.

Glissant, Édouard. 1997. *Poetics of Relation*. Ann Arbor: The University of Michigan Press.

Glorius, Birgit. 2020. Migrationsgeschichte Ostdeutschlands I. Von der Zeit der DDR bis in die 1990er-Jahre. In *Regionalentwicklung in Ostdeutschland*, edited by Sören Becker and Matthias Naumann, 211–22. Berlin: Springer Spektrum.

Goldberg, David Theo. 2003. *The Anatomy of Racism*. Minneapolis: University of Minnesota.

González Ferrin, Emilio. 2006. *Historía General de Al Andalus*. Córdoba: Almuzara.

González Ferrin, Emilio. 2017. *Cuando fuimos árabes*. Córdoba: Almuzara.

Gordon, Lewis. 2005. Through the zone of nonbeing a reading of Black skin, White Masks in celebration of Fanon's eightieth birthday. *The CLR James Journal* 11, no. 1: 1–43.

Gorer, Geoffrey. 1965. *Death, Grief and Mourning in Contemporary Britain*. London: Cresset.

Gready, Paul, and Simon Robins. 2014. From transitional to transformative justice: A new agenda for practice. *International Journal of Transitional Justice* 8, no. 3: 339–61.

Grosfoguel, Ramón. 2000. Modernity, and dependency theory in Latin America. *Nepantla: Views From South* 1, no. 2: 347–74.

Grosfoguel, Ramón. 2016. What is racism? *Journal of World-System Research* 22, no. 1: 9–15.

Güleç, Ayşe. 2015. Fordern, überfordern, verweigern. Bild- und Raumpolitik(en) in der Migrationsgesellschaft. In *Gespräche über Rassismus. Perspektiven & Widerstände*, edited by Çetin, Zülfukar and Savaş Taş, 189–215. Berlin: Yılmaz Günay.

Güleç, Ayşe. 2018a. Vermittlung von Realitäten: The society of friends of Halit. *Art Education Research* 8, no. 14: 1–10. https://sfkp.ch/resources/files/2018/03/n°14_Ayse_Gulec_DE.pdf (accessed September 2022).

Güleç, Ayşe. 2018b. The society of friends of Halit: Migrant-situated knowledge and affirmative sabotage*. *Documenta Studies*, no. 1: 1–11.

Güleç, Ayşe, and Cana Bilir-Meier. 2018. Bewegungen zwischen Archiven – Dekolonisierung von Disziplinen/Movements between archives – Decolonizing disciplines. *Camara Austria* 141: 33–44.

Güleç, Ayşe, and Johanna Schaffer. 2017. Empathie, Ignoranz und migrantisch situiertes Wissen: Gemeinsam an der Auflösung des NSU-Komplexes arbeiten. In *Den NSU Komplex analysieren*, edited by Juliane Karakayali, Çağrı Kahveci, Doris Liebscher, and Carl Melchers, 57–79. Bielefeld: Transcript.

Güleç, Ayşe, and Lee Hielscher. 2015. Zwischen Hegemonialität und Multiplizität des Erinnerns. Suchbewegungen einer gesellschaftlichen Auseinandersetzung mit dem NSU. In *Der NSU in bester Gesellschaft. Zwischen Neonazismus, Rassismus und Staat*, edited Sebastian Friedrich, Regina Wamper, and Jens Zimmermann, 144–58. Münster: Unrast.

Gunn Allen, Paula. 1992 [1986]. *The Sacred Hoop: Recovering the Feminine in American Indian Traditions*. Boston: Beacon Press.

Gutiérrez Rodríguez, Encarnación. 1999. *Intellektuelle Migrantinnen. Subjektivitäten im Zeitalter der Globalisierung. Eine dekonstruktive postkoloniale Analyse von Prozessen der Ethnisierung und Vergeschlechtlichung*. Münster: Opladen.

Gutiérrez Rodríguez, Encarnación. 2010. *Migration, Domestic Work and Affect*. New York: Routledge.

Gutiérrez Rodríguez, Encarnación. 2014a Domestic work-affective labor: On feminization and the coloniality of labor. *Women's Studies International Forum* 46: 45–53.

Gutiérrez Rodríguez, Encarnación. 2014b. The precarity of feminisation: On domestic work, heteronormativity and the coloniality of labour. *International Journal of Politics, Culture and Society* 27, no. 2: 191–202.

Gutiérrez Rodríguez, Encarnación. 2015. Archipelago Europe: On creolizing conviviality. In *Creolizing Europe: Legacies and Transformations*, edited by Encarnación Gutiérrez Rodríguez and Shirley Anne Tate, 80–99. Liverpool: Liverpool University Press.

Gutiérrez Rodríguez, Encarnación. 2016. 'Flüchtlingskrise', Kolonialität und Rassismus – Eine andere Grammatik der Krise des Kapitalismus denken. *Das Argument* 319, no. 58: 1–18.

Gutiérrez Rodríguez, Encarnación. 2018a. The coloniality of migration and the 'refugee crisis': On the asylum-migration nexus, the transatlantic white European settler colonialism-migration and racial capitalism. *Refuge: Canada's Journal on Refugees* 34, no. 1: 16–28.

Gutiérrez Rodríguez, Encarnación. 2018b. Political subjectivity, transversal mourning and a caring common: Responding to deaths in the Mediterranean. *Critical African Studies* 10, no. 3: 345–60.

Gutiérrez Rodríguez, Encarnación. 2020. Creolising conviviality: Thinking relational ontology and decolonial ethics through Ivan Illich and Édouard Glissant. In *Conviviality at the Crossroads: The Poetics and Politics of Everyday Encounters*, edited by Oscar Hemer, Maja Povrzanović Frykman, and Per-Markku Ristilammi, 105–24. Springer Nature.

Gutiérrez Rodríguez, Encarnación. 2021. Entangled migrations: The coloniality of migration and creolizing conviviality. Mecila Working Paper No. 35. https://www.iai.spk-berlin.de/fileadmin/dokumentenbibliothek/Veroeffentlichungen/Mecila_Working_Papers/WP_35_Gutiérrez_Rodr%C3%ADguez_Online.pdf (accessed September 2022).

Gutiérrez Rodríguez, Encarnación. 2024. Precarious inclusion: Refugees in higher education in Germany. In *Ethics, Rights, Culture and the Humanization of Refugees*, edited by Anna Kirova, Yasemin Abu-Laban, Reza Hasmath, and Michael Frishkopf. Edmonton: University of Athabasca Press.

Gutiérrez Rodríguez, Encarnación, and Pinar Tuzcu. 2021. *Migrantischer Feminismus in der deutschen Frauenbewegung, 1985–2000*. Münster: Edition assemblage.

Gutiérrez Rodríguez, Encarnación, and Rhoda Reddock. 2021. *Decolonial Perspectives on Entangled Inequalities: Europe and the Caribbean*. New York: Anthem Press.

Gutiérrez Rodríguez, Encarnación, and Shirley Anne Tate. 2015. *Creolizing Europe: Legacies and Transformations*. Liverpool: Liverpool University Press.

Gün, Ali Kemal. 2023. Transgenerational vererbte Trauma. In *Solingen, 30 Jahre nach dem Brandanschlag*, edited by Birgül Demirtaş, Adelheid Schmitz, Derya Gür-Şeker, and Çağrı Kahveci, 303–316. Bielefeld: transcript.

Ha, Kien Nghi. 2012a. *Asiatische Deutsche: Vietnamesische Diaspora and Beyond*. Berlin: Assoziation.

Ha, Kien Nghi. 2012b. Rostock-Lichtenhagen. Die Rückkehr des Verdrängten. Blog *Asiatische Deutsche. Vietnamesische Diaspora and Beyond*. https://asiatischedeutsche.wordpress.com/2012/09/19/rostock-lichtenhagen-die-ruckkehr-des-verdrangten/ (accessed September 2022).

Ha, Kien Nghi. 2012c. Rostock-Lichtenhagen – (K)ein Thema für die vietnamesische Community? Blog *Asiatische Deutsche. Vietnamesische Diaspora and Beyond*. https://asiatischedeutsche.wordpress.com/2012/08/23/rostock-lichtenhagen-kein-thema-fur-die-vietnamesische-community/ (accessed September 2022).

Hall, Stuart. 1994. Cultural identity and diaspora. In *Colonial Discourse and Postcolonial Theory: A Reader*, edited by Patrick Williams and Laura Christman, 227–37. London: Harvester Wheatsheaf.

Hall, Stuart. 1996. Who needs 'identity'? In *Questions of Cultural Identity*, edited by Stuart Hall and Paul du Gay. London: SAGE.

Hall, Stuart. 1997. Old and new identities, old and new ethnicities. In *Culture, Globalization, and the World-System*, edited by Anthony D. King, 41–68. Minneapolis: University of Minnesota Press.

Hall, Stuart, Chas Critcher, Tony Jefferson, John Clarke, and Brian Roberts. 2013 [orig. 1978]. *Policing the Crisis: Mugging, the State and Law and Order*. Second Edition, Enlarged. London: Palgrave MacMillan.

Hansen, Peo and Stefan Jonsson. 2015. *Euroafrica: The Untold History of European Integration and Colonialism*. London: Bloomsbury.

Haritaworn, Jin, Adi Kuntsman, and Silvia Posocco. 2014. *Queer Necropolitics*. New York: Routledge.

Harris, Christopher Paul. 2021. (Caring for) the world that must be undone. *Contemporary Political Theory* 29: 890–925.

Hartman, Saidiya. 1997. *Scenes of Subjection: Terror, Slavery, and Self-Making in Nineteenth-Century America.* Oxford: Oxford University Press.

Hartmann, Heidi I. 1979. The unhappy marriage of Marxism and feminism: Towards a more progressive union. *Capital & Class* 3, no. 2: 1–33.

Held, Nina. 2022. As queer refugees, we are out of category, we do not belong to one, or the other: LGBTIQ+ refugees' experiences in "ambivalent" queer spaces. *Ethnic and Racial Studies*: 1–21.

Held, Virginia (ed.). 2006. *The Ethics of Care: Personal, Political, Global.* New York: Oxford University Press.

Hernández, Castillo, and Rosalva Aída. 2014. Cuerpos femeninos, violencia y acumulación por desposesión. In *Des/posesión: Género, Territorio y luchas por la autodeterminación*, edited by Marisa Belausteguigoitia Ruis and María Josefina Saldaña-Portillo, 79–100. México: UNAM-PUEG.

Herzog Astaburuaga, Oscar. 2023. The Hanau massacre and state (in)action: A dossier. *Race & Class*: 1–14. https://journals.sagepub.com/doi/10.1177/03063968231156376 (accessed March 2023).

Hesse, Barnor, and Debra Thompson. 2022. Introduction: Antiblackness—Dispatches from Black political thought. *South Atlantic Quarterly* 121, no. 3: 447–75.

Heyden, Ulrich van der, Wolfgang Semmler, and Ralf Straßburg. 2014. *Mosambikanische Vertragsarbeiter in der DDR-Wirtschaft. Hintergründe – Verlauf – Folgen.* Münster: Lit Verlag.

Hielscher, Lee. 2016. Das Staatsgeheimnis ist Rassismus. Migrantisch-situiertes Wissen und die Bedeutungsebene des NSU-Terrors. Movements 2, no. 1: 187–97.

Higgins, Charlotte. 2018. Banu Cennetoğlu: 'As long as I have resources, I will make The List more visible'. *The Guardian*, 20 June 2018. https://www.theguardian.com/world/2018/jun/20/banu-cennetoglu-interview-turkish-artist-the-list-europe-migrant-crisis (accessed August 2022).

Hillmann, Felicitas. 2005. Riders on the storm: Vietnamese in Germany's two migration systems. In *Asian Migrants and European Labor Markets*, edited by Ernst Spaan, Felicitas Hillmann, and Ton van Naerssen, 80–100. London and New York: Routledge.

Hine, Darlene Clark, Trica Danielle Keaton, and Stephen Small (eds.). 2009. *Black Europe and the African Diaspora.* Champaign: University of Illinois Press.

Hinton, Elizabeth K. 2016. *From the War on Poverty to the War on Crime: The Making of Mass Incarceration in America.* Cambridge, MA: Harvard University Press.

Hirschkind, Charles. 2021. *The Feeling of History: Islam, Romanticism and Andalusia.* Chicago: Chicago University Press.

Honig, Bonnie. 1995. Towards an agonistic feminism. In *Feminist Interpretations of Hannah Arendt*, edited by Bonnie Honig, 135–66. Philadelphia, PA: Pennsylvania State University Press.

Honig, Bonnie. 2009. Antigone's Laments, Creon's grief: Mourning, membership, and the politics of exception. *Political Theory* 37, no. 1: 5–43.

Honig, Bonnie. 2013. *Antigone Interrupted.* Cambridge: Cambridge University Press.

Honkasalo, Julian. 2016. *Sisterhood, natality, queer: Reframing feminist interpretation of Hannah Arendt.* Dissertation submitted at the University of Helsinki.

Hooker, Juliet. 2017. Black protest/white grievance: On the problem of white political imaginations not shaped by loss. *The South Atlantic Quarterly* 116, no. 3: 483–504.

Horkheimer, Max, and Theodor W. Adorno. 2002 [1947]. *Dialectic of Enlightment*, edited by Gunzelin Schmid Noeri and translated by Edmund Jephcott. Stanford: Stanford University Press.

Horsti, Karina, and Klaus Neumann. 2019. Memorializing mass deaths at the border: Two cases from Canberra (Australia) and Lampedusa (Italy). *Ethnic and Racial Studies* 42, no. 2: 141–58.

Hügel, Ika, Chris Lange, and May Ayim (eds.). 1993. *Entfernte Verbindungen: Rassismus, Antisemitismus, Klassenunterdrückung.* Berlin: Orlanda.

Iberoamérica Social. 2020. *El femicidio, la massacre cotidiana en Iberoamérica* XIV, no. 8. https://iberoamericasocial.com/ojs/index.php/IS/issue/view/17 (accessed August 2022).

Illich, Ivan. 1973. *Tools for Conviviality.* New York: Harper & Row; London: Calder & Boyars.

Inan, Çiğdem. 2022. "Not this time". On the dispossession of grief. *Texte zur Kunst* 126. https://www.textezurkunst.de/en/126/cigdem-inan-not-this-time/ (accessed March 2023).

Inda, Jonathan Xavier. 2020. Fatal prescriptions: Immigration detention, mismedication, and the necropolitics of uncare. *Death Studies* 44, no. 11: 699–708.

Initiative 19. Februar Hanau 2021. Wir klagen an und fordern Taten statt Worte. In *Rassismus.Macht.Vergessen*, edited by Onur Suzan Nobrega, Matthias Quent, and Jonas Zipf, 77–80. Bielefeld: Transcript.

International Feminist Collective 1972. 2017. Statement of the international feminist collective. In *The New York Wages for Housework Committee 1972–77: History, Theory and Documents*, edited by in Silvia Federici and Arlen Austin, 30–31. New York: Autonomedia.

International Women Space. 2015. *In Our Own Words. Refugee Women in Germany Tell Their Stories.* Berlin: International Women Space.

Isaac, Jeffrey C. 1998. *Democracy in Dark Times.* Ithaca: Cornell Univesity Press.

Istanbul Protocolls. 2004 [1991]. *Manual on the Effective Investigation and Documentation of Torture and Other Cruel, Inhuman or Degrading Treatment or Punishment.* Professional Training Series no. 8, rev. 1. New York/Geneva: United Nations.

Itzu, Diana Itzu. 2022. *Una cuota de energía al tejido de la vida.* Buenos Aires: Consejo Latinoamericano de Ciencias Sociales; San Cristóbal de Las Casas, Chiapas: Cooperativa Editorial Retos; Guadalajara, Jalisco: Cátedra Jorge Alonso: Universidad de Guadalajara.

Jabardo Velasco, Mercedes. 2006. *Senegaleses en España. Conexiones entre origen y destino.* Madrid: Ministerio de Trabajo y Asuntos Sociales.

Jäger, Siegfried, and Jürgen Link (eds.). 1993. *Die Vierte Gewalt. Rassismus in den Medien.* Duisburg: Duisburger Institut für Sprach- und Sozialforschung (DISS).

Jaggar, Alison M. 1989. Love and knowledge: Emotion in feminist epistemology. *Inquiry* 32, no. 2: 151–76.

James, C. L. R. 2001 [1938]. *The Black Jacobins: Toussaint L'Ouverture and the San Domingo Revolution.* London: Penguin.

James, Joy. 2003. All power to the people! Hannah Arendt's theory of communicative power in a racialized democracy. In *Race and Racism in Continental Philosophy*, edited by Robert Bernasconi and Sybol Cook, 249–67. Bloomington: Indiana University Press.

Jenkins, Destin, and Justin Leroy. 2021. *Histories of Racial Capitalism.* New York: Columbia University Press.

John, Barbara. 2014. *Unsere Wunden kann die Zeit nicht heilen. Was der NSU-Terror für die Opfer und Angehörigen bedeutet.* Bonn: Bundeszentrale für politische Bildung.

Johnson, Clarence Sholé. 2009. Reading between the lines: Kathryn Gines on Hannah Arendt and antiblack racism. *The Southern Journal of Philosophy* 47: 77–83.

Jones, Claudia. 2016. *Beyond Containment: Autobiographical Reflections*, edited by Carole Boyce Davies. Banbury: Ayebia Clarke.

Jones, Ernest. 1975. *Life and Work of Sigmund Freud.* New York: Basic Books.

Joralemon, Donald. 2016. *Mortal Dilemmas: The Troubled Landscape of Death.* New York: Routledge.

Kahvaci, Çağrı. 2017. *Migrantische Selbstorganisierung im Kampf gegen Rassismus.* Münster: Unrast.

Kahveci, Çağrı. 2023. Ein kurzer Überblick über Rassismus und Antirassismus in Deutschland im Kontext türkeistämmiger Migrant*innen. In *Solingen, 30 Jahre nach dem Brandanschlag*, edited by Birgül Demirtaş, Adelheid Schmitz, Derya Gür-Şeker, and Çağrı Kahveci, 171–182. Bielefeld: transcript.

Karakayali, Juliane, Çağrı Kahveci, Doris Liebscher, and Carl Melchers (eds.). 2017. *Den NSU-Komplex analysieren: Aktuelle Perspektiven aus der Wissenschaft.* Bielefeld: Transcript.

Karakayalı, Serhat. 2008. *Gespenster der Migration. Zur Genealogie illegaler Einwanderung in der Bundesrepublik Deutschland.* Bielefeld: transcript.

Karakayalı, Serhat, and Vasilis Tsianos. 2002. Migrationsregimes in der Bundesrepublik Deutschland. Zum Verhältnis von Staatlichkeit und Rassismus. In *Konjunkturen des Rassismus*, edited by Alex Demerović and Manuela Bojadžijev, 246–267. Münster: Westfälisches Dampfboot.

Kateb, George. 2000. Political action: Its nature and advantages. In *The Cambridge Companion to Hannah Arendt*, edited by Dana Villa, 130–48. Cambridge: Cambridge University Press.

Keller, Jean, and Eva Feder Kittay. 2017. Feminist ethics of care. In *The Routledge Companion to Feminist Philosophy*, edited by Ann Garry, Serene J. Khader, and Alison Stone, 540–55. New York: Routledge.

Kermoal, Nathalie, and Isabel Altamirano-Jiménez. 2016. *Living on the Land: Indigenous Women's Understanding of Place.* Athabasca University Press.

King, Richard H. 2004. *Race, Culture, and the Intellectuals, 1940–1970.* Baltimore: Johns Hopkins University Press.

Klee, Ernst (ed.). 1972. *Gastarbeiter. Analysen und Berichte.* Frankfurt am Main: Edition Suhrkamp.

Kleffner, Heike. 2014. 24. Oktober 1991 Fünf Monate „Antirassistisches Zentrum" – Die Besetzung der TU Berlin 1991/92. *Der Berlin-Blog von apabiz.* https://rechtsaussen .berlin/2014/04/fuenf-monate-antirassistisches-zentrum-die-besetzung-der-tu-berlin -199192/ (accessed September 2022).

Kleffner, Heike. 2021. Die mörderische Gewalt der »Generation Terror« und die Verdrängung ihrer Opfer aus dem kollektiven Gedächtnis. In *Rassismus.Macht. Vergessen*, edited by Onur Suzan Nobrega, Matthias Quent, and Jonas Zipf, 257–72. Bielefeld: Transcript.

Kleffner, Heike, and Adreas Feser. 2013. Der NSU-Untersuchungsausschuss. *Bundeszentrale für politische Bildung.* https://www.bpb.de/themen/rechtsextremismus/ dossier-rechtsextremismus/172857/der-nsu-untersuchungsausschuss/.

Klesse, Christian. 2014. Poly economics—Capitalism, class, and polyamory. *International Journal of Politics, Culture, and Society* 27, no. 2: 203–20.

Knortz, Heike. 2008. *Diplomatische Tauschgeschäfte. Gastarbeiter in der westdeutschen Diplomatie und Beschäftigungspolitik 1953–1973*. Köln: Böhlau.

Kobelinsky, Carolina. 2020. Border beings: Present absences among migrants in the Spanish enclave of Melilla. *Death Studies* 44, no. 11: 709–17.

Kocatürk-Schuster, Bengü, and Ceren Türkmen. 2021. The history of racist violence, between structural racism, political mourning and the struggle for civil rights: An oral history perspective. In *Interkultur Ruhr 2016–2021*, edited by Johann-Yasirra Kluhs, Aurora Rodonò, Fabian Saavedra-Lara, and Nesrin Tunç, 102–13. Köln: StrzeleckiBooks.

Kocatürk-Schuster, Bengü, and Kutlu Yurtseven im Gespräch mit A. Schmitz. 2023. Warum wir erinnern. In *Solingen, 30 Jahre nach dem Brandanschlag*, edited by Birgül Demirtaş, Adelheid Schmitz, Derya Gür-Şeker, and Çağrı Kahveci, 353–372. Bielefeld: transcript.

Koller, Christian. 2006. The recruitment of colonial troops in Africa and Asia and their deployment in Europe during the first world war. *Immigrants & Minorities* 26, no. 1/2: 111–33.

Koller, Christian. 2011. Representing otherness: African, Indian, and European soldiers' letters and memoirs. In *Race, Empire and First World War Writing*, edited by Santanu Das, 127–42. Cambridge: Cambridge University Press.

Kourabas, Veronika. 2021. *Die Anderen ge-brauchen. Eine rassismustheoretische Analyse von >Gastarbeit< im migrationsgesellschaftlichen Deutschland*. Bielefeld: Transcript.

Kubaşık, Gamze. 2014. Ich will nicht ewig Opfer sein. In *Unsere Wunden kann die Zeit nicht heilen. Was der NSU-Terror für die Opfer und Angehörigen bedeutet*, edited by Barbara John, 121–34. Bonn: Bundeszentrale für politische Bildung Band.

Kujala, Will. 2021. Hannah Arendt, antiracist rebellion, and the counterinsurgent logic of the social. *European Journal of Political Theory*. https://journals.sagepub.com/doi/10.1177/14748851211009206https://journals.sagepub.com/doi/10.1177/14748851211009206 (accessed August 2022).

Lagarde y de los Ríos, Marcela. 2006a. *Feminicidio. La política del asesinato de mujeres*. Mexico: UNAM.

Lagarde y de los Ríos, Marcela. 2006b. Del femicidio al feminicidio. *Desde el jardín de Freud* 6: 216–25. https://repositorio.ciem.ucr.ac.cr/jspui/bitstream/123456789/9/3/RCIEM002.pdf (accessed September 2022).

Lagarde y de los Ríos, Marcela. 2007. Por los derechos humanos de las mujeres: La Ley General de Acceso de las Mujeres a una Vida Libre de Violencia. *Revista Mexicana de Ciencias Políticas y Sociales* 49, no. 200: 143–65.

Lagarde y de los Ríos, Marcela. 2008. Antropologia, feminismo y politica. Violencia feminicide y derechos humanos de las las mujeres. In *Ankulegi. Revista De Antropología Social, special issue Retos teóricos y nuevas practicas*, edited by Margaret Louise Bullen and María Carmen Diez Mintegui, 209–40.

Lambourne, Wendy. 2014. Transformative justice, reconciliation and peacebuilding. In *Transitional Justice Theories*, edited by Susanne Buckley Zistel, Teresa Koloma Beck, Christian Braun, and Friederike Mieth, 19–39. Routledge: New York.

LASA Forum. 2019. Special issue: Violencias contra líderes y lideresas defensores del territorio y el ambiente en América Latina. *LASA Forum* 50: 4.

Lee, Richard E. 2018. Lessons of the longe durée: The legacy of Fernand Braudel. *Historia Crítica* 69: 66–77.

Lee, You Jae. 2014. Glückauf der Kyopos – 50 Jahre koreanische Arbeitsmigration in Deutschland. Heinrich-Böll-Stiftung, Heimatkunde – migrationspolitisches Portal.

29.01.2014. https://heimatkunde.boell.de/de/2014/01/29/glueckauf-der-kyopos-50 -jahre-koreanische-arbeitsmigration-deutschland (accessed April 2023).

Legarreta Iza, Matxalen. 2013. El tiempo como herramienta para la economía feminista. In *IV Congreso de Economía Feminista*.

Lerner, Gerda. 1986. *The Creation of Patriarchy*. Oxford: Oxford University Press.

Lewicki, Aleksandra. 2017. 'The dead are coming': Acts of citizenship at Europe's borders. *Citizenship Studies* 21: 275–90.

Leyva Solano, Xochitl. 2019a. Abertura. In *En tiempos de muerte: Cuerpos, Rebeldias, Resistencias*, edited by Xochitl Leyva Solano and Rosalba Icaza, 11–26. Buenos Aires/Chiapas/La Haya: Cooperative Editorial Retos. CLACSO. Institute of Social Studies-Erasmus University Rotterdam.

Leyva Solano, Xochitl. 2019b. 'Poner el cuerpo' para des(colonizer)patriarcalizar nuestro conocimiento, la academia, nuestra vida. In *En tiempos de muerte: Cuerpos, Rebeldias, Resistencias*, edited by Xochitl Leyva Solano and Rosalba Icaza, 339–62. Buenos Aires/Chiapas/La Haya: Cooperative Editorial Retos. CLACSO. Institute of Social Studies-Erasmus University Rotterdam.

Leyva Solano, Xochitl, and Rosalba Icaza. 2019. *En tiempos de muerte: Cuerpos, Rebeldias, Resistencias, Series: Prácticas Otras de Conocimiento*, Vol. IV. Buenos Aires/Chiapas/La Haya: Cooperative Editorial Retos. CLACSO. Institute of Social Studies-Erasmus University Rotterdam.

Lewicki, Aleksandra. 2017. The dead are coming: Acts of citizenship at Europe's borders. *Citizenship Studies* 21, no. 3: 275–290.

Lidia, Clara E. 1997. *Immigración y Exilio. Reflexiones sobre el caso español*. México D.F./ Madrid: Siglo XXI.

Liebscher, Doris. 2017. Der NSU-Komplex vor Gericht: Zur Notwendigkeit einer Perspektivenerweiterung in der rechtlichen Auseinandersetzung mit institutionellen Rassismus. In *Den NSU-Komplex analysieren: Aktuelle Perspektiven aus der Wissenschaft*, edited by Juliane Karakayali, Çağrı Kahveci, Doris Liebscher, and Carl Melchers, 81–106. Bielefeld: Transcript.

Loick, Daniel, and Vanessa Eileen Thompson. 2022. *Abolitionismus. Ein Reader*. Frankfurt a.M.: Suhrkamp.

Loick, Daniel, and Vanessa Eileen Thompson. 2021. Abolitionist futures. prefigurations beyond violence. Special Issue in *Behemoth. A Journal of Civilization* 14, no. 3. https://ojs .ub.uni-freiburg.de/behemoth/issue/view/93 (accessed September 2022).

Lowney, Chris. 2005. *A Vanished World: Muslims, Christians, and Jews in Medieval Spain*. Oxford: Oxford University Press.

Lozano, Lerma, and Betty Ruth. 2019. Asesinato de mujeres y acumulación global. El caso del bello Puerto del mar, mi Buenaventura. In *En tiempo de muerte: Cuerpos, Rebeldias, Resistencias*, edited by Xoxitl Leyva Solano and Rosalba Icaza, 47–66. Series: Prácticas Otras de Conocimiento, Vol. IV. Buenos Aires/Chiapas/La Haya: Cooperative Editorial Retos. CLACSO. Institute of Social Studies-Erasmus University Rotterdam.

Lugones, María. 2007. Heterosexualism and the colonial/modern gender system. *Hypatia* 22, no. 1: 186–209.

Lugones, María. 2008. The coloniality of gender. Worlds & Knowledges Otherwise *(Spring)*.

Lugones, María. 2010. Toward a decolonial feminism. *Hypatia* 25, no. 4: 742–59.

Lugones, María. 2020. Gender and universality in colonial methodology. *Critical Philosophy of Race* 8, nos. 1–2: 25–47.

Luxemburg, Rosa. (in German orig. 1913). 2015. *The Accumulation of Capital.* Oxford: Benediction Classics.

MacCormack, Patricia. 2020. Embracing death, opening the world. *Australian Feminist Studies* 35, no. 104: 101–15.

Macharia, Keguro. 2015. Mbiti & Glissant. *The New Inquiry*, 9 March. https://thenewinquiry.com/blog/mbiti-glissant/ (accessed April 2023).

Mack, Ashley Noel, and Tiara R. Na'puti. 2019. Our bodies are not Terra Nullius: Building a decolonial feminist resistance to gendered violence. *Women's Studies in Communication* 42, no. 3: 347–70.

Madley, Benjamin. 2005. From Africa to Auschwitz: How German South West Africa incubated ideas and methods adopted and developed by the Nazis in Eastern Europe. *European History Quarterly* 35, no. 3: 429–64.

Malatino, Hill. 2020. *Trans Care.* Minneapolis: University of Minnesota Press.

Maldonado Torres, Nelson. 2007. On the coloniality of being. *Cultural Studies* 21, nos. 2–3: 240–270.

Malkki, Liisa H. 1994. *Purity and Exile: Violence, Memory, and National Cosmology Among Hutu Refugees in Tanzania.* Chicago: University of Chicago Press.

Mamani, Carlos. 2019. *Tinku y Pachakuti. Geopolíticas indígenas originarias y estado plurinacional en Bolivia.* Tuxtla Gutiérrez, Chiapas: Universidad de Ciencias y Artes de Chiapas/ Buenos Aires: CLACSO.

Mantena, Karuna. 2010. Genealogies of catastrophe: Arendt on the logic and legacy of imperialism. In *Politics in Dark Times: Encounters With Hannah Arendt*, edited by Seyla Benhabib, 83–112. Cambridge: Cambridge University Press.

Marchesoni, Stefano. 2016. *Walter Benjamins Konzept des Eingedenkens.* Berlin: Kadnos.

Márquez, Francia. 2016. Entre vientos de paz, y el pueblo afrocolombiano sin la garantía de sus derechos. In *Des/DIBUJANDO EL PAIS/aje. Aportes para la paz con los pueblos afrodescendientes e indígenas: Territorio, autonomía y buen vivir*, edited by Sheila Gruner, Melquiceded Blandón Mena, Jader Gómez Caicedo, and Charo Mina-Rojas, 133–45. Medellin: Ediciones Poder Negro y Centro Popular Afrodescendiente (cepafro.org).

Márquez, Francia, and Camilo Salcedo. 2012. Defensa del territorio y resistencia afrocolombiana en el norte del Cauca. In *Minería Territorio y Conflicto en Colombia*, edited by Catalina Toro-Péreu, Julio Fierro-Morales, Sergio Coronado Delgado, and Tatiana Roa Avendaño, 427–36. Bogotá: Universidad Nacional de Colombia.

Márquez Macías, Rosario. 1995. *La emigración Española a América (1765–1824).* Oviedo: Universidad de Oviedo.

Marschall, Annika, and Ann-Christine Simke. 2022. Forensic architecture in the theatre and the gallery: A reflection on counterhegemonic potentials and pitfalls of art institutions. *Theatre Research International* 47, no. 2: 142–59.

Martín-Díaz, Emma, and Beltrán Roca. 2017. Spanish migration to Europe: From the fordist model to the flexible economy. *Journal of Mediterranean Studies* 26, no. 2: 189–207.

Martínez-Andrade, Luis. 2022. Necropolitics and coloniality of power in Latin America. In *Crossing Racial Borders: The Epistemic Empowerment of the Subaltern*, edited by Lenita Perrier and Luis Martínez-Andrade. Lanham: Lexington Books.

Martín-Márquez, Susan. 2008. *Disorientations: Spanish Colonialism in Africa and the Performance of Identity.* New Haven: Yale University Press.

Martinez-López, Fernando (ed.). 2014. *Los andaluces en el exilio del 39*. Sevilla: Fundación Pública Andaluza – Centro de Estudios Andaluces.

Marx, Karl, and Friedrich Engels. 2004 [1845–6]. *The German Ideology*, edited by C. J. Arthur. New York: International Publishers.

Marx, Karl, and Friedrich Engels (Das Kapital and Vorarbeiten). 1990 [1887]. Chapter XXIII: Simple reproduciton. In *Capital: A Critical Analysis of Capitalist Production*, 493–503. London: MEGA, Vol. 9. Berlin: Dietz Verlag.

Maus, Andreas. 2016. *Documentary: Der Kuaför aus der Keupstrasse*. Köln.

Mayer, Hans. 1992a. *Vorlesung zum 100. Geburtstag Walter Benjamin*. Inaugural Lecture, University Leipzig. https://www.grimmchronik.com/hans-mayer-zum-100 -geburtstag-von-walter-benjamin/ (accessed August 2022).

Mayer, Hans. 1992b. *Der Zeitgenosse Walter Benjamin*. Frankfurt am Main: Jüdischer/ Suhrkamp Verlag.

Mbembe, Achille. 2001. *On the Postcolony*. Los Angeles: University of California Press.

Mbembe, Achille. 2003. Necropolitics. *Public Culture* 1, no. 15: 11–40.

Mbembe, Achille. 2013. *Critique de la raison nègre*. Paris: La Découverte.

Mbembe, Achille. 2019. *Necropolitics*. Durham: Duke University Press.

McKittrick, Katherine. 2014. Mathematics black life. *The Black Scholar* 44, no. 2: 16–28.

McIvor, David W. 2012. Bringing ourselves to grief: Judith Butler and the politics of mourning. *Political Theory* 40, no. 4: 409–36.

McIvor, David W. 2016. *Mourning in America: Race and the Politics of Loss*. Ithaca: Cornell University Press.

McIvor, David W., and Alexander Keller Hirsch. 2019. Rituals of re-entry: An interview with Bonnie Honig. In *The Democratic Arts of Mourning: Political Theory and Loss*, 207–18. Lanham: Lexington Books.

McIvor, David W., Juliet Hooker, Ashley Atkins, Athena Athanasiou, and George Shulman. 2021. Mourning work: Death and democracy during a pandemic. *Contemporary Political Theory* 20: 165–99.

Mecklenburg, Jens (ed.). 1996. *Handbuch Deutscher Rechtsextremismus*. Berlin: Elefanten Press.

Medina, José. 2012. *The Epistemology of Resistance: Gender and Racial Oppression, Epistemic Injustice, and Resitant Imaginations*. Oxford: Oxford University Press.

Mehrabi, Tara. 2020. Queer ecologies of death in the lab: Rethinking waste, decomposition and death through a queerfeminist lens. *Australian Feminist Studies* 35, no. 104: 138–54.

Mehrländer, Ursula. 1984. Ausländerpolitik und ibre sozialen Folgen. In *Der gläserne Fremde*, edited by Hartmut M. Griese, 89–102. Leverkusen: Leske und Budrich.

Memmi, Dominique. 2004. Administrer une matière sensible. Conduites raisonnables et pédagogie par corps autour de la naissance et de la mort. In *Le gouvernement des corps*, edited by Didier Fassin and Dominique Memmi, 135–54. Paris: Éditions de l'EHESS.

Memmi, Dominique, and Emmanuel Taïeb. 2009. Les recompositions du 'faire mourir': vers une biopolitique d'institution. *Presses de Sciences Po, Sociétés Contemporaines* 3, no. 75: 5–15.

Mendoza, Breny. 2014. *Ensayos de crítica feminista en nuestra América*. Mexico D.F.: Herder Editorial.

Mendoza, Breny. 2015. Coloniality of gender and power. In *The Oxford Handbook of Feminist Theory*, edited by Lisa Disch and Mary Hawkesworth, 100–121. Oxford: Oxford University Press.

Mendoza, Breny, and Daniela Paredes Grijalva. 2022. The epistemology of the south, coloniality of gender, and Latin American feminism. *Hypatia* 37, no. 3: 510–522.

Mezzadri, Alessandra. 2022. Social reproduction and pandemic neoliberalism: Planetary crises and the reorganization of life, work and death. *Organization* 29, no. 3: 379–400.

Michaelsen, Anja. 2015. Nicht-Trauern-Können und demonstratives Trauern. Affektive Folgen rassistischer Gewalt. In *I, is for Impasse. Affektive Queerverbindungen in Theorie_Aktivismus_Kunst*, edited by Käthe von Bose, Ulrike Klöppel, Katrin Köppert, Karin Michalski, and Pat Treusch, 33–44. Berlin: b_books.

Michael, Theodor. 2015. *Deutsch sein und Schwarz dazu. Erinnerungen eines Afro-Deutschen*. München: dtv Verlag.

Michel, Verónica. 2020. Judicial reform and legal opportunity structure: The emergence of strategic litigation against femicide in Mexico. In *Studies in Law, Politics, and Society*, edited by Austin Sarat, 27–54, Vol. 82. Bingley: Emerald Publishing Limited.

Mies, Maria. 1986. *Patriarchy and Accumulation on a World Scale: Women in the International Division of Labour*. London: Zed Books.

Mies, Maria, Veronika Benholdt-Thomsen, and Claudia von Werlhof. 1988. *Women: The Last Colony*. London: Zed Books.

Millar, Katharine M., Yuna Han, Martin J. Bayly, Katharina Kuhn, and Irene Morlino. 2020. Confronting the COVID-19 pandemic: Grief, loss, and social order. http://eprints.lse.ac.uk/106739/1/Confronting_the_covid_19_pandemic_grief_loss_and_social_order.pdf (accessed August 2022).

The Minnesota Protocol on the Investigation of Potentially Unlawful Death. 2016 [1991]. New York/Geneva: United Nations Human Rights Office of the High Commissioner.

Mokre, Monika. 2015. *Solidarität als Übersetzung. Überlegungen zum Refugee Protest Camp Vienna*. Bielefeld: Transversal.

Mole, Richard C. M. 2021. *Queer Migration and Asylum in Europe*. London: UCL Press.

Molina Vargas, Herma'ny, Camila Marambio, and Nina Lykke. 2020. Decolonising mourning: World-making with the Selk'nam people of Karokynka/Tierra Del Fuego. *Australian Feminist Studies* 35, no. 104: 186–201.

Monárrez Fragoso, Julia. 2002. Feminicidio sexual serial en Ciudad Juárez: 1993–2001. *Debate Feminista* 25: 279–305.

Monárrez Fragoso, Julia. 2014. Ciudad Juarez: Surviving, superfluos lives and the banality of death. Alter/Nativas, *Latin American Cultural Studies Journal* 3.

Monárrez Fragoso, Julia. 2019. Feminicidio sexual sistémico: Impunidad histórica constante en Ciudad Juárez, víctimas y perpetradores. *Estado & comunes, revista de políticas y problemas públicos* 1, no. 8: 85–110.

Morrison, Toni. 08.08.2019. I wanted to carve out a world both culture specific and race-free. *The Guardian*. https://www.theguardian.com/books/2019/aug/08/toni-morrison-rememory-essay (accessed August 2022).

Mortensen, Mette, and Hans-Jörg Trenz. 2016. Media morality and visual icons in the age of social media: Alan Kurdi and the emergence of an impromptu public of moral spectatorship. *Javnost – The Public* 23, no. 4: 343–362.

Movement for Black Lives. 2016. *A Vision for Black Lives: Policy Demands for Black Power, Freedom, and Justice*. policy.m4bl.org/downloads/.

Mujeres Creando. 2015. No Hay Libertad Política Sin Libertad Sexual. https://www.verkami.com/locale/es/projects/13037-mujeres-creando-no-hay-libertad-politica-sin-libertad-sexual (accessed March 2023).

Muñoz, José Esteban. 1999. *Disidentifications: Queers of Color and the Performance of Politics*. Minnesota: Minnesota University Press.

Muñoz, José Esteban. 2006. Feeling Brown, feeling down: Latina affect, the performativity of race, and the depressive position. *Signs* 31, no. 35: 675–88.

Naas, Michael. 2014. *When It Comes to Mourning*. New York: Routledge.

Neeley, Abigail H., and Patricia J. Lopez. 2022. Toward healthier futures in post-pandemic times: Political ecology, racial capitalism and black feminist approaches to care. *Geography Compass* 16, no. 2. https://compass.onlinelibrary.wiley.com/doi/full/10.1111/gec3.12609 (accessed August 2022).

Ngari, Elizabeth. 2020. Frauen im Lager extrem gefährdet. Interview with Elizabeth Ngari. *Taz*. 24.11.2020. https://taz.de/Mehrfachdiskriminierung-von-Fluechtlingen/!5727323/ (accessed September 2022).

Nguyen, Dan Thy, and Matthias N. Lorenz. 2022. "Es ging darum, dass die eigene Geschichte nicht vergessen wird". Autor Dan Thy Nguyen über wehrhafte Opfer, fragile Netzwerke und die begrenzte Mittel der Literatur. In *Rechte Gewalt erzählen*. LiLi: Studien der Literaturwissenschaft und Linguistik 1, 233–44. Stuttgart: J.B. Metzler.

Ni Una Menos. 2017. Llamamiento al Paro Internacional de Mujeres – 8 de marzo 2017. https://m.facebook.com/nt/screen/?params=%7B%22note_id%22%3A2733343383648814%7D&path=%2Fnotes%2Fnote%2F (accessed March 2023).

Nitzschke, Bernd. 1996. *Wir und der Tod: Essays über Sigmund Freuds Leben und Werk*. Paderborn: Brill Deutschland.

Nitzschke, Bernd (ed.). 2011. *Die Psychoanalyse Sigmund Freuds. Konzepte und Begriffe*. Wiesbaden: VS Verlag.

Noble, Denise, and Lisa Amanda Palmer. 2022. Misogynoir: Anti-blackness, patriarchy, and refusing the wrongness of black women. In *The Palgrave Handbook of Critical Race and Gender*, edited by Shirley Anne Tate and Encarnación Gutiérrez Rodríguez, 227–45. London: Palgrave.

Nobrega, Onur Suzan. 2014. *Postmigrant Theatre and Cultural Diversity in the Arts: Race, Precarity and Artistic Labour in Berlin*. Dissertation submitted in the Department of Media and Communication, Goldsmiths, University of London.

Nobrega, Onur Suzan, Matthias Quent, and Jonas Zipf. 2021a. *Rassismus, Macht, Vergessen*. Bielefeld: Transcript.

Nobrega, Onur Suzan in conversation with Ibrahim Arslan. 2021b. Seit Mölln, 23. November 1992. Ein drei Jahrzenter langer Weg, auf dem nicht alle Wunden heilen. In *Rassismus, Macht, Vergessen*, edited by Onur Suzan Nobrega, Matthias Quent, and Jonas Zipf, 25–42. Bielefeld: Transcript.

Nobrega, Onur Suzan in conversation with Elif and Gamze Kubaşık. 2021c. Es it das Recht eines jeden Menschen. In *Rassismus.Macht.Vergessen*, edited by Onur Suzan Nobrega, Matthias Quent, and Jonas Zipf, 61–76. Bielefeld: Transcript.

Norget, Kristin. 2006. *Days of Death, Days of Life: Ritual in the Popular Culture of Oaxaca*. New York: Columbia University Press.

Norton, Anne. 1995. Heart of darkness: Africa and African Americans in the writings of Hannah Arendt. In *Feminist Interpretations of Hannah Arendt*, edited by Bonnie Honig, 247–61. University Park: Pennsylvania State University Press.

Odabaşı, Mirza. 2013. Documentary: 93/13 – 20 Jahre nach Solingen. *Landesintegrationsrat NRW*.

Odugbesan, Abimbola, and Schwiertz, Helge. 2018. We are here to stay – Refugee struggles in Germany between unity and division. In *Protest Movements in Asylum and Deportation*, edited by Sieglinde Rosenberger, Verena Stern, and Nina Merhaut, 185–204. Cham: Springer (IMISCOE Research Series).

Oguntoye, Katharina. 2020. *Schwarze Wurzeln. Afro-deutsche Familiengeschichten von 1884 bis 1950*. Berlin: Orlanda.

Oguntoye, Katharina, Dagmar Schulz, and May Ayim (eds.). 1987. *Farbe Bekennen. Afrodeutsche Frauen auf den Spuren ihrer Geschichte*. Berlin: Orlanda Frauenverlag.

Ojakangas, Mika. 2020. *Polis* and *Oikos*: The art of politics in the Greek city-state. *The European Legacy* 25, no. 4: 404–420.

Oliver, José F. A. 1997. *Austernfischer, Marinero, Vogelfrau. Liebesgedichte und andere Miniaturen*. Berlin: Das Arabische Buch.

Oliver, José F. A. 2000. *Fernlautmetz. Gedichte*. Frankfurt am Main: Suhrkamp.

Oliver, Pamela. 2021. Special issue: Black lives matter in context. *Mobilization: An International Quaterly* 26, no. 4.

Ortega, Mariana. 2019. Bodies of color, bodies of sorrow: On resistant sorrow, aesthetic unsettlement, and becoming-with. *Critical Philosophy of Race* 7, no. 1: 124–43.

Owens, Patricia. 2017. Racism in the theory canon: Hannah Arendt and 'the one great crime in which america was never involved'. *Millennium* 45, no. 3: 403–24.

Oyewumi, Oyeronke. 1997. *The Invention of Women: Makingan African Sense of Western Gender Discourses*. Minneapolis: University of Minnesota Press.

Özdamar, Emine Sevgi. 1990. *Mutterzunge*. Cologne: Kiepenheuer & Witsch.

Özüdoğru, Tülin. 2014. Wir gehören doch dazu! In *Unsere Wunden kann die Zeit nicht heilen. Was der NSU-Terror für die Opfer und Angehörigen bedeutet*, edited by Barbara John, 48–54. Bonn: Bundeszentrale für politische Bildung Band.

Pagonakis, Pagonis. 2013. *Documentary: Alle sind noch da, nur die Toten fehlen – 20 Jahre nach dem Brandanschlag in Solingen, WDR-Archive*, Germany.

Panagiotopoulos, Anastasia, and Diana Espírito Santo. 2019. *Articulate Necrographies: Comparative Perspectives on the Voices and Silences of Dead*. New York/Oxford: Berghahn.

Panayi, Panikos. 1994. Racial violence in the new Germany 1990–93. *Contemporary European History* 3, no. 3: 265–87.

Paredes, Julieta. 2010. Hilando fino desde el feminismo indígena comunitarion. In *Aproximaciones críticas a las prácticas teóricas políticas del feminismo latinoamericano*, edited by Yuderkys Espinosa Miñoso, 117–120. Buenos Aires: En la Frontera.

Paredes, Julieta. 2013. *Hilando fino desde el Feminismo Comunitario*. Mexico: El Reboso, Zapateándole, Lente Flotante. https://sjlatinoamerica.files.wordpress.com/2013/06/paredes-julieta-hilando-fino-desde-el-feminismo-comunitario.pdf (accessed March 2023), En cortito que's palargo y Ali Fem AC.

Park, Chan-Kyong, and Klaus Fehling. 2003. *Koreans Who Went to Germany*. Stuttgart: Noonbit.

Partridge, Damani J. 2012. *Hypersexuality and Headscarves: Race, Sex, and Citizenship in the New Germany*. Bloomington: Indiana University Press.

Pasinato, Wania, and Thiago Pierobom de Ávila. 2022. Criminalization of femicide in Latin America: Challenges of legal conceptualization. *Current Sociology*. https://journals.sagepub.com/doi/full/10.1177/00113921221090252 (accessed September 2022).

Patterson, Orlando. 2018 [1981]. *Slavery and Social Death: A Comparative Study*. Cambridge: Harvard University Press.

Pereira, Godofredo. 2020. Caring for the dead: The afterlives of collective bodies. In *Rights of Future Generations: Conditions*, edited by Adrian Lahoud and Andrea Bagnato, 36–40. Ostfildern: Hatje Cantz.

Pérez Orozco, Amaia. 2014. *Subversión feminista de la economia: Aportes para un debate sobre el conflicto capital-vida*. Madrid: Traficantes de Sueños.

Perinelli, Massimo, and Lydia Lierke. 2020. *Erinnern Stören. Der Mauerfall aus migrantischer und jüdischer Perspektive*. Berlin: Verbrecher Verlag.

Perraudin, Michael, and Jürgen Zimmerer (eds.). 2010. *German Colonialism and National Identity*. New York: Routledge.

Peters, Michael A. 2018. The refugee camp as the biopolitical paradigm of the west. *Educational Philosophy and Theory* 50, no. 13: 1165–68.

Petuya Ituarte, Begoña, Antonio Muñoz Sánchez, and Miguel Montero Lange. 2014. Annäherung an die Situation der spanischen Bürger/innen in Deutschland. In *Arbeitsmigration nach Deutschland. Analysen zur neuen Arbeitsmigration aus Spanien vor dem Hintergrund der Migration seit 1960*, edited by Christian Pfeffer-Hoffmann, 241–80. Berlin: Mensch & Buch Verlag.

Piasek, Sebastián Luis. 2015. El duelo ante la ausencia del cuerpo. In *Acta Academica: VII Congreso Internacional de Investigación y Práctica Profesional en Psicología XXII Jornadas de Investigación XI Encuentro de Investigadores en Psicología del MERCOSUR*, 206–207. Buenos Aires: Facultad de Psicología - Universidad de Buenos Aires.

Piasek, Sebastián Luis, Noailles Gervasio, and Gutiérrez, Carlos Edgardo Francisco. 2016. El duelo en los familiares de los desaparecidos. Los juicios por crímenes de lesa humanidad y las condiciones de posibilidad de elaboración del duelo. In *Acta Academica: VIII Congreso Internacional de Investigación y Práctica Profesional en Psicología XXIII Jornadas de Investigación XII Encuentro de Investigadores en Psicología del MERCOSUR*, 158–60. Buenos Aires: Facultad de Psicología - Universidad de Buenos Aires.

Pichl, Maximilian. 2015. Der NSU-Mord in Kassel. Eine Geschichte deutscher Staatsapparate und ihrer Skandale. *Kritische Justiz* 48, no. 3: 275–87.

Pichl, Maximilian. 2018. Von Aufklärung keine Spur: 20 Jahre NSU-Komplex. *Blätter für deutsche und internationale Politik*, 33–44. https://www.blaetter.de/ausgabe/2018/januar/von-aufklaerung-keine-spur-20-jahre-nsu-komplex (accessed September 2022).

Piesche, Peggy. 2020. *Labor 89. Intersektionale Bewegungsgeschite*n aus West und Ost*. Berlin: Yılmaz Günay.

Plümecke, Tino, Claudia S. Wilopo, and Tarek Naguib. 2022. Effects of racial profiling: The subjectivation of discriminatory police practices. *Ethnic and Racial Studies*. https://www.tandfonline.com/doi/pdf/10.1080/01419870.2022.2077124?casa_token=wB98I2YTpU4AAAAA:T4pa0NTN3SzvxQrriG4j8QnXTlAQ0iyx4A0bF1qfjvYaML-nQ9Add1Aa2oXU1MS2_zBg6d3G6M4U12o (accessed September 2022).

Plutarch. 1919. *The Parallel Lives*, published in Volume VIII, Web Classical Library: https://penelope.uchicago.edu/Thayer/E/Roman/Texts/Plutarch/Lives/Phocion*.html.

Portillo, Lourdes. 2001. Documentary: Señorita Extraviada. https://www.lourdesportillo.com/senorita-extraviada (accessed September 2022).

Poutrus, Patrice G. 2005. Die DDR, ein anderer deutscher Weg? Zum Umgang mit Ausländern im SED-Staat. In *Zuwanderungsland Deutschland. Migrationen 1500–2005*, edited by Rosmarie Beier-de Haan, 120–33. Berlin: Edition Minerva.

Poutrus, Patrice G. 2019. *Umkämpftes Asyl. Vom Nachkriegsdeutschland bis in die Gegenwart*. Berlin: Ch. Links Verlag.

Poutrus, Patrice G. 01.09.2022. 'Rostock-Lichtenhagen: Rassistische Gewalt wurde zum Argument', interviewed by Nelli Tügel. *woz*. https://www.woz.ch/2235/rostock-lichtenhagen/rostock-lichtenhagen-rassistische-gewalt-wurde-zum-argument/%21HETXDAG6BVRF (accessed September 2022).

Precarias a la Deriva. 2004. *A la Deriva: Por los circuitos de la precariedad femenina*. Madrid: Traficantes de Sueños.

Prenzel, Thomas. 2005. 'Das sind doch keine Menschen.' Die Debatte um das Grundrecht auf Asyl und die Ereignisse von Rostock-Lichtenhagen. *Indes. Zeitschrift für Politik und Gesellschaft* 4, no. 1: 79–85.

Prieto, Marina, and Carolina Quinteros. 2004. Never the twain shall meet? Women's organisations and trade unions in the *maquila* industry in Central America. *Development in Practice* 14, nos. 1–2: 149–57.

Projekt Migration. 2005. *Katalog zur Ausstellung im Kölner Kunstverein, 2005/2006*. Köln: Dumont Verlag.

Quijano, Anibal. 1981. Sociedad y sociología en América Latina (notas para una discusión). *Revista De Ciencias Sociales*, nos. 1–2: 223–49. https://revistas.upr.edu/index.php/rcs/article/view/8665.

Quijano, Anibal. 1988. *Modernidad, Identidad y Utopía en América Latina*. Quito: Editorial El Conejo.

Quijano, Anibal. 2000a. Coloniality of power and eurocentrism in Latin America. *Nepantla* 1, no. 3: 533–80.

Quijano, Anibal. 2000b. Colonialidad del poder y clasificación social. *Journal of World Systems Research* 6, no. 2: 342–86.

Quijano, Anibal. 2008. Coloniality of power, eurocentrism, and social classification. In *Coloniality at Large: Latin America and the Postcolonial Debate*, edited by Mabel Moraña, Enrique D. Dussel, and Carlos A. Jáuregui, 181–224. Durham: Duke University Press.

Quijano, Anibal. 2020. *Cuestiones y horizontes: De la dependencia histórico-estructural a la colonialidad/descolonialidad del poder*. Ciudad Autónoma de Buenos Aires: CLACSO; Lima: Universidad Nacional Mayor de San Marcos.

Quijano, Anibal, and Immanuel Wallerstein. 1992. La americanidad como concepto, o América en el moderno sistema mundial. *International Social Sciences Journal (ISSJ)* 134: 549–557.

Radford, Jill, and Diana E. H.Russell (eds.). 1992. *Femicide: The Politics of Woman Killing*. New York: Twayne.

Radomska, Marietta. 2020. Deterritorialising death: Queerfeminist biophilosophy and ecologies of the non/living in contemporary art. *Australian Feminist Studies* 35, no. 104: 116–37.

Radomska, Marietta, Tara Mehrabi, and Nina Lykke. 2020. Queer death studies: Death, dying and mourning from a queerfeminist perspective. *Australian Feminist Studies* 35, no. 104: 81–100.

Ramelsberger, Annette. 2020. Wir waren ihnen kein Wort wert. *Süddeutsche Zeitung*, 30 April 2020. https://www.sueddeutsche.de/politik/nsu-rechtsextremismus-terror-urteil-kritik-1.4893697 (accessed September 2022).

Rancière, Jacques. 2007 [1992]. *On the Shores of Politics*. London, New York: Verso.

Rankine, Claudia. 22.01.2015. The condition of black life is one of mourning. *The New York Times Magazine*. https://www.nytimes.com/2015/06/22/magazine/the-condition-of-black-life-is-one-of-mourning.html (accessed August 2022).

Reddock, Rhoda. 1994. *Women, Labour and Politics in Trinidad and Tobago: A History*. Kingston, Jamaica: Ian Randle.

Reddock, Rhoda. 2014. Radical Caribbean social thought: Race, class identity and the postcolonial nation. *Current Sociology* 62, no. 4: 493–511.

Reddock, Rhoda. 2022. Pan-Africanism and feminism in the early thwentieth-century British Colonial Caribbean. In *Palgrave Handboof of Critical Race and Gender*, edited by Shirley Anne Tate and Encarnación Gutiérrez Rodríguez, 143–66. London: Palgrave.

Reinhardt, Mala. 2018. Documentary: *The second attack/Der zweite Anschlag*. In Mai-Phương Kollath, Ibrahim Arslan, Özge Pınar Sarp, Gülüstan Ayaz-Avcı, Osman Taşköprü, and Ayşe Güleç. Germany. https://derzweiteanschlag.de/__trashed/?lang=en (accessed September 2022).

Renshaw, Layla. 2016. *Exhuming Loss: Memory, Materiality and Mass Graves of the Spanish Civil War*. New York: Routledge.

Restrepo, Gabriel. 2016. Seguir los pasos de Orlando Fals Borda: Religión, música, mundos de la vida y carnaval. *Investigación & Desarrollo* 24, no. 2: 199–239.

Ribas, Cristina. 2014. Infraestructura: Maternidade/Paternidade/Economia do Cuidado/Trabalho. In *Vocabulário político para processos estéticos*, edited by Cristina Ribas. Rio de Janeiro: Editora Aplicação. http://vocabpol.cristinaribas.org/infraestrutura/.

Ricard, Nathalie. 2014. Testimonies of LGBTIQ refugees as cartographies of political, sexual and emotional borders. *Journal of Language and Sexuality* 3, no. 1: 28–59.

Rich, Adrienne. 1979. Conditions for work: the common world of women. In *On Lies, Secrets, and Silence: Selected Prose, 1966–1978*. New York: Norton.

Richards, Michael. 1998. *A Time of Silence: Civil War and the Culture of Repression in Franco's Spain, 1936–1945*. Cambridge: Cambridge University Press.

Rio, Ruiz, and Manuel Ángel. 2003. *Violencia étnica y destierro. Dinámicas de cuatro disturbios antigitanos en Andalucía*. Granada: Fundación Secretariado General Gitano: Editorial Maristán.

Rispoli, Tania, and Miriam Tola. 2020. Reinventing socio-ecological reproduction: Designing as feminist logistics: Perspectives from Italy. *Feminist Studies* 46, no. 3: 663–73.

Rivera Cusicanqui, Silvia. 2010. The notion of 'rights' and the paradoxes of postcolonial modernity: Indigenous peoples and women in Bolivia. *Qui Parle*, vol. 18, no. 2: 29–54.

Rivera Cusicanqui, Silvia. 2012. Ch'ixinakax utxiwa: A reflection on the practices and discourses of decolonization. *The South Atlantic Quartely* 111, no. 1: 95–109.

Robinson, Cedric J. 1983. *Black Marxism: The Making of the Black Radical Tradition*. Chapel Hill, NC: University of Carolina.

Rocha, Luciane. 2014. *Outraged Mothering: Black Women, Racial Violence, and the Power of Emotions in Rio de Janeiro's African Diaspora*. Anthropology Department, The University of Texas, Austin. https://repositories.lib.utexas.edu/handle/2152/25886 (accessed September 2022).

Rocha, Luciane. 2020. Estamos em Marcha! Anti-racism, political struggle, and the leadership of black Brazilian women. In *Black and Indigenous Resistance in the Americas: From Multiculturalism to Racist Backlash*, edited by Juliet Hooker, 159–88. New York: Lexington Books.

Rodríguez, Aguilera, and Metzli Yoalli. 2021. *Grieving Geographies, Mourning Waters: Race, Gender and Environmental Struggles on the Coast of Oaxaca, Mexico*. Dissertation Submitted. The University of Texas, Austin. https://repositories.lib.utexas.edu/handle/2152/88054 (accessed August 2022).

Rodríguez, Aguilera, and Metzli Yoalli. 2022. Grieving geographies, mourning waters: Life, death, and environmental gendered racialized struggles in Mexico. *Feminist Anthropology* 3, no. 1: 28–43.

Rodríguez Castro, Laura. 2021. *Decolonial Feminisms, Power and Place. Sentipensando With Rural Women in Colombia.* London: Palgrave.

Rose, Gillian. 1992. *The Broken Middle: Out of Our Ancient Society.* New York: Wiley-Blackwell.

Rose, Gillian. 1996. *Mourning Has Become the Law: Philosophy and Representation.* Cambridge: Cambridge University Press.

Ruído, María. 2002. Documentary: The inner memory/La Memoría interior. http://www.workandwords.net/en/projects/view/485 (accessed August 2022).

Rushdy, Ashraf H.A. 1990. "Rememory": Primal scenes and constructions in Toni Morrison's novels. *Contemporary Literature* 31, no. 3: 300–23.

Ruvituso, Clara I. 2020. From the south to the north: The circulation of Latin American dependency theories in the Federal Republic of Germany. *Current Sociology* 68, no. 1: 22–40.

Rygiel, Kim. 2016. Dying to live: Migrant deaths and citizenship politics along European borders: Transgressions, disruptions, and mobilizations. *Citizenship Studies* 20, no. 5: 545–60.

Saciak, Gözde. 2021. Auch eine Frage des Geldes. Materielle Gerechtigkeit für Betroffene rassistischer und antisemitischer Gewalt. In *Rassismus.Macht.Vergessen*, edited by Onur Suzan Nobrega, Matthias Quent, and Jonas Zipf, 93–108. Bielefeld: Transcript.

Sagot Rodríguez, Montserrat. 2017. ¿Un mundo sin femicidios? Las propuestas del feminismo para erradicar la violencia contra las mujeres. *CLACSO: RCIEM201.* Costa Rica: Centro de Investigación en Estudios de la Mujer.

Samuels, Robert, and Toluse Olorunnipa. 2022. *His name is George Floyd: one man's life and the struggle for social justice.* New York: Viking.

Sánchez, Antonio Muñoz. 2001. Una Introducción a La Historia de La Emigración Española en la República Federal de Alemania (1960–1980). *Iberoamericana* 12, no. 46: 23–42.

Sánchez-Alonso, Blanca. 2000. Those who left and those who stayed behind: Explaining emigration from the regions of Spain, 1880–1914. *The Journal of Economic History* 60, no. 3: 730–55.

Sánchez-Alonso, Blanca. 2001. Visiones de la emigracion en el siglo XX: De emigrantes a inmigrantes. In *Las claves de la España del siglo XX. La modernización social*, edited by Antonio Morales, 101–18. Madrid: Sociedad Estatal Nuevo Milenio.

Sánchez, Antonio Muñoz. 2012. Una introducción a la historia de la emigración española en la República Federal de Alemania (1960–1980). *Iberoamericana* 12, no. 46: 23–42.

Sander-Staudt, Maureen. 2006. The unhappy marriage of care ethics and virtue ethics. *Hypatia* 21, no. 4: 21–39.

Sänger, Eva. 2015. Obstetrical care as a matter of time: Ultrasound screening, temporality and prevention. *History and Philosophy of the Life Sciences* 37, no. 1: 105–20.

Sarkin, Jeremy. 2009. *Colonial Genocide and Reparations Claims in the Twenty-First Century: The Socio-Legal Context of Claims Under International Law by the Herero Against Germany for Genocide in Namibia, 1904–1908.* Westport: Greenwood.

Sauer, Walter. 2012. Habsburg colonial: Austria-Hungary's role in European Overseas expansion reconsidered. *Austrian Studies* 20: 5–23.

Sauerländer, Willibald. 2006. *Set in Stone: The Face in Medieval Sculpture.* New York: Metropolitan Museum of Art.

Schatzker, Chaim. 1995. Eingedenken – Das Gedächtnis der oder in der jüdischen Tradition. In *Generation und Gedächtnis. Erinnerungen und kollektive Identitäten*, edited by Kristin Platt und Mihran Dabag, 107–14. Wiesbaden: Verlag für Sozialwissenschaften.

Scheinfeld, Emily, Kendyl Barney, Katlyn Gangi, Erin C. Nelson, and Catherine C. Sinardi. 2021. Filling the void: Grieving and healing during a socially isolating global pandemic. *Journal of Social and Personal Relationships* 38, no. 10: 2817–37.

Schenck, Marcia C. 2016. From Luanda and Maputo to Berlin: Uncovering Angolan and Mozambican migrants. *African Economic History* 44: 202–34.

Schick, Kate. 2012. *Gillian Rose: A Good Enough Justice*. Edinburgh: Edinburgh University Press.

Schild, Verónica. 2019. Feminisms, the environment and capitalism: On the necessary ecological dimension of a critical Latin American feminism. *Journal of International Women's Studies* 20, no. 6. https://vc.bridgew.edu/jiws/vol20/iss6/3 (accessed August 2022).

Schmincke, Imke, and Jasmin Siri (eds.). 2013. *NSU Terror. Ermittlunggen am rechten Abgrund. Ereignisse, Kontexte, Diskurse*. Bielefeld: Transcript.

Schneider, Jan, and Axel Kreienbrink. 2010. *Rückkehrunterstützung in Deutschland: Programme und Strategien zur Förderung von unterstützter Rückkehr und zur Reintegration in Drittstaaten; Studie I/2009 im Rahmen des Europäischen Migrationsnetzwerks (EMN)*. (Working Paper/ Bundesamt für Migration und Flüchtlinge (BAMF) Forschungszentrum Migration, Integration und Asyl (FZ), 31). Nürnberg: Bundesamt für Migration und Flüchtlinge (BAMF) Forschungszentrum Migration, Integration und Asyl (FZ); Bundesamt für Migration und Flüchtlinge (BAMF) Nationale Kontaktstelle für das Europäische Migrationsnetzwerk (EMN).

Schröttle, Monika, Maria Arnis, Marceline Naudi, Lara Dimitrijevic, Martina Farrugia, Emily Galea, Alexia Shakou, Christiana, Elina Kouta, Susana Pavlou, Camila Iglesias, Carolina Magalhães Dias, Cátia Pontedeira, Maria José Magalhães, Susana Coimbra, Ivana Paust, Lea Pölzer, Chaime Marcuello Servós, Santiago Boira Sarto, Patricia Almaguer, Antonio Eito, and Paz Olaciregui Rodríguez. 2021. Comparative report on femicide research and data in five countries (Cyprus, Germany, Malta, Portugal, Spain). FEM-UnitED Project.

Schwenkel, Christina. 2014. Rethinking Asian mobilities: Socialist migration and postsocialist repatriation of vietnamese contract workers in East Germany. *Critical Asian Studies* 46, no. 2: 235–58.

Schweppenhäuser, Hermann. 1999. Zum Geschichtsbegriff Walter Benjamins. In *Geschichte denken*, edited by Karl Rahner Akademie, 95–106. Münster: Lit Verlag.

Sedgwick, Eve Kosofsky. 2003. *Touching Feelings: Affect, Pedagogy, Performativity*. Durham: Duke University Press.

Sedgwick, Eve Kosofsky, and Adam Frank (eds.). 1995a. *Shame and Its Sisters: A Silvan Tomkins Reader*. Durham: Duke University Press.

Sedgwick, Eve Kosofsky, and Adam Frank. 1995b. Shame in the cybernetic fold: Reading Silvan Tomkins. *Critical Inquiry* 21, no. 2: 496–522.

Segato, Rita Laura. 2003. *Las estructuras elementales de la violencia: Ensayos sobre género entre la antropología, el psicoanálisis y los derechos humanos*. Bernal: Universidad Nacional de Quilmes.

Segato, Rita Laura. 2008. La escritura en el cuerpo de las mujeres asesinadas en Ciudad Juárez: Territorio, soberanía y crímenes de segundo estado. *Debate Feminista* 37: 78–102.

Segato, Rita Laura. 2014. *Las nuevas formas de la guerra y el cuerpo de las mujeres*. Puebla: Pez en el Árbol.

Segato, Rita Laura. 2016. *La guerra contra las mujeres* (Primera edición). Madrid: Traficantes de Sueños.

Segato, Rita Laura. 2019. La escritura en el cuerpo de las mujeres asesinadas de Ciudad Juarez. In *En tiempo de muerte: Cuerpos, Rebeldías, Resistencias*, edited by Xoxitl Leyva Solano and Rosalba Icaza, 67–88. Series: Prácticas Otras de Conocimiento, Vol. IV. Buenos Aires/Chiapas/La Haya: Cooperative Editorial Retos. CLACSO. Institute of Social Studies-Erasmus University Rotterdam.

Sempértegui, Andrea. 2021a. *Weaving Resistance: The Amazonian Women's Struggle against Extractivism in Ecuador*. Dr.Phil., Faculty of Social Sciences and Cultural Studies, Justus-Liebig-Universität-Giessen.

Sempértegui, Andrea. 2021b. Indigenous women's activism, ecofeminism, and extractivism: Partial connections in the Ecuadorian Amazon. *Politics & Gender* 17: 197–224.

Sempértegui, Andrea. 2022. Sustaining the struggle, taking over the space: Amazonian women and the indigenous movement in Ecuador. In *The Palgrave Handbook of Critical Race and Gender*, edited by Shirley Anne Tate and Encarnación Gutiérrez Rodríguez, 651–72. London: Palgrave Macmillan.

Seremetakis, Nadia C. 1991. *The Last Word: Women, Death, and Divination in Inner Mani*. Chicago: Chicago University Press.

Sharpe, Christina. 2016. *The Wake: On Blackness and Being*. Durham, DC: Duke University Press.

Silva-Tapia, Andrea, and Rosario Fernandez Ossandón. 2022. Feminist movements in Chile: New configurations and the intensification of their critical power. In *The Palgrave Handbook of Critical Race and Gender*, edited by Shirley Anne Tate and Encarnación Gutiérrez Rodríguez, 265–83. London: Palgrave Macmillan.

Simon, Jonathan. 2021. Dignity and its discontents: Towards an abolitionist rethinking of dignity. *European Journal of Criminology* 18, no. 1:33–51.

Simone, AbdouMaliq. 2004. People as infrastructure: Intersecting fragments in Johannesburg. *Public Culture* 16, no. 3: 407–29.

Simone, AbdouMaliq. 2021. Ritornello: "People as Infrastructure". *Urban Geography* 42, no. 9: 1341–48.

Simpson, Leanne Betasamosake. 2014. Land as pedagogy: Nishnaabeg intelligence and rebellious transformation. *Decolonization: Indigeneity, Education & Society* 3, no. 3: 1–15.

Simpson, Leanne Betasamosake. 2017. *As We Have Always Done: Indigenous Freedom Through Radical Resistance*. Minneapolis: University of Minnesota Press.

Şimşek, Semiya (with Peter Schwarz). 2013. *Schmerzliche Heimat, Deutschland und der Mord an meinem Vater*. Berlin: Rowohlt.

Smythe, S. A. 2018. Black mediterranean and the politics of imagination. *Middle East Report* 286: 3–9.

Snorton, Riley C., and Jin Haritaworn. 2013. Trans necropolitics: A transnational reflection on violence, death, and the trans of color afterlife. In *The Transgender Studies Reader*, 2nd Edition, edited by Susan Stryker and Aren Aizura, 66–76. New York: Routledge.

Sontag, Susan. 2005 [1977]. *On Photography*. New York: RosettaBooks.

Souza de, Natália Maria Felix. 2019. When the body speaks (to) the political: Feminist activism in Latin America and the quest for alternative democratic futures. *Contexto Internacional* 41, no. 1: 89–112.

Souza de, Natália Maria Félix, and Lara Martim Rodrigues Selis. 2022. Gender violence and feminist resistance in Latin America. *International Feminist Journal of Politics* 24, no. 1: 5–15.

Spade, Dean. 2020. *Mutual Aid: Building Solidarity During This Crisis (And the Next)*. London: Verso.

Spillers, Hortense J. 2003. *Black, White, and in Color: Essays on American Literature and Culture*. Chicago: The University of Chicago Press.

Spinoza, Benedictus de. 1994. The ethics. In *A Spinoza Reader: The Ethics and Other Works*, edited by Edwin Curley, 85–265. Princeton: Princeton University Press.

Spivak, Gayatri Chakravorty. 1987. *In Other Worlds: Essays in Cultural Politics*. New York: Routledge.

Spivak, Gayatri Chakravorty. 1994. Responsibility. *Boundary 2* 21, no. 3: 16–94.

Spivak, Gayatri Chakravorty. 2012. *An Aesthetic Education in the Era of Globalization*. Harvard: Harvard University Press.

Squire, Vicky. 2015. *Post/Humanitarian Border Politics Between Mexico and the USA. People, Places, Things*. London: Palgrave.

Squire, Vicky. 2020. *Europe's Migration Crisis: Border Deaths and Human Dignity*. Cambridge: Cambridge University Press.

Stanley, Liz. 2002. Mourning becomes …: The work of feminism in the spaces between lives lived and lives written. *Women's Studies International Forum* 25, no. 1: 1–17.

Stewart, Abibi. 2021. Feminism for the 99% or solidarity in the house of difference? Intersectionality and social reproduction theory. *Femina Politica* 2, no. 30: 23–35.

Stewart, Terah J. 2020. Hard grief for hard love: Writing through doctoral studies and the loss of my mother. In *Narratives of Hope and Grief in Higher Education*, edited by Stephanie Anne Shelton and Nicole Sieben, 27–37. London: Palgrave Macmillan.

Stierl, Maurice. 2016. Contestation in death – The role of grief in migration struggles. *Citizenship Studies* 20, no. 2: 173–91.

Stierl, Maurice. 2019. *Migrant Resistance in Contemporary Europe*. New York: Routledge.

Strasser, Petra. 2003. Trauer versus Melancholie aus psychoanalytischer Sicht. In *Trauer*, edited by Wolfram Mauser and Joachim Pfeffer, 37–52. Würzburg: Königshausen & Neumann.

Suárez-Navaz, Liliana. 2004. *Rebordering of the Mediterranean: Boundaries and Citizenship in Southern Europe*. Oxford/New York: Berghahn Books.

Strathern, Marilyn. 2004 [1991]. *Partial Connections*. Walnut Creek: Altamira Press.

Sutton, David E. 2004. Ritual, continuity and change: Greek reflections. *History and Anthropology* 15, no. 2: 91–105.

Svampa, Maristella. 2019. *Neo-Extractivism in Latin America: Socio-Environmental Conflicts, the Territorial Turn, and New Political Narratives*. Cambridge: Cambridge University Press.

Taïeb, Emmanuel. 2006a. Avant-propos: Du biopouvoir au thanatopouvoir. *Quaderni*, no. 62: 5–15.

Taïeb, Emmanuel. 2006b. La peine de mort en République, un 'faire mourir' souverain? *Quaderni* 62: 17–26.

Tate, Shirley-Anne. 2015. *Black Women's Bodies and the Nation: Race, Gender and Culture*. London: Palgrave Macmillan.

Tate, Shirley-Anne. forthcoming. No human involved/no theory involved: The (im)possibility of black studies in the United Kingdom and Canadian Prairie academia. In *Critical University Studies*, edited by Dina Belluigi, Andre Keet, and Jason Arday. Stellenbosch: African Sun Media.

Taylor, Keeanga-Yamahtta. 2016. *From #BlackLivesMatter to Black Liberation.* 1st ed. Haymarket Books. https://www.haymarketbooks.org/books/778-from -blacklivesmatter-to-black-liberation. Chicago: Haymarket Books.

Teraoka, Arlene Akiko. 1987. Gastarbeiterliteratur: The other speaks back. *Cultural Critique*, no. 7: 77–101.

The Voice. 2014. "20 Jahre sind nicht genug!" – Vereint gegen Abschiebung und soziale Ausgrenzung. http://thecaravan.org/files/caravan/faltblatt_de.pdf (accessed September 2022).

Thompson, Vanessa Eileen. 2018. There is no justice, there is just us! Ansätze zu einer post-kolonialen-feministischen Kritik der Polizei am Beispiel von Racial Profiling. In *Kritik der Polizei*, edited by Daniel Loick, 197–222. Frankfurt/Main: Campus.

Thompson, Vanessa Eileen. 2021a. Policing in Europe: Disability justice and abolitionist intersectional care. *Race & Class* 62, no. 3: 61–76.

Thompson, Vanessa Eileen. 2021b. Policing difference, feminist oblivions and the (im-) possibilities of intersectional abolition. In *Transitioning to Gender Equality*, edited by Christa Binswanger and Andrea Zimmermann, 27–42. Basel: MDPI.

Thompson, Vanessa Eileen. 2021c. 'There is no justice, there is just us!' Towards a postcolonial feminist critique of policing using the example of racial profiling in Europe. In *Contesting Carceral Logic: Towards Abolitionist Futures*, edited by Michael J. Coyle and Mechthild Nagel, 90–104. New York: Routledge.

Thompson, Vanessa Eileen. 2022. From Minneapolis to Dessau, from Moira to Tripoli, from the shores to the land and the sea: Geographies of abolition. In *Disembodied Territories*, curated and designed by Sara Salem, Menna Agha, Engy Mohsen, Frederick Kannemeyer, and Rudo Mpisaunga. London: London School of Economics and Vlaans Architectuurinstituut. https://disembodiedterritories.com/ From-Minneapolis-to-Dessau-from-Moria-to-Tripoli-from-the-shores-to (accessed September 2022).

Thränhardt, Dietrich. 1995. The political uses of Xenophobia in England, France and Germany. *Party Politics* 1, no. 3: 323–45.

Thym, Daniel. 2018. Vom 'Fremdenrecht' über die 'Denizenship' zur 'Bürgerschaft'. Gewandeltes Selbstverständnis im deutschen Migrationsrecht. *Der Staat* 57: 77–117.

Ticktin, Miriam. 2016. Thinking beyond Humanitarian borders. *Social Research* 83, no. 2: 255–71.

Todd, Zoe. 2017. Fish, kin, and hope: Tending to water violations in amiskwaciwâskahikan and treaty six territory. *Afterall: A Journal of Art, Context and Inquiry* 43, no. 1: 102–7.

Tomkins, Silvan S. 2008 (orig. 1962–1963). *Affect, Imagery, Consciousness.* Volume I and II. New York: Springer Publishing.

Tomkins, Silvan S., and Robert McCarter. 1964. What and where are the primary affects? Some evidence for a theory. *Perceptual and Motor Skills* 18, no. 1: 119–58.

Touray, Maimuna. 2021. Plotting liberation: A scheme for the commons as reparations. *ATM Magazine* 2. https://www.atm-magazine.com (accessed September 2022).

Tran, Minh Thu, and Vanessa Vu (Rice & Shine). 27.12.2021. Podcast: Hamburg 1980: Als der rechte Terror wieder aufflammte. https://www.ardaudiothek.de/episode/rice -and-shine/hamburg-1980-als-der-rechte-terror-wieder-aufflammte-archiv/cosmo /10569269/ (accessed September 2022).

TRIBUNALE - NSU Komplex Auflösen. 2021. Berlin/Hamburg: Assoziation A.

Tribunal NSU-Komplex auflösen, Wir klagen an!. 2017. https://www.nsu-tribunal.de/ wp-content/uploads/2017/10/NSU-Tribunal_Anklageschrift_DE_V3.pdf

Trinidad Galván, Ruth. 2016. Collective memory of violence of the female brown body: A decolonial feminist public pedagogy engagement with the feminicides. *Pedagogy, Culture & Society* 24, no. 3: 343–57.

Tronto, Joan. 1994. *Moral Boundaries: A Political Argument for an Ethic of Care*. New York: Routledge.

Tronto, Joan. 2006. Women and caring: What can feminists learn about morality from caring? In *Justice and Care: Essential Readings in Feminist Ethics*, edited by Virginia Held, 101–15. Boulder: Westview Press.

Tronto, Joan. 2011. A feminist democratic ethics of care and global care workers: Citizenship and responsibility. In *Feminist Ethics and Social Policy: Towards a New Global Political Economy of Care*, edited by Rianne Mahon and Fiona Robinson, 162–78. Vancouver: University of British Columbia Press.

Tronto, Joan. 2013. *Caring Democracy: Markets, Equality, and Justice*. New York: New York University Press.

Tronto, Joan. 2015. *Who Cares? How to Reshape a Democratic Politics*. Ithaca and London: Cornell University Press.

Trouillot, Michel-Rolph. 2015 [1995]. *Silencing the Past: Power and the Production of History*. Boston: Beacon Press.

Trudy. 2013. Misogyny, in general vs. anti-black misogyny (misogynoir), specifically. *Gradient Lair*. September 11. https://www.gradientlair.com/post/60973580823/general-misogyny-versus-misogynoir (accessed September 2022).

Trudy. 2014. Explanation of Misogynoir. *Gradient Lair*, April 28. https://www.gradientlair.com/post/84107309247/define-misogynoir-anti-black-misogyny-moya-bailey-coined (accessed September 2022).

Truth, Soujourner. 1851. "Ain'I a Woman?". Modern history sourcebook. History Department, Fordham University, New York. https://sourcebooks.fordham.edu/mod/sojtruth-woman.asp (accessed March 2023).

Tsosie, Rebecca. 2012. Indigenous peoples and epistemic injustice: Science, ethics, and human rights. *Washington Law Review* 87, no. 4: 1132–202.

Tuck, Eve, and K. Wayne Yang. 2012. Decolonization is not a metaphor. *Decolonization: Education, Indigeneity & Society* 1, no. 1: 1–40.

Türkmen, Ceren. 16.10.2018. 'Duisburg 1984'. ak – Analyse und kritik. Zeitung für linke Debatten und Praxis. https://www.akweb.de/gesellschaft/rassistischer-brandanschlag-duisburg-1984/ (accessed September 2022).

Türkmen, Ceren. 2020. Migration und Rassismus in der Bonner Republik. Der Brandanschlag in Duisburg 1984. In *Erinnern Stören. Migrantische und jüdische Perspektiven auf den Mauerfall*, 99–133. Berlin: Verbrecher Verlag.

Türkmen, Ceren in Interview mit Garip Bali. 17.03.2020. Was können wir vom migrantischen Selbstschutz der 1990er lernen?, ak – Analyse und kritik. *Zeitschrift für linke Politik*. https://www.akweb.de/ausgaben/658/was-koennen-wir-vom-migrantischen-selbstschutz-der-1990er-lernen/ (accessed September 2022).

Turner, Simon, and Zachary Whyte. 2022. Introduction: Refugee camps as carceral junctions. *Incarceration: An International Journal of Imprisonment, Detention and Coercive Confinement*, April. https://journals.sagepub.com/doi/full/10.1177/26326663221084591?casa_token=oMQ0fyBzLmAAAAAA:mPY7CGeG_wKKsn7wP1WlXArglIvtt_oPOE5t3IMVA4J4vqgcX5GT3JPwCib12yottAUCsUrY_GiIsl4 (accessed September 2022).

Tzul Tzul, Gladys. 2018a. Sistemas de Gobierno Comunal Indígena: La organizacion de la reproduccion de la vida. In *Epistemologias del Sur: Epistemologias Do Sul*, edited by Maria Paula Menese and Karina Bidaseca, 385–96. Buenos Aires: CLACSO.

Tzul Tzul, Gladys. 2018b. Rebuilding communal life: Ixil women and the desire for life in Guatemala. *NACLA-Report on the Americas* 50, no. 4: 404–6.

Tzul Tzul, Gladys. 2019a. *Sistemas de Gobierno Comunal Indígena. Mujeres y tramas de parentesco Enchuimeq'ena.* Guatemala: Instituto Amaq.

Tzul Tzul, Gladys. 2019b. Archipiélago y tejido de asambleas: Algunas claves criticas para comprender la tensa relación entre Estado guatemalteco y comunidades indígenas. In *Vuelta a la autonomía: Debates y experiencias para la emancipación social desde América Latina*, edited by Gaya Makaran, Pabel Lopez, and Juan Wahren, 101–14. Mexico: Baja Tierra.

Tzul Tzul, Gladys. 2019c. La forma comunal de la resistencia. Abya Yala Dossiert. Revista de la Universidad de Mexico. https://www.revistadelauniversidad.mx/articles /7a052353-5edf-45fe-a7ab-72c6121665b4/la-forma-comunal-de-la-resistencia.

Ulrich, George. 2001. *Unforgiving Remembrance: The Concept and Practice of Eingedenken in Walter Bejanmin's Late Work.* PhD submitted Department of Philosophy, University of Toronto.

Ulu, Turgay. 2013. Eine Widerstandserfahrung der Flüchtlinge in Deutschland. In *Wer MACHT Demo_kratie? Kritische Beiträge zu Migration und Machtverhältnissen*, edited by Duygu Gürsel, Zülfukar Çetin, and V. Allmende, 117–36. Münster: Edition Assemblage.

Unfried, Berthold. 2022. International labor migration within the socialist world: Cuban contract laborers in the German Democratic Republic, 1975–1990. In *Yearbook of Transnational History* 5, edited by Thomas Adam, 131–73. Lanham: Rowman & Littlefield.

Unvar, Serpil Temiz. 2023. Kampf für Aufklärung und Gerechtigkeit in Hanau – und darüber hinaus. In *Solingen, 30 Jahre nach dem Brandanschlag*, edited by Birgül Demirtaş, Adelheid Schmitz, Derya Gür-Şeker, and Çağrı Kahveci, 397–398. Bielefeld: transcript.

Ünsal, Nadiye. 2015. Challenging 'refugees' and 'supporters'. Intersectional power structures in the refugee movement in Berlin. Online journal Movement 2, no. 1. https://movements-journal.org/issues/02.kaempfe/09.ünsal--refugees-supporters -oplatz-intersectionality.html (accessed April 2023).

Ünsal, Nadiye, Tijana Vukmirović, and Zerrin Güneş. 2018. *Zusammen haben wir eine Chance.* Berlin: Verlag Yılmaz-Günay.

Utlu, Deniz. 2013. *Für Trauer und für Zorn. Plädoyer gegen eine Ökonomie des Gedenkens.* Berlin: Rosa Luxemburg Stiftung Standpunkte.

Valencia, Sayak. 2010. *Capitalismo gore.* Barcelona: Melusina.

Valencia, Sayak. 2018. *Gore Capitalism.* Pasadena, CA: Semiotext(e).

Valencia, Sayak, and Olga Arnaiz Zhuravleva. 2019. Necropolitics, postmortem/ transmortem politics, and transfeminisms in the sexual economies of death. *TSQ* 6, no. 2: 180–93.

Valle Escalante, Emilio del. 2014. Self-determination: A perspective from Abya Yala. https://www.e-ir.info/2014/05/20/self-determination-a-perspective-from-abya -yala/ (accessed August 2022).

Vega Solís, Cristina. 2019. Reproducción social y cuidados en la reinvención de lo común. Aportes conceptuales y analíticos desde los feminismos. *Revista de Estudios Sociales* 70: 49–63.

Vega Solís, Cristina, Raquel Martínez Buján, and Myriam Paredes Chauca. 2018. *Cuidado, comunidad y común*. Madrid: Traficantes de Sueños.

Veillette, Anne-Marie. 2021. Racialized popular feminism: A decolonial analysis of women's struggle with police violence in Rio de Janeiro's favelas. *Latin American Perspectives* 239: 87–104.

Velásquez, Nimatuj, and Irma Alicia. 2019. Las abuelas de Sepur Zurco. Esclavitud sexual y Estado Criminal en Guatemala. In *En tiempo de muerte: Cuerpos, Rebeldias, Resistencias*, edited by Xoxitl Leyva Solano and Rosalba Icaza, 89–112. Series: Prácticas Otras de Conocimiento, Vol. IV. Buenos Aires/Chiapas/La Haya: Cooperative Editorial Retos. CLACSO. Institute of Social Studies-Erasmus University Rotterdam.

Vickstrom, Erik R. 2019. *Pathways and Consequences of Legal Irregularity. Senagalese Migrants in France, Italy and Spain*. (IMISCOE Research Series). Cham: Springer Nature.

Vigil-Villodres, Anabel. 2021. Extractivismo Agrario e Industria Agroalimentaria en Andalucía. *ANDULI, Revista Andaluza De Ciencias Sociales* 20: 35–58.

Villa, Dana. 2000. *The Cambridge Companion to Hannah Arendt*. Cambridge: Cambridge University Press.

Villaplana Ruíz, Virginia. 2010. *El instante de la memoria. Una novela documental*. Madrid: Traficantes de Sueños.

Voice, Paul. 2014. Labour, work and action. In *Hannah Arendt. Key Concepts*, 36–53. London: Routledge.

Wallerstein, Immanuel. 1976. *The Modern World-System I: Capitalist Agriculture and the Origins of the European World-Economy in the Sixteenth Century*. New York: Academic Press.

Wallerstein, Immanuel. 2004. *World-System Analysis: An Introduction*. Durham, NC: Duke University Press.

Wallerstein, Immanuel. 2011a. *The Modern World-System II: Mercantilism and the Consolidation of the European World-Economy, 1600–1750*. Berkeley: University of California Press.

Wallerstein, Immanuel. 2011b. *The Modern World-System III: Second Era of Great Expansion of the Capitalist World-Economy, 1730s–1840s*. Berkeley: University of California Press.

Wallerstein, Immanuel. 2011c. *The Modern World-System IV: Centrist Liberalism Triumphant, 1789–1914*. Berkeley: University of California Press.

Wallerstein, Immanuel. 2013. Structural Crisis, or why capitalist can no longer find capitalism rewarding. In *Does Capitalism have a Future?*, edited by Immanuel Wallerstein, Randall Collins, Michael Mann, Georgi Derluguian, and Craig Calhoun, 9–36. Oxford: Oxford University Press.

Walter, Tony. 2020. *Death in the Modern World*. London: Sage.

Weheliye, Alexander G. 2014. *Habeas Viscus: Racializing Assemblages, Biopolitics, and Black Feminist Theories of the Human*. Durham, DC: Duke University Press.

Wekker, Gloria. 2016. *White Innocence: Paradoxes of Colonialism and Race*. Durham: Duke University Press.

Wells, Ida B. 2005 [1892]. *Southern Horrors: Lynch Law in All Phases*. The Project Gutenberg Ebook. https://www.gutenberg.org/files/14975/14975-h/14975-h.htm (accessed March 2023).

Wells, Ida B. 2020 [1895]. *The Red Record*. Bristol: Read & Co.

Whitebook, Joel. 2017. *Freud: An Intellectual Biography*. Cambridge: Cambridge University Press.

Williams, Eric. 1994 [1944]. *Capitalism and Slavery*. Chapel Hill: University of North Carolina.

Wimmer, Andreas. 1997. Explaining xenophobia and racism: A critical review of current research approaches. *Ethnic and Racial Studies* 20, no. 1: 17–41.

Winter, Yves. 2012. Violence and visibility. *New Political Science* 34, no. 2: 195–202.

Wollheim, Richard. 1987. *Painting as an Art*. London: Thames and Hudson.

Women in Exile. 2022. *Breaking Borders to Build Bridges. 20 Years Women in Exile*. Münster: edition assemblage.

Women in Exile, the Voice, the Caravan for the Rights of Refugees and Migrants, International Women Space and other international refugee organisations. 2013. International Refugee Tribunal Statement. http://thecaravan.org/node/3857 (accessed April 2023).

Women in Exile and Duygu Gürsel. 2013. The struggle has to continue, we do not give up! Wer MACHT Demo_kratie? Kritische Beiträge zu Migration und Machtverhältnissen. In *Wer MACHT Demo_kratie? Kritische Beiträge zu Migration und Machtverhältnissen*, edited by Duygu Gürsel, Zülfukar Çetin, and V. Allmende, 88–98. Münster: Edition Assemblage.

Wright, Melissa W. 2006. *Disposable Women and Other Myths of Global Capitalism*. New York: Routledge.

Wright, Melissa W. 2011. Necropolitics, narcopolitics, and femicide: Gendered violence on the Mexico–US border. *Signs: Journal of Women in Culture and Society* 36, no. 3: 707–31.

Wynter, Sylvia. 1984. The ceremony must be found: After humanism. *Boundary 2: A Journal of Post Modern Literature and Culture* XII, no. 3, and Vol. XIII, no. 1: 19–69.

Wynter, Sylvia. 1994. No humans involved: An open letter to my colleagues. In Forum N.H.I: Knowledge for the 21st Century 1, no. 1: 1–17.

Wynter, Sylvia. 1995. 1492: A new world view. In *Race, Discourse, and the Origin of the Americas: A New World View*, edited by Vera Lawrence Hyatt and Rex Nettleford, 5–57. Washington: Smithsonian Institution Press.

Wynter, Sylvia. 2003. Unsettling the coloniality of being/power/truth/freedom: Towards the human, after man, its overrepresentation – An argument. *The New Centennial Review* 3, no. 3: 257–337.

Yazzi, Melanie, and Cutcha Risling Baldy. 2018. Introduction: Indigenous peoples and the politics of water. *Decolonization: Indigeneity, Education and Society* 7, no. 1: 1–18.

Yildirim, Gürsel. 26.05.2021. Im Feuer. Todestag von Semra Ertan. *taz*. https://taz.de/Todestag-von-Semra-Ertan/!5774155/ (accessed September 2022).

Yimer, Dagmawi. 2015. *Asmat (Video)*. Rome: Archivio delle Memorie Migranti/The Archive of Migrant Memories.

Yozgat, İsmail. 13.03.2014. Sehr geehrter Herr Vorsitzender. Speech at the Higher Regional Court (Oberlandesgericht) Munich. Munich.

Zimmerer, Jürgen. 2021. *German Rule, African Subjects: State Aspirations and the Reality of Power in Colonial Namibia*. New York/Oxford: Berghahn.

Zinzi, D. Bailey, and J. Robin Moon. 2020. Racism and the political economy of COVID-19: Will we continue to resurrect the past? *Journal of Health Politics, Policy and Law* 1, no. 45: 937–50.

Zlomislić, Marko. 2007. *Jacques Derrida's Aporetic Ethics*. Lanham: Lexington Books.

Zölls, Philip. 2019. *Regieren der Migration. Von Einwanderungsprozessen und staatliche Regulierungspolitiken*. München: Allitera Verlag.

INDEX

Hanau, 22.08.2020
Copyright: Encarnación Gutiérrez Rodríguez

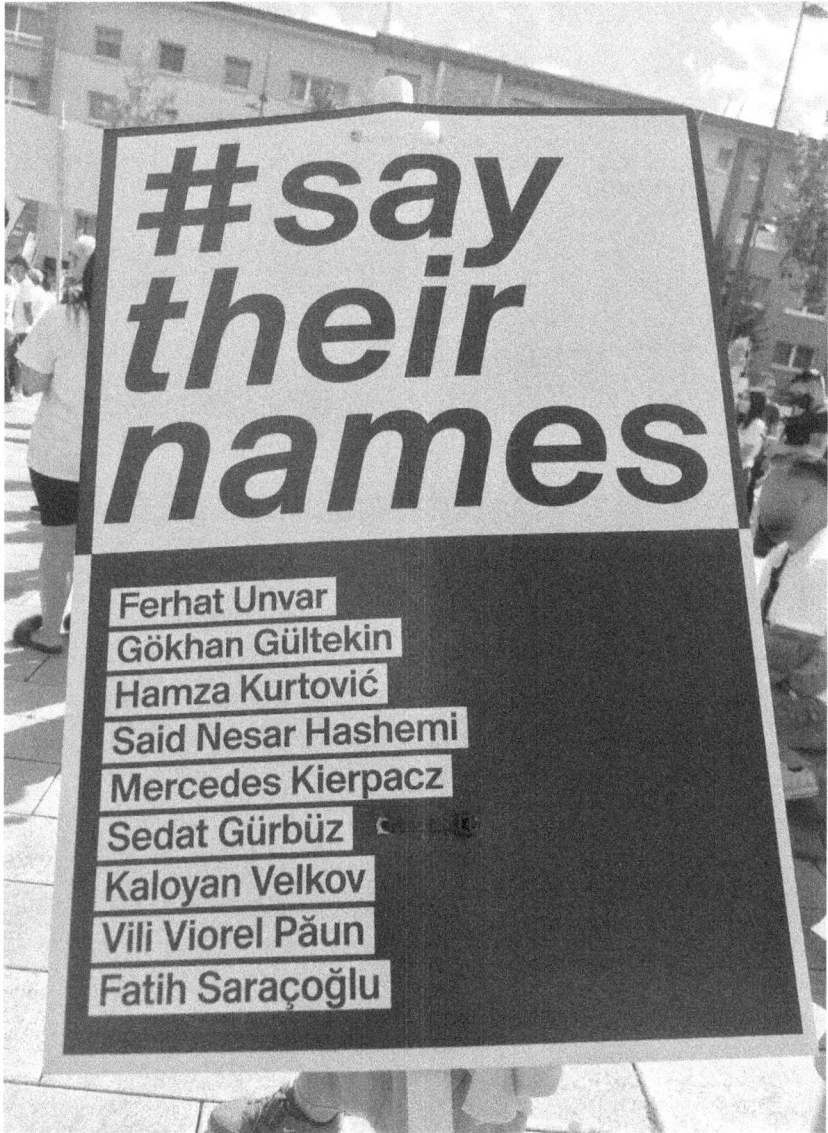

Hanau, 22.08.2020
Copyright: Encarnación Gutiérrez Rodríguez